Oracle8 DBA: SQL and PL/SQL

The Cram Sheet

This Cram Sheet contains the distilled, key facts about Oracle8 in the area of SQL and PL/SQL. Review this information right before you enter the test room, paying special attention to those areas you feel you need to review the most. You can transfer any of these facts from your head onto a blank piece of paper before beginning the exam.

SQL COMMANDS

1. SQL consists of DDL, DCL, and DML statements.

2. DDL (Data Definition Language) consists of commands used to define or alter database internal structures such as tables, views, indexes, and so on. DDL commands include **CREATE**, **ALTER**, **DROP**, and **TRUNCATE**.

3. DCL (Data Control Language) consists of commands used to control data access, such as the several forms of the **GRANT** command.

4. DML (Data Manipulation Language) consists of commands used to populate or alter database data contents. DML commands include **INSERT**, **UPDATE**, **DELETE**, and **SELECT**.

5. SQL has intrinsic functions that allow for data type conversion and data manipulation.

6. SQL has operators that define operations between values and expressions.

7. **SELECT** statements make use of joins, which can be one of the following types:
   - *Equijoins*—State equality or inequality operations.
   - *Outer joins*—Used when one of the tables is deficient in data to complete the specified relationship.
   - *Self-joins*—Used when a table is joined to itself by use of table aliases.

8. SQL supports **SORT**, **COLLECTION**, and **SET** operations.

PRECEDENCE OF OPERATORS

9. The precedence of operators is as follows:
   - *(+) and (−)*—Unary operators (positive and negative number indicators) and the **PRIOR** operators.
   - *(*) and (/)*—Multiplication and division operators.
   - *Binary (=)*—Arithmetic operators (such as addition "+" and subtraction "−") and the concatenation operator (‖).
   - *All comparison operators*—This includes the **NOT**, **AND**, and **OR** logical operators.

10. Parentheses always override precedence. Operators inside parentheses are always evaluated first.

FUNCTIONS

11. Functions are either scalar (single row) or aggregate (group) in nature. A single-row function returns a single result row for each row of a queried table or view, whereas an aggregate function returns a single value for a group of rows.

42. Special roles such as **OSOPER**, **OSDBA**, **CONNECT**, **RESOURCE**, and **DBA** are automatically created:

- **OSOPER**—Grants all rights except the ability to create a database.
- **OSDBA**—Grants **OSOPER** and the right to create databases.
- **CONNECT**—Grants a basic set of privileges.
- **RESOURCE**—Grants a set of privileges that specifically apply to a developer.
- **DBA**—Grants almost unlimited rights that a DBA would use.

DATABASE DESIGN

43. The five-step system development cycle consists of:

1. *Strategy and analysis*—Users are interviewed and requirements are generated. Design documents are written. Entities, attributes, and relationships are identified as well as relationships.

2. *Design*—The actual system is designed in detail. Entity relationship diagrams (ERDs), function decompositions, and data flow diagrams are created. In object-oriented design, Universal Modeling Language (UML) diagrams may be used instead of ERDs.

3. *Build and document*—The system is built mapping the ERD to tables and columns (or objects) and relationships to primary key and foreign key relationships (or **REF** values). The function decompositions and data flows are used to create forms, reports, and other application modules.

4. *Transition*—The system is moved from development into production. During this period, user acceptance testing is performed and final documentation is generated.

5. *Production*—The system is placed into production, code is locked down, and a firm change control process is implemented. This is the final stage.

44. Entities (or objects) can be either parent, child, dependent, or independent. An entity (or object) is a thing of importance.

45. Relationships (or **REF**s) are named associations between things of significance and have cardinality and optionality. Relationships can be one-to-one, one-to-many, or even many-to-many, although most should be either required or optional one-to-manys. A **REF** can be only a one-one relationship from child back to parent record.

46. Normalization is the process where repeating values (attributes) are removed from an entity until all attributes in the entity relate only to the entity's unique identifier. The most common form of normalization is third normal form.

- Alter a column to **NOT NULL** if it has rows with null values in that column.
- Rename a column.
- Drop a column.
- Change a column's data type to an incompatible data type.

DATA DICTIONARY

19. At its lowest level, the data dictionary consists of **X$** and **K$** C structs, not normally viewable or used by DBA.

20. The data dictionary has **V$** virtual views or tables, which contain variable data such as statistics.

21. The data dictionary has dollar ($) tables, which actually contain database metadata about tables, views, indexes, and other database structures.

22. At the uppermost layer, the data dictionary has **DBA_** views about all objects, **ALL_** views about all objects a user can access, and **USER_** views about all objects a user owns.

PL/SQL

23. PL/SQL consists of the PL/SQL engine, which can be incorporated in the forms, SQL*Plus, or reports executables. The PL/SQL engine processes procedural statements and passes the SQL statements to the SQL processor.

24. A PL/SQL procedure may return one or more values. It is used to perform many functions, such as table input, table output, and value processing.

25. A PL/SQL function must return one and only one value and cannot be used to perform input and output. A function should be used only to manipulate existing data; this ties in with the concept of function purity.

26. A procedure consists of header, declarative, and executable (which may contain an exception handling block) sections.

27. An anonymous PL/SQL block is an externally stored PL/SQL block that is not named and contains at a minimum an executable block. It may, however, contain a declarative and executable (with or without exception handling block) section. An anonymous PL/SQL block

can be called from any Oracle environment. An anonymous PL/SQL block is used to form the heart of table triggers.

28. To process **SELECT** commands, PL/SQL uses either an explicit cursor (which usually returns more than one row) or an implicit cursor (which can return only one row or an exception will be raised).

29. Flow control in PL/SQL uses loops, which can be counted **FOR** loops, conditional **WHILE** loops, or conditional infinite loops.

30. Conditional flow control uses the **IF...THEN...ELSE** construct in PL/SQL.

31. Multiple **IF** constructs can be nested using the **IF...ELSIF** construct.

32. The **GOTO** is used for unconditional branching in PL/SQL.

33. The **NULL** command is a special command in PL/SQL used to fulfill the requirement for a flow control command to be followed by an executable command. Although **NULL** is an executable command, it does nothing.

34. SQL in the form of DML can be used in PL/SQL. Generally speaking, without using specially provided procedure packages, DDL cannot be used in PL/SQL.

35. **COMMIT** is used in PL/SQL to commit changed data explicitly.

36. **ROLLBACK** is used in PL/SQL to return altered data to its previous state.

USERS AND GRANTS

37. Users can be created, altered, and dropped using the **CREATE**, **ALTER**, and **DROP** commands.

38. Users are granted profiles, roles, and privileges.

39. Profiles are used to limit resource usage and can be used to enforce password limitations.

40. Roles are used to group a collection of privileges, roles, and grants that can then be granted en masse to a user or another role.

41. Grants and privileges are given at the system, table, or column level.

12. A single-value function can appear in a **SELECT** if the **SELECT** doesn't contain a **GROUP BY** clause. Single-value functions can also appear in **WHERE, START WITH,** and **CONNECT BY** clauses. Single-row functions can also be nested.

LIMITS ON A VIEW

13. A view can't be updated if:
    - It has a join.
    - It uses a **SET** operator.
    - It contains a **GROUP BY** clause.
    - It uses any group function.
    - It uses a **DISTINCT** operator.
    - It has flattened subqueries.
    - It uses nested table columns.
    - It uses **CAST** and **MULTISET** expressions.

DELETE AND TRUNCATE COMMANDS

14. The **DELETE** command is used to remove some or all rows from a table allowing **ROLLBACK** of the command if no **COMMIT** is executed.

15. The **TRUNCATE** command is used to remove all rows from a table, and no **ROLLBACK** is allowed.

OUTER JOINS

16. The restrictions on outer joins are:
    - The (+) operator can appear only in the **WHERE** clause and can apply only to a table or view.
    - If there are multiple join conditions, the (+) operator must be used in all of these conditions.
    - The (+) operator can be applied to a column only, not to an expression. However, it can be applied to a column inside an arbitrary expression.
    - A condition containing a column with a (+) cannot be **OR** related to another condition; neither can it be used in an **IN** condition.
    - A column marked with the (+) operator cannot be compared to a subquery.
    - Only one table in a multitable join can have the (+) operator applied to its joins to one other table.

THE ALTER TABLE COMMAND

17. The following are things you can do with the **ALTER TABLE** command:
    - Use the **ADD** clause to add columns that have null values to any table.
    - Use the **MODIFY** clause to increase the size of columns or to change the precision of numeric columns.
    - Use the **MODIFY** clause to change columns with all null values so that the columns are shorter or have a different data type.
    - Alter the **PCTFREE, PCTUSED, INITRANS,** or **MAXTRANS** values for any table.
    - Use the **STORAGE** clause to alter the storage parameters for any table.
    - Use the **PARALLEL** clause to change or remove the parallelism of a table.
    - Use **CACHE** or **NOCACHE** to specify whether a table is to be cached or not.
    - Use the **DROP** clause to remove a constraint.
    - Use the **DEFAULT** value clause to add a default value to any column.
    - Use the **DISABLE** clause to disable a constraint. (This is the only way to disable a constraint.) When the **CASCADE** option is specified with **DISABLE**, it also disables all dependent integrity constraints.
    - Use the **DEALLOCATE UNUSED** clause to deallocate space that is not being used. (You can use the **KEEP** option to specify a safety margin above the high-water mark.)
    - Use the **ENABLE** clause to enable a constraint that was created as disabled. (The **ENABLE** clause can be used only in **CREATE** and **ALTER TABLE** commands.)
    - Use the **ADD CONSTRAINT** clause to add a primary, not null, check, or foreign key constraint to an existing table.

18. The things you can't do with the **ALTER TABLE** command include:
    - Modify a column that has values to be shorter or to be a different data type than it already is.
    - Add a **NOT NULL** column to a table that has rows in a single step operation with only the **ALTER TABLE** command.

Oracle8 DBA:
SQL and PL/SQL

Michael R. Ault

Oracle8 DBA: SQL and PL/SQL Exam Cram

The Coriolis Group, LLC
14455 N. Hayden Road
Suite 220
Scottsdale, Arizona 85260

480/483-0192
FAX 480/483-0193
http://www.coriolis.com

Library of Congress Cataloging-in-Publication Data
Ault, Michael R.
   Oracle8 DBA : SQL and PL/SQL exam cram/by Michael R. Ault.
     p. cm.
   Includes index.
   ISBN 1-57610-577-6
   1. Electronic data processing personnel--Certification. 2. Database management--Examinations--Study guides. 3. SQL (Computer program language) 4. Oracle (Computer file) I. Title.
QA76.3.A95 2000
005.75'85--dc21   00-021907
                               CIP

President, CEO
Keith Weiskamp

Publisher
Steve Sayre

Acquisitions Editor
Jeff Kellum

Marketing Specialist
Cynthia Caldwell

Project Editor
Meredith Brittain

Technical Reviewer
Pete Sharman

Production Coordinator
Wendy Littley

Cover Design
Jesse Dunn

Layout Design
April Nielsen

Printed in the United States of America
10 9 8 7 6 5 4 3 2 1

14455 North Hayden Road • Suite 220 • Scottsdale, Arizona 85260

Coriolis: The Smartest Way To Get Certified™

To help you reach your goals, we've listened to readers like you, and we've designed our entire product line around you and the way you like to study, learn, and master challenging subjects.

In addition to our highly popular *Exam Cram* and *Exam Prep* books, we offer several other products to help you pass certification exams. Our *Practice Tests* and *Flash Cards* are designed to make your studying fun and productive. Our *Audio Reviews* have received rave reviews from our customers—and they're the perfect way to make the most of your drive time!

The newest way to get certified is the *Exam Cram Personal Trainer*—a highly interactive, personalized self-study course based on the best-selling *Exam Cram* series. It's the first certification-specific product to completely link a customizable learning tool, exclusive *Exam Cram* content, and multiple testing techniques so you can study what, how, and when you want.

Exam Cram Insider—a biweekly newsletter containing the latest in certification news, study tips, and announcements from Certification Insider Press—gives you an ongoing look at the hottest certification programs. (To subscribe, send an email to **eci@coriolis.com** and type "subscribe insider" in the body of the email.) We also sponsor the Certified Crammer Society and the Coriolis Help Center—two other resources that will help you get certified even faster!

Help us continue to provide the very best certification study materials possible. Write us or email us at **cipq@coriolis.com** and let us know how our books have helped you study. Tell us about new features that you'd like us to add. Send us a story about how we've helped you; if we use it in one of our books, we'll send you an official Coriolis shirt!

Good luck with your certification exam and your career. Thank you for allowing us to help you achieve your goals.

Keith Weiskamp
President and CEO

Look For These Other Books From The Coriolis Group:

Oracle8 DBA: Network Administration Exam Cram
by Barbara Ann Pascavage

Oracle DBA 7.3 to 8 Upgrade Exam Cram
by Robert Freeman

Oracle8 DBA: Database Administration Exam Cram
by Paul Collins

I would like to dedicate this book first and foremost to my loving wife Susan and my daughters Marie and Michelle. Their patience and love have made the hard work and long hours bearable. I would also like to dedicate this book to my mother and father, Mary and Tom Ault, who taught me anything worth doing was worth doing well. I would like to also dedicate this to my brother Chris, who has always been there for me. Last but not least, I would like to dedicate this work as a part of my ongoing testament to doing the best that God allows me to through his love and guidance.

About The Author

Michael R. Ault began working with database systems as a nuclear chemist in the mid-'80s. He developed a chemistry results tracking database on the HP9845C computer using arrays and enhanced HP-Basic and HPGL. Mike then worked with Informix and INGRES databases until 1990 as a product manager with Nuclear Data, Inc. (now a part of Canberra Industries).

Mike began working with Oracle in 1990 with Oracle version 5 and moved rapidly into Oracle version 6. Almost immediately, Mike began publishing papers and articles on the use, tuning, and management of Oracle—first at DECUS conferences, then at Oracle Open World events, and finally at the IOUG-A, OOW, ECO, and EOUG events. Mike has published articles in *Oracle Magazine*, *DBMS Magazine*, *SELECT Magazine*, *Computer World*, and *Oracle Internals*, as well as several other publications.

Mike has published seven books on Oracle (including this one), one on Unix, and dozens of articles and papers. Mike also is the moderator of the **www.revealnet.com** DBA Pipeline forum and participates in the IOUG, ORAFANS, TECHNET, and METALINK Oracle forums.

Mike was asked by Educational Testing Services to help develop the Chauncey Oracle7 certification test, and he helped with quality control for the Oracle7 OCP certification questions for Self Test Software. He also obtained the Oracle6 certification offered by Oracle in the early 1990s. Mike holds five Oracle Master Certificates and the Oracle7, Oracle8, and Oracle8i OCP-DBA certifications.

In his Oracle career, Mike has worked for Aerojet, a GenCorp company, Marion-Merrell-DOW (Now Heorschst Marion Rochelle), PacBell, TeleTV/TeleItalia, BellSouth Business Systems, Tennessee Valley Authority (TVA), AGCO, and Adidas as either an in-house DBA or as a consultant, as well as for many other companies as a troubleshooter/consultant.

Mike is the Chief Technical Officer, as well as one of the founders and owners, of the DBMentors International, Inc. consulting, training, and remote monitoring company. Mike's company can be reached at **www.dbmentors.com**, and Mike's email address is **mikerault@earthlink.net**.

Acknowledgments

I would like to thank Meredith Brittain, Jeff Kellum, and Catherine E. Oliver from The Coriolis Group for their unwavering confidence as well as their gentle (and not so gentle) kicks from behind. In spite of numerous delays caused by personal problems on my end, they still supported and encouraged me to complete the book. Thanks also to the rest of the Coriolis team: Wendy, Cynthia, Jesse, and April. I would also like to thank Pete Sharman from Oracle for his technical review (in spite of my sharp retorts to some of his comments, I still appreciate the hard work), without which the book would not have been as accurate or technically strong. Finally, I want to thank the unsung heroes at any publishing house—the proofreaders, page markup folks, and the ones who do all the odd, complex jobs that take a bunch of electronic ghosts and convert them into a book.

Contents At A Glance

Table Of Contents

Introduction

Welcome to *Oracle8 DBA: SQL and PL/SQL Exam Cram*! This book will help you get ready to take—and pass—the first of the five-part series of exams for Oracle Certified Professional-Oracle8 Certified Database Administrator (OCP-DBA) certification. In this Introduction, I talk about Oracle's certification programs in general and how the *Exam Cram* series can help you prepare for Oracle8's certification exams.

Exam Cram books help you understand and appreciate the subjects and materials you need to pass Oracle certification exams. The books are aimed strictly at test preparation and review. They do not teach you everything you need to know about a topic. Instead, I present and dissect the questions and problems that you're likely to encounter on a test.

Nevertheless, to completely prepare yourself for any Oracle test, I recommend that you begin by taking the Self-Assessment included in this book immediately following this Introduction. This tool will help you evaluate your knowledge base against the requirements for an OCP-DBA under both ideal and real circumstances.

Based on what you learn from that exercise, you might decide to begin your studies with some classroom training or by reading one of the many DBA guides available from Oracle and third-party vendors. I also strongly recommend that you install, configure, and fool around with the software or environment that you'll be tested on, because nothing beats hands-on experience and familiarity when it comes to understanding the questions you're likely to encounter on a certification test. Book learning is essential, but hands-on experience is the best teacher of all!

The Oracle Certified Professional (OCP) Program

The OCP program for DBA certification currently includes five separate tests. I cover the first one in this first book in the series. A brief description of each test follows, and Table 1 shows the required exams for the OCP certification:

Table 1 OCP-DBA Requirements*

All 5 of these tests are required		
Test 1	Exam 1Z0-001	Introduction to Oracle: SQL and PL/SQL
Test 2	Exam 1Z0-013	Oracle8: Database Administration
Test 3	Exam 1Z0-015	Oracle8: Backup and Recovery
Test 4	Exam 1Z0-014	Oracle8: Performance Tuning
Test 5	Exam 1Z0-016	Oracle8: Network Administration

* If you are currently an OCP certified in Oracle7.3, you need take only the upgrade exam (Oracle8: New Features for Administrators, Exam 1Z0-010) to be certified in Oracle8.

➤ *Introduction to Oracle: SQL And PL/SQL (Exam 1Z0-001)*—Test 1 is the base test for the series. Knowledge tested in Test 1 will also be used in all other tests in the DBA series. Besides testing knowledge of SQL and PL/SQL language constructs, syntax, and usage, Test 1 covers Data Definition Language (DDL), Data Manipulation Language (DML), and Data Control Language (DCL). Also covered in Test 1 are basic data modeling and database design.

➤ *Oracle8: Database Administration (Exam 1Z0-013)*—Test 2 deals with all levels of database administration in Oracle8 (primarily version 8.0.5 and above). Topics include architecture, startup and shutdown, database creation, managing database internal and external constructs (such as redo logs, rollback segments, and tablespaces), and all other Oracle structures. Database auditing, use of National Language Support (NLS) features, and use of SQL*Loader and other utilities are also covered.

➤ *Oracle8: Backup And Recovery (Exam 1Z0-015)*—Test 3 covers one of the most important parts of the Oracle DBA's job: database backup and recovery operations. Test 3 tests knowledge in backup and recovery motives, architecture as it relates to backup and recovery, backup methods, failure scenarios, recovery methodologies, archive logging, supporting 24×7 shops, troubleshooting, and use of Oracle8's standby database features. The test also covers the use of the Recovery Manager (RMAN) product from Oracle, new in Oracle8.

➤ *Oracle8: Performance Tuning (Exam 1Z0-014)*—Test 4 covers all aspects of tuning an Oracle8 database. Topics in both application and database tuning are covered. The test tests knowledge in diagnosis of tuning problems, database optimal configuration, shared pool tuning, buffer cache tuning, Oracle block usage, tuning rollback segments and redo mechanisms, monitoring and detection lock contention, tuning sorts, tuning in OLTP, DSS, and mixed environments, and load optimization.

➤ *Oracle8: Network Administration (Exam 1Z0-016)*—Test 5 covers all
parts of the Net8 product: NET8, Oracle Names Server, the listener
process, lsnrctl (the listener control utility), and the NET8 configuration
files sqlnet.ora, tnsnames.ora, and listener.ora.

To obtain an OCP certificate in database administration, an individual must
pass all five exams. You do not have to take the tests in any particular order.
However, it is usually better to take the examinations in order because the
knowledge tested builds from each exam. The core exams require individuals
to demonstrate competence with all phases of Oracle8 database lifetime activities. If you already have your Oracle7.3 certification, you need to take only one
exam—Oracle8: New Features for Administrators (Exam 1Z0-010)—to upgrade your status.

It's not uncommon for the entire process to take a year or so, and many individuals find that they must take a test more than once to pass. The primary
goal of the *Exam Cram* series is to make it possible, given proper study and
preparation, to pass all of the OCP-DBA tests on the first try.

Finally, certification is an ongoing activity. Once an Oracle version becomes
obsolete, OCP-DBAs (and other OCPs) typically have a six-month time frame
in which they can become recertified on current product versions. (If an individual does not get recertified within the specified time period, his certification
becomes invalid.) Because technology keeps changing and new products con-
tinually supplant old ones, this should come as no surprise.

The best place to keep tabs on the OCP program and its various certifications is on
the Oracle Web site. The current root URL for the OCP program is at **http://
education.oracle.com/certification**. Oracle's certification Web site changes frequently, so if this URL doesn't work, try using the Search tool on Oracle's site
(**www.oracle.com**) with either "OCP" or the quoted phrase "Oracle Certified
Professional Program" as the search string. This will help you find the latest
and most accurate information about the company's certification programs.

Taking A Certification Exam

Alas, testing is not free. You'll be charged $125 for each test you take, whether
you pass or fail. In the United States and Canada, tests are administered by
Sylvan Prometric. Sylvan Prometric can be reached at 1-800-755-3926 or
1-800-891-EXAM, any time from 7:00 A.M. to 6:00 P.M., Central Time, Mon-
day through Friday. If you can't get through at this number, try 1-612-896-7000
or 1-612-820-5707.

To schedule an exam, call at least one day in advance. To cancel or reschedule
an exam, you must call at least one day before the scheduled test time (or you

may be charged the $125 fee). When calling Sylvan Prometric, please have the following information ready for the telesales staffer who handles your call:

➤ Your name, organization, and mailing address.

➤ The name of the exam you want to take.

➤ A method of payment. (The most convenient approach is to supply a valid credit card number with sufficient available credit. Otherwise, payments by check, money order, or purchase order must be received before a test can be scheduled. If the latter methods are required, ask your order-taker for more details.)

An appointment confirmation will be sent to you by mail if you register more than five days before an exam, or it will be sent by fax if less than five days before the exam. A Candidate Agreement letter, which you must sign to take the examination, will also be provided.

On the day of the test, try to arrive at least 15 minutes before the scheduled time slot. You must supply two forms of identification, one of which must be a photo ID.

All exams are completely closed book. In fact, you will not be permitted to take anything with you into the testing area. I suggest that you review the most critical information about the test you're taking just before the test. (*Exam Cram* books provide a brief reference—The Cram Sheet, located inside the front of this book—that lists the essential information from the book in distilled form.) You will have some time to compose yourself, to mentally review this critical information, and even to take a sample orientation exam before you begin the real thing. I suggest you take the orientation test before taking your first exam; they're all more or less identical in layout, behavior, and controls, so you probably won't need to do this more than once.

When you complete an Oracle8 certification exam, the testing software will tell you whether you've passed or failed. Results are broken into several topical areas. Whether you pass or fail, I suggest you ask for—and keep—the detailed report that the test administrator prints for you. You can use the report to help you prepare for another go-round, if necessary, and even if you pass, the report shows areas you may need to review to keep your edge. If you need to retake an exam, you'll have to call Sylvan Prometric, schedule a new test date, and pay another $125.

Tracking OCP Status

Oracle generates transcripts that indicate the exams you have passed and your corresponding test scores. After you pass the necessary set of five exams, you'll be certified as an Oracle8 DBA. Official certification normally takes anywhere from four to six weeks (generally within 30 days), so don't expect to get your credentials overnight. Once certified, you will receive a package with a Welcome Kit that contains a number of elements:

➤ An OCP-DBA certificate, suitable for framing.

➤ A license agreement to use the OCP logo. Once it is sent into Oracle and your packet of logo information is received, the license agreement allows you to use the logo for advertisements, promotions, documents, letterhead, business cards, and so on. An OCP logo sheet, which includes camera-ready artwork, comes with the license.

Many people believe that the benefits of OCP certification go well beyond the perks that Oracle provides to newly anointed members of this elite group. I am starting to see more job listings that request or require applicants to have an OCP-DBA certification, and many individuals who complete the program can qualify for increases in pay and/or responsibility. As an official recognition of hard work and broad knowledge, OCP certification is a badge of honor in many IT organizations.

How To Prepare For An Exam

At a minimum, preparing for OCP-DBA exams requires that you obtain and study the following materials:

➤ The Oracle8 Server version 8.0.5 Documentation Set on CD-ROM.

➤ The exam preparation materials, practice tests, and self-assessment exams on the Oracle certification page (**http://education.oracle.com/certification**). Find the materials, download them, and use them!

➤ This *Exam Cram* book. It's the first and last thing you should read before taking the exam.

In addition, you'll probably find any or all of the following materials useful in your quest for Oracle8 DBA expertise:

➤ *OCP resource kits*—Oracle Corporation has a CD-ROM with example questions and materials to help with the exam; generally, these are provided free by requesting them from your Oracle representative. They have also been offered free for the taking at most Oracle conventions, such as IOUGA-Alive! and Oracle Open World.

➤ *Classroom training*—Oracle, TUSC, LearningTree, and many others offer classroom and computer based training-type material that you will find useful to help you prepare for the exam. But a word of warning: these classes are fairly expensive (in the range of $300 per day of training). However, they do offer a condensed form of learning to help you brush up on your Oracle knowledge. The tests are closely tied to the classroom training provided by Oracle, so I would suggest taking at least the introductory classes to get the Oracle-specific (and classroom-specific) terminology under your belt.

➤ *Other publications*—You'll find direct references to other publications and resources in this book, and there's no shortage of materials available about Oracle8 DBA topics. To help you sift through some of the publications out there, I end each chapter with a "Need To Know More?" section that provides pointers to more complete and exhaustive resources covering the chapter's subject matter. This section tells you where to look for further details.

➤ *The Oracle Support CD-ROM*—Oracle provides a Support CD-ROM on a quarterly basis. This CD-ROM contains useful white papers, bug reports, technical bulletins, and information about release-specific bugs, fixes, and new features. Contact your Oracle representative for a copy.

➤ *The Oracle Administrator and PL/SQL Developer*—These are online references from RevealNet, Inc., an Oracle and database online reference provider. These online references provide instant lookup on thousands of database and developmental topics and are an invaluable resource for study and learning about Oracle. Demo copies can be downloaded from **www.revealnet.com**. Also available at the RevealNet Web site are the DBA and PL/SQL Pipelines, online discussion groups where you can obtain expert information from Oracle DBAs worldwide. The costs of these applications run about $400 each (current pricing is available on the Web site) and are worth every cent.

These required and recommended materials represent a nonpareil collection of sources and resources for Oracle8 DBA topics and software. In the section that follows, I explain how this book works and give you some good reasons why this book should also be on your required and recommended materials list.

About This Book

Each topical *Exam Cram* chapter follows a regular structure, along with graphical cues about especially important or useful material. Here's the structure of a typical chapter:

➤ *Opening hotlists*—Each chapter begins with lists of the terms, tools, and techniques that you must learn and understand before you can be fully conversant with the chapter's subject matter. I follow the hotlists with one or two introductory paragraphs to set the stage for the rest of the chapter.

➤ *Topical coverage*—After the opening hotlists, each chapter covers a series of topics related to the chapter's subject. Throughout this section, I highlight material most likely to appear on a test using a special Exam Alert layout, like this:

> This is what an Exam Alert looks like. Normally, an Exam Alert stresses concepts, terms, software, or activities that will most likely appear in one or more certification test questions. For that reason, any information found offset in Exam Alert format is worthy of unusual attentiveness on your part. Indeed, most of the facts appearing in The Cram Sheet appear as Exam Alerts within the text.

Even if material isn't flagged as an Exam Alert, *all* the contents of this book are associated, at least tangentially, to something test-related. This book is tightly focused for quick test preparation, so you'll find that what appears in the meat of each chapter is critical knowledge.

I have also provided tips that will help build a better foundation of data administration knowledge. Although the information may not be on the exam, it is highly relevant and will help you become a better test-taker.

> This is how tips are formatted. Keep your eyes open for these, and you'll become a test guru in no time!

➤ *Practice questions*—A section at the end of each chapter presents a series of mock test questions and explanations of both correct and incorrect answers. I also try to point out especially tricky questions by using a special icon, like this:

Ordinarily, this icon flags the presence of an especially devious question, if not an outright trick question. Trick questions are calculated to "trap"

you if you don't read them carefully, and more than once at that. Although they're not ubiquitous, such questions make regular appearances in the Oracle8 exams. That's why exam questions are as much about reading comprehension as they are about knowing DBA material inside out and backward.

➤ *Details and resources*—Every chapter ends with a section titled "Need To Know More?". This section provides direct pointers to Oracle and third-party resources that offer further details on the chapter's subject matter. In addition, this section tries to rate the quality and thoroughness of each topic's coverage. If you find a resource you like in this collection, use it, but don't feel compelled to use all these resources. On the other hand, I recommend only resources I use on a regular basis, so none of my recommendations will be a waste of your time or money.

The bulk of the book follows this chapter structure slavishly, but there are a few other elements that I would like to point out. Chapter 11 includes a sample test that provides a good review of the material presented throughout the book to ensure you're ready for the exam. Chapter 12 provides an answer key to the sample test. In addition, you'll find a handy glossary and an index.

Finally, look for The Cram Sheet, which appears inside the front of this *Exam Cram* book. It is a valuable tool that represents a condensed and compiled collection of facts, figures, and tips that I think you should memorize before taking the test. Because you can dump this information out of your head onto a piece of paper before answering any exam questions, you can master this information by brute force—you need to remember it only long enough to write it down when you walk into the test room. You might even want to look at it in the car or in the lobby of the testing center just before you walk in to take the test.

How To Use This Book

If you're prepping for a first-time test, I've structured the topics in this book to build on one another. Therefore, some topics in later chapters make more sense after you've read earlier chapters. That's why I suggest you read this book from front to back for your initial test preparation.

If you need to brush up on a topic or you have to bone up for a second try, use the index or table of contents to go straight to the topics and questions that you need to study. Beyond the tests, I think you'll find this book useful as a tightly focused reference to some of the most important aspects of topics associated with being a DBA, as implemented under Oracle8.

Given all the book's elements and its specialized focus, I've tried to create a tool that you can use to prepare for—and pass—the Oracle OCP-DBA set of examinations. Please share your feedback on the book with me, especially if you have ideas about how I can improve it for future test-takers. I'll consider everything you say carefully, and I try to respond to all suggestions. You can reach me via email at **mikerault@earthlink.net**. Or you can send your questions or comments to **cipq@coriolis.com**. Please remember to include the title of the book in your message; otherwise, I'll be forced to guess which book of mine you're making a suggestion about. Also, be sure to check out the Web pages at **www.certificationinsider.com,** where you'll find information updates, commentary, and certification information.

Thanks, and enjoy the book!

Self-Assessment

I've included a Self-Assessment in this *Exam Cram* to help you evaluate your readiness to tackle Oracle Certified Professional-Oracle8 Certified Database Administrator (OCP-DBA) certification. It should also help you understand what you need to master the topic of this book—namely, Exam 1Z0-001 (Test 1), "Introduction to Oracle: SQL and PL/SQL." But before you tackle this Self-Assessment, let's talk about the concerns you may face when pursuing an Oracle8 OCP-DBA certification, and what an ideal Oracle8 OCP-DBA candidate might look like.

Oracle8 OCP-DBAs In The Real World

In the next section, I describe an ideal Oracle8 OCP-DBA candidate, knowing full well that only a few actual candidates meet this ideal. In fact, my description of that ideal candidate might seem downright scary. But take heart; although the requirements to obtain an Oracle8 OCP-DBA may seem pretty formidable, they are by no means impossible to meet. However, you should be keenly aware that it does take time, requires some expense, and consumes a substantial effort.

You can get all the real-world motivation you need from knowing that many others have gone before you. You can follow in their footsteps. If you're willing to tackle the process seriously and do what it takes to obtain the necessary experience and knowledge, you can take—and pass—the certification tests. In fact, the *Exam Crams* and the companion *Exam Preps* are designed to make it as easy as possible for you to prepare for these exams. But prepare you must!

The same, of course, is true for other Oracle certifications, including:

➤ Oracle7.3 OCP-DBA, which is similar to the Oracle8 OCP-DBA certification but requires only four core exams

➤ Application Developer, Oracle Developer Rel 1 OCP, which is aimed at software developers and requires five exams

➤ Application Developer, Oracle Developer Rel 2 OCP, which is aimed at software developers and requires five exams

➤ Oracle Database Operators OCP, which is aimed at database operators and requires only one exam

➤ Oracle Java Technology Certification OCP, which is aimed at Java developers and requires five exams

The Ideal Oracle8 OCP-DBA Candidate

Just to give you some idea of what an ideal Oracle8 OCP-DBA candidate is like, here are some relevant statistics about the background and experience such an individual might have. Don't worry if you don't meet these qualifications (or if you don't even come close), because this world is far from ideal, and where you fall short is simply where you'll have more work to do. The ideal candidate will have:

➤ Academic or professional training in relational databases, Structured Query Language (SQL), performance tuning, backup and recovery, and Net8 administration

➤ Three-plus years of professional database administration experience, including experience installing and upgrading Oracle executables, creating and tuning databases, troubleshooting connection problems, creating users, and managing backup and recovery scenarios

I believe that well under half of all certification candidates meet these requirements. In fact, most probably meet less than half of these requirements (that is, at least when they begin the certification process). But, because all those who have their certifications already survived this ordeal, you can survive it, too—especially if you heed what this Self-Assessment can tell you about what you already know and what you need to learn.

Put Yourself To The Test

The following series of questions and observations is designed to help you figure out how much work you'll face in pursuing Oracle certification and what kinds of resources you may consult on your quest. Be absolutely honest in your answers, or you'll end up wasting money on exams you're not ready to take. There are no right or wrong answers, only steps along the path to certification. Only you can decide where you really belong in the broad spectrum of aspiring candidates.

Two things should be clear from the outset, however:

➤ Even a modest background in computer science will be helpful.

➤ Hands-on experience with Oracle products and technologies is an essential ingredient to certification success.

Educational Background

1. Have you ever taken any computer-related classes? [Yes or No]

   If Yes, proceed to question 2; if No, proceed to question 4.

2. Have you taken any classes on relational databases? [Yes or No]

   If Yes, you will probably be able to handle Oracle's architecture and network administration discussions. If you're rusty, brush up on the basic concepts of databases and networks. If the answer is No, consider some basic reading in this area. I strongly recommend a good Oracle database administration book I wrote: *Oracle8 Administration and Management* (Wiley, 1998). Or, if this title doesn't appeal to you, check out reviews for other, similar titles at your favorite online bookstore.

3. Have you taken any networking concepts or technologies classes? [Yes or No]

   If Yes, you will probably be able to handle Oracle's networking terminology, concepts, and technologies (but brace yourself for frequent departures from normal usage). If you're rusty, brush up on basic networking concepts and terminology. If your answer is No, you might want to check out the Oracle technet Web site (**http://technet.oracle.com**) and read some of the white papers on Net8. If you have access to the Oracle MetaLink Web site, or the Technet Web site, download the Oracle SQL and PL/SQL User's Guides for Oracle8 version 8.0.5.

4. Have you done any reading on relational databases or networks? [Yes or No]

   If Yes, review the requirements from questions 2 and 3. If you meet those, move to the next section, "Hands-On Experience." If you answered No, consult the recommended reading for both topics. This kind of strong background will be of great help in preparing you for the Oracle exams.

Hands-On Experience

Another important key to success on all of the Oracle tests is hands-on experience. If I leave you with only one realization after taking this Self-Assessment, it should be that there's no substitute for time spent installing, configuring, and using the various Oracle products upon which you'll be tested repeatedly and in depth.

5. Have you programmed in and worked with SQL and PL/SQL using SQL*Plus? [Yes or No]

   If Yes, make sure you understand basic concepts as covered in Exam 1Z0-001 (Test 1), "Introduction to Oracle: SQL and PL/SQL."

You can download the candidate certification guide, objectives, practice exams, and other information about Oracle exams from the company's Training and Certification page on the Web at **http://education.oracle.com/certification**.

If you haven't worked with Oracle, you must obtain a copy of Oracle8 or Personal Oracle8. Then, learn about SQL and PL/SQL as they are implemented in Oracle8.

For any and all of these Oracle exams, the candidate guides for the topics involved are a good study resource. You can download them free from the Oracle Web site (**http://education.oracle.com**). You can also download information on purchasing additional practice tests ($99 per exam).

If you have the funds or your employer will pay your way, consider taking a class at an Oracle training and education center.

Before you even think about taking any Oracle exam, make sure you've spent enough time with database design, SQL, and PL/SQL to understand how they are used, particularly in the SQL*Plus environment, and how to troubleshoot SQL and PL/SQL programs when things go wrong. Additionally, you should be conversant with the database utilities such as import, export, and SQL*Loader. This will help you in the exam—as well as in real life.

Testing Your Exam-Readiness

Whether you attend a formal class on a specific topic to get ready for an exam or use written materials to study on your own, some preparation for the Oracle certification exams is essential. At $125 a try, pass or fail, you want to do everything you can to pass on your first try. That's where studying comes in.

I have included in this book several practice exam questions for each chapter and a sample test, so if you don't score well on the chapter questions, you can study more and then tackle the sample test at the end of the book. If you don't earn a score of at least 70 percent after this test, you'll want to investigate the other practice test resources I mention in this section.

For any given subject, consider taking a class if you've tackled self-study materials, taken the test, and failed anyway. If you can afford the privilege, the opportunity to interact with an instructor and fellow students can make all the difference in the world. For information about Oracle classes, visit the Training and Certification page at **http://education.oracle.com**.

If you can't afford to take a class, visit the Training and Certification page anyway, because it also includes free practice exams that you can download. Even if you can't afford to spend much, you should still invest in some low-cost practice exams from commercial vendors.

6. Have you taken a practice exam on your chosen test subject? [Yes or No]

   If Yes—and you scored 70 percent or better—you're probably ready to tackle the real thing. If your score isn't above that crucial threshold, keep at it until you break that barrier. If you answered No, obtain all the free and low-budget practice tests you can find (or afford) and get to work. Keep at it until you can comfortably break the passing threshold.

 There is no better way to assess your test readiness than to take a good-quality practice exam and pass with a score of 70 percent or better. When I'm preparing, I shoot for 80-plus percent, just to leave room for the "weirdness factor" that sometimes shows up on Oracle exams.

Assessing Your Readiness For Exam 1Z0-001 (Test 1)

In addition to the general exam-readiness information in the previous section, other resources are available to help you prepare for the Introduction to Oracle: SQL and PL/SQL exam. For starters, visit the Revealnet pipeline (**www.revealnet.com**) or **http://technet.oracle.com**. These are great places to ask questions and get good answers, or simply to observe the questions that others ask (along with the answers, of course).

Oracle exam mavens also recommend checking the Oracle Knowledge Base from RevealNet. You can get information on purchasing the RevealNet software at **www.revealnet.com.**

For Introduction to Oracle: SQL and PL/SQL preparation in particular, I'd also like to recommend that you check out one or more of these books as you prepare to take the exam:

➤ Ault, Michael. *Oracle8 Administration and Management.* John Wiley and Sons, New York, New York, 1998.

➤ Honour, Dalberth, and Mehta Kaplan. *Oracle8 How-To.* Waite Group Press, Corte Madera, California, 1998. ISBN 1-57169-123-5.

➤ *Oracle8 Server SQL Reference, Release 8.0,* Volumes 1 and 2. Oracle Corporation, Redwood Shores, California, June 1997. Part No. A54648-01 and A54649-01.

One last note: Hopefully, it makes sense to stress the importance of hands-on experience in the context of the Introduction to Oracle: SQL and PL/SQL exam. As you review the material for this exam, you'll realize that hands-on experience with Oracle8 commands, tools, and utilities is invaluable.

Onward, Through The Fog!

Once you've assessed your readiness, undertaken the right background studies, obtained the hands-on experience that will help you understand the products and technologies at work, and reviewed the many sources of information to help you prepare for a test, you'll be ready to take a round of practice tests. When your scores come back positive enough to get you through the exam, you're ready to go after the real thing. If you follow my assessment regime, you'll not only know what you need to study, but when you're ready to make a test date at Sylvan. Good luck!

Oracle OCP
Certification Exams

Terms you'll need to understand:

√ Radio button

√ Checkbox

√ Exhibit

√ Multiple-choice question formats

√ Careful reading

√ Process of elimination

Techniques you'll need to master:

√ Assessing your exam-readiness

√ Preparing to take a certification exam

√ Practicing (to make perfect)

√ Making the best use of the testing software

√ Budgeting your time

√ Saving the hardest questions until last

√ Guessing (as a last resort)

As experiences go, test-taking is not something that most people anticipate eagerly, no matter how well they're prepared. In most cases, familiarity helps ameliorate test anxiety. In plain English, this means you probably won't be as nervous when you take your fourth or fifth Oracle certification exam as you will be when you take your first one.

But no matter whether it's your first test or your tenth, understanding the exam-taking particulars (how much time to spend on questions, the setting you'll be in, and so on) and the testing software will help you concentrate on the material rather than on the environment. Likewise, mastering a few basic test-taking skills should help you recognize—and perhaps even outfox—some of the tricks and gotchas you're bound to find in some of the Oracle test questions.

In this chapter, I'll explain the testing environment and software, as well as describe some proven test-taking strategies you should be able to use to your advantage.

Assessing Exam-Readiness

Before you take any Oracle exam, I strongly recommend that you read through and take the Self-Assessment included with this book (it appears just before this chapter, in fact). This will help you compare your knowledge base to the requirements for obtaining an OCP, and it will also help you identify parts of your background or experience that may be in need of improvement, enhancement, or further learning. If you get the right set of basics under your belt, obtaining Oracle certification will be that much easier.

Once you've gone through the Self-Assessment, you can remedy those topical areas where your background or experience may not measure up to an ideal certification candidate. But you can also tackle subject matter for individual tests at the same time, so you can continue making progress while you're catching up in some areas.

Once you've worked through an *Exam Cram*, have read the supplementary materials, and have taken the practice test at the end of the book, you'll have a pretty clear idea of when you should be ready to take the real exam. Although I strongly recommend that you keep practicing until your scores top the 70 percent mark, 75 percent would be a good goal to give yourself some margin for error in a real exam situation (where stress will play more of a role than when you practice). Once you hit that point, you should be ready to go. But if you get through the practice exam in this book without attaining that score, you should keep taking practice tests and studying the materials until you get there. You'll find more information about other practice test vendors in the

Self-Assessment, along with even more pointers on how to study and prepare. But now, on to the exam itself!

The Testing Situation

When you arrive at the Sylvan Prometric Testing Center where you scheduled your test, you'll need to sign in with a test coordinator. He or she will ask you to produce two forms of identification, one of which must be a photo ID. Once you've signed in and your time slot arrives, you'll be asked to leave any books, bags, or other items you brought with you, and you'll be escorted into a closed room. Typically, that room will be furnished with anywhere from one to half a dozen computers, and each workstation is separated from the others by dividers designed to keep you from seeing what's happening on someone else's computer.

You'll be furnished with a pen or pencil and a blank sheet of paper, or in some cases, an erasable plastic sheet and an erasable felt-tip pen. You're allowed to write down any information you want on this sheet, and you can write stuff on both sides of the page. I suggest that you memorize as much as possible of the material that appears on The Cram Sheet (inside the front of this book), and then write that information down on the blank sheet as soon as you sit down in front of the test machine. You can refer to the sheet any time you like during the test, but you'll have to surrender it when you leave the room.

Most test rooms feature a wall with a large window. This allows the test coordinator to monitor the room, to prevent test-takers from talking to one another, and to observe anything out of the ordinary that might go on. The test coordinator will have preloaded the Oracle certification test you've signed up for, and you'll be permitted to start as soon as you're seated in front of the machine.

All Oracle certification exams permit you to take up to a certain maximum amount of time (usually 90 minutes) to complete the test (the test itself will tell you, and it maintains an on-screen counter/clock so that you can check the time remaining any time you like). Each exam consists of between 60 and 70 questions, randomly selected from a pool of questions.

 The passing score varies per exam and the questions selected. For Exam 1Z0-001, the passing score is 72 percent.

All Oracle certification exams are computer generated and use a multiple-choice format. Although this might sound easy, the questions are constructed not just to check your mastery of basic facts and figures about Oracle8 DBA topics, but also require you to evaluate one or more sets of circumstances or requirements. Often, you'll be asked to give more than one answer to a question; likewise, you may be asked to select the best or most effective solution to a problem from a range of choices, all of which technically are correct. The tests are quite an adventure, and they involve real thinking. This book will show you what to expect and how to deal with the problems, puzzles, and predicaments you're likely to find on the tests—in particular, Exam 1Z0-001, "Introduction to Oracle: SQL and PL/SQL."

Test Layout And Design

A typical test question is depicted in Question 1. It's a multiple-choice question that requires you to select a single correct answer. Following the question is a brief summary of each potential answer and why it was either right or wrong.

Question 1

You issue this SQL*Plus command:

```
SAVE my_file REPLACE
```

What task has been accomplished?

- ○ a. A new file was created.
- ○ b. An existing file was replaced.
- ○ c. The command was continued to the next line of the SQL prompt.
- ○ d. No task was accomplished because a file extension was not designated.

The correct answer is b. The **SAVE** command has only one option: **REPLACE**. **SAVE** without **REPLACE** requires that the file not exist; **SAVE** with **REPLACE** replaces an existing file. No file extension is required, the default is ".sql." Answer a is incorrect because the **REPLACE** option is specified. With just a **SAVE**, a new file is created; with a **SAVE...REPLACE**, an existing file is replaced. Answer c is incorrect because the continuation of a line is done automatically when you hit Return. Answer d is incorrect because if a suffix isn't specified, a default one is added.

This sample question corresponds closely to those you'll see on Oracle certification tests. To select the correct answer during the test, you would position the cursor over the radio button next to answer b and click the mouse to select that particular choice. The only difference between the certification test and this question is that the real questions are not immediately followed by the answers.

Next, I'll examine a question where one or more answers are possible. This type of question provides checkboxes, rather than radio buttons, for marking all appropriate selections.

Question 2

Which three ways can the SQL buffer be terminated?

- ❏ a. Enter a slash (/).
- ❏ b. Press Return (or Enter) once.
- ❏ c. Enter an asterisk (*).
- ❏ d. Enter a semicolon (;).
- ❏ e. Press Return (or Enter) twice.
- ❏ f. Press Esc twice.

The correct answers for this question are a, d, and e. A slash (/) is usually used for termination of PL/SQL blocks, procedures, and functions, but it can also be used for SQL commands. A semicolon (;) is generally used for terminating SQL commands. Pressing the Return key (or the Enter key on many keyboards) twice in succession will also tell the buffer your command is complete, but will not execute it. Most of the time, the slash or semicolon will also result in execution of the previous command (except within a PL/SQL block); a subsequent entry of the slash, the semicolon, or an "r" (short for run) will be required to execute the command(s) terminated with a double Return.

For this type of question, one or more answers must be selected to answer the question correctly. For Question 2, you would have to position the cursor over the checkboxes next to items a, d, and e to obtain credit for a correct answer.

These two basic types of questions can appear in many forms. They constitute the foundation on which all the Oracle certification exam questions rest. More complex questions may include so-called "exhibits," which are usually tables or data-content layouts of one form or another. You'll be expected to use the information displayed in the exhibit to guide your answer to the question.

Other questions involving exhibits may use charts or diagrams to help document a workplace scenario that you'll be asked to troubleshoot or configure.

Paying careful attention to such exhibits is the key to success—be prepared to toggle between the picture and the question as you work. Often, both are complex enough that you might not be able to remember all of either one.

Using Oracle's Test Software Effectively

A well-known test-taking principle is to read over the entire test from start to finish first, but to answer only those questions that you feel absolutely sure of on the first pass. On subsequent passes, you can dive into more complex questions, knowing how many such questions you have to deal with.

Fortunately, Oracle test software makes this approach easy to implement. At the bottom of each question, you'll find a checkbox that permits you to mark that question for a later visit. (Note that marking questions makes review easier, but you can return to any question by clicking the Forward and Back buttons repeatedly until you get to the question.) As you read each question, if you answer only those you're sure of and mark for review those that you're not, you can keep going through a decreasing list of open questions as you knock the trickier ones off in order.

 There's at least one potential benefit to reading the test over completely before answering the trickier questions: Sometimes, you find information in later questions that sheds more light on earlier ones. Other times, information you read in later questions might jog your memory about Oracle8 DBA facts, figures, or behavior that also will help with earlier questions. Either way, you'll come out ahead if you defer those questions about which you're not absolutely sure of the answer(s).

Keep working on the questions until you are absolutely sure of all your answers or until you know you'll run out of time. If there are still unanswered questions, you'll want to zip through them and guess. No answer guarantees no credit for a question, and a guess has at least a chance of being correct. (Oracle scores blank answers and incorrect answers as equally wrong.)

At the very end of your test period, you're better off guessing than leaving questions blank or unanswered.

Taking Testing Seriously

The most important advice I can give you about taking any Oracle test is this: Read each question carefully. Some questions are deliberately ambiguous; some use double negatives; others use terminology in incredibly precise ways. I've taken numerous practice tests and real tests myself, and in nearly every test I've missed at least one question because I didn't read it closely or carefully enough.

Here are some suggestions on how to deal with the tendency to jump to an answer too quickly:

➤ Make sure you read every word in the question. If you find yourself jumping ahead impatiently, go back and start over.

➤ As you read, try to restate the question in your own terms. If you can do this, you should be able to pick the correct answer(s) much more easily.

➤ When returning to a question after your initial read-through, reread every word again—otherwise, the mind falls quickly into a rut. Sometimes seeing a question afresh after turning your attention elsewhere lets you see something you missed before, but the strong tendency is to see what you've seen before. Try to avoid that tendency at all costs.

➤ If you return to a question more than twice, try to articulate to yourself what you don't understand about the question, why the answers don't appear to make sense, or what appears to be missing. If you chew on the subject for a while, your subconscious might provide the details that are lacking, or you may notice a "trick" that will point to the right answer.

Above all, try to deal with each question by thinking through what you know about being an Oracle8 DBA—utilities, characteristics, behaviors, facts, and figures involved. By reviewing what you know (and what you've written down on your information sheet), you'll often recall or understand things sufficiently to determine the answer to the question.

Question-Handling Strategies

Based on the tests I've taken, a couple of interesting trends in the answers have become apparent. For those questions that take only a single answer, usually two or three of the answers will be obviously incorrect, and two of the answers will be plausible. But, of course, only one can be correct. Unless the answer leaps out at you (and if it does, reread the question to look for a trick; sometimes those are the ones you're most likely to get wrong), begin the process of answering by eliminating those answers that are obviously wrong.

Things to look for in the "obviously wrong" category include spurious command choices or table or view names, nonexistent software or command options, and terminology you've never seen before. If you've done your homework for a test, no valid information should be completely new to you. In that case, unfamiliar or bizarre terminology probably indicates a totally bogus answer. As long as you're sure what's right, it's easy to eliminate what's wrong.

Numerous questions assume that the default behavior of a particular Oracle utility (such as SQL*Plus or SQL*Loader) is in effect. It's essential, therefore, to know and understand the default settings for SQL*Plus, SQL*Loader, and Server Manager utilities. If you know the defaults and understand what they mean, this knowledge will help you cut through many Gordian knots.

Likewise, when dealing with questions that require multiple answers, you must know and select all of the correct options to get credit. This, too, qualifies as an example of why careful reading is so important.

As you work your way through the test, another counter that Oracle thankfully provides will come in handy—the number of questions completed and questions outstanding. Budget your time by making sure that you've completed one-fourth of the questions one-quarter of the way through the test period (between 13 and 17 questions in the first 22 or 23 minutes). Check again three-quarters of the way through (between 39 and 51 questions in the first 66 to 69 minutes).

If you're not through after 85 minutes, use the last five minutes to guess your way through the remaining questions. Remember, guesses are potentially more valuable than blank answers, because blanks are always wrong, but a guess might turn out to be right. If you haven't a clue with any of the remaining questions, pick answers at random, or choose all a's, b's, and so on. The important thing is to submit a test for scoring that has an answer for every question.

Mastering The Inner Game

In the final analysis, knowledge breeds confidence, and confidence breeds success. If you study the materials in this book carefully and review all of the questions at the end of each chapter, you should be aware of those areas where additional studying is required.

Next, follow up by reading some or all of the materials recommended in the "Need To Know More?" section at the end of each chapter. The idea is to become familiar enough with the concepts and situations that you find in the sample questions to be able to reason your way through similar situations on a real test. If you know the material, you have every right to be confident that you can pass the test.

Once you've worked your way through the book, take the practice test in Chapter 11. The test will provide a reality check and will help you identify areas you need to study further. Make sure you follow up and review materials related to the questions you miss before scheduling a real test. Only when you've covered all the ground and feel comfortable with the whole scope of the practice test, should you take a real test.

> If you take the practice test (Chapter 11) and don't score at least 75 percent correct, you'll want to practice further. At a minimum, download the practice tests and the self-assessment tests from the Oracle Education Web site's download page (its location appears in the next section). If you're more ambitious or better funded, you might want to purchase a practice test from one of the third-party vendors that offers them.

Armed with the information in this book and with the determination to augment your knowledge, you should be able to pass the certification exam. But if you don't work at it, you'll spend the test fee more than once before you finally do pass. If you prepare seriously, the execution should go flawlessly. Good luck!

Additional Resources

By far, the best source of information about Oracle certification tests comes from Oracle itself. Because its products and technologies—and the tests that go with them—change frequently, the best place to go for exam-related information is online.

If you haven't already visited the Oracle certification pages, do so right now. As I'm writing this chapter, the certification home page resides at **http:// education.oracle.com/certification/** (see Figure 1.1).

> *Note: It might not be there by the time you read this, or it may have been replaced by something new and different, because things change regularly on the Oracle site. Should this happen, please read the section titled "Coping With Change On The Web," later in this chapter.*

The menu options in the left column of the page point to the most important sources of information in the certification pages. Here's what to check out:

➤ *FAQ's*—Frequently Asked Questions, yours may get answered here.

➤ *What's New*—Any new tests will be described here.

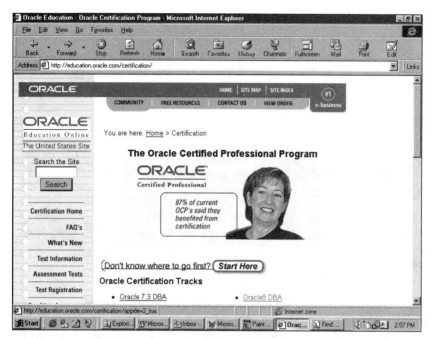

Figure 1.1   The Oracle certification page should be your starting point for further investigation of the most current exam and preparation information.

➤ *Test Information*—This is a detailed section that provides many jump points to detailed test descriptions for the several OCP certifications.

➤ *Assessment Tests*—This section provides a download of the latest copy of the assessment test after you fill out an online questionnaire.

➤ *Test Registration*—This section provides information for phone registration and a link to the Prometric Web page for online registration. Also, this section provides a list of testing sites outside of the USA.

➤ *Candidate Agreements*—Just what are you agreeing to be by becoming Oracle certified?

➤ *Oracle Partners*—This link provides information about test discounts and other offers for Oracle Partner companies.

Of course, these are just the high points of what's available in the Oracle certification pages. As you browse through them—and I strongly recommend that you do—you'll probably find other things I didn't mention here that are every bit as interesting and compelling.

Coping With Change On The Web

Sooner or later, all the specifics I've shared with you about the Oracle certification pages, and all the other Web-based resources I mention throughout the rest of this book, will go stale or be replaced by newer information. In some cases, the URLs you find here might lead you to their replacements; in other cases, the URLs will go nowhere, leaving you with the dreaded "404 File not found" error message.

When that happens, please don't give up. There's always a way to find what you want on the Web—if you're willing to invest some time and energy. To begin with, most large or complex Web sites—and Oracle's qualifies on both counts—offer a search engine. As long as you can get to Oracle's home page (and I'm sure that it will stay at **www.oracle.com** for a long while yet), you can use this tool to help you find what you need.

The more particular or focused you can make a search request, the more likely it is that the results will include information you can use. For instance, you can search the string "training and certification" to produce a lot of data about the subject in general, but if you're looking for the Preparation Guide for the Oracle DBA tests, you'll be more likely to get there quickly if you use a search string such as this:

```
"DBA" AND "preparation guide"
```

Likewise, if you want to find the training and certification downloads, try a search string such as this one:

```
"training and certification" AND "download page"
```

Finally, don't be afraid to use general search tools such as **www.search.com**, **www.altavista.com**, or **www.excite.com** to search for related information. Even though Oracle offers the best information about its certification exams online, there are plenty of third-party sources of information, training, and assistance in this area that do not have to follow a party line like Oracle does. The bottom line is this: If you can't find something where the book says it lives, start looking around. If worse comes to worse, you can always email me! I just might have a clue. My email address is **mikerault@earthlink.net**.

DML: Using The INSERT, UPDATE, And DELETE Commands

2

Terms you'll need to understand:

√ DECODE

√ INSERT

√ UPDATE

√ DELETE

√ TRUNCATE

√ COMMIT

√ ROLLBACK

Techniques you'll need to master:

√ Using intrinsic SQL functions to perform operations and conversions on data

√ Using **INSERT** to place data into tables

√ Using **UPDATE** to change data in tables

√ Using **DELETE** to perform partial data removal from tables

√ Using and applying **COMMIT** and **ROLLBACK** commands in Oracle to make changes permanent or remove them

Database structures, objects, and files aren't useful unless you have a means of putting data into the database, altering stored values, retrieving that data when needed, and removing that data when it's no longer needed. This manipulation of database data is handled with Data Manipulation Language (DML) statements. In this chapter, I'll cover the Oracle DML elements. The test this book covers encompasses SQL (Structured Query Language) and PL/SQL (Procedural Language/SQL). SQL consists of Data Definition Language (DDL), Data Manipulation Language (DML), and Data Control Language (DCL). You should be able to:

➤ Identify improper command syntax.

➤ Analyze tables to determine the SQL needed to generate appropriate result sets.

➤ Use Oracle-intrinsic SQL functions.

➤ Understand how basic SQL statements operate against a database.

It's vital for the database administrator (DBA) to have a complete understanding of SQL, DDL, DML, DCL, and PL/SQL.

DML Elements

The actual command elements that form the DML portion of SQL are few in number; they are: **INSERT, UPDATE, DELETE, SELECT,** and **TRUNCATE.** Oracle also contains operators (unary and binary) and functions. I'll discuss operators and functions first because they're used to construct parts of the DML commands. The **SELECT** command is covered in Chapter 3.

Oracle Operators

Oracle has two types of operators: unary and binary. Unary operators operate on only one operand and are shown in the format:

Operator operand

A binary operator operates on two operands and generally is shown in the format:

Operator operand, operand

Special operators also exist that can operate on more than two operands.

If an operator is given a **NULL** argument, and if it's any operator other than the concatenation operator (a double pipe: ||), its results are **NULL.**

Precedence governs the order in which operands are evaluated. Those with high precedence are evaluated before those with low precedence, and those with equal precedence are evaluated left to right.

Precedence of operators (from highest to lowest) is as follows:

➤ *(+) and (-)*—Unary operators (positive and negative number indicators) and the **PRIOR** operator.

➤ *(*) and (/)*—Multiplication and division operators.

➤ *Binary (=)*—Arithmetic operators (such as addition [+] and subtraction [-]) and the concatenation (||) operator.

➤ *All comparison operators*—The **NOT, AND,** and **OR** logical operators.

 Parentheses always override precedence. Operators inside parentheses are always evaluated first.

Set operators are also supported in Oracle SQL. The set operators are:

➤ **UNION**—Shows all nonduplicate results from queries A and B.

➤ **UNION ALL**—Shows all results from queries A and B (including duplicates).

➤ **INTERSECT**—Shows common results from queries A and B.

➤ **MINUS**—Shows only noncommon results from queries A and B.

 All set operators have equal precedence.

Comparison operators allow the comparison of two values. The comparison operators are:

➤ (=)—Does A equal B?

➤ (!=)—Does A not equal B?

➤ (^=)—Does A not equal B?

➤ (<>)—Does A not equal B?

➤ (>)—Is A greater than B?

➤ (<)—Is A less than B?

➤ (>=)—Is A greater than or equal to B?

➤ (<=)—Is A less than or equal to B?

➤ IN—Is A in this set?

➤ NOT IN—Is A not in this set?

➤ ANY, SOME—Combines with certain operators—(=), (!=), (<),(>), (<=), (>=)—and compares a value to each value in a list returned from a query. Evaluates to **FALSE** if no rows are returned.

➤ ALL—Combines with certain operators—(=), (!=), (<), (>), (<=), (>=)— and says that a value must relate to the entire list or to the subquery as indicated.

➤ [NOT] BETWEEN *x* AND *y*—Checks for inclusion between *x* and *y* values, inclusive of the values *x* and *y*.

➤ EXISTS—Evaluates to **TRUE** if a subquery returns at least one row.

➤ *X* [NOT] LIKE *y* [ESCAPE 'z']—Evaluates to **TRUE** if *x* does not match the pattern *y*. The *y* value can contain the wildcard characters % (percent) and _ (underscore). Any character except % and _ can follow the **ESCAPE** clause to allow comparison against restricted characters such as the wildcards. A wildcard can be used if it is preceded by the **ESCAPE** character. The default escape character is the \ character on some platforms.

➤ IS [NOT] NULL—Tests for **NULL** values and is the only valid method to test for nulls. **NULL** values cannot be tested for using equality or nonequality operators because, by definition, a **NULL** is undefined.

The logical operator most used in SQL is probably the **AND** operator because it is used to add more conditional clauses to a **WHERE** clause. The logical operator used to search a list of values is the **IN** operator. The operator most used in single-row subqueries is the equal operator.

SQL Functions

SQL functions allow the manipulation of values, and they return a result. Functions can have multiple arguments yet always return a single value. Functions have the general format:

```
Function(arg1, arg2, ...)
```

If possible, functions will do implicit conversion of data types if a type other than the one needed is specified to them. Calling most functions with a NULL will return a NULL. The only functions that don't return a NULL are:

➤ CONCAT—Concatenates strings.

➤ DECODE—Performs explicit conversions.

➤ DUMP—Dumps a value.

➤ NVL—Allows for NULL value substitution.

➤ REPLACE—Allows for string replacement.

Functions are either *scalar* (single row) or *aggregate* (group) in nature. A single-row function returns a single result row for each row of a queried table or view. An aggregate function returns a single value for a group of rows.

A single-value function can appear in a SELECT statement if the SELECT statement doesn't contain a GROUP BY clause. Single-value functions can also appear in WHERE, START WITH, and CONNECT BY clauses. Single-value functions can also be nested.

Group functions can be used in select lists and HAVING clauses. If a SELECT statement uses group functions, the GROUP BY clause must include all columns not affected by group functions.

Functions are divided into NUMBER, CHARACTER, and DATE functions.

The SQL Numeric Single-Value Functions

In the NUMBER functions listed in this section, n can be an expression. If the accuracy is not specified in the following list, it can be up to 38 places. The NUMBER functions are:

➤ ABS(n)—Returns the absolute value of n.

➤ ACOS(n)—Returns the arc-cosine of n. Accurate to 30 places.

➤ ASIN(n)—Returns the arc-sine of n. Accurate to 30 places.

➤ ATAN(n)—Returns the arc-tangent of n. Accurate to 30 places.

➤ ATAN2(n,m)—Returns the arc-tangent of n and m outputs in the range of $-pi$ to pi, depending on the signs of n and m. Results are expressed in radians. Accurate to 30 places.

➤ CEIL(n)—Rounds n up.

➤ COS(n)—Returns the cosine of n. Accurate to 36 places.

➤ COSH(*n*)—Returns the hyperbolic cosine of *n*. Accurate to 36 places.

➤ EXP(*n*)—Returns *e* raised to the *n*th power (natural log). Accurate to 36 places.

➤ FLOOR(*n*)—Rounds *n* down.

➤ LN(*n*)—Returns the natural log of *n* where *n* is greater than zero. Accurate to 36 places.

➤ LOG(*m,n*)—Returns the logarithm, base *m*, of *n*. The base can be any positive number other than 0 or 1, and *n* can be any positive number. Accurate to 36 places.

➤ MOD(*m,n*)—Returns the remainder of *m* divided by *n*. Returns *m* if *n* is 0.

➤ POWER(*m,n*)—Returns *m* raised to the *n*th power.

➤ ROUND(*n* [,*m*])—Returns *n* rounded to *m* decimal places; *m* can be positive or negative, depending on which side of the decimal you wish to round.

➤ SIGN(*n*)—Returns -1 if *n* is less than 0. Returns 0 if *n* equals 0. Returns 1 if *n* is more than 0.

➤ SIN(*n*)—Returns the sine of *n*. Accurate to 36 places.

➤ SINH(*n*)—Returns the hyperbolic sine of *n*. Accurate to 36 places.

➤ SQRT(*n*)—Returns the square root of *n*. Accurate to 36 places.

➤ TAN(*n*)—Returns the tangent of *n*. Accurate to 36 places.

➤ TANH(*n*)—Returns the hyperbolic tangent of *n*. Accurate to 36 places.

➤ TRUNC(*n* [,*m*])—Returns *n* truncated to *m* decimal places. If *m* is omitted, truncates to zero decimal places.

Numeric functions provide great calculation abilities within Oracle. You can perform almost any arithmetic operation with the proper combination of these functions and operators.

Character Functions That Return Character Values

Oracle also provides a rich function set for character data. Character data— such as **CHAR** and **VARCHAR2** values—can be altered, translated, truncated, or appended to through the use of functions. **VARCHAR2** data types are limited to 4,000 bytes, and **CHAR** data types are limited to 2,000 bytes in Oracle8.

If any result exceeds the maximum size for its data type, the result is truncated to that length and no error is returned.

The character functions included in Oracle are:

➤ CHR(*n*)—Returns the character having the ASCII-code equivalent to *n* in the current character set for the database.

➤ CONCAT(*char1*, *char2*)—Returns *char1* concatenated to *char2*.

➤ INITCAP(*char*)—Returns *char* with the first letter of each word in uppercase.

➤ LOWER(*char*)—Returns *char* with all characters lowercase.

➤ LPAD(*char1*,n [,*char2*])—Returns *char1* left, padded with either blanks or the value of *char2*.

➤ LTRIM(*char1* [,*set*])—Returns *char1* left-trimmed of blanks if *set* isn't specified, or trimmed of *set* characters if it is.

➤ NLS_INITCAP(*char* [, '*nlsparams*'])—Returns *char* with all initial letters capitalized. The *nlsparams* entry determines the **NLS_SORT** setting or is set to **BINARY**.

➤ NLS_LOWER(*char* [, '*nlsparams*'])—Returns *char* all lowercase. The *nlsparams* values are the same as for **NLS_INITCAP**.

➤ NLS_SORT(*char*[, '*nlsparams*'])—Returns a string of bytes used to sort *char*. The value of *nlsparams* can have the form: **NLS_SORT** = *sort*, where *sort* is a linguistic sort sequence or **BINARY**. If the *nlsparams* setting is left off, the default setting for your session is used.

➤ NLS_UPPER (*char* [, '*nlsparams*'])—Returns *char* all uppercase. The *nlsparams* values are the same as for **NLS_INITCAP**.

➤ REPLACE(*char*, *search_string*[, *replacement_string*])—In *char*, replaces all instances of *search_string* with the value of *replacement_string*. Removes all instances of *search_string* if no *replacement_string* is specified.

➤ RPAD(*char1*, n [,*char2*])—Right-pads *char1* with the value of *char2*, or with a blank if *char2* isn't specified to a length of *n*.

➤ RTRIM(*char* [,*set*])—Returns *char* with the rightmost characters in *set* removed. If *set* isn't specified, all rightmost blanks are removed.

➤ SOUNDEX(*char*)—Returns the soundex equivalent of the value of *char*. This is useful in searching for words that sound alike but are spelled differently.

➤ SUBSTR(*char* *m* [,*n*])—Returns the substring located in *char*, starting at *m* and ending at *n*. If *n* isn't specified, it returns the value, starting at *m* and going to the end of the *char* value. The value for *m* can be positive to search forward or negative to search backwards.

➤ SUBSTRB(*char* *m* [,*n*])—Returns the byte substring located in *char*, starting at *m* bytes and ending at *n*. If *n* is unspecified, it returns the value, starting at *m* bytes and going to the end of the *char* value. The value for *m* can be positive to search forward or negative to search backwards. For single-byte character sets, the effect is the same as with **SUBSTR**.

➤ TRANSLATE(*char*, *from*, *to*)—Returns *char* with the values in *from* translated to the values in *to*.

➤ UPPER(*char*)—Returns *char* in all uppercase.

Character Functions That Return Numeric Values

The following functions return numeric values from character inputs. Outputs, such as length or position, are generated by these functions:

➤ ASCII(*char*)—Returns the ASCII equivalent of the first byte of *char*. This is the inverse of the **CHR()** function. If you need to know the value to insert into a **CHR()** for a specific character, use **SELECT ASCII**(*char*) **FROM DUAL** to get it.

➤ INSTR(*char*1, *char*2 [, *n*[, *m*]])—Returns the numeric position of the *m*th occurrence of *char*2 in *char*1, starting at the *n*th character. The value of *m* must be positive if specified. If the value is not specified, it defaults to 1 (one). The value of *n*, if negative, says to search backwards. If this returns zero, the search was not successful.

➤ INSTRB(*char*1, *char*2 [, *n*[, *m*]])—Returns the numeric byte position of the *m*th occurrence of *char*2 in *char*1, starting at the *n*th byte. The value of *m* must be positive if specified. The value of *n*, if negative, says to search backwards. If this returns zero, the search wasn't successful. The effect is the same as **INSTR()** for single-byte character sets.

➤ LENGTH(*char*)—Returns the length in characters of *char*. If *char* is a **CHAR**, it includes trailing blanks. If *char* is null, it returns a **NULL**.

➤ LENGTHB(*char*)—Returns the length in bytes of *char*. If *char* is a **CHAR**, it includes trailing blanks. If *char* is null, it returns a **NULL**. It's the same as **LENGTH** for single-byte character sets.

Date And Time Functions

Almost all databases pertain to dates and times. Humans are time-based crea-tures who want to know "when" as well as "what, who, and how." Databases require the ability to deal with date and time values. Oracle provides numerous date and time functions, including the following:

➤ ADD_MONTHS(*d,n*)—Adds *n* months to date *d*. Returns a **DATE** value.

➤ LAST_DAY(*d*)—Returns the last day of the month that contains date *d*. Returns a **DATE** value.

➤ MONTHS_BETWEEN(*d*1, *d*2)—Returns either the positive or the negative difference between date *d*1 and date *d*2. Returns a numeric value.

➤ NEW_TIME(*d*, *z*1, *z*2)—Returns the date and time in time zone *z*2 when date *d* is in time zone *z*1.

➤ NEXT_DAY(*d*, *char*)—Returns the first weekday named by *char* that is later than date *d*. Returns a **DATE** value.

➤ ROUND(*d*[,*fmt*])—Returns date *d* rounded to the unit specified by the *fmt* string. For example, a *fmt* of **YEAR** will return only the year portion of the specified date value.

➤ SYSDATE—Has no arguments and returns the current system date and time. It can't be used in a **CHECK** constraint.

➤ TRUNC(*d*[,*fmt*])—Returns date *d* with the time truncated to the unit specified by the format string *fmt*. If *fmt* is left off, the entire time portion of *d* is removed.

The **ROUND** and **TRUNC** functions use standard date-formatting sequences:

➤ *CC*—Both CC and SCC return one number greater than the first two digits of a four-digit year (for example, returns 20 for 1999).

➤ *SCC*—Returns 20 for 1999.

➤ *SYYYY*—The various forms of the year format round up as of July 1 for any year. Returns 1999 for 1999.

➤ *YYYY*—Returns 1999 for 1999.

➤ *YEAR*—Returns NINETEEN NINTY-NINE for 1999.

➤ *SYEAR*—Returns NINETEEN NINTY-NINE for 1999.

➤ *YYY*—Returns 956 for 1956.

- ➤ *YY*—Returns 56 for 1956.

- ➤ *Y*—Returns 6 for 1956.

- ➤ *IYYY*—Use of the "I" with the year produces the ISO year format. Returns 1956 for 1956.

- ➤ *IYY*—Returns 956 for 1956.

- ➤ *IY*—Returns 56 for 1956.

- ➤ *I*—Returns 6 for 1956.

- ➤ *Q*—Rounds up on the 16th day of the second month of the quarter. Returns the number of the current quarter.

- ➤ *MONTH*—Month (rounds up on the 16th day of the month). Returns the month spelled out.

- ➤ *MON*—First three letters of the month.

- ➤ *MM*—Numeric month.

- ➤ *RM*—A really useful format, the roman numeral month.

- ➤ *WW*—Rounds to the same day of the week as the first day of the year. Gives the current week's number. For August 8, 1999, returns 32.

- ➤ *IW*—Rounds to the same day of the week as the first day of the ISO year. For August 8, 1999, returns 31.

- ➤ *W*—Rounds to the same day of the week as the first day of the month, and the number of the week in the month. For August 8, 1999, returns 2.

- ➤ *DDD*—Day of the year. For August 8, 1999, returns 220.

- ➤ *DD*—Two-place numeric day (01).

- ➤ *J*—Julian day (for August 8, 1999, returns 2451399).

- ➤ *DAY*—Rounds to starting day of the week. Spells out the day (SUNDAY).

- ➤ *DY*—Abbreviation for day of week (SUN).

- ➤ *D*—Day (numeric) of week (1).

- ➤ *HH*—Hour (defaults to 12-hour format); 2 P.M.=02.

- ➤ *HH12*—Forces 12-hour format (2 P.M.=02).

- ➤ *HH24*—Forces 24-hour format (2 P.M.=14).

- ➤ *MI*—Minute.

Remember that MM is for months and MI is for minutes. If you specify a time value as HH:MM:SS, you will get a constant value returned in the minutes area that will correspond to the current month.

Starting day of the week is determined from the setting of the **NLS_TERRITORY** setting.

Subtraction of two date values (when converted with the **TO_DATE** function) results in the difference in days between the two dates.

Any appropriate date-format string can also use the date suffixes shown in Table 2.1.

Special modifiers for date-format models can also be applied to date values. These modifiers are **FM** or **FX** (which can also be lowercase, **fm** and **fx**). The **FM** modifier specifies "fill mode," which suppresses blank padding in the return from a **TO_CHAR** call with a date. The **FX** mode means "format exact"; it requires an exact matching for the character argument and the date-format model of a **TO_DATE** function call.

Conversion Functions

Oracle provides conversion routines for standard data-type conversions. In many cases, Oracle will do implicit conversions for compatible data types; however, it's recommended that explicit conversions be done to prevent performance problems inherent in some implicit conversions. The conversion functions are:

➤ CHARTOROWID(*char*)—Converts *char* to Oracle's internal **ROWID** format. The value of *char* must follow **ROWID** data-type guidelines.

➤ CONVERT(*char, dest_char_set* [,*source_char_set*])—Converts *char* to the character set specified in *dest_char_set*. If *char* is in a different character set than the database default, *source_char_set* must be included to specify the character set of the *char* value.

➤ HEXTORAW(*char*)—Converts the hexadecimal value in *char* to its equivalent **RAW** value.

Table 2.1 Date suffixes.			
Suffix	**Meaning**	**Example Element**	**Example Value**
TH	Ordinal number	DDTH	4TH
SP	Spelled number	DDSP	FOUR
SPTH or THSP	Spelled, ordinal number	FOURTH	

➤ RAWTOHEX(*raw*)—Converts the raw data value in *raw* to its hexadecimal equivalent.

➤ ROWIDTOCHAR(*rowid*)—Converts the row ID value in *rowid* to its character equivalent.

➤ TO_CHAR(d, [, *fmt* [, '*nlsparams*']]), TO_CHAR(*label* [, *fmt*]), or TO_CHAR(*number*)—Converts from a date value, *d*, to a character value in the format specified by *fmt*, using any guidelines in the *nlsparams* variable. It can also convert the label specified in *label* to the specified character format in *fmt*, or convert the number value in *number* to a character value. (A *label* is a tag used in Oracle secure server; it is not on the test so unless you use it, don't worry about it.) It also formats using date, number, or label format strings to specify the proper output form.

➤ TO_DATE(*char* [, *fmt* [, '*nlsparams*']])—Converts the specified character value in *char* to the internal Oracle **DATE** value as translated via the *fmt* and, if specified, the *nlsparams* value.

➤ TO_MULTI_BYTE(*char*)—Converts the character value *char* to its equivalent multibyte representation.

➤ TO_NUMBER(*char* [, *fmt* [, '*nlsparams*']])—Converts the number represented in the character value *char* to a number based on translation in the format string *fmt* (if specified) and the *nlsparams* value.

➤ TO_SINGLE_BYTE(*char*)—Converts the multibyte value in *char* to its single-byte equivalent.

➤ TRANSLATE (*text* USING {*CHAR_CS* | *NCHAR_CS*})—Translates the value of *text* into the character set specified by either *CHAR_CS* or *NCHAR_CS*. Using *CHAR_CS* output is **VARCHAR2**; using *NCHAR_CS* output is **NVARCHAR2**.

Other Functions

Other functions in Oracle don't quite fit in any category. These functions are described here:

➤ BFILENAME ('*directory*','*filename*')—Used to create a **BFILE** entry. The *directory* value is the internal **DIRECTORY** specification set with the **CREATE DIRECTORY** command. The *filename* value is the name of the external file containing the external **LOB** data. The actual operating-system directory used in the **BFILENAME** function is not verified to exist or to be accessible until the **BFILE** access is attempted by an application.

➤ DUMP (*expr*[, *return_format* [,*start_position* [, *length*]]])—Returns a VARCHAR2 value containing the data type code, length in bytes, and internal representation of *expr*. The *return_format* tells Oracle to return the value as octal (8), decimal (10), hexadecimal (16), or single characters (17). The *start_position* and *length* values determine which portion of the representation to return.

➤ EMPTY_[B|C]LOB()—Returns an empty **LOB** (either **BLOB** or **CLOB**) locator, which can be used to initialize a **LOB** variable or can be used in an **INSERT** or **UPDATE** statement to create an **EMPTY LOB** value for subsequent use.

➤ GREATEST(*expr* [,*expr*] ...)—Returns the greatest of the specified values.

➤ LEAST(*expr* [,*expr*] ...)—Returns the least of the specified values.

➤ NLS_CHARSET_DECL_LEN(*bytcnt, csid*)—Returns the declaration width, in number of characters, of an **NCHAR** column. The *bytcnt* value is the width in bytes of the columns. The *csid* value is the character set for the column.

➤ NLS_CHARSET_ID(*text*)—Returns the NLS character set number that corresponds to the NLS character set specified by *text*. Use of **CHAR_CS** as the value for *text* returns the server's database character set ID number. **NCHAR_CS** returns the server's national character set.

➤ NLS_CHARSET_NAME(*n*)—Returns the name of the character set with *n* as its ID number. Note that *n* can also be an expression, such as a call to **NLS_CHARSET_ID()**.

➤ NVL(*expr*1, *expr*2)—Returns *expr*1 if *expr*1 isn't null, or *expr*2 if *expr*1 is null. Be careful with any conversion routines or substitution functions when used in mathematical formulas, especially in division. Don't substitute a zero for a **NULL** in division $Y / (NVL(X,0))$, or a divide-by-zero exception will result.

➤ UID—Has no arguments and returns the user ID of the current user.

➤ USER—Has no arguments and returns the username of the current user.

➤ USERENV(*option*)—Returns the specified setting for the current environment. The *option* argument is always surrounded by single quotes. Possible values of *option* are:

  ➤ ISDBA—Returns **TRUE** if the OSDBA role is enabled for this user on Unix using OS authentication, or if the user has logged in with the **AS SYSDBA** clause with username and password, or if the user has the group ORA_[<sid>]_DBA on NT and has logged in with no username or password (such as svrmgrl / AS SYSDBA).

➤ **ENTRYID**—Returns the available auditing-entry identifier.

➤ **INSTANCE**—Returns the instance-identification number of the current instance.

➤ **LANG**—Returns the ISO language setting for this session.

➤ **LANGUAGE**—Returns the language and territory used by this session.

➤ **SESSIONID**—Returns your auditing session ID.

➤ **TERMINAL**—Returns the operating system ID of this session's terminal.

➤ **VSIZE**(*expr*)—Returns the number of bytes in the internal representation of *expr*.

Object-Reference Functions

Oracle8 object-reference functions manipulate **REF** values in Oracle8 objects (UDTs, or User-Defined Types). The object-reference functions are:

➤ **DEREF**(*e*)—Returns the object reference of argument *e*. Argument *e* must resolve to a valid **REF** value.

➤ **MAKE_REF**(*table, key* [,*key*...])—Creates a **REF** to a row of an object view using the value(s) of *key* as the primary key.

➤ **REFTOHEX**(*r*)—Returns the hexadecimal equivalent of argument *r*.

Oracle Group Functions

Oracle also provides group functions to act on groups of values, rather than individual items. You should know how to use these functions in conjunction with **SELECT, INSERT, UPDATE,** and **DELETE.** The group functions are:

➤ **ALL**—Returns all values, including duplicates, for the specified data-set grouping.

➤ **AVG**([DISTINCT|ALL] *n*)—Returns the average value for the specified set of numbers. You can exclude duplicates by using **DISTINCT** or include them with **ALL,** which is the default.

➤ **COUNT**({* | [DISTINCT|ALL] *expr*})—Returns the count of rows (*), distinct values using **DISTINCT,** all values (the default) using **ALL,** or all values that satisfy the values generated from the expression in *expr*.

➤ DISTINCT—Returns only unique values for the specified data-set grouping.

➤ MAX([DISTINCT|ALL] *expr*)—Returns the maximum value generated from the expression in *expr*.

➤ MIN([DISTINCT|ALL] *expr*)—Returns the minimum value generated from the expression in *expr*. The expression can be numeric or character data. If the value is a character, the sum of the ASCII values for the letters is used to determine what value is minimum.

➤ STDDEV([DISTINCT|ALL] *expr*)—Returns the standard deviation of the values generated from the expression in *expr*. For this function, standard deviation is calculated as the square root of the variance as calculated in the **VARIANCE** function.

➤ SUM([DISTINCT|ALL] *expr*)—Returns the sum of the values generated from the expression in *expr*.

➤ VARIANCE([DISTINCT|ALL] *expr*)—Returns the variance of the values generated from the expression in *expr*. The **VARIANCE** function uses the standard *n-1* statistics variance formula.

The *expr* Clause

In many of the commands, function definitions, and statement definitions, you may see the term *expr*. This clause represents several possible expressions that can be placed in commands, functions, and statements. Not all commands, however, will accept all forms of the *expr* formats. In particular, expressions are used in:

➤ **SELECT** select lists

➤ **WHERE** and **HAVING** clauses

➤ **CONNECT BY, START WITH,** and **ORDER BY** clauses

➤ The **VALUES** clause of the **SELECT** statement

➤ The **SET** clause of the **UPDATE** statement

Lists can contain up to 254 expressions. Figures 2.1 through 2.11 show the various forms of the *expr* clause.

Form 1 of the *expr* clause, shown in Figure 2.1, is used when the expression represents any of the following: a pseudo-column—such as **LEVEL, ROWID,** or **ROWNUM**—in a table; a constant; a sequence number; or a **NULL** value. Pseudo-column use is restricted to tables. **NCHAR** and **NVARCHAR2** are

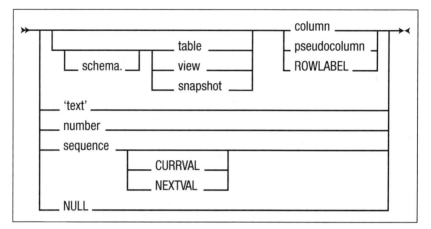

Figure 2.1 Form 1 of the *expr* clause.

not valid pseudo-column or **ROWLABEL** data types. **ROWLABEL** is applicable only to trusted Oracle.

Form 2 of the **expr** clause, shown in Figure 2.2, is used as a host variable with an optional indicator variable. This form can be used only in embedded SQL or through the Oracle Call Interface (OCI).

Form 3 of the **expr** clause, shown in Figure 2.3, is used when you're calling an implicit SQL function.

Form 4 of the **expr** clause, shown in Figure 2.4, is used when you're calling a user-defined function.

Form 5 of the **expr** clause, shown in Figure 2.5, is used when a combination of

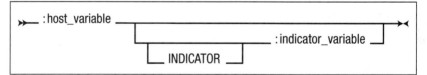

Figure 2.2 Form 2 of the *expr* clause.

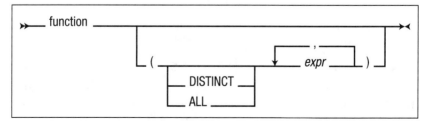

Figure 2.3 Form 3 of the *expr* clause.

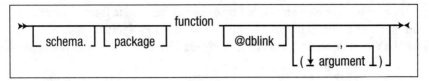

Figure 2.4   Form 4 of the *expr* clause.

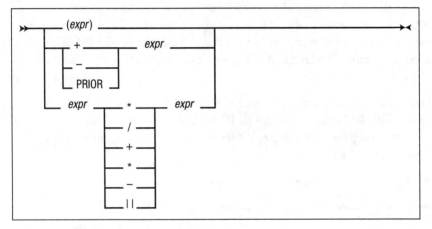

Figure 2.5   Form 5 of the *expr* clause.

other expressions is required. Some combinations are inappropriate, such as use of a **LENGTH** expression in a **GROUP BY** clause. In the case of an inappropriate combination of expressions, the combination will be rejected.

Form 6 of the *expr* clause, shown in Figure 2.6, is used to call a type constructor when using objects in Oracle. The *type_name* is an object type, and *type_argument_list* is an ordered list of any arguments where the argument types correspond to the type attribute-data types. Any embedded type in the

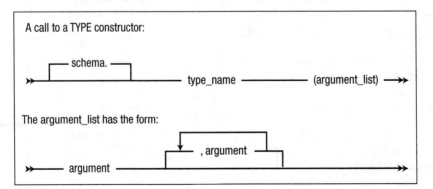

Figure 2.6   Form 6 of the *expr* clause.

master type will have an embedded type constructor inside form 6. The maximum number of attributes in a type expression is 999. Nested types—such as **VARRAY** or a nested table specification—can have zero arguments, creating an empty collection.

Form 7 of the *expr* clause, shown in Figure 2.7, is used to cast the collection-typed values of one type into another collection type. The collection that is cast can be the result of an embedded subquery, or it can be a collection type of **VARRAY** or a nested table. The target *type_name* must be an existing, compatible type. If a subquery results in multiple rows, the **MULTISET** keyword must be specified. Scalar **SELECT** operations are not allowed in the subquery of a **CAST** expression.

Form 8 of the *expr* clause, shown in Figure 2.8, is used to return a nested cursor. This is similar to a PL/SQL **REF** cursor. The nested cursor is opened implicitly when the containing row is fetched from the parent cursor. The nested cursor is closed when:

➤ The user explicitly closes the nested cursor.

➤ Re-execution of the parent cursor occurs.

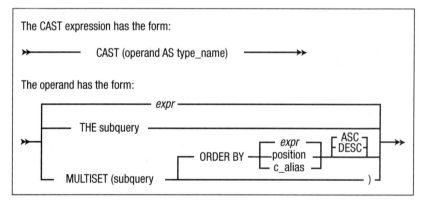

Figure 2.7   Form 7 of the *expr* clause.

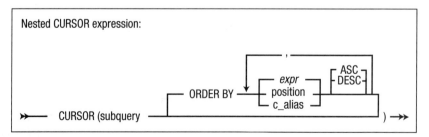

Figure 2.8   Form 8 of the *expr* clause.

➤ The parent cursor is closed.

➤ The parent cursor is canceled.

➤ An error closes the parent cursor and it is closed during cleanup.

Form 8 can be used only when:

➤ It is in a non-nested **SELECT** statement, except if the **SELECT** is in the parent cursor.

➤ It is in the outermost **SELECT** list of the query.

➤ It is not in a view.

BIND and **EXECUTE** operations cannot be performed on nested queries.

Form 9 of the *expr* clause, shown in Figure 2.9, is used to construct a reference (REF) value. The *argument* is not a table name, but is a table alias as specified in the main statement. The clause returns a **REF** value, which is bound to the variable or row selected.

Form 10 of the *expr* clause, the **VALUE** expression (don't confuse it with the **VALUES** clause of the **INSERT** command), returns the actual row object from a referenced object. The **VALUE** expression takes a table alias as its argument and returns the corresponding row rather than the **REF** value. Figure 2.10 shows form 10 of the *expr* clause.

Form 11 of the *expr* clause, shown in Figure 2.11, specifies attribute reference and method invocation for types. The *column* value is either a **REF** or an object column.

When an expression contains a numeric value or a character value enclosed in

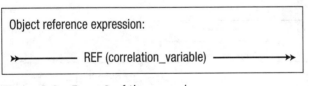

Figure 2.9   Form 9 of the *expr* clause.

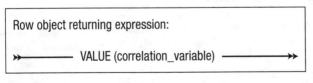

Figure 2.10   Form 10 of the *expr* clause.

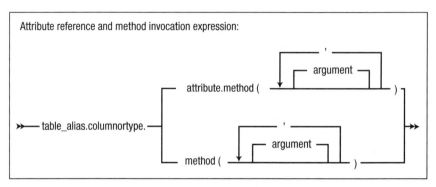

Figure 2.11   Form 11 of the *expr* clause.

single quotes, these values are known as *literals*. Literals can be concatenated to other literals or to column values. The simplest literal would be a blank space enclosed with single quotes. Special characters, such as the forward slash (/) and percent sign (%), can be used in a literal if they're preceded by the escape character. An escape character is either the backslash (\) or the character designated with the **ESCAPE** clause in a **LIKE** operator statement.

The **DECODE** Function

The **DECODE** function is important in that it can be used to perform quasi if...then processing inside SQL statements and to enable value specific ordering and translation. Figure 2.12 shows the format to use for the **DECODE** function.

When the **DECODE** function is invoked, Oracle compares *expr* to each *search* value one by one. If the values of *expr* and *search* match, *result* is substituted. If *default* is not specified, the null value is returned; otherwise, *default* is returned.

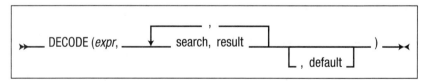

Figure 2.12   The format for the **DECODE** function.

The **CONDITION** Clause

The entire purpose of SQL is to allow the insertion, updating, deletion, and retrieval of data. Limiting retrieval of data to just what we want requires some means of limiting the return set of data. The **CONDITION** clause lets us weed out data that's not wanted or needed. Just like the *expr* clause, the **CONDITION** clause has several forms. A **CONDITION** clause can be used in **DELETE, SELECT**, or **UPDATE** statements. A **CONDITION** clause can also be used in the **WHERE, START WITH, CONNECT BY**, and **HAVING** clauses of the **SELECT** statement.

Figures 2.13 through 2.20 show the various forms of the **CONDITION** clause:

➤ *Form 1*—The **CONDITION** clause in Figure 2.13 shows a comparison with expressions or subquery results.

➤ *Form 2*—The **CONDITION** clause in Figure 2.14 shows a comparison with any or all members in a list or subquery.

➤ *Form 3*—The **CONDITION** clause in Figure 2.15 shows a comparison to test for membership in a group or subquery.

➤ *Form 4*—The **CONDITION** clause in Figure 2.16 tests for inclusion in a range.

➤ *Form 5*—The **CONDITION** clause in Figure 2.17 tests for nulls. (You must implicitly test for nulls in some situations—such as when you're checking for values not to exist or using **COUNT**—or the rows will be ignored.)

➤ *Form 6*—The **CONDITION** clause in Figure 2.18 checks for the existence of rows in a subquery.

➤ *Form 7*—The **CONDITION** clause in Figure 2.19 performs pattern matching.

➤ *Form 8*—The **CONDITION** clause in Figure 2.20 is a combination conditional clause.

The various forms of the **CONDITION** clause can be combined using logical operators such as **AND, OR,** and **NOT**. Clauses grouped by use of parentheses are checked as a set of conditions that must be met to move on to the next condition.

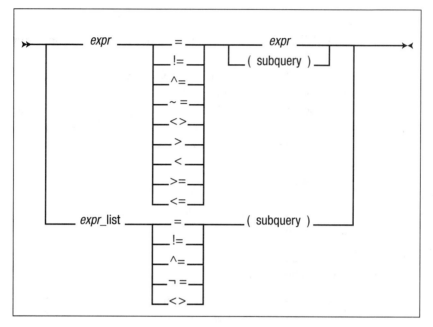

Figure 2.13 Form 1 of the **CONDITION** clause.

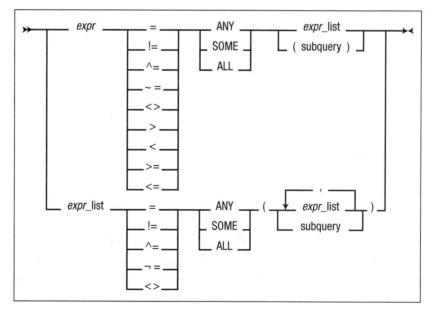

Figure 2.14 Form 2 of the **CONDITION** clause.

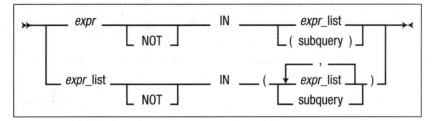

Figure 2.15   Form 3 of the **CONDITION** clause.

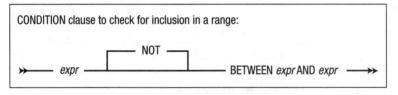

Figure 2.16   Form 4 of the **CONDITION** clause.

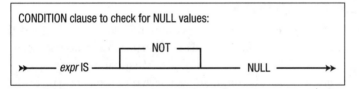

Figure 2.17   Form 5 of the **CONDITION** clause.

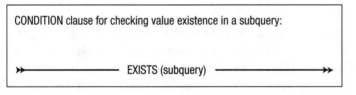

Figure 2.18   Form 6 of the **CONDITION** clause.

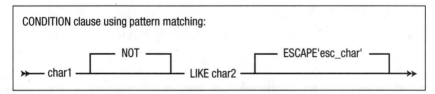

Figure 2.19   Form 7 of the **CONDITION** clause.

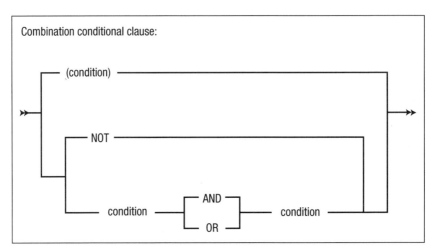

Figure 2.20   Form 8 of the **CONDITION** clause.

DML Commands

I'll cover **INSERT** first because the other commands do you little good if there's no data in the database to manipulate. Insertions can't override constraints, such as **NOT NULL** or **UNIQUE**. Insertions can't specify nonconverted values that can't be implicitly converted to the data type in the destination table.

The **INSERT** Command

The **INSERT** command is used to add new data into existing database tables, a view's base table, a table's partition, an object table, or an object view's base table from SQL and PL/SQL. In order to **INSERT** into a table, you must have **INSERT** privilege on the table or have the **INSERT ANY TABLE** system privilege. In order to **INSERT** into a view's base table, the owner of the view must have **INSERT** privilege on the table or have the **INSERT ANY TABLE** system privilege.

The syntax of the **INSERT** command is shown in Figure 2.21.

The parameters have the following definitions:

➤ **schema**—The owner of the table or view.

➤ **table, view**—Name of the table or updatable view.

➤ **PARTITION**—Clause used to specify the partition of a partitioned table in which to insert the data.

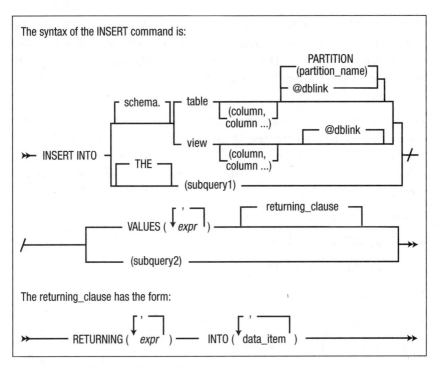

The syntax of the INSERT command is:

The returning_clause has the form:

Figure 2.21   Syntax of the **INSERT** command.

➤ **dblink**—The database link for a remote table or view.

➤ **column**—The name(s) of the column(s) in which data will be inserted. If the names are omitted, all the table or view columns must have a matching value or **subquery2** item.

➤ **THE**—Clause used to flatten a nested object, such as a **VARRAY** or a nested table.

➤ **subquery1**—The query that returns the **VARRAY** or nested table values.

➤ *expr*—An expression or a list of values corresponding to the inserted values.

➤ **subquery2**—A subquery that returns rows or values to be inserted.

➤ **RETURNING**—Clause used to specify the data items returned (such as **REF** values). This clause cannot be used with parallel DML or with remote objects.

An **INSERT** that uses a **VALUES** clause can insert only a single row of data into a table. On the other hand, a query with a subselect instead of a **VALUES** clause can insert multiple rows. The number of items in a subquery that's used to fetch items for insertion must match the number of items in the column list **VALUES** clause list. Also, the items must be of the same or a convertible data type. If no column list or **VALUES** clause is included, then the subquery must have a one-to-one relation between its returned values and the target table's attributes.

The **INSERT** command is used to add table values, and it can also be used to insert data into an updatable view's base table. If a view is to have data inserted into it, and if that view has a **WITH CHECK OPTION** clause with its definition, then the inserted rows must meet the criteria in the view's defining query.

A view can't have data inserted into it if:

➤ It has a **JOIN**.

➤ It uses a **SET OPERATOR**.

➤ It contains a **GROUP BY** clause.

➤ It uses any group function.

➤ It uses a **DISTINCT** operator.

➤ It has a nested table column.

➤ It has flattened subqueries.

➤ It uses **CAST** and **MULTISET** expressions.

The **INSERT** command causes any triggers on the table or underlying tables acted on by the **INSERT** to fire. It can't be used to do the following: force the insertion of data of an incorrect data type or of a nonimplicitly convertible data type into a noncompatible row; violate a **NOT NULL, UNIQUE,** or **CHECK** constraint limitation; or violate foreign or primary key constraints.

AN **INSERT** statement using a **RETURNING** clause retrieves any inserted rows into the specified PL/SQL or bind variables. **ROWID**s and **REF**s may also be returned in a **RETURNING** clause.

Examples Using the **INSERT** Command

The **INSERT** command is used to initially insert data into tables either directly or through views. The **INSERT** command can use subqueries and the **THE** object clause. The **INSERT** command can also use the **RETURNING** clause to return inserted values to variables. The **RETURING** clause cannot be used with Parallel DML or with remote objects. Listing 2.1 shows the various forms of the **INSERT** command.

Listing 2.1   Example **INSERT** commands.

```
SQL> CREATE TABLE test1 (table_name varchar2(30),
  2  owner varchar2(30));

Table created.

SQL> INSERT INTO test1 SELECT table_name,owner FROM all_tables

11 rows created.

SQL> COMMIT;

Commit complete.

SQL> INSERT INTO test1 VALUES ('TEST_TABLE','NO_ONE');

1 row created.

SQL> INSERT INTO test1(table_name) VALUES('TEST2_TABLE');

1 row created.

SQL> VAR t1 varchar2(30);
SQL> VAR t2 varchar2(30);
SQL> INSERT INTO test1 VALUES ('TEST3_TABLE','TEST3_OWNER')
  2  RETURNING table_name,owner INTO :t1,:t2;

1 row created.

SQL> PRINT t1

T1
--------------------------------
TEST3_TABLE

SQL> PRINT t2

T2
--------------------------------
TEST3_OWNER
```

The examples in Listing 2.1 show various uses of the **INSERT** command. The first example is an insert using a subquery. The second example shows an insert of an entire row. You should be aware that if a column list is not provided, a value must be present in the **VALUES** clause or subquery result for each column in the table. The third example shows a partial row insert. The final example shows the use of the **RETURNING** clause.

The **UPDATE** Command

The **UPDATE** command is used to change the contents of an existing table row column or columns or the base columns for an updatable view. You must have **UPDATE** privilege on the table being updated or have the **UPDATE ANY TABLE** system privilege. To update views, the owner of the view must have the **UPDATE ANY TABLE** system privilege.

The syntax for an **UPDATE** command is shown in Figure 2.22.

The parameters have the following definitions:

➤ **schema**—Owner of the table, view, or snapshot.

➤ **table, view, snap**—Table or updatable view or snapshot to be updated.

➤ **dblink**—A database link to the update item's remote location (if needed).

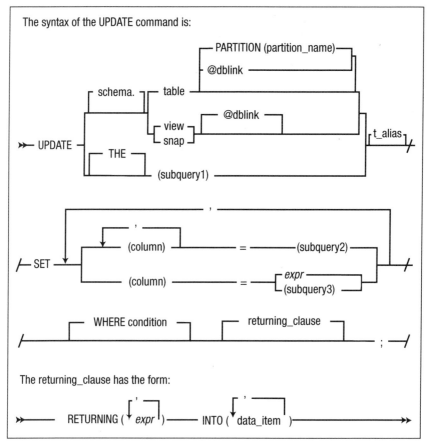

Figure 2.22 Syntax of the **UPDATE** command.

➤ **THE**—This clause flattens the corresponding subquery when it returns values from a nested table or **VARRAY**.

➤ **subquery1**—A subquery that's in the same format as a view definition.

➤ **t_alias**—Alias for object name to be used in subqueries and in **WHERE** clauses to make them more readable or more logical. A column or table alias cannot exceed 30 characters.

➤ **column**—A column or list of columns to be updated. Lists must be in parentheses. If a column is not mentioned in the clause, that column's value is not updated.

➤ **subquery2**—A subquery that returns values to be used to update the object.

➤ *expr*—New value or values assigned to the subquery or to the column list.

➤ **subquery3**—A subquery that returns a single value.

➤ **WHERE**—A clause used to limit which rows are updated by the **UPDATE** command. If a **WHERE** clause is not specified, then all rows are updated.

➤ **RETURNING**—The returning clause retrieves the rows affected by the **UPDATE** statement. Returned values are limited to scalar, **LOB**, **ROWID**, or **REF** types. The **RETURNING** clause cannot be used with Parallel DML or with remote objects.

➤ **INTO**—Shows Oracle the variables in which the values returned are to be stored.

➤ **data_item**—This is a PL/SQL variable or bind variable in which to store the returned value. This variable must match the value's data type, or the value's data type must be convertible to the specified data type of the variable.

The **UPDATE** command is used to change table values, and it can be used to update an updatable view's base table. The **UPDATE** command will fire any **UPDATE** triggers that have been specified for the table, or any **INSTEAD OF** triggers on an **UPDATE** to a view. If a view is to be updated, and that view has a **WITH CHECK OPTION** clause with its definition, the updated rows must meet the criteria in the view's defining query.

A view can't be updated if:

➤ It has a **JOIN**.

➤ It uses a **SET OPERATOR**.

➤ It contains a **GROUP BY** clause.

➤ It uses any group function.

➤ It uses a **DISTINCT** operator.

➤ It has flattened subqueries.

➤ It uses nested table columns.

➤ It uses **CAST** and **MULTISET** expressions.

When you're updating a partition, you must specify all of the partition columns in the update. (A *partition column* is one of the possible set of columns that determine how to partition the table.) A partition update that could force a row to migrate will be rejected with an error in Oracle8.

If a subquery in an **UPDATE** statement refers back to the updated table, this situation is called a *correlated update*, and the subquery will be evaluated once for each row updated. Usually, to use a subquery to perform a correlated update, you will specify a table alias.

When you're using a **RETURNING** clause, you must be sure to specify scalar return variables for scalar updates, and to provide bind arrays for any **UPDATE** that will return multiple rows, or an error will be returned.

Examples Using The **UPDATE** Command

The **UPDATE** command can only change existing rows; it cannot create new rows. The **UPDATE** clause can use the **WHERE** clause, subqueries, the **RETURNING** clause, and the **THE** object-related clause. Listing 2.2 shows examples of the **UPDATE** command.

Listing 2.2   Example **UPDATE** commands.

```
SQL> UPDATE emp SET ename='Michael Ault'
  2  WHERE ename='Mike Ault';

1 row updated.

SQL> COMMIT;

Commit complete.

SQL> SELECT ename,enumber FROM emp;

ENAME                ENUMBER
-------------------- --------
Michael Ault               1
George Petrod              3
```

```
Carol Smith                    4
Francine Lenord                2

SQL> UPDATE emp SET ename='Frank Lenord' WHERE enumber=2;

1 row updated.

SQL> COMMIT;

Commit complete.

SQL> SELECT ename,enumber FROM emp;

ENAME                   ENUMBER
--------------------    --------
Michael Ault                  1
George Petrod                 3
Carol Smith                   4
Frank Lenord                  2

SQL> UPDATE emp SET assignment='None';

4 rows updated.

SQL> COL assignment FORMAT a10
SQL> SELECT ename,enumber,assignment FROM emp;

ENAME                   ENUMBER ASSIGNMENT
--------------------    -------- ----------
Michael Ault                  1 None
George Petrod                 3 None
Carol Smith                   4 None
Frank Lenord                  2 None

SQL> SELECT * FROM assignments;

   ENUMBER COMPANY_NAME
-------- ----------------------------------
         1 Internal
         2 Practical Software, Inc.
         3 The Phone Company
         4 Internal

SQL> UPDATE emp a SET a.assignment=(SELECT b.company_name
  2                                 FROM assignments b
  3                                 WHERE a.enumber=b.enumber);

4 rows updated.
```

```
SQL> COL assignment FORMAT a24
SQL> SELECT ename,enumber,assignment FROM emp;

ENAME                   ENUMBER ASSIGNMENT
--------------------    -------- ------------------------
Michael Ault                  1 Internal
George Petrod                 3 The Phone Company
Carol Smith                   4 Internal
Frank Lenord                  2 Practical Software, Inc.

SQL> UPDATE emp SET ename='Michael R. Ault'
  2  WHERE ename='Michael Ault'
  3  RETURNING ename INTO :e;

1 row updated.

SQL> print e

E
--------------------------------
Michael R. Ault

SQL> DESC art
 Name                           Null?    Type
 -------------------------      -------- ------------------
 PICTURE_DATE                            DATE
 PICTURE_CONTENTS                        PICTURE_PART_V
 ARTIST                                  ARTIST_LIST

SQL> UPDATE THE(SELECT artist FROM art a
  2  WHERE a.picture_date='23-aug-99') artists
  3  SET artists.last_name='Smith';

2 rows updated.

SQL> COL artists FORMAT a59
SQL> SELECT THE(SELECT artist FROM art a
  2  WHERE a.picture_date='23-aug-99') artists
  3  FROM art;

ARTISTS(LAST_NAME, FIRST_NAME, MIDDLE_INITIAL, SSN)
-----------------------------------------------------------
ARTIST_LIST(ARTIST_T('Smith', 'Mike', 'R', '222-33-4444'),
ARTIST_T('Smith', 'Susan', 'K', '333-44-5555'))

SQL> UPDATE emp SET edept=NULL WHERE edept IS DANGLING;

1 row updated.
```

In the examples in Listing 2.2, you first see two simple single-row updates using the **WHERE** clause to restrict the **UPDATE** to a single row. The next example shows the use of **UPDATE** to update a single column in the entire table. The next few examples show the use of a subquery, a **RETURNING** clause, and the **THE** clause for a nested table. The final example shows how to set **DANGLING REF** values to **NULL**.

The **DELETE** Command

After a table has been loaded with data, it may be necessary periodically to remove rows from the data set that results. This removal of data is accomplished with one of two commands. The **DELETE** command is used to remove some or all rows from a table, and a **ROLLBACK** of the command is allowed if no **COMMIT** is executed. The **TRUNCATE** command is used to remove all rows from a table, and no **ROLLBACK** is allowed.

The syntax of the **DELETE** command is shown in Figure 2.23.

The parameters have the following definitions:

➤ **schema**—Name of the object owner.

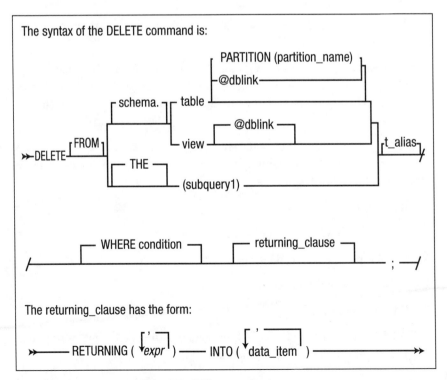

Figure 2.23   Syntax of the **DELETE** command.

➤ **table, view**—Name of the table or view whose base table will have data deleted from it.

➤ **dblink**—Database link to remote instance if the object is not local.

➤ **THE**—This clause tells Oracle that the column value returned is a nested table and not a scalar value. I prefer to think of it as **THE TABLE** instead of just **THE**.

➤ **subquery1**—A subquery that selects data to be deleted. This subquery is executed, and the resulting rows are deleted. The subquery can't query a table that appears in the same **FROM** clause as the subquery.

➤ **t_alias**—Shorthand for the table, view, or subquery, for use in the **WHERE** clause. A column or table alias cannot exceed 30 characters.

➤ **WHERE** condition—Allows deletion of only those rows that meet the specified condition.

➤ **RETURNING**—This clause retrieves the rows affected by the **DELETE** statement. Returned values are limited to scalar, **LOB, ROWID**, or **REF** types. The **RETURNING** clause cannot be used with Parallel DML or with remote objects.

➤ **INTO**—Shows Oracle the variables in which the values returned are to be stored.

➤ **data_item**—This is a PL/SQL variable or bind variable in which to store the returned value. The variable must match the value's data type, or the value's data type must be convertible to the specified data type of the variable.

The **DELETE** command is used to remove table values, and it can be used to remove rows from an updatable view's base table. A view can't have data deleted from it if:

➤ It has a **JOIN**.

➤ It uses a **SET OPERATOR**.

➤ It contains a **GROUP BY** clause.

➤ It uses any group function.

➤ It uses a **DISTINCT** operator.

A **DELETE** will fire any **DELETE** triggers specified on the tables or underlying tables of the **DELETE** command.

If you **DELETE** data from a specified partition in a partitioned table, you can avoid using a complex **WHERE** clause.

Examples Using The **DELETE** Command

The **DELETE** command is used to remove records from tables. The **DELETE** command can use the **WHERE** clause, subqueries, the **RETURNING** clause, and the **THE** object-related clause. Listing 2.3 shows examples of the **DELETE** command.

Listing 2.3   Example **DELETE** commands.

```
SQL> SELECT ename,enumber FROM emp;

ENAME                   ENUMBER
--------------------    ---------
Michael R. Ault               1
George Petrod                 3
Carol Smith                   4
Frank Lenord                  2

SQL> DELETE emp;

4 rows deleted.

SQL> SELECT ename,enumber FROM emp;

no rows selected

SQL> ROLLBACK;

Rollback complete.

SQL> SELECT ename,enumber FROM emp;

ENAME                   ENUMBER
--------------------    ---------
Michael Ault                  1
George Petrod                 3
Carol Smith                   4
Frank Lenord                  2

SQL> DELETE emp WHERE enumber=1;

1 row deleted.

SQL> SELECT ename,enumber FROM emp;
```

```
ENAME                    ENUMBER
-------------------- ----------
George Petrod                  3
Carol Smith                    4
Frank Lenord                   2

SQL> ROLLBACK;

Rollback complete.

SQL> DELETE emp e WHERE e.ename=(SELECT d.ename
  2  FROM emp d WHERE d.enumber=1);

1 row deleted.

SQL> SELECT ename,enumber FROM emp;

ENAME                    ENUMBER
-------------------- ----------
George Petrod                  3
Carol Smith                    4
Frank Lenord                   2

SQL> ROLLBACK;

Rollback complete.
SQL> DELETE emp e WHERE e.ename=(SELECT d.ename
FROM emp d
WHERE d.enumber=1)
  4  RETURNING enumber,ename INTO :e1,:e2;

1 row deleted.

SQL> PRINT e1

        E1
---------
         1

SQL> PRINT e2

E2
--------------------------------
Michael Ault

SQL> ROLLBACK;

Rollback complete.
```

```
SQL> DELETE THE(SELECT artist FROM art a
  2             WHERE a.picture_date='23-aug-99') artists
  3  WHERE artists.first_name='Mike';

1 row deleted.

SQL> SELECT THE(SELECT artist FROM art a
  2             WHERE a.picture_date='23-aug-99') artists
  3  FROM art;

ARTISTS(LAST_NAME, FIRST_NAME, MIDDLE_INITIAL, SSN)
-------------------------------------------------------------
ARTIST_LIST(ARTIST_T('Ault', 'Susan', 'K', '333-44-5555'))

SQL> rollback;

Rollback complete.

SQL> SELECT THE(SELECT artist FROM art a
  2             WHERE a.picture_date='23-aug-99') artists
  3  FROM art;

ARTISTS(LAST_NAME, FIRST_NAME, MIDDLE_INITIAL, SSN)
-----------------------------------------------------------
ARTIST_LIST(ARTIST_T('Ault', 'Mike', 'R', '222-33-4444'),
ARTIST_T('Ault', 'Susan', 'K', '333-44-5555'))
```

In the first example in Listing 2.3, you see the deletion of an entire table using the **DELETE** command with no **WHERE** clause. the next example shows a simple single-row delete using a **WHERE** clause. The next few examples show the use of a subquery, a **RETURNING** clause, and the **THE** clause for a nested table.

The **COMMIT** And **ROLLBACK** Commands

The **COMMIT** command converts temporary records into permanent records. If a user exits from a session normally, a **COMMIT** is automatically performed. Many of the DBMS package procedures provided by Oracle do implicit commits.

The **ROLLBACK** command rolls back (undoes the actions of) any changes that haven't been committed by a **COMMIT** (either implicit or explicit).

The **ROLLBACK** and **COMMIT** commands are demonstrated in several of the previous listings.

Practice Questions

Question 1

Which command is used to add new rows to an existing table?

- ○ a. **UPDATE**
- ○ b. **INTO**
- ○ c. **INSERT**
- ○ d. **CREATE**
- ○ e. **ADD**

The correct answer is c. Answer a is incorrect because the **UPDATE** command is used to alter existing rows, not to insert new ones. Answer b is incorrect because **INTO** is actually a required part of the **SELECT** command when it is used in PL/SQL, and it has nothing to do with **INSERT**. Answer d is incorrect because the **CREATE** command is a DDL and not a DML command, and it has nothing to do with putting data into a table. Answer e is incorrect because **ADD** is a part of the DDL command **ALTER** and has nothing to do with insertion of data into tables.

Question 2

After examining Table 2.2, evaluate this command:

```
DELETE FROM products
WHERE cost < 5.00 AND receive_date >
   to_date(15-oct-1999, 'dd-mon-yyyy');
```

Which **PROD_ID** would be deleted?

- ○ a. 27025
- ○ b. 27027
- ○ c. 27023
- ○ d. 27028
- ○ e. 34081
- ○ f. 34096
- ○ g. 27026
- ○ h. 47025

Table 2.2   The **PRODUCTS** table.

PROD_ID	DESCRIPTION	SUPPLIER_ID	INVENTORY	COST	RECEIVE_DATE
27025	Lables	avery111	100	2.10	10-jun-99
27027	Cable	canon222	100	0.50	11-oct-99
27023	Pen set	bic333	80	8.25	19-apr-99
27028	Barrel pen	blick777	200	2.50	30-oct-99
34081	Copy paper	ibm999	50	20.00	25-jul-99
34096	Address book	taft666	100	2.50	11-sep-99
27026	Ledger book	taft666	100	3.50	31-jan-99
47025	Reference set	wiley000	10	25.00	15-sep-99

The correct answer is d, 27028. None of the other answers meet the criteria of having a **COST** less than 5.00 and a **RECEIVE_DATE** greater than 15-oct-1999.

Question 3

> What is the purpose of the **ROLLBACK** command?
>
> O a. Insert data into the database.
>
> O b. Change existing data in the database.
>
> O c. Make any pending changes permanent in the database.
>
> O d. Move a transaction back to a predetermined statement.
>
> O e. Discard all pending data changes or inserts.

The correct answer is e. A **ROLLBACK** command discards all pending data changes or inserts. Answer a is incorrect because this is the purpose of the **INSERT** command. Answer b is incorrect because this is the purpose of the **UPDATE** command. Answer c is incorrect because this is the purpose of the **COMMIT** command (the inverse command from **ROLLBACK**). Answer d is incorrect because this is the purpose of a **SAVEPOINT** command.

Question 4

> What command is used to alter existing data in a table?
>
> O a. **INSERT**
>
> O b. **UPDATE**
>
> O c. **DELETE**
>
> O d. **SELECT**

The correct answer is b, **UPDATE**. Answer a is incorrect because the **INSERT** command places new data into a table. Answer c is incorrect because the **DELETE** command removes data from a table. Answer d is incorrect because the **SELECT** command is used to retrieve data from a table.

Question 5

> Which of the following actions will happen when a **CREATE** command is issued?
>
> ○ a. The system crashes.
>
> ○ b. The system automatically exits the active session.
>
> ○ c. An automatic **ROLLBACK** is issued.
>
> ○ d. An automatic **COMMIT** is issued.

The correct answer is d. Whenever a DDL command is issued, an automatic **COMMIT** is generated upon successful completion.

Question 6

> What will happen if an **ALTER** command is issued in the middle of a transaction?
>
> ○ a. The transaction will end.
>
> ○ b. The system will crash.
>
> ○ c. An error will be generated and processing will continue to the end of the transaction.
>
> ○ d. The results will be deferred until the transaction ends.

The correct answer is a. Because **ALTER** is a DDL command, any **ALTER** command will result in a **COMMIT** upon its completion, which will end the current transaction.

Question 7

> What is true about a DML transaction?
>
> ○ a. Only one statement per transaction is allowed.
>
> ○ b. Multiple actions such as a credit and debit can be performed.
>
> ○ c. Automatic **COMMIT** commands are generated after each statement.
>
> ○ d. Transaction logic doesn't apply to DML operations.

The correct answer is b. In DML, multiple DML statements can be entered before a **COMMIT** or ROLLBACK terminates the transaction.

Question 8

You perform the following operations:

1. Create table **USERS**.

2. Insert four records into table **USERS**.

3. Grant **SELECT** privilege on **USERS** to **PUBLIC**.

At this point, the system crashes because someone unplugged it.

What is the state of the **USERS** table on instance restart?

○ a. Because no **COMMMIT** was completed before the crash, there is no **USERS** table.

○ b. Because no **COMMIT** was completed before the crash, there are no rows in the **USERS** table.

○ c. There are four rows in a pending state for the **USERS** table.

○ d. There are four permanent records in the **USERS** table.

The correct answer is d. Because the **GRANT** command in Step 3 performs an implicit **COMMIT** command, the records were committed prior to the system crash.

Question 9

Evaluate this command:

```
DELETE test_scores;
```

Which task will this command accomplish?

○ a. Delete the **test_scores** column.

○ b. Delete all the values in the columns of the **test_scores** table that don't have **NOT NULL** constraints.

○ c. Drop the **test_scores** table.

○ d. Delete all records from the **test_scores** table.

The correct answer is d. **DELETE** is a DML command, so it only affects data. A nonrestricted **DELETE** removes all rows from the specified table unless the table is a parent table and child records exist. Because you have not been told that **test_scores** is a parent table, you have to assume d is the correct answer to this question.

Question 10

Which two commands will cause an implicit **COMMIT** command? [Choose two]

❑ a. **GRANT**

❑ b. **SELECT**

❑ c. **INSERT**

❑ d. **UPDATE**

❑ e. **CREATE**

❑ f. **DELETE**

The correct answers are a and e. Answer a is correct because **GRANT** is a DCL command, and DCL commands always cause an implicit **COMMIT**. Answer e is correct because **CREATE** is a DDL command, and DDL commands always cause an implicit **COMMIT**. Answers b, c, d, and f are incorrect because they are DML commands, and DML commands do not cause an implicit **COMMIT**.

Need To Know More?

Ault, Michael R. *Oracle8 Administration and Management.* John Wiley & Sons, New York, New York, 1998. ISBN 0-471-19234-1. This book covers virtually all aspects of Oracle8 administration, including command syntax, tuning, and management topics.

Honour, Edward, Dalberth, Paul, Kaplan, Ari, and Atul Mehta. *Oracle8 HOW-TO.* Waite Group Press, Corte Madera, California, 1998. ISBN 1-57169-123-5. This book provides an excellent resource for general Oracle how-to information and covers topics from installation to how to use the Web server.

Oracle8 Server SQL Reference Manual, Release 8.0. Oracle Corporation, Redwood Shores, California, June 1997. Part No. A54649-01, parts one and two. This is the source book for all Oracle SQL for version 8.0. This book can be found on the Web, at the time of writing, at **http://technet.oracle.com**. This site has free membership and has all current versions of Oracle documentation available online in Acrobat format (PDF files).

DML: Using The
SELECT Command

. . . .

Terms you'll need to understand:

√ **SELECT**

√ Equijoin

√ Self-join

√ Outer join

√ Cartesian product

Techniques you'll need to master:

√ Using the **SELECT** command to retrieve data
  from tables

√ Using the equijoin to relate multiple tables to
  each other

√ Using the self-join to flatten hierarchical data

√ Using the outer join to return data from a second table
  even if the join value is not present

√ Structuring **SELECT** statements to avoid Cartesian
  products

In Chapter 2, I discussed the use of the **INSERT, UPDATE,** and **DELETE** commands to place data into tables, manipulate data values, and remove data from tables. In this chapter, you'll learn about the **SELECT** command. The **SELECT** command allows you to retrieve values from a table or set of tables, optionally performing conversions using the functions I discussed in Chapter 2. The **SELECT** command is the major command most users execute against the database, so it will be your biggest source of headaches in the realm of tuning and maintaining performance in the database environment.

The **SELECT** Command

The **SELECT** command is used to retrieve values that have been stored in a table or set of tables; the retrieval is based on some selection criteria. An unrestricted **SELECT** retrieves all values from the specified table, view, or snapshot. A restricted **SELECT** contains a **WHERE** clause with some restricting clauses. The **SELECT** command is also the basis for all subqueries in all other commands.

In order to **SELECT** from a table, you must have the **SELECT** privilege on the table or have the **SELECT ANY TABLE** system privilege. To **SELECT** from the base table(s) of a view, the owning schema of the view must have the **SELECT** privilege on the table or have the **SELECT ANY TABLE** system privilege.

Unless forced by the **DESC** qualifier into descending order, all **SELECT** query results using an **ORDER BY** clause or retrieved by way of an indexed-column lookup are returned in ascending (**ASC**) order.

At the absolute minimum, a **SELECT** statement consists of a **SELECT** command with an expression and a **FROM** clause that specifies from where the data is to be selected. This is why the **DUAL** table is required with nondirected **SELECT** statements, such as **FROM** sequences or non–table-related, single-value functions such as **SYSDATE**.

Figure 3.1 shows the complete syntax of the **SELECT** command.

The parameters have the following definitions:

➤ DISTINCT—Returns only one copy of any duplicate rows or of specific columns, as determined by the position of the **DISTINCT** parameter and returned by the **SELECT** statement. If the **DISTINCT** parameter is placed immediately following the **SELECT** statement, all combinations of the columns that follow will be distinct.

➤ ALL—Returns all rows with duplicates (default value).

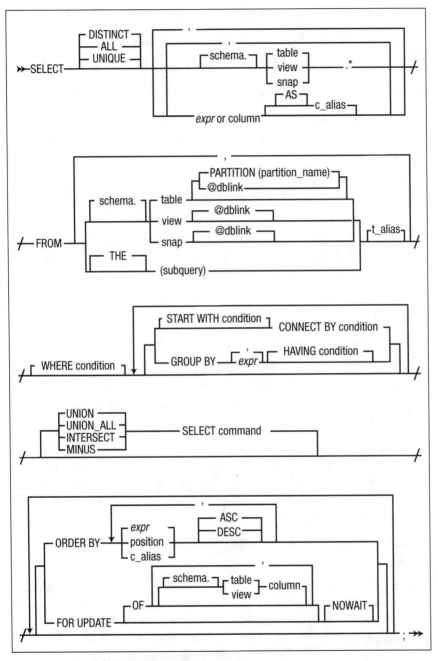

Figure 3.1   Syntax of the **SELECT** command.

➤ **schema**—Owner of the table, view, or snapshot.

➤ **table, view, snap**—Name of the object from which values are selected.

➤ *****—Used to return all columns from the specified table, view, or snapshot.

➤ *expr*—Selects an expression.

➤ **c_alias**—Column alias, used in subsequent statements in the **SELECT** command to refer to its column. A column alias cannot exceed 30 characters.

➤ **PARTITION (partition_name)**—This is used when you know that the data is located in a particular partition of a base table (such as monthly or quarterly data).

➤ **dblink**—The database link to the remote instance where the object of the **SELECT** command is located. If a link is not specified, the object must be local.

➤ **THE**—Tells Oracle that a column is actually a nested object, such as a nested table or **VARRAY**, and instructs Oracle to flatten the return set.

➤ **subquery**—Subquery that's specified identically to a view query definition.

➤ **t_alias**—Table alias, used in subsequent subqueries or in **WHERE** conditions. Once a table alias is specified, the table name can no longer be used, or an error will be generated. A table alias cannot exceed 30 characters.

➤ **WHERE**—Used to restrict the returned rows to a designated subset. Only **WHERE** clauses result in the use of indexes. A **SELECT** command without a **WHERE** clause will return all rows of the specified tables, joined in a Cartesian product. A Cartesian product is wasteful of resources and is generally not the desired result.

➤ **START WITH...CONNECT BY**—Returns rows in a hierarchical order.

➤ **GROUP BY**—Groups the rows based on the specified column's values. The *expr* for the statement must include at least one grouping function, such as **COUNT()**. All columns not participating in the grouping functions must be included in the **GROUP BY** column list. **GROUP BY** does not restrict values; it merely groups them. A **GROUP BY** clause, unless overridden with the **ORDER BY** sort option **DESC**, always returns values sorted in ascending order. A **GROUP BY** clause can use the column name but not the column-position specification or the column alias.

➤ HAVING—Restricts the **GROUP BY** clause to those groups for which the **HAVING** clause is **TRUE**. You can't have a **HAVING** clause without a **GROUP BY** clause.

➤ UNION, UNION ALL, INTERSECT, MINUS—Specify the set operation for the **SELECT** commands specified.

➤ ORDER BY—Forces ordering of the returned rows to either ascending (**ASC**): from least to most, which is the default order, or descending: from highest to lowest, with the descending (**DESC**) operator. The **ORDER BY** clause doesn't restrict rows, but only orders the returned data set. The **ORDER BY** clause can use the column name, column-order specifier, or column alias to identify the columns to be used in the sort. The columns specified for a sort are sorted in left-to-right order, so the values returned are sorted first by the leftmost column, then by the next, and so forth, until all columns have been sorted.

➤ ASC, DESC—Determine the ordering of the returned set of values.

➤ FOR UPDATE—Locks the selected rows.

➤ OF—Locks the rows of only the specified table or table columns.

➤ NOWAIT—Returns control to you if the **SELECT** command attempts to lock a row that is locked by another user. Otherwise, the **SELECT** command waits for any locked rows to be free and returns the results when they are free.

If two or more tables have the same column names in a **SELECT** statement, the table name or table alias must be used to differentiate them.

Column aliases can be used in **ORDER BY**, but in no other clauses.

If **DISTINCT** is used, the total number of bytes selected in all select list expressions is limited to the size of a data block minus some overhead.

Hints can be used to tell the Oracle optimizer how to optimize the query, thus forcing query behavior to what you want, instead of what the optimizer thinks it should be.

If all you could do with a **SELECT** command was look at data from one table, it would be pretty useless. We'll take a look at joins and subqueries in the following subsections.

Any common named columns in joined tables must be prefixed by table names, view names, snapshot names, or a specified alias.

Hierarchical Queries

Hierarchical joins occur when one column in the join relates to another, such as in a bill-of-materials table or in the **explain_plan** table created by execution of the UTLXPLAN.SQL script and used by the **EXPLAIN PLAN** command. Hierarchial queries are usully resolved using self-joins. In tables that may have hierarchical joins, the **START WITH...CONNECT BY...WHERE** combination allows you to break out this relationship:

➤ The **START WITH** clause specifies the root row of the hierarchy.

➤ The **CONNECT BY** clause specifies the relationship between the parent and child rows. This clause must contain a **PRIOR** operator to refer to the parent row.

➤ The **WHERE** clause is used to restrict the rows returned by the query without affecting other rows of the hierarchy.

The **LEVEL** clause creates a level pseudo-column that returns an integer corresponding to the row's level within the hierarchy.

Hierarchical queries are restricted in that the same **SELECT** command that performs a hierarchical query cannot perform a join, nor can it contain an **ORDER BY** clause.

Joins

Joins are **SELECT** commands that retrieve data from two or more tables. One thing to remember is that a table can be joined to itself by the use of table aliases. The **WHERE** clause usually provides the join conditions that determine how data is selected from each table in the join to fill in the specified columns in the select list.

The minimum number of joins required to relate a set of tables is the number of tables in the join minus one (so, for three tables, two joins at a minimum will be required). If you use fewer than n-1 joins, the properly joined tables will have their results Cartesian-joined to the table or tables that are left out. In a test of a join of the **DBA_TABLES, DBA_TAB_COLUMNS, DBA_TAB_PRIVS,** and **DBA_OBJECTS** views—using a join between the **TABLE_NAME** columns and leaving the join to the **OBJECT_NAME** column out of the conditions—a count of 607,662 was returned. When the proper joins between **TABLE_NAME** and **OBJECT_NAME** and between **DBA_TABLES** and **DBA_OBJECTS** were added, the result count dropped to 210.

An *equijoin* uses any of the equality operators. Depending on the optimizer algorithm chosen, the total size of the columns in the equijoin of a single table may be limited to **db_block_size** bytes minus overhead. An equijoin is generally used to display data from two (or more) tables that have common values residing in corresponding columns.

A *self-join* joins a table to itself. Employing this option requires that table aliases be used.

A *Cartesian product* results if two or more tables are specified in a **SELECT** statement without a qualifying **WHERE** clause and join condition. This statement generates a result set with all possible combinations of the rows in the tables, such that the number of rows returned is equal to the product of the number of rows in each table. (That is, if table A has 10 rows, and table B has 20 rows, 200 rows will be returned. Obviously if we extrapolate this concept to a couple of million row tables, you can see that a Cartesian product is not a desirable outcome the majority of the time.)

An *outer join* extends the results of a simple query. It returns all rows that satisfy the join condition and those rows from one of the tables for which no rows from the other table satisfy the join condition. The outer-join operator is (+)—the plus sign surrounded by parentheses. The operator is placed on the side of the join statement deficient in information. The outside-join operator can appear only in the **WHERE** clause applied to a column name. If the specified tables have multiple join conditions, the operator must be present in all of the specified conditions. The outer join can't be used in an **OR** expression, and the outer-join operator can't be applied to a column compared using an **IN** condition or subquery.

The basic format for an outer join is shown in Figure 3.2.

The restrictions on outer joins are:

➤ The (+) operator can appear only in the **WHERE** clause and can apply only to a table or view.

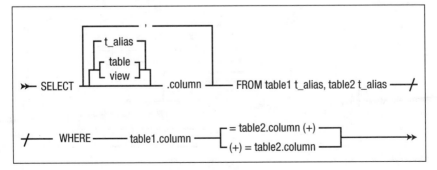

Figure 3.2   Basic syntax of an outer join.

➤ If there are multiple join conditions, the (+) operator must be used in all of these conditions.

➤ The (+)operator can be applied only to a column, not to an expression. But it can be applied to a column inside an arbitrary expression.

➤ A condition containing a column with a (+) cannot be **OR**-related to another condition; neither can it be used in an **IN** condition.

➤ A column marked with the (+) operator cannot be compared to a subquery.

➤ Only one table in a multitable join can have the (+) operator applied to its joins to one other table.

Subqueries

Subqueries are used to return one or more values or sets of values to be used for comparison purposes. A subquery using a single-row comparison operator can return only a single value. A subquery can't use ordering clauses, such as **ORDER BY** or **GROUP BY**, and it cannot contain a **FOR UPDATE** clause. The subquery must return a single value if it's used in an equality comparison, but if it's used with **IN**, a subquery can return multiple values. Other than the restriction on the use of **ORDER BY, GROUP BY,** and **FOR UPDATE,** the syntax of the subquery is nearly identical to a standard **SELECT** statement.

To allow subqueries against nested tables, a **TABLE** clause has been added to the **FROM** clause, as shown in Figure 3.3.

NULL Operations

Oracle supports **NULL** operations. You should be familiar with how the operations involving **NULL** values will be evaluated.

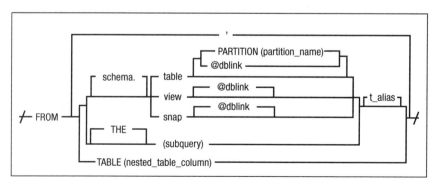

Figure 3.3 Addition of **TABLE** to **FROM** in subselect.

Any operation that involves a one-sided **NULL** (multiply by **NULL**, divide by **NULL**, add **NULL**, subtract **NULL**) will result in a **NULL**. Almost all functions, if called with a **NULL** operand, will return a **NULL** (with the exception of **NVL** and **DECODE**, which can be used to convert **NULL** values). The special clauses **IS NULL** and **IS NOT NULL** must be used when **NULL**s are expected.

If a column contains a **NULL** value, it is ignored for most mathematical operations, such as **SUM**, **AVG**, **MIN**, **MAX**, and **COUNT**. The comparison operators—such as =, !=, <, >, and <>—will not work against **NULL** values. An example would be:

```
SELECT COUNT(*) FROM restrictions WHERE use_restrict!='ADMIN';
```

The return from the above **SELECT** statement will be only columns that have values that don't match '**ADMIN**', excluding **NULL** values. For the **SELECT** statement to include **NULL** values, it will have to be rewritten as:

```
SELECT COUNT(*) FROM restrictions WHERE use_restrict!='ADMIN'
AND use_restrict IS NULL;
```

Examples Using The **SELECT** Command

Generally speaking, you should be familiar with the following **SELECT** command topics:

➤ Selecting rows

➤ Limiting selected rows

➤ Using single-row functions

➤ Displaying data from multiple tables

➤ Using group functions

➤ Using subqueries

This chapter will examine each of these topics and show examples using data-dictionary views and tables for each type of query.

Selecting Rows

The command used for selecting rows is, of course, the **SELECT** command. Probably the simplest form of the **SELECT** command is the totally unrestricted, select-everything form:

```
SELECT * FROM dba_objects;
```

The problem with a simple **SELECT** of everything in a table comes when the table has:

➤ Very long rows or data items, such as **LOBs**, **REFs**, or **LONG** data types, or

➤ A large number of rows.

In both of these situations, you must restrict either the number of columns or the number of rows returned. Table 3.1 shows the structure of the **DBA_OBJECTS** data-dictionary view. Notice the number of columns and the total length possible for a single row.

The total length of a single row could exceed 250 bytes if we did an unrestricted query from the **DBA_OBJECTS** view. In many cases, the maximum length of a row that can be viewed without wrapping is 132 bytes. The **DBA_OBJECTS** view may have several thousand rows, so we will want to restrict the number of rows returned as well as the number, and perhaps size, of columns.

To begin simply, let's first restrict the number of rows returned; we'll do this by filtering against the **OWNER** column. Let's search for all rows that have objects owned by the user **SYSTEM**:

```
SELECT * FROM dba_objects WHERE owner='SYSTEM';
```

Table 3.1	The structure of the **DBA_OBJECTS** data-dictionary view.	
Name	**Null?**	**Type**
OWNER	Y	VARCHAR2(30)
OBJECT_NAME	Y	VARCHAR2(128)
SUBOBJECT_NAME	Y	VARCHAR2(30)
OBJECT_ID	Y	NUMBER
DATA_OBJECT_ID	Y	NUMBER
OBJECT_TYPE	Y	VARCHAR2(15)
CREATED	Y	DATE
LAST_DDL_TIME	Y	DATE
TIMESTAMP	Y	VARCHAR2(19)
STATUS	Y	VARCHAR2(7)
TEMPORARY	Y	VARCHAR2(1)
GENERATED	Y	VARCHAR2(1)
Total bytes:		approximately 250 bytes

Notice that we restricted the rows returned by simply specifying a **WHERE** clause.

How do we limit the number of columns? To restrict the number of columns in a result set from a **SELECT** command, we list only those column names that we wish to see in our result set. For example, if we wanted to see only **owner, object_name, object_type,** and the last time the object was modified, **last_ddl_time,** we'd use the following:

```
SELECT owner, object_name, object_type, last_ddl_time
  FROM dba_objects
WHERE owner='SYSTEM';
```

Restricting the length of returned columns can be done in one of two ways. If you are in the SQL*Plus environment you can use **COLUMN** commands to format how each column is displayed. If you are in PL/SQL or other non-interactive environments then you will have to use Oracle functions to restrict the size or format of a data item. Restricting the length of returned columns can be done in two ways. If you are working in the SQL*Plus environment, you can use **COLUMN** commands to format how each column is displayed. If you are working in PL/SQL or other noninteractive environments, then you have to use Oracle functions to restrict the size or format of a data item. Functions such as **SUBSTR(), RTRIM(), LTRIM(), TRUNC(),** and **TO_CHAR()** can be used to restrict the length or to force formatting of data items. These are single-row functions. An example use of functions would be:

```
DMDB:select substr(owner,1,10) owner,
  2   substr(object_name,1,10) object_name,
  3   substr(object_type, 1,10) object_type,
  4   to_char(last_ddl_time,'dd-mon-yyyy hh24:mi') last_ddl_time
  5   from dba_objects
  6*  where owner='SYSTEM'
```

OWNER	OBJECT_NAM	OBJECT_TYP	LAST_DDL_TIME
SYSTEM	AQDEF_AQ	VIEW	03-aug-1998 11:56
SYSTEM	AQDEF_AQ	VIEW	03-aug-1998 11:56
SYSTEM	AQ$_QIDSEQ	SEQUENCE	03-aug-1998 11:53
SYSTEM	AQ$_QUEUES	TABLE	03-aug-1998 11:53
SYSTEM	AQ$_QUEUES	INDEX	03-aug-1998 11:53
SYSTEM	AQ$_QUEUES	INDEX	03-aug-1998 11:53
SYSTEM	USER_PRIVS	VIEW	03-aug-1998 12:20
SYSTEM	USER_PROFI	TABLE	03-aug-1998 12:20

Notice that several objects appear to have identical names and object types (**SYS_LOB000**); this is not allowed. Actually, they are all named differently, but the **SUBSTR()** function sliced away the unique portion of the names, leaving us to scratch our heads over which is which. You might think that using the **RTRIM()** function would do the trick, but unfortunately, although it trims away the trailing blanks for the data items, it leaves the default length as is.

As was stated above, inside SQL*Plus, we can use the **COLUMN** command (usually shortened to **COL**) to restrict each column's output length. One nice feature of the **COLUMN** command is that it allows the column value to wrap if the column value exceeds the specified format length; thus, no data is lost. Let's look at a select using the **COLUMN** commands in SQL*Plus to format the output:

```
DMDB: COL owner FORMAT a10 HEADING 'Owner'
DMDB: COL object_name FORMAT a10 HEADING 'Object|Name'
DMDB: COL object_type FORMAT a10 HEADING 'Object|Type'
DMDB: COL last_ddl_time FORMAT a16 HEADING 'Last|DDL Time'
DMDB: SELECT owner, object_name, object_type,
   2  TO_CHAR(last_ddl_time,'dd-mon-yyyy hh24:mi') last_ddl_time
   3  FROM dba_objects
   4* WHERE owner='SYSTEM'
```

Owner	Object Name	Object Type	LAST_DDL_TIME
SYSTEM	AQDEF_AQCALL	VIEW	03-aug-1998 11:56
SYSTEM	AQDEF_AQERROR	VIEW	03-aug-1998 11:56
SYSTEM	AQ$_QIDSEQ	SEQUENCE	03-aug-1998 11:53
SYSTEM	AQ$_QUEUES	TABLE	03-aug-1998 11:53
SYSTEM	AQ$_QUEUES_CHECK	INDEX	03-aug-1998 11:53
SYSTEM	AQ$_QUEUES_PRIMARY	INDEX	03-aug-1998 11:53
SYSTEM	AQ$_QUEUE_TABLES	TABLE	03-aug-1998 11:53
SYSTEM	USER_PRIVS	VIEW	03-aug-1998 12:20
SYSTEM	USER_PROFILE	TABLE	03-aug-1998 12:20

So, to limit the number of columns returned, we simply list—in the body of the **SELECT** command—only those columns from which we want to see data. To limit the size of returned columns, we can use internal Oracle functions, such as **SUBSTR()**, or—if we are using the SQL*Plus interface—we can use the **COLUMN** command to reformat data volumes without losing information due to truncation of their values.

What do we do if we want to enforce an order on returned rows? That's covered next.

Enforcing Order

You can impose order on **SELECT** command result sets by using the **ORDER BY** clause. The **ORDER BY** clause accepts as its argument either a single order column or a set of order columns. The **ORDER BY** clause can also accept positional indicators and column-alias values as its arguments. The **ORDER BY** clause can enforce ascending (**ASC**) or descending (**DESC**) orders based on the columns specified. Listing 3.1 shows the results of various **ORDER BY** clauses.

Listing 3.1   Sample **SELECT** statements using the **ORDER BY** clause.

```
SQL> SELECT username, default_tablespace FROM dba_users;

USERNAME                        DEFAULT_TABLESPACE
----------------------------    ----------------------------
SYS                             SYSTEM
SYSTEM                          TOOLS
OUTLN                           SYSTEM
MIGRATE                         SYSTEM
REPMAN                          TOOLS
DBSNMP                          SYSTEM
GRAPHICS_DBA                    GRAPHICS_DATA
AULTM                           USER_DATA
ORDSYS                          SYSTEM

9 rows selected.

SQL> SELECT username, default_tablespace FROM dba_users
  2   ORDER BY username;

USERNAME                        DEFAULT_TABLESPACE
----------------------------    ----------------------------
AULTM                           USER_DATA
DBSNMP                          SYSTEM
GRAPHICS_DBA                    GRAPHICS_DATA
MIGRATE                         SYSTEM
ORDSYS                          SYSTEM
OUTLN                           SYSTEM
REPMAN                          TOOLS
SYS                             SYSTEM
SYSTEM                          TOOLS

9 rows selected.

SQL> SELECT username, default_tablespace FROM dba_users
  2   ORDER BY username desc;
```

```
USERNAME                          DEFAULT_TABLESPACE
------------------------------    ------------------------------
SYSTEM                            TOOLS
SYS                               SYSTEM
REPMAN                            TOOLS
OUTLN                             SYSTEM
ORDSYS                            SYSTEM
MIGRATE                           SYSTEM
GRAPHICS_DBA                      GRAPHICS_DATA
DBSNMP                            SYSTEM
AULTM                             USER_DATA

9 rows selected.

SQL> SELECT username, default_tablespace FROM dba_users
  2  ORDER BY default_tablespace,username;

USERNAME                          DEFAULT_TABLESPACE
------------------------------    ------------------------------
GRAPHICS_DBA                      GRAPHICS_DATA
DBSNMP                            SYSTEM
MIGRATE                           SYSTEM
ORDSYS                            SYSTEM
OUTLN                             SYSTEM
SYS                               SYSTEM
REPMAN                            TOOLS
SYSTEM                            TOOLS
AULTM                             USER_DATA

9 rows selected.
```

In Listing 3.1, first we see a non-ordered **SELECT** statement, which will return the rows selected either by inserted order in the table or by indexed order if an index is used to resolve the query. Next, we see examples using a single-column **ORDER BY** on the **username** column using both the default **ASCENDING** sort and a forced **DESC (DESCENDING)** sort. In Listing 3.1, we also see a two-column sort where the return is sorted by **default_tablespace**; then, for each set of values for each **default_tablespace** value, the result set is also sorted by **username**.

Using the **ORDER BY** clause always results in a **SORT**. This can have a performance impact if the result set exceeds the initialization parameter **SORT_AREA_SIZE** in size or exceeds the value of the parameter **SORT_AREA_RETAINED_SIZE** (if that parameter is set).

Other, more complex ordering methods involve using an index and then ensuring that the **SELECT** statement uses that index to return values in order. The **GROUP BY** clause is another sort method, but it's usually used when grouping functions such as **SUM()** or **COUNT()** are used in a **SELECT** statement. If all columns in the result set are used to sort the result set, then the **GROUP BY** clause can be used to sort the returned rows; otherwise, all columns not affected by functions must be included in the **GROUP BY** clause. If one or more columns affected by grouping functions are present in a query along with one or more nongrouped columns, the nongrouped columns must all be present in the **GROUP BY** clause. Listing 3.2 shows several examples of the **GROUP BY** clause in **SELECT** statements.

Listing 3.2   Sample **SELECT** statements using the **GROUP BY** clause.

```
SQL> SELECT username, default_tablespace FROM dba_users
  2   GROUP BY default_tablespace,username;

USERNAME                         DEFAULT_TABLESPACE
-----------------------------    ------------------------------
GRAPHICS_DBA                     GRAPHICS_DATA
DBSNMP                           SYSTEM
MIGRATE                          SYSTEM
ORDSYS                           SYSTEM
OUTLN                            SYSTEM
SYS                              SYSTEM
REPMAN                           TOOLS
SYSTEM                           TOOLS
AULTM                            USER_DATA

12 rows selected.

SQL> SELECT username, default_tablespace FROM dba_users
  2   GROUP BY default_tablespace;

SELECT username, default_tablespace
       *
ERROR at line 1:
ORA-00979: not a GROUP BY expression


SQL> SELECT COUNT(username) users, default_tablespace
  2   FROM dba_users
```

```
  3  GROUP BY default_tablespace
SQL> /

   USERS DEFAULT_TABLESPACE
-------- -----------------------------
       1 GRAPHICS_DATA
       5 SYSTEM
       2 TOOLS
       1 USER_DATA
```

In the examples in Listing 3.2, we see a **GROUP BY** clause that uses all of the columns returned in the result set. The next example in Listing 3.2 shows the error that will result if a nongrouping function altered column is left out of the column list in the clause. The final example shows a **GROUP BY** clause with a grouping function applied to a column.

Multiple grouping functions can be applied to the same result set, but their effect will be limited to the major **GROUP BY** subsets. The **GROUP BY** clause has the **HAVING** subclause, which is used to restrict the rows returned. Listing 3.3 shows an example of a single column **GROUP BY** clause using multiple grouping functions.

Listing 3.3   Example of a **SELECT** statement with multiple groupings and a **GROUP BY** clause.

```
SQL> SELECT owner, COUNT(*) objects, SUM(bytes) bytes
  2  FROM dba_extents
  3  GROUP BY owner;

OWNER                           OBJECTS     BYTES
------------------------------- -------- ----------
GRAPHICS_DBA                         21   8724480
OUTLN                                 6     98304
REPMAN                              176   7208960
SYS                                 670  52912128
SYSTEM                               61   2662400

5 rows selected.
```

Joins

What if we need data from more than one table? As long as there is a relationship between the tables, we can join them in a query statement and pull the related information out of both tables. If there is no relationship, we can form a **SELECT** statement that gets information from both tables, but the data will be returned in an "all-or-nothing" arrangement.

Joins can be simple or complex. The simplest join in most cases is the equijoin, which establishes a simple equality or inequality relationship between two tables. The relationship takes the form: tab1.col1 = tab2.col2. The data types of the two columns must be the same or be convertible into a compatible type. Any forced conversion of data types (from number to character, for example) will result in the query not being able to use any indexes associated with the converted column. Listing 3.4 demonstrates several equijoins.

Listing 3.4 Sample equijoins.

```
SQL> SELECT a.table_name,b.column_name
  2  FROM dba_tables a, dba_tab_columns b
  3  WHERE a.table_name = b.table_name
  4  AND a.tablespace_name = 'GRAPHICS_DATA';
```

```
TABLE_NAME                        COLUMN_NAME
-------------------------------   -----------
GRAPHICS_TABLE                    BFILE_ID
GRAPHICS_TABLE                    BFILE_TYPE
GRAPHICS_TABLE                    BFILE_LOC
GRAPHICS_USERS                    USERNAME
GRAPHICS_USERS                    USER_FUNCTION
INTERNAL_GRAPHICS                 GRAPHIC_ID
INTERNAL_GRAPHICS                 GRAPHIC_TYPE
INTERNAL_GRAPHICS                 GRAPHIC_BLOB

8 rows selected.
```

```
SQL> SELECT a.table_name,b.column_name, c.created
  2  FROM dba_tables a, dba_tab_columns b, dba_objects c
  3  WHERE a.table_name = b.table_name
  4  AND a.table_name = c.object_name
  5  AND a.tablespace_name = 'GRAPHICS_DATA'
  6 AND object_type = 'TABLE';
```

```
TABLE_NAME                        COLUMN_NAME                     CREATED
-------------------------------   ---------------------------     ---------
GRAPHICS_TABLE                    BFILE_ID                        11-MAY-99
GRAPHICS_TABLE                    BFILE_LOC                       11-MAY-99
GRAPHICS_TABLE                    BFILE_TYPE                      11-MAY-99
GRAPHICS_USERS                    USERNAME                        23-MAY-99
GRAPHICS_USERS                    USER_FUNCTION                   23-MAY-99
INTERNAL_GRAPHICS                 GRAPHIC_ID                      11-MAY-99
INTERNAL_GRAPHICS                 GRAPHIC_BLOB                    11-MAY-99
INTERNAL_GRAPHICS                 GRAPHIC_TYPE                    11-MAY-99

15 rows selected.
```

The examples in Listing 3.4 are simple two-table and three-table equijoins. (Well, actually, in this case, they are views, but the principle is still the same.) One thing to notice is that in order to ensure that you get the proper rows returned, there must be *n-1* join conditions, where *n* is the number of tables. If *n-1* join conditions are not present, a Cartesian join will be performed against the nonequijoined table.

Another type of join is the outer join. An *outer join* is used when one of the tables participating in the join is deficient in data. For example, suppose that you have a department that has no employees yet, and you want the department to be listed in a report. In this case, an outer join would be required.

An outer join is performed when the outer-join indicator is placed at the end of the table name for the table deficient in data. The outer-join indicator is a plus sign surrounded by parentheses: "(+)". Listing 3.5 demonstrates an outer join using some simple tables.

Listing 3.5   Sample outer join.

```
SQL> SELECT * FROM department;

    DEPTNO DEPT_DESC
--------- ------------------------------
        1 Administration
        2 Sales
        3 Marketing
        4 Consulting
        5 Training
        6 Remote Monitoring

6 rows selected.

SQL> SELECT * FROM employee;

    EMP_NO   DEPT_NO NAME
--------- --------- ----------------------
       100         1 Joe Boss
       101         1 Ann Assistant
       102         1 Fred Fumbles
       103         1 Frank Receives
       104         2 Sam Salesman
       105         2 Eliza Can
       106         2 Bill Cant
       107         3 Sara Smiles
       108         3 John Dont
       109         4 Gilles Gogeter
       110         4 Gomer Newbie

11 rows selected.
```

```
SQL> SELECT a.dept_desc, b.emp_no, b.name
  2  FROM department a, employee b
  3  WHERE a.deptno = b.dept_no ORDER BY dept_no;


DEPT_DESC                             EMP_NO NAME
------------------------------------- --------- ------------------------
Administration                           100 Joe Boss
Administration                           101 Ann Assistant
Administration                           102 Fred Fumbles
Administration                           103 Frank Receives
Sales                                    104 Sam Salesman
Sales                                    105 Eliza Can
Sales                                    106 Bill Cant
Marketing                                107 Sara Smiles
Marketing                                108 John Dont
Consulting                               109 Gilles Gogeter
Consulting                               110 Gomer Newbie


11 rows selected.

SQL> SELECT a.dept_desc, b.emp_no, b.name
  2  FROM department a, employee b
  3  WHERE a.deptno=b.dept_no(+) ORDER BY dept_no;


DEPT_DESC                             EMP_NO NAME
------------------------------------- --------- ------------------------
Administration                           100 Joe Boss
Administration                           101 Ann Assistant
Administration                           102 Fred Fumbles
Administration                           103 Frank Receives
Sales                                    104 Sam Salesman
Sales                                    105 Eliza Can
Sales                                    106 Bill Cant
Marketing                                107 Sara Smiles
Marketing                                108 John Dont
Consulting                               109 Gilles Gogeter
Consulting                               110 Gomer Newbie
Training
Remote Monitoring


13 rows selected.
```

In Listing 3.5, we see two tables: **department** and **employee**. In the **department** table, each department has employees, with the exception of the **Training** and **Remote Monitoring** departments. In the first join (not using the outer-join indicator), we get back 11 rows, and the departments without employees are ignored. When we add the outer-join indicator, as is shown in the second **SELECT** statement, the result set includes the two empty departments, as well as the nonempty departments, giving us 13 rows.

Self-Joins

A self-join is used when a table relates back to itself. This can happen in an **employee** table where the department and title information is included (for example, when a manager is also managed), or in the classic BOM (bill-of-materials) breakout problem (when a part is a subcomponent in a larger subassembly that is a component of a larger subassembly). A good example of a self-join is the **plan_table** created by the utlxplan.sql script for use with the **EXPLAIN PLAN** and **TKPROF** utilities. The **plan_table** contains the columns **ID** and **PARENT_ID**, which are used to join the table to itself. Another example is the case in which a table may have duplicate rows. To identify the duplicate rows for removal, you'd use a query including the **ROWID** hidden column and the column values that cause duplication. Another use for the self-join is to eliminate rows based on a specific criterion, such as when a specific column or columns contains no data. Listing 3.6 demonstrates some of these examples.

Listing 3.6   Sample self-joins.

```
DMDB:EXPLAIN PLAN SET STATEMENT_ID='TEST1'
  2* FOR SELECT * FROM dba_temp WHERE rep_order>5

Explained.

DMDB:SELECT operation,options, object_name, id, parent_id
  2  FROM plan_table
  3  WHERE statement_id='TEST1'
  4* ORDER BY id

OPERATION            OPTIONS    OBJECT_NAME           ID PARENT_ID
-------------------- ---------- -------------------- -- ---------
SELECT STATEMENT                                      0
TABLE ACCESS         FULL       DBA_TEMP              1         0

DMDB:SELECT
  2  LPAD('   ',2*LEVEL)||operation||' '||object_name query_plan
  3  FROM plan_table WHERE statement_id='TEST1'
  4  CONNECT BY PRIOR id=parent_id
  5  START WITH id=0;
```

```
QUERY_PLAN
-------------------------------------------------------------------
  SELECT STATEMENT
    TABLE ACCESS DBA_TEMP

DMDB:CREATE TABLE test_self_join (id number, desc_id varchar2(10))

Table created.

DMDB:INSERT INTO test_self_join VALUES (1,'TEST1');

1 row created.

...

DMDB:INSERT INTO test_self_join VALUES (4,'TEST4')

1 row created.

DMDB:COMMIT;

Commit complete.

DMDB:SELECT * FROM test_self_join;

        ID DESC_ID
--------- ----------
         1 TEST1
         1 TEST1
         1 TEST1
         2 TEST2
         3 TEST3
         3 TEST3
         4 TEST4

7 rows selected.

DMDB:SELECT a.rowid FROM test_self_join a
  2  WHERE a.rowid > (SELECT MIN (b.rowid)
  3  FROM test_self_join b
  4* WHERE b.id=a.id);

ROWID
------------------
AAAC4xAAPAAAADUAAB
AAAC4xAAPAAAADUAAC
AAAC4xAAPAAAADUAAF
```

```
DMDB:DELETE FROM test_self_join a
   2  WHERE a.rowid > (SELECT MIN (b.rowid)
   3  FROM test_self_join b
   4  WHERE b.id=a.id);

3 rows deleted.

DMDB:COMMIT;

Commit complete.

DMDB:SELECT * FROM test_self_join;

      ID DESC_ID
--------- ----------
       1 TEST1
       2 TEST2
       3 TEST3
       4 TEST4

DMDB:DESC sql_garbage
 Name                           Null?    Type
 ----------------------------   -------- ----
 USERS                                   VARCHAR2(30)
 GARBAGE                                 NUMBER
 GOOD                                    NUMBER

DMDB:select * from sql_garbage;

 USERS                          GARBAGE      GOOD
 ----------------------------   --------  --------
 ASAP                            680879
 ASAP                                     2182475
 ESTOECKE                                   88203
 JKISKEL                                   214491
 QDBA                                     2456368
 SYS                              33236
 SYS                                      1210234
 SYSTEM                         1245629
 SYSTEM                                    119171

9 rows selected.

DMDB:SELECT
   2  AVG(b.good/(b.good+a.garbage))*100 avg_reuse
   3  FROM sql_garbage a, sql_garbage b
   4  WHERE a.users=b.users
```

```
5    AND a.garbage IS NOT NULL
6    AND b.good IS NOT NULL;
```

```
AVG_REUSE
---------
61.895823
```

In Listing 3.6, we see three types of self-joins: one using the **CONNECT BY** clause; one using a subquery; and the final one using an alias join structure to relate the table to itself. Some items to note about the self-joins in Listing 3.6:

➤ The **CONNECT BY** clause must have a root value to start from. In this example, the root value is zero.

➤ The subquery must use multiple aliases for the table.

➤ The join of the table to itself, using the alias join, must also use multiple aliases.

Cartesian Products

If a join is performed and no join condition is specified, then a Cartesian product results. A *Cartesian product* is a result set that is the product of the two tables' total rows. If table "a" has 10 rows and table "b" has 100 rows, and a Cartesian product is developed, the result set will have 1,000 rows. If a query joins three or more tables, the optimizer may find a way to choose a join order that precludes a Cartesian product, but don't count on it.

Hash Joins And Anti-Joins

Two new types of joins became available in late Oracle7 and in Oracle8; these are the hash join and the anti-join.

Hash Joins

The hash join has nothing to do with hash clusters or the **TABLE ACCESS HASH** method. A *hash join* compares two tables in memory. The first table is full-table scanned, and a hashing function is applied to the data in memory. Then, the second table is full-table scanned, and the hashing function is used to compare the values. Matching values are returned to the user. The user usually has nothing to do with this process, which is completely controlled by the optimizer. However, a hash join can be used only by the cost-based optimizer. To use hash joins, you must set the **HASH_JOIN_ENABLED** initialization parameter to true.

Several **HASH** parameters affect how hash joins are used. These parameters are:

> ➤ HASH_JOIN_ENABLED—Set to true to use hash joins.

> ➤ HASH_AREA_SIZE—A large value reduces the cost of hash joins so they are used more frequently. (Set this parameter to half the square root of the size of the smaller of the two objects, but not less than 1 megabyte.) Suggested range is 8 to 32 megabytes.

> ➤ HASH_MULTIBLOCK_IO_COUNT—A large value reduces the cost of hash joins so they are used more frequently. Suggested size is 4 blocks.

Anti-Joins

To use anti-joins, you must set the initialization parameter **ALWAYS_ANTI_JOIN** to **HASH** or **MERGE**. This causes the **NOT IN** clause in queries to always be resolved using a parallel-hash or parallel-merge anti-join. If the **ALWAYS_ANTI_JOIN** parameter is set to anything other than **HASH** or **MERGE**, the **NOT IN** clause will be evaluated as a correlated subquery. You can force Oracle to perform a specific query as an **ANTI-JOIN** by using the **MERGE_AJ** or **HASH_AJ** hints.

Subqueries

We have already looked at a subquery example back in Listing 3.6. We have also learned that if a **NOT IN** clause is declared and the initialization parameters aren't set to use the **HASH** or **ANTI_JOIN** types of joins, then a correlated subquery is generated to resolve the **NOT IN** condition. When a subquery is included in a **FROM** clause, the subquery can also be considered an inline view. Listing 3.7 shows some examples of subqueries.

Listing 3.7   Sample **SELECT** statements using subqueries.

```
DMDB:SELECT COUNT(*) num_owned, a.owner
  2  FROM dba_objects a
  3  WHERE 10<(SELECT COUNT(*) FROM dba_objects b
  4  WHERE a.owner=b.owner)
  5  GROUP BY a.owner;


NUM_OWNED OWNER
---------- ----------------------------
      3016 ASAP
      1954 DMADMIN
        38 EBOND
        14 EDI
      1605 PUBLIC
```

```
      67 QDBA
    1407 SYS
      90 SYSTEM
```

8 rows selected.

```
DMDB:SELECT COUNT(*) num_owned, a.owner
  2  FROM dba_objects a
  3  WHERE 100<(SELECT COUNT(*) FROM dba_objects b
  4  WHERE a.owner=b.owner)
  5  GROUP BY a.owner;


NUM_OWNED OWNER
--------- ------------------------------
     3016 ASAP
     1954 DMADMIN
     1605 PUBLIC
     1407 SYS


DMDB:SELECT COUNT(*) num_owned, a.owner
  2  FROM dba_objects a
  3  WHERE a.owner NOT IN (SELECT b.owner FROM dba_objects b
  4  WHERE b.owner LIKE 'SYS%')
  5  GROUP BY a.owner;


NUM_OWNED OWNER
--------- ------------------------------
     3016 ASAP
     1954 DMADMIN
       38 EBOND
       14 EDI
     1605 PUBLIC
       67 QDBA
```

6 rows selected.

```
DMDB:SELECT COUNT(*) num_owned, a.owner
  2  FROM dba_objects a
  3  WHERE a.owner NOT IN (SELECT b.owner FROM dba_objects b
  4  WHERE b.owner LIKE 'S%')
  5  GROUP BY a.owner;


NUM_OWNED OWNER
--------- ------------------------------
     3016 ASAP
     1954 DMADMIN
       38 EBOND
       14 EDI
```

```
   1605 PUBLIC
     67 QDBA
```

6 rows selected.

```
DMDB:SELECT a.owner
   2  FROM (SELECT DISTINCT b.owner FROM dba_objects b
   3  WHERE b.owner LIKE 'S%') a;
```

```
OWNER
------------------------------
SYS
SYSTEM
```

Using The **SET** Operators **UNION, UNION ALL, INTERSECT, And MINUS**

Sometimes you may need to merge the results of two disparate queries. In some cases, there are no logical ways to join two sets of tables, but you want to display their contents in a single report. How can you accomplish these types of SELECTs without generating Cartesian products? The answers to these problems are the SET operators. The SET operators are UNION, UNION ALL, INTERSECT, and MINUS.

➤ A UNION merges the results of two queries and discards any duplicate rows.

➤ A UNION ALL merges the results of two queries and leaves in duplicate values.

➤ The INTERSECT merges the results from two queries and leaves only the distinct rows.

➤ The MINUS operator returns all distinct rows selected by the first query but not the second.

In a SET operation, if the column names don't match, aliases must be used. The SET operators cannot be used with the object clauses **THE** or **MULTISET**, or with the **FOR UPDATE** clause. Listing 3.8 demonstrates the various SET operators.

Listing 3.8   Sample **SELECT** statements using the **SET** operators.

```
SQL> SELECT object_name FROM dba_objects
   2  WHERE object_type = 'TABLE' AND owner = 'GRAPHICS_DBA';
```

```
OBJECT_NAME
--------------------------------------------------------------------
ART
ARTIST_STORE
BASIC_LOB_TABLE
GRAPHICS_TABLE
GRAPHICS_USERS
INTERNAL_GRAPHICS

6 rows selected.

SQL> SELECT object_name FROM dba_objects WHERE owner = 'GRAPHICS_DBA';

OBJECT_NAME
--------------------------------------------------------------------
ART
ARTIST_LIST
ARTIST_STORE
ARTIST_T
ART_T
BASIC_LOB_TABLE
GET_BFILES
GRAPHICS_SEC
GRAPHICS_SEC
GRAPHICS_TABLE
GRAPHICS_TABLE_SEQ
GRAPHICS_USERS
IMAGE_SEQ
INTERNAL_GRAPHICS
PICTURE_PART_V
PK_INTERNAL_GRAPHICS

16 rows selected.

SQL> SELECT object_name FROM dba_objects
  2   WHERE object_type = 'TABLE' AND owner = 'GRAPHICS_DBA'
  3   UNION
  4   SELECT object_name FROM dba_objects
  5   WHERE owner = 'GRAPHICS_DBA';

OBJECT_NAME
--------------------------------------------------------------------
ART
ARTIST_LIST
ARTIST_STORE
ARTIST_T
ART_T
BASIC_LOB_TABLE
```

```
GET_BFILES
GRAPHICS_SEC
GRAPHICS_TABLE
GRAPHICS_TABLE_SEQ
GRAPHICS_USERS
IMAGE_SEQ
INTERNAL_GRAPHICS
PICTURE_PART_V
PK_INTERNAL_GRAPHICS

15 rows selected.

SQL> SELECT object_name FROM dba_objects
  2  WHERE object_type = 'TABLE' AND owner = 'GRAPHICS_DBA'
  3  UNION ALL
  4  SELECT object_name FROM dba_objects
  5  WHERE owner = 'GRAPHICS_DBA';

OBJECT_NAME
-----------
ART
ARTIST_STORE
BASIC_LOB_TABLE
GRAPHICS_TABLE
GRAPHICS_USERS
INTERNAL_GRAPHICS
ART
ARTIST_LIST
ARTIST_STORE
ARTIST_T
ART_T
BASIC_LOB_TABLE
GET_BFILES
GRAPHICS_SEC
GRAPHICS_SEC
GRAPHICS_TABLE
GRAPHICS_TABLE_SEQ
GRAPHICS_USERS
IMAGE_SEQ
INTERNAL_GRAPHICS
PICTURE_PART_V
PK_INTERNAL_GRAPHICS

22 rows selected.

SQL> SELECT object_name FROM dba_objects
  2  WHERE object_type = 'TABLE' AND owner = 'GRAPHICS_DBA'
  3  INTERSECT
```

```
  4  SELECT object_name FROM dba_objects
  5  WHERE owner = 'GRAPHICS_DBA';

OBJECT_NAME
-----------
ART
ARTIST_STORE
BASIC_LOB_TABLE
GRAPHICS_TABLE
GRAPHICS_USERS
INTERNAL_GRAPHICS

6 rows selected.

SQL> SELECT object_name FROM dba_objects
  2  WHERE object_type = 'TABLE' AND owner = 'GRAPHICS_DBA'
  3  MINUS
  4  SELECT object_name FROM dba_objects
  5  WHERE owner = 'GRAPHICS_DBA';

no rows selected

SQL> SELECT object_name FROM dba_objects
  2  WHERE owner = 'GRAPHICS_DBA'
  3  MINUS
  4  SELECT object_name FROM dba_objects
  5  WHERE object_type = 'TABLE' AND owner = 'GRAPHICS_DBA';

OBJECT_NAME
-----------
ARTIST_LIST
ARTIST_T
ART_T
GET_BFILES
GRAPHICS_SEC
GRAPHICS_TABLE_SEQ
IMAGE_SEQ
PICTURE_PART_V
PK_INTERNAL_GRAPHICS

9 rows selected.
```

The examples in Listing 3.8 show the results of the two nonmerged queries and then the various results from using the **SET** operators. Note that the order for the **UNION** and **UNION ALL SELECT** operators is not important, but the order for the **INTERSECT** and **MINUS** operators is critical, as is demonstrated by the last two examples.

Practice Questions

Question 1

> Which clause restricts the groups of rows returned in a **GROUP BY** clause to those groups meeting a specified condition?
>
> ○ a. **SELECT**
>
> ○ b. **FROM**
>
> ○ c. **WHERE**
>
> ○ d. **HAVING**

The correct answer is d. The **HAVING** clause restricts the groups of rows returned to those groups meeting a specified condition. Answer a is incorrect because a **SELECT** by itself doesn't group results. For that matter, **SELECT** is a command, not a clause. Answer b is incorrect because the **FROM** clause tells **SELECT** where to get its data, and it has nothing to do with ordering or grouping. Answer c is incorrect because the **WHERE** clause has nothing to do with sorting or grouping; it deals with what data to retrieve.

Question 2

> You query the database with this command:
>
> ```
> SELECT id_number, 100/nvl(quantity,0)
> FROM inventory;
> ```
>
> Which value is displayed when the quantity value is null?
>
> ○ a. 0
>
> ○ b. The command will error out
>
> ○ c. The keyword **NULL**
>
> ○ d. 100

The correct answer is b; the command will error out. Answers a and d are incorrect because any operation involving the **NVL** function will substitute the provided value for the **NULL**; 100/0 is indeterminate, so an error is generated.

Answer c is incorrect because a null response is a blank space, not any special keyword. Also, because we are using the **NVL** function, no **NULL** value is present in the answer.

Question 3

> Which operator would be most appropriate to use to search through a list of values?
>
> ○ a. **LIKE**
>
> ○ b. =
>
> ○ c. **BETWEEN**
>
> ○ d. **IN**

The correct answer is d, **IN**. Answer a is incorrect because the **LIKE** operator only compares a value against a single template value using one or more wildcards. Answer b is incorrect because an equality can be used to compare against only a single value, not a list of values. Answer c in incorrect because **BETWEEN** is used to find values inside a specified minimum and maximum value, not inside a list of possible values.

Question 4

> After reviewing Table 3.2, evaluate this command:
>
> ```
> SELECT product_id
> FROM products
> WHERE price BETWEEN 5.00 AND 50.00
> ORDER BY description, supplier_id;
> ```
>
> Which **product_id** would be displayed first?
>
> ○ a. 30079
>
> ○ b. 23026
>
> ○ c. 23021
>
> ○ d. 23023

Table 3.2 PRODUCTS table contents.

PRODUCT_ID	DESCRIPTION	SUPPLIER_ID	STOCK_ON_HAND	PRICE	SHIP_DATE
23023	Tennis balls	1334	255	10.57	10-jun-99
23025	Tennis rackets	1335	50	34.99	15-jul-99
23021	Elbow guards	1336	25	5.28	15-jul-99
23026	Shin guards	1336	50	10.22	15-jul-99
30079	Tennis shorts	1335	10	32.56	10-jun-99

The correct answer is c, 23021. All of the **PRICE** column values fall into the **BETWEEN** values, so there is no restriction based on the **BETWEEN**. Because the first **ORDER BY** is on the **DESCRIPTION** column, the rows will be ordered by that column and then reordered by duplicate **SUPPLIER_ID** values in the default order, which is ascending if not specified. This places the value of elbow guards—23021—at the top of the list.

Question 5

You need to display the column **order_date**, which is a date data type, in this format:

25TH OF FEBRUARY 1997

Which **SELECT** statement could you use?

○ a.
```
SELECT order_date('fmDD "OF" MONTH YYYY')
FROM inventory;
```

○ b.
```
SELECT
TO_CHAR(order_date,'fmDDTH "OF" MONTH YYYY')
FROM inventory;
```

○ c.
```
SELECT
TO_CHAR(order_date,('fmDDspth "OF" MONTH YYYY')
FROM inventory;
```

○ d.
```
SELECT
order_date('fmDDspth "OF" MONTH YYYY')
FROM inventory;
```

The correct answer is b. Answers a and d are incorrect because they are syntactically incorrect; they don't include the **TO_CHAR** function. Answer c is incorrect because its format line is incorrect and can't produce the desired output.

Question 6

You have four tables in a **SELECT** statement, with two join conditions specified for three of the tables. What will happen when the query is run?

- ○ a. Three of the tables will have their results properly restricted, and the results will be Cartesian-joined to the fourth table.

- ○ b. Two of the tables will have their contents properly joined and restricted, and the results will be Cartesian-joined to the other two tables.

- ○ c. Nothing; an error will be returned because you have only two join conditions for four tables.

- ○ d. An error will be returned because you can't join more than three tables in Oracle.

The correct answer is a. Answer b is incorrect because you have joins between three tables, not just two. Answer c is incorrect because you will get processing, just not what you expect. Answer d is incorrect because the number of tables joined in Oracle is essentially limited to the amount of physical memory you have available on your machine (unlimited).

Question 7

Evaluate this command:

```
SELECT manufacturer_id
"Manufacturer Identification Code", SUM(price)
FROM inventory
WHERE price > 6.00
GROUP BY "Manufacturer Identification Code"
ORDER BY 2
```

Which two clauses will cause errors?

❏ a.
```
SELECT manufacturer_id
"Manufacturer Identification Code", SUM(price)
```

❏ b.
```
FROM inventory
```

❏ c.
```
WHERE price >  6.00
```

❏ d.
```
GROUP BY "Manufacturer Identification Code"
```

❏ e.
```
ORDER BY 2
```

The correct answers are a and d. Answer a is correct because you can't have a column alias longer than 30 characters. Answer d is correct because you can't perform a **GROUP BY** on a column alias. The rest of the clauses shown are correct in their syntax.

Question 8

You query the database with this command:

```
SELECT manufacturer_id
FROM inventory
WHERE manufacturer_id LIKE
'%N\%P\%O%' ESCAPE \;
```

For which character pattern is the **LIKE** operator searching?

○ a. NPO

○ b. N\%P\%O

○ c. N\P\O

○ d. N%P%O

Trick! question

The correct answer is d. When you're evaluating a **LIKE** statement, always check to see if it includes the **ESCAPE** clause. If there's an **ESCAPE** clause, note which character it specifies to treat as an escape. Any character that's preceded by the escape character will be treated as a normal character and will have no special meaning. In this case, with answer d, the percent signs in front of the P and O characters have been escaped, indicating that they're to be treated as a part of the search string and not as wildcards. The leading and trailing percent signs have not been escaped, so they're treated as wildcards. The other answers are incorrect because they're not what the specified string translates into.

Question 9

Your **parts** table contains a **subassembly** column and a **part_no** column. If you want to find out which parts are contained in which subassemblies, what type of join should you use? [Choose the most complete answer]

○ a. A self-join

○ b. An equijoin

○ c. A self-join with an equijoin

○ d. A self-join containing a hierarchical query

The correct answer is d. Answer a is incorrect because, although correct in that you need a self-join, it doesn't mention the hierarchical query. Answer b is incorrect because, although you may need to do an equijoin, it doesn't mention the self-join or the hierarchical query. Answer c is incorrect because, although it may be true that you will need a self-join and maybe an equijoin, it doesn't mention the hierarchical query. Answer d is the most complete answer because this query will require a hierarchical query and a self-join.

Question 10

Which clauses cannot contain a subquery? [Choose three]

❑ a. **WHERE**

❑ b. **SELECT**

❑ c. **HAVING**

❑ d. **ORDER BY**

❑ e. **GROUP BY**

The correct answers are b, d, and e. Of the clauses listed, only **WHERE** and **HAVING** are allowed to have a subquery.

Need To Know More?

 Ault, Michael R. *Oracle8 Administration and Management.* John Wiley & Sons, New York, New York, 1998. ISBN 0-471-19234-1. This book covers virtually all aspects of Oracle8 administration, including command syntax, tuning, and management topics.

 Honour, Edward, Dalberth, Paul, Kaplan, Ari, and Atul Mehta. *Oracle8 HOW-TO.* Waite Group Press, Corte Madera, California, 1998. ISBN 1-57169-123-5. This book provides an excellent resource for general Oracle how-to information and covers topics from installation to how to use the Web server.

Oracle8 Server SQL Reference Manual, Release 8.0. Oracle Corporation, Redwood Shores, California, June1997. Part No. A54649-01, parts one and two. This is the source book for all Oracle SQL for version 8.0. This book can be found on the Web, at the time of writing, at **http://technet.oracle.com.** This site has free membership and has all current versions of Oracle documentation available online in Acrobat format (PDF files).

DDL: Using The CREATE Command For All Objects

Terms you'll need to understand:

√ Data Definition Language (DDL)

√ Tablespace

√ Storage clause

√ Initial extents

√ **INITIAL**

√ **NEXT**

√ **MINEXTENTS**

√ **MAXEXTENTS**

√ **PCTINCREASE**

√ **PCTFREE**

√ **PCTUSED**

√ **INITRANS**

√ **MAXTRANS**

Techniques you'll need to master:

√ Using all storage parameters

√ Using the **CREATE** command for all objects (databases, tablespaces, relational tables, object tables, types, indexes, clusters, sequences, views, synonyms, rollback segments, and control files)

The OCP exam covers the storage parameters and their various uses in great detail. A DBA (database administrator) must know all of the ins and outs of the storage parameters, particularly those dealing with the prevention of chaining and fragmentation.

Data Definition Language (DDL) includes all commands used to create, alter, and drop database objects. These objects include tables, indexes, clusters, sequences, triggers, procedures, functions, and packages (including package bodies). The **CREATE** command is used to create all of these objects (with differing modifiers and options). Likewise, the **ALTER** command is used to alter database objects, and the **DROP** command is used to drop them. This first DDL chapter is dedicated to the most complex of these command sets: the CREATE command.

The **CREATE** Command

The CREATE command is used to make all database objects. This command and its optional **STORAGE** clause will be the subject of most of the DDL-related questions on the exam.

The **CREATE** Command For Databases

All things in an Oracle database reside in the database. Therefore, the first CREATE command we'll discuss is the **CREATE DATABASE** command. Some systems require the user to have the OSDBA or SYSDBA role to use the command. Figure 4.1 shows the format for this command.

The **CREATE DATABASE** command has the following parameters:

➤ database_name—Name of the database. Composed of a maximum of eight characters.

➤ file_specs—File specifications for data files are of the format: 'filename' SIZE integer K or M REUSE. K is for kilobytes, M is for megabytes, and REUSE specifies that if the file already exists, reuse it. Usually a file name is a full path file name such as /data1/oracle/ortest1/data/psdata01.dbf.

Note: File specifications for log files depend on the operating system.

➤ AUTOEXTEND—Used to allow your data files to automatically extend as needed. Be very careful with this command because it can use up a great deal of disk space rather rapidly if a mistake is made during table builds or inserts.

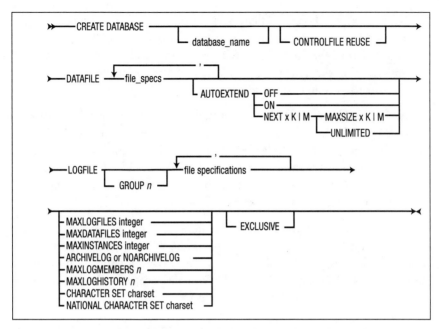

Figure 4.1 The syntax of the **CREATE DATABASE** command.

➤ **MAXLOGFILES, MAXDATAFILES,** and **MAXINSTANCES**—Set hard limits for the database and should be set to the maximum you ever expect.

➤ **ARCHIVELOG**—Used to set archive logging.

➤ **NOARCHIVELOG**—Used if you don't need to set archive logging.

➤ **MAXLOGMEMBERS** and **MAXLOGHISTORY**—Set hard limits. **MAXLOGMEMBERS** specifies the maximum number of redo logs in a single log group. **MAXLOGHISTORY** specifies the maximum number of redo log switches to record in the control file.

 There is a bug in all Oracle8 and 8i databases that the **MAXLOGHISTORY** setting will not overwrite as it is supposed to once it is reached, causing a database crash. Make sure you set this high enough.

➤ **CHARACTER SET**—Determines the character set that data will be stored in. This value is operating-system dependent.

➤ NATIONAL CHARACTER SET—Specifies the national character set used to store data in columns specifically defined as **NCHAR**, **NCLOB**, or **NVARCHAR2**. You can't change the national character set after creating the database. If not specified, the national character set defaults to the database character set.

➤ **EXCLUSIVE or PARALLEL**—Databases are in either **EXCLUSIVE** or **PARALLEL** mode. A database must be altered into **PARALLEL** mode after creation. **EXCLUSIVE** mode sets the database so that only one instance of Oracle at a time has access. **PARALLEL** mode allows one or more instances to have access to the same database, but requires an additional license purchase from Oracle.

The **CREATE DATABASE** command allows the initial specification of database maximum values, such as the maximum allowed number of database data files, log files, and log file groups. It also allows for specification of the initial database data file for the **SYSTEM** tablespace, as well as specification of other data files used with other tablespaces.

The **CREATE** Command For Tablespaces

All objects in an Oracle database are stored in *tablespaces*, which are the units of logical storage for an Oracle database. The **CREATE TABLESPACE** command allows you to create a tablespace and one or more initial data files. It also allows you to specify default storage parameters. Figure 4.2 shows the **CREATE TABLESPACE** syntax.

The **CREATE TABLESPACE** command has the following keywords and parameters:

➤ **tablespace_name**—Name of the tablespace to be created.

➤ DATAFILE—Specifies the data file or files used to compose the tablespace.

➤ AUTOEXTEND—Enables or disables the automatic extension of the data file:

  ➤ ON—Enables **AUTOEXTEND**.

  ➤ OFF—Disables **AUTOEXTEND** if it's turned on. **NEXT** and **MAXSIZE** are set to zero. After **AUTOEXTEND** is disabled, to re-enable the feature, you must specify values again for **NEXT** and **MAXSIZE** in additional **ALTER TABLESPACE AUTOEXTEND** commands.

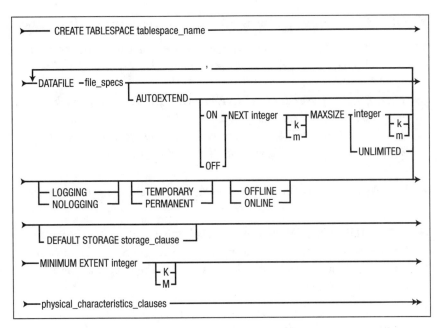

Figure 4.2   The syntax of the **CREATE TABLESPACE** command.

> ➤ **NEXT**—Specifies disk space to allocate to the data file when more
>   extents are required.

> ➤ **MAXSIZE**—Specifies the maximum disk space allowed for
>   allocation to the data file.

> ➤ **UNLIMITED**—Tells Oracle to set no limit on allocating disk
>   space to the data file.

➤ **LOGGING/NOLOGGING**—Specifies the default logging attributes
  of all tables, indexes, and partitions within the tablespace. **LOGGING** is
  the default. If **NOLOGGING** is specified, no undo and redo logs are
  generated for operations that support the **NOLOGGING** option on the
  tables, indexes, and partitions within the tablespace. The tablespace-level
  logging attribute can be overridden by logging specifications at the table,
  index, and partition levels.

➤ **TEMPORARY**—Specifies that the tablespace will be used only to hold
  temporary objects—for example, segments used by implicit sorts to
  handle **ORDER BY** clauses.

➤ **PERMANENT**—Specifies that the tablespace will be used to hold
  permanent objects. This is the default.

➤ OFFLINE—Makes the tablespace unavailable immediately after creation.

➤ ONLINE—Makes the tablespace available immediately after creation to users who have been granted access to the tablespace.

Note: If you omit both the ONLINE and OFFLINE options, Oracle creates the tablespace online by default. The data dictionary view DBA_TABLESPACES indicates whether each tablespace is online or offline. Similarly, LOGGING and OFF are defaults.

➤ DEFAULT STORAGE—Specifies the default storage parameters for all objects created in the tablespace.

➤ MINIMUM EXTENTS—Integer clause that controls free-space fragmentation in the tablespace by ensuring that every used and/or free extent size in a tablespace is at least as large as the integer and is a multiple of the integer.

The major decisions when you use the **CREATE TABLESPACE** command are the placement of the data files and the specification of the default storage options. You should be familiar with file placement and with what happens to objects created using the default storage options. The **STORAGE** clause and its options are shown in Figure 4.3.

The **STORAGE** clause has the following parameters:

➤ INITIAL—Size in bytes of the initial extent of the object segment. The default is 10,240 bytes. The minimum is 4,096 bytes. The maximum is 4,095 megabytes. All values are rounded to the nearest Oracle block size.

➤ NEXT—Size for the next extent after **INITIAL** is used. The default is 5 blocks, the minimum is 1 block, the maximum is 4,095 megabytes.

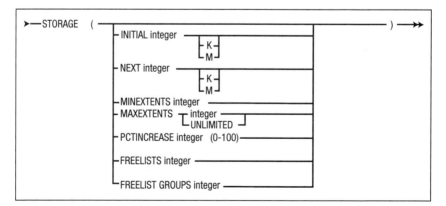

Figure 4.3 The syntax of the **STORAGE** clause.

This is the value that will be used for each new extent if **PCTINCREASE** is set to 0.

➤ MINEXTENTS—Number of initial extents for the object. Generally, except for rollback segments, it's set to 1. If a large amount of space is required and if there's not enough contiguous space for the table setting, using a smaller extent size and specifying several extents may solve the problem.

➤ MAXEXTENTS—Largest number of extents allowed for the object. This defaults to the maximum allowed for your block size.

➤ PCTINCREASE—Parameter that tells Oracle how much to grow each extent after the **INITIAL** and **NEXT** extents are used. A specification of 50 will grow each extent after **NEXT** by 50 percent for each subsequent extent. This means that for a table created with one initial and a next extent, any further extents will increase in size by 50 percent over their predecessor. In Oracle7.2 and later versions, this parameter is applied only against the size of the previous extent. Increase this value if you don't know how much the table will grow, but know only that it will grow significantly. The value of **PCTINCREASE** indicates a growth *rate* for subsequent extents. A tablespace with a default storage setting for **PCTINCREASE** of zero will not be automatically coalesced.

➤ FREELISTS—For objects other than tablespaces, specifies the number of freelists for each of the freelist groups for the table, index, or cluster. The minimum value is 1, and the maximum is block-size dependent.

➤ FREELIST GROUPS—Parameter that specifies the number of freelist groups to maintain for a table or index. This parameter is generally meaningful only for parallel server databases.

Tablespaces are subject to fragmentation as their chief space-related problem. As objects grow and shrink, extents are allocated and dropped. This frequent deallocation of extents results in fragmented tablespaces. In Chapter 6, I'll cover the **ALTER TABLESPACE** command, which allows coalescence of contiguous free-space areas (deallocated extents that lie next to each other).

The **CREATE** Command For Relational And Object Tables

Tables are structures in an Oracle database that contain header and data sections. In Oracle8, the command to create tables has expanded extensively. Tables can now be index-only, partitioned, relational, and object (user-defined type).

However, each table still contains the same elements, with the exception of the object table, which uses an OID (object identifier) as well as **ROWID**.

The table contains segment and block headers. The segment header contains freelist information, the block header contains transaction entries, and the row header contains row-length and data-type indicators. (The row length is 1 byte if less than 256 bytes; otherwise, 3 bytes if longer than 256 bytes.) The data, or row sections, contains the actual data values. The header grows from the bottom up, whereas the data area grows from the top down.

Table placement in relation to other database objects is important for optimal database performance. You should attempt to minimize contention by placing tables away from their associated indexes and away from other I/O-intensive database objects, such as redo logs and rollback segments.

 For some large tables, you may want to consider partitioning across several disks. This is not a labor-intensive operation, but before considering its use, you must thoroughly understand how your data is used. This partitioning of tables involves manual striping tablespace data files across several disks in previous versions but is now part of the **CREATE** and **ALTER TABLE** commands; however, the data files where the partitions are to be placed must already exist.

Because all other database objects depend completely on tables for existence (such as indexes) or operate against tables (functions, procedures, packages) or provide data for tables (sequences), it makes sense to discuss the **CREATE** command in relation to tables next. Figure 4.4 shows the **CREATE TABLE** command syntax for relational tables.

The **CREATE TABLE** commands have the following parameters in Oracle8:

➤ **schema**—The schema to contain the table. If you omit **schema**, Oracle creates the table in your own schema.

➤ **table**—The name of the table (or object table) to be created. A partitioned table cannot be a clustered table or an object table.

➤ **column**—Specifies the name of a column of the table. A table can have up to 1,000 columns in Oracle8. You can omit column definitions only when you're using the **AS** subquery clause.

➤ **datatype**—The data type of a column. You can omit **datatype** only if the statement also designates the column as part of a foreign key in a

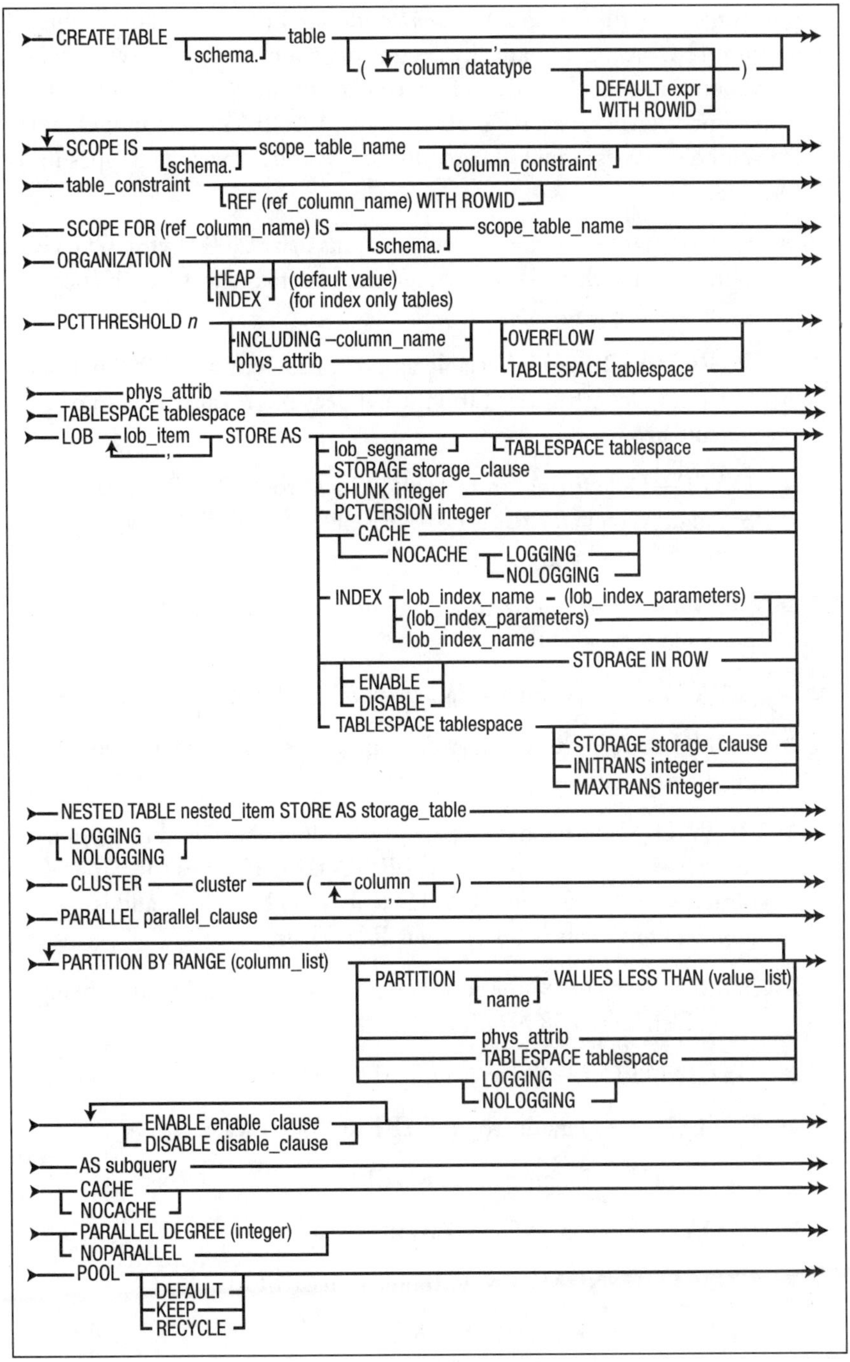

Figure 4.4 The syntax of the **CREATE TABLE** command.

referential integrity constraint. (*Constraints* are limits placed on a table or a column.) Oracle automatically assigns the column the data type of the corresponding column of the referenced key of the referential-integrity constraint. Object types, **REF objcct_type, VARRAYs,** and nested tables are valid data types. The following list shows the allowed data types in Oracle8:

➤ **CHAR(size)**—Character-type data; max size 2,000 bytes. **CHAR** is right-side padded to specified length. It defaults to 1 byte if the value for size is not specified.

➤ **VARCHAR2(size)**—Variable length character up to 4,000 bytes. It must have length specification when declared because it has no default size.

➤ **DATE**—Date format from 1/1/4712 B.C. to 12/31/4712 A.D. Standard Oracle format is (10-APR-99). A DATE datatype is always 7 bytes long.

➤ **LONG**—Character up to 2 gigabytes long. Only one **LONG** per table.

➤ **RAW(size)**—Raw binary data, max of 2,000 bytes under Oracle8.

➤ **LONG RAW**—Raw binary data in hexadecimal format, two gigabytes maximum.

➤ **ROWID**—Internal data type, not user definable. Used to uniquely identify table rows. An extended **ROWID** is 10 bytes (new in Oracle8) and restricted **ROWID** which is 6 bytes long and is identical to Oracle7 and previous **ROWIDs**.

➤ **NUMBER(p,s)**—Numeric data with p being precision and s being scale. Defaults to 38 p, null s.

➤ **DECIMAL(p,s)**—Same as numeric.

➤ **INTEGER**—Defaults to **NUMBER(38)**, no scale.

➤ **SMALLINT**—Same as **INTEGER**.

➤ **FLOAT**—Same as **NUMBER(38)**.

➤ **FLOAT(b)**—**NUMBER** with precision of 1 to 126.

➤ **REAL**—Same as **NUMBER(63)**.

➤ **DOUBLE PRECISION**—Same as **NUMBER(38)**. If no scale is specified for numeric data types where it's allowed, then the value is treated as a floating point.

The following data types are provided for compatibility, but are treated internally the same as **NUMBER**:

➤ **NUMERIC**(precision, scale)

➤ **DECIMAL**(precision, scale)

➤ **DEC**(precision, scale)

➤ **INTEGER**

➤ **INT**

➤ **SMALLINT**

➤ **FLOAT**(size)

➤ **DOUBLE PRECISION**

➤ **REAL**

The following are Large Object data types:

➤ **BLOB**—Up to 4 gigabytes in size.

➤ **CLOB**—Up to 4 gigabytes in size.

➤ **NCLOB**—Up to 4 gigabytes in size.

➤ **BFILE**—Pointer to an external data file that can be up to 4 gigabytes in size.

➤ **DEFAULT**—Specifies a value to be assigned to the column if a subsequent **INSERT** statement omits a value for the column. The data type of the expression must match the data type of the column. The column must also be large enough to hold this expression. A **DEFAULT** expression cannot contain references to other columns, to the pseudo-columns **CURRVAL, NEXTVAL, LEVEL,** and **ROWNUM,** or for date constants that are not fully specified.

➤ **WITH ROWID**—Stores the **ROWID** and the **REF** value in a column or attribute. Storing a **REF** value with a **ROWID** can improve the performance of dereferencing operations, but will also use more space. Default storage of **REF** values is without **ROWIDs**.

➤ **SCOPE IS** scope_table_name—Restricts the scope of the column **REF** values to **scope_table_name**. The **REF** values for the column must come from **REF** values obtained from the object table specified in the clause. You can specify only one scope table per **REF** column. The **scope_table_name** is the name of the object table in which object instances (of the same type as the **REF** column) are stored. The values in the **REF** column point to objects in the scope table. You must have **SELECT** privilege on the table or **SELECT ANY TABLE** system privilege.

➤ **column_constraint**—Used to specify constraints. It's a statement of the format:

```
CONSTRAINT constraint_type
```

Constraints also may be of the form:

➤ **NULL CONSTRAINT** constraint_name

➤ **NOT NULL CONSTRAINT** constraint_name

➤ **PRIMARY KEY CONSTRAINT** constraint_name

➤ **UNIQUE CONSTRAINT** constraint_name

➤ **CHECK** condition **CONSTRAINT** constraint_name

➤ **REFERENCES** table name (column name) **CONSTRAINT** constraint_name

➤ **DEFAULT** default_value_clause

In these formats, the **CONSTRAINT** constraint_name is optional. There can be unlimited **CHECK**-type constraints per column, and a **NOT NULL** is converted internally into a **CHECK** constraint by Oracle. A **CHECK** constraint requires that a condition be true or unknown for each value in the column it affects. Check constraints are the only constraints allowed to call system functions such as **USER** or **SYSDATE**. **NOT NULL** constraints can be defined only at the column level. Constraints can be added, enabled, disabled, or dropped. The **DEFAULT** value clause is not an actual constraint, but because it acts similar to one I have included it here.

Tables may also have the additional constraints. Although they are named the same, they are formatted differently because they are not directly associated with a column except by reference. Each should be prefaced by the **CONSTRAINT** constraint_name clause to prevent Oracle from using default naming:

```
FOREIGN KEY (column, column)
REFERENCES table_name (column, column)
PRIMARY KEY (column, column)
USING INDEX TABLEPACE tablespace_name
STORAGE (storage_clause)
CONSTRAINT constraint_name
```

The foreign key constraint is enforced such that its values must match its corresponding primary or unique key values. However, no index is automatically generated. Indexes should be maintained on foreign keys to prevent excessive full-table scans and to reduce locking problems by allowing key lookups to be resolved in the index. A primary key will automatically have an index-generated name for the constraint. A primary key automatically forces its column or columns to be not null, and if a single column—unique, and for a composite set of columns—the resulting combined set must result in a unique value. Foreign and primary key constraints are referred to as *referential constraints*. Referential integrity violations occur when a parent record is deleted and child records still exist: Orphan records are not permitted in the child table of a parent-child relationship where primary and foreign key constraints are in place.

User-defined constraints are used to enforce business rules. Users should not create constraints that enforce typing (such as inserts of number-into-number columns), which are column constraints. These are generally enforced with no action on the part of the DBA or designer.

Declarative constraints, though they provide instant feedback to the users, can make it difficult to get an overview of which declarative constraints are in effect on the database. Declarative constraints deal with such things as column value verification.

➤ **table_constraint**—Defines an integrity constraint as part of the table definition.

➤ **REF (ref_column_name)**—Refers to a row in an object table. You can specify either a **REF** column name of an object or relational table or an embedded **REF** attribute within an object column as **ref_column_name**.

➤ **SCOPE FOR (ref_column_name) IS scope_table_name**—Restricts the scope of the **REF** values in **ref_column_name** to **scope_table_name**. The **REF** values for the column must come from **REF** values obtained from the object table specified in the clause. The **ref_column_name** is the name of a **REF** column in an object table or an embedded **REF** attribute within an object column of a relational table. The values in the **REF** column point to objects in the scope table. You must have **SELECT** privilege on the table or the **SELECT ANY TABLE** system privilege. Use this format for tables with multiple **REF** columns.

➤ **ORGANIZATION HEAP**—Specifies that the data rows of the table are stored in no particular order. This is the default.

➤ **ORGANIZATION INDEX**—Specifies that the table is created as an index-only table. In an index-only table, the data rows are held in an index defined on the primary key for the table.

➤ **PCTTHRESHOLD**—Specifies the percentage of space reserved in the index block for the index-only table row. Any portion of the row that exceeds the specified threshold is stored in the area. If **OVERFLOW** is not specified, then rows exceeding the **THRESHOLD** limit are rejected. **PCTTHRESHOLD** must be a value from 0 to 50.

➤ **INCLUDING column_name**—Specifies a column at which to divide an index-only table row into index and overflow portions. All columns that follow **column_name** are stored in the overflow data segment. A **column_name** is the name of either the last primary key column or any non–primary-key column.

➤ **phys_attrib**—This clause gives the physical storage attributes for the object. The physical attributes are:

   ➤ **PCTFREE**—Specifies the percentage of space in each of the table's, object table's **OIDINDEX**, or partition's data blocks reserved for future updates to the table's rows. **PCTFREE** must be a value from 0 to 99. A value of 0 allows the entire block to be filled by inserts of new rows. The default value is 20. This value reserves 20 percent of each block for updates to existing rows and allows inserts of new rows to fill a maximum of 80 percent of each block.

   PCTFREE has the same function in the **PARTITION** description clause and in the commands that create and alter clusters, indexes, snapshots, and snapshot logs. The combination of **PCTFREE** and **PCTUSED** determines whether inserted rows will go into existing data blocks or into new blocks. For nonpartitioned tables, the value specified for **PCTFREE** is the actual physical attribute of the segment associated with the table. For partitioned tables, the value specified for **PCTFREE** is the default physical attribute of the segments associated with the table. The default value of **PCTFREE** applies to all partitions specified in the **CREATE** statement (and on subsequent **ALTER TABLE ADD PARTITION** statements) unless you specify **PCTFREE** in the **PARTITION** description clause.

You must understand row chaining (row migration). Row chaining is caused when a row is updated and there is insufficient space available to insert the new data. Row migration usually happens with **VARCHAR2** and **NUMBER** types that can vary in size, but more so with **VARCHAR2**. Other data types that may vary in length (such as **RAW, LONG,** and **LONG RAW**) can also cause row chaining. Row chaining causes Oracle to have to perform multiple disk reads to get a single row, most times forcing the read head for the disk to jump from a smooth read to reading all over the disk.

This increase in disk I/O can cause extreme performance degradation. A large value for **PCTFREE** can reduce or eliminate row chaining, but can also reduce increased storage requirements. Remember that unless the **PCTUSED** and **PCTFREE** are set so their sum exactly equals 100, an increase or decrease in one may have no effect on the other. Block migration happens when the initial size of a row exceeds the size of a block forcing the row to occupy more than one block from the start.

➤ PCTUSED—Specifies the minimum percentage of used space allowed for each data block of the table, the object table OIDINDEX, or the overflow data segment of the index-only table. A block becomes a candidate for row insertion when its used space falls below PCTUSED. PCTUSED is specified as a positive integer from 1 to 99 and defaults to 40.

PCTUSED has the same function in the PARTITION description clause and in the commands that create and alter clusters, snapshots, and snapshot logs. For nonpartitioned tables, the value specified for PCTUSED is the actual physical attribute of the segment associated with the table. For partitioned tables, the value specified for PCTUSED is the default physical attribute of the segments associated with the table partitions. The default value of PCTUSED applies to all partitions specified in the CREATE statement (and on subsequent ALTER TABLE ADD PARTITION statements) unless you specify PCTUSED in the PARTITION description clause. PCTUSED is not a valid table-storage characteristic if you're creating an index-only table (ORGANIZATION INDEX). The sum of PCTFREE and PCTUSED must be less than 100. You can use PCTFREE and PCTUSED together to use space within a table more efficiently.

➤ INITRANS—Specifies the initial number of transaction entries allocated within each data block allocated to the table, object table OIDINDEX, partition, LOB index segment, or overflow data segment. This value can range from 1 to 255 and defaults to 1. In general, you should not change the INITRANS value from its default.

Each transaction that updates a block requires a transaction entry in the block. The size of a transaction entry depends on your operating system. This parameter ensures that a minimum number of concurrent transactions can update the block and helps avoid the overhead of dynamically allocating a transaction entry.

The INITRANS parameter serves the same purpose in the PARTITION description clause and in clusters, indexes, snapshots, and snapshot logs as in tables. The minimum and default INITRANS value for a cluster or index is 2, rather than 1. For nonpartitioned tables, the value specified for INITRANS is the actual physical attribute of the segment associated with the table. For partitioned tables, the value specified for INITRANS is the default physical attribute of the segments associated with the table partitions. The default value of INITRANS applies to all partitions specified in the CREATE statement (and on subsequent ALTER TABLE ADD PARTITION statements) unless you specify INITRANS in the PARTITION description clause.

➤ MAXTRANS—Specifies the maximum number of concurrent transactions that can update a data block allocated to the table, object table OIDINDEX, partition, LOB index segment, or index-only overflow data segment. This limit does not apply to queries. This value can range from 1 to 255 and the default is a function of the data block size. According to Oracle's SQL and tuning manuals, you should not change the MAXTRANS value from its default. If the number of concurrent transactions updating a block exceeds the INITRANS value, Oracle dynamically allocates transaction entries in the block until either the MAXTRANS value is exceeded or the block has no more free space.

The MAXTRANS parameter serves the same purpose in the PARTITION description clause, clusters, snapshots, and snapshot logs as in tables. For nonpartitioned tables, the value specified for MAXTRANS is the actual physical attribute of the segment associated with the table. For partitioned tables, the value specified for MAXTRANS is the default physical attribute of the segments associated with the table partitions. The default value of MAXTRANS applies to all partitions specified in the CREATE statement (and on subsequent ALTER TABLE ADD PARTITION statements) unless you specify MAXTRANS in the PARTITION description clause.

➤ TABLESPACE—Specifies the tablespace in which Oracle creates the table, object table **OIDINDEX**, partition, **LOB** storage, **LOB** index segment, or overflow data segment of the index-only table. If you omit this option, then Oracle creates the relevant segment, or partition in the default tablespace of the owner of the schema containing the table.

For nonpartitioned tables, the value specified for **TABLESPACE** is the actual physical attribute of the segment associated with the table. For partitioned tables, the value specified for **TABLESPACE** is the default physical attribute of the segments associated with the table partitions. The default value of **TABLESPACE** applies to all partitions specified in the **CREATE** statement (and on subsequent **ALTER TABLE ADD PARTITION** statements) unless you specify **TABLESPACE** in the **PARTITION** description clause.

➤ STORAGE—Specifies the storage characteristics for the table, object table **OIDINDEX**, partition, **LOB** storage, **LOB** index segment, or overflow data segment of the index-only table. This clause has performance ramifications for large tables. Storage should be allocated to minimize dynamic allocation of additional space. For nonpartitioned tables, the value specified for **STORAGE** is the actual physical attribute of the segment associated with the table. For partitioned tables, the value specified for **STORAGE** is the default physical attribute of the segments associated with the table partitions. The default value of **STORAGE** applies to all partitions specified in the **CREATE** statement (and on subsequent **ALTER TABLE ADD PARTITION** statements) unless you specify **STORAGE** in the **PARTITION** description clause.

➤ OVERFLOW—Specifies that an index-only table's data rows exceeding the specified threshold are placed in the data segment listed in this clause.

➤ LOB—Specifies the **LOB** storage characteristics.

➤ lob_item—The **LOB** column name or **LOB** object attribute for which you are explicitly defining tablespace and storage characteristics that are different from those of the table.

➤ STORE AS lob_segname—Specifies the name of the **LOB** data segment. You cannot use **lob_segname** if more than one **lob_item** is specified.

➤ CHUNK integer—The unit of **LOB** value allocation and manipulation. Oracle allocates each unit of **LOB** storage as **CHUNK integer**. You can also use K or M to specify this size in kilobytes or megabytes. The default value of integer is 1K and the maximum is 32K. For efficiency, use a multiple of the Oracle block size.

➤ PCTVERSION integer—The maximum percentage of overall **LOB** storage space used for creating new versions of the **LOB**. The default value is 10, meaning that older versions of the **LOB** data are not over-written until 10 percent of the overall **LOB** storage space is used.

➤ INDEX lob_index_name—The name of the **LOB** index segment. You cannot use **lob_index_name** if more than one **lob_item** is specified.

➤ NESTED TABLE nested_item STORE AS storage_table—Specifies **storage_table** as the name of the storage table in which the rows of all **nested_item** values reside. You must include this clause when you're creating a table with columns or column attributes whose type is a nested table. The **nested_item** is the name of a column or a column-qualified attribute whose type is a nested table. The **storage_table** is the name of the storage table. The storage table is created in the same schema and the same **tablespace** as the parent table.

➤ LOGGING—Specifies that the creation of the table (and any indexes required because of constraints), partition, or **LOB** storage characteristics will be logged in the redo log file. LOGGING also specifies that subsequent operations against the table, partition, or **LOB** storage are logged in the redo file. This is the default. If the database is run in **ARCHIVELOG** mode, media recovery from a backup will re-create the table (and any indexes required because of constraints). You cannot specify **LOGGING** when using **NOARCHIVELOG** mode.

For nonpartitioned tables, the value specified for **LOGGING** is the actual physical attribute of the segment associated with the table. For partitioned tables, the value specified for **LOGGING** is the default physical attribute of the segments associated with the table partitions. The default value of **LOGGING** applies to all partitions specified in the **CREATE** statement (and on subsequent **ALTER TABLE ADD PARTITION** statements) unless you specify **LOGGING** in the **PARTITION** description clause.

Note: In future versions of Oracle, the LOGGING keyword will replace the RECOVERABLE option. RECOVERABLE is still available as a valid keyword in Oracle8 when you're creating nonpartitioned tables, but it is not recommended. You must specify LOGGING if you're creating a partitioned table.

➤ RECOVERABLE—See **LOGGING** previously. **RECOVERABLE** is not a valid keyword for creating partitioned tables or **LOB** storage characteristics.

➤ NOLOGGING—Specifies that the creation of the table (and any indexes required because of constraints), partition, or **LOB** storage characteristics will not be logged in the redo log file. **NOLOGGING** also specifies that subsequent operations against the table or **LOB** storage are not logged in the redo file. As a result, media recovery will not re-create the table (or any indexes required because of constraints).

For nonpartitioned tables, the value specified for **NOLOGGING** is the actual physical attribute of the segment associated with the table. For partitioned tables, the value specified for **NOLOGGING** is the default physical attribute of the segments associated with the table partitions. The default value of **NOLOGGING** applies to all partitions specified in the **CREATE** statement (and on subsequent **ALTER TABLE ADD PARTITION** statements) unless you specify **NOLOGGING** in the **PARTITION** description clause.

Using this keyword makes table creation faster than using the **LOGGING** option because redo log entries are not written. **NOLOGGING** is not a valid keyword for creating index-only tables.

*Note: In future versions of Oracle, the **NOLOGGING** keyword will replace the **UNRECOVERABLE** option. **UNRECOVERABLE** is still available as a valid keyword in Oracle when you're creating nonpartitioned tables, but it is not recommended. You must specify **NOLOGGING** if you're creating a partitioned table.*

➤ UNRECOVERABLE—See **NOLOGGING** previously. This keyword can be specified only with the **AS** subquery clause. **UNRECOVERABLE** is not a valid keyword for creating partitioned or index-only tables.

➤ CLUSTER—Specifies that the table is to be part of the cluster. The columns listed in this clause are the table columns that correspond to the cluster's columns. Generally, the cluster columns of a table are the column or columns that make up its primary key or a portion of its primary key. Specify one column from the table for each column in the cluster key. The columns are matched by position, not by name. Because a clustered table uses the cluster's space allocation, do not use the **PCTFREE, PCTUSED, INITRANS,** or **MAXTRANS** parameters, the **TABLE-SPACE** option, or the **STORAGE** clause with the **CLUSTER** option because they are ignored if specified.

➤ PARALLEL parallel_clause—Specifies the degree of parallelism for creating the table and the default degree of parallelism for queries on the table after it's created. This is not a valid option when you're creating index-only tables.

➤ PARTITION BY RANGE—Specifies that the table is partitioned on ranges of values from column_list.

➤ column_list—An ordered list of columns used to determine in which partition a row belongs. You cannot specify more than 16 columns in column_list. The column_list cannot contain the ROWID pseudo-column or any columns of data type ROWID or LONG.

➤ PARTITION partition_name—Specifies the physical partition clause. If partition_name is omitted, Oracle generates a name with the form SYS_Pn for the partition. The partition_name must conform to the rules for naming schema objects and their parts.

➤ VALUES LESS THAN—Specifies the noninclusive upper bound for the current partition.

➤ value_list—An ordered list of literal values corresponding to column_list in the PARTITION BY RANGE clause. You can substitute the keyword MAXVALUE for any literal value in value_list. Specifying a value other than MAXVALUE for the highest partition bound imposes an implicit integrity constraint on the table.

➤ MAXVALUE—Specifies a maximum value that will always sort higher than any other value, including NULL.

➤ ENABLE—Enables an integrity constraint.

➤ DISABLE—Disables an integrity constraint.

Constraints specified in the ENABLE and DISABLE clauses of a CREATE TABLE statement must be defined in the statement. You can also enable and disable constraints with the ENABLE and DISABLE keywords of the CONSTRAINT clause. If you define a constraint but do not explicitly enable or disable it, Oracle enables it by default. You cannot use the ENABLE and DISABLE clauses in a CREATE TABLE statement to enable and disable triggers.

➤ AS subquery—Inserts the rows returned by the subquery into the table upon its creation. The number of columns in the table must equal the number of expressions in the subquery. The column definitions can specify only column names, default values, and integrity constraints, not

data types. Oracle derives data types and lengths from the subquery.
Oracle also follows these rules for integrity constraints:

➤ Oracle automatically defines any **NOT NULL** constraints on
columns in the new table if those constraints existed on the corresponding columns of the selected table and if the subquery selects
the column rather than an expression containing the column.

➤ A **CREATE TABLE** statement cannot contain both an **AS** clause
and a referential-integrity constraint definition.

➤ If a **CREATE TABLE** statement contains both the **AS** clause and a
CONSTRAINT clause or an **ENABLE** clause with the **EXCEP-
TIONS** option, Oracle ignores the **EXCEPTIONS** option. If any
rows violate the constraint, Oracle does not create the table and
returns an error message.

➤ If all expressions in the subquery are columns, rather than expressions, you can omit the columns from the table definition entirely. In
this case, the names of the columns in the table are the same as the
columns in the subquery.

➤ CACHE—Specifies that the data will be accessed frequently, so the blocks
retrieved for this table are placed at the most recently used end of the LRU
list in the buffer cache when a full table scan is performed. This option is
useful for small lookup tables. **CACHE** as a parameter in the **LOB**
storage clause specifies that Oracle allocates and retains **LOB** data values
in memory for faster access. **CACHE** is the default for index-only tables.

➤ NOCACHE—Specifies that the data will not be accessed frequently, so
the blocks retrieved for this table are placed at the least recently used end
of the LRU list in the buffer cache when a full table scan is performed.
For **LOBs**, the **LOB** value is not placed in the buffer cache. This is the
default behavior except when you're creating index-only tables. This is
not a valid keyword when you're creating index-only tables. **NOCACHE**
as a parameter in the **LOB** storage clause specifies that **LOB** values are
not allocated in memory. This is the **LOB** storage default.

➤ PARALLEL DEGREE (integer)—This parameter is used to specify
the degree of parallel processing for the table.

➤ NOPARALLEL—This parameter turns off parallel processing for the
table.

➤ POOL—With the **DEFAULT, KEEP,** and **RECYCLE** options,
determines the buffer pool area in which the table will be cached. The

DEFAULT pool is the standard Oracle buffer pool. If configured, the optional **KEEP** and **RECYCLE** pools provide for keeping objects (the **KEEP** pool) or having them quickly recycle out of the pool (the **RECYCLE** pool). Both the **KEEP** and **RECYCLE** sections are subsets of the **DEFAULT** pool area. If the **KEEP** and **RECYCLE** areas aren't configured, buffer pool behavior is the same as in Oracle7, even if the **POOL** qualifier is used.

Oracle8 Object Tables

In Oracle8, you also have object tables. For you to create an object table, there must be existing UDTs (User-Defined Types) to use. In light of this, let's first look at the creation command for User-Defined Types (UDTs) in Oracle8.

The **TYPE** creation command is shown in Figure 4.5. The command to create an **INCOMPLETE TYPE** is shown in Figure 4.6.

An incomplete type would be used when a type referred to a second type, which referred to the first type (a circular reference such as emp-supervisor). An incomplete type can be referred to before it is completed. However, before a table can be constructed from an incomplete type, the type must be completed.

The command to create a **VARRAY TYPE** is shown in Figure 4.7. A **VARRAY** should be used when the number of items to be stored in the type is:

➤ Known and fixed

➤ Small (this is a relative term; remember that data is stuffed into a **RAW** and stored in line with the rest of the type's data)

A **VARRAY** cannot be used in a partitioned table. The command to create a **NESTED TABLE TYPE** is shown in Figure 4.8.

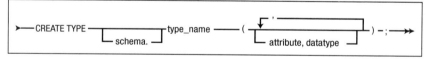

Figure 4.5   **TYPE** creation command.

Figure 4.6   **INCOMPLETE TYPE** command.

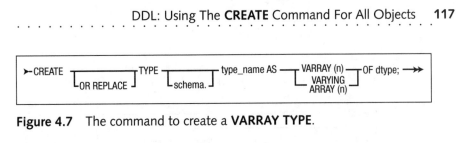

Figure 4.7   The command to create a **VARRAY TYPE**.

Figure 4.8   The command to create a **NESTED TABLE TYPE**.

A **NESTED TABLE** should be used when:

➤ The number of items is large or unknown.

➤ The storage of the items needs to be managed.

A **NESTED TABLE** is stored in a **STORE TABLE,** which must be specified in the **CREATE TABLE** command for each **NESTED TABLE** type used. The **NESTED TABLE** type cannot be used in partition tables. Some early documentation releases incorrectly state that Oracle itself specifies the store table name. Nested tables cannot contain **VARRAY**s or other nested tables.

Object Types

If you will be using the **TYPE** command to build an object table that will be REFed by a second table, the object table must be constructed as an **OBJECT** type and thus include an object ID (OID). Nested tables and **VARRAY**s are limited in the types of **TYPE**s they can store, but a second object table is not. In cases where the entity relation diagram (ERD) shows a series of one-to-many type relationships, object tables will have to be used to show this relationship structure under the object-oriented paradigm in Oracle8.

The command to create an **OBJECT TYPE** is shown in Figure 4.9.

The constraints for the **PRAGMA** line are:

➤ **RNDS**—Reads no database state.

➤ **WNDS**—Writes no database state.

➤ **RNPS**—Reads no package state.

➤ **WNPS**—Writes no package state.

> *Note: These can be specified in any order, but no duplicates are allowed. Object types cannot be used in partition tables.*

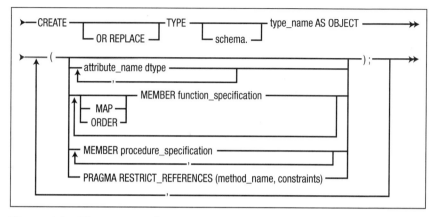

Figure 4.9 The command to create an **OBJECT TYPE**.

The possible data type specifications are the same as those for the **CREATE TABLE** command.

Keywords And Parameters For The TYPE Commands

The **TYPE** commands have the following keywords and parameters:

➤ **OR REPLACE**—Re-creates the type if it already exists. You can use this option to change the definition of an existing type without first dropping it. Users previously granted privileges on the re-created object type can use and refer to the object type without being granted privileges again.

➤ **schema**—The schema to contain the type. If this is omitted, Oracle creates the type in the user's default schema.

➤ **type_name**—The name of an object type, a nested table type, or a **VARRAY** type.

➤ **AS OBJECT**—Creates the type as a user-defined object type. The variables that form the data structure are called *attributes*. The member procedures and functions that define the object's behavior are called *methods*.

➤ **AS TABLE**—Creates a named nested table of type **datatype**. When **datatype** is an object type, the nested table type describes a table whose columns match the name and attributes of the object type. When **datatype** is a scalar type, then the nested table type describes a table with a single, scalar type column called **column_value**.

➤ **AS VARRAY(limit)**—Creates the type as an ordered set of elements, each of which has the same data type. You must specify a name and a maximum limit of zero or more. The array limit must be an integer literal. Only variable-length arrays are supported. Oracle does not support anonymous **VARRAY**s. The type name for the objects contained in the **VARRAY** must be one of the following:

    ➤ A scalar data type

    ➤ A **REF**

    ➤ An object type, including an object with **VARRAY** attributes

The type name for the objects contained in the **VARRAY** cannot be any of the following:

    ➤ An object type with a nested table attribute

    ➤ A **VARRAY** type

    ➤ A **TABLE** type

    ➤ A **LOB** data type

The **(limit)** value is an unsigned integer in the range of 1 to $2^{31}-1$ (2,147,483,647). Of course, because the **VARRAY** is stored as a **RAW** value in line with the other data in a table, specifications of extremely large limits would be foolish because they would cause chaining and performance degradation. For a large number of elements, use a **NESTED TABLE** instead.

➤ **OF dtype**—The name of any Oracle built-in data type or library type. **ROWID**, **LONG**, and **LONG RAW** are not valid data types for this specification.

➤ **REF object_type_name**—Associates an instance of a source type with an instance of the target object. A **REF** logically identifies and locates the target object. The target object must have an object identifier.

➤ **type_name**—The name of a user-defined object type, a nested table type, or a **VARRAY** type.

➤ **attribute_name**—An object attribute name. Attributes are data items with a name and a type specifier that form the structure of the object.

➤ **method**—Specifies a function or procedure subprogram method associated with the object type that is referred to as an attribute. You must specify a corresponding method body in the object-type body for each procedure or function specification.

➤ procedure_specification—The specification of a procedure subprogram.

➤ function MEMBER_specification—The specification of a function subprogram.

➤ MAP MEMBER function_specification—Specifies a member function (MAP method) that returns the relative position of a given instance in the ordering of all instances of the object. A MAP method is called implicitly and induces an ordering of object instances by mapping them to values of a predefined scalar type. PL/SQL uses the ordering to evaluate Boolean expressions and to perform comparisons. A scalar value is always manipulated as a single unit. Scalars are mapped directly to the underlying hardware. An integer, for example, occupies 4 or 8 contiguous bytes of storage, in memory or on disk. An object specification can contain only one MAP method, which must be a function. The result type must be a predefined SQL scalar type, and the MAP function can have no arguments other than the implicit SELF argument.

You can define either MAP method or ORDER method in a type specification, but not both. If a MAP or an ORDER method is not specified, only comparisons for equality or inequality can be performed, and thus the object instances cannot be ordered. No comparison method needs to be specified to determine the equality of two object types.

➤ ORDER MEMBER function_specification—Specifies a member function (ORDER method) that takes an instance of an object to be compared as an explicit argument and the implicit SELF argument (the current value of the type) and returns either a negative integer, zero, or a positive integer. The negative, positive, or zero indicates that the implicit SELF argument is less than, equal to, or greater than the explicit argument. When instances of the same object-type definition are compared in an ORDER BY clause, the order method function_specification is invoked.

An object specification can contain only one ORDER method, which must be a function having the return type INTEGER. You can declare either a MAP method or an ORDER method, but not both. If you declare either method, you can compare object instances in SQL. If you do not declare either method, you can only compare object instances for equality or inequality. Note that instances of the same type definition are equal only if each pair of their corresponding attributes is equal. No comparison method needs to be specified to determine the equality of two object types.

➤ **PRAGMA RESTRICT_REFERENCES**—A compiler directive that denies member functions read/write access to database tables, packaged variables, or both, and thereby helps to avoid side effects. The arguments for this directive are:

> ➤ **method_name**—The name of the **MEMBER** function or procedure to which the **PRAGMA** is being applied.

> ➤ **RNDS**—Specifies that the function reads no database state (does not query database tables).

> ➤ **WNDS**—Specifies that the function writes no database state (does not modify database tables).

> ➤ **RNPS**—Specifies that the function reads no package state (does not refer to packaged variables).

> ➤ **WNPS**—Specifies that the function writes no package state (does not modify packaged variables).

Creation Of Object Tables

The command to create object tables is shown in Figure 4.10.

The Keywords And Parameters For The Oracle8 Object **CREATE TABLE** Command

The CREATE TABLE command for Oracle8 object tables has the following parameter definitions in Oracle8 (note that items with the same definition as in a relational table creation have been omitted):

➤ **OF object_type**—Explicitly creates an object table of type **object_type**. The columns of an object table correspond to the top-level attributes of type **object_type**. Each row will contain an object instance, and each instance will be assigned a unique, system-generated object identifier (OID) when a row is inserted. If you omit **schema**, Oracle creates the object table in your own schema. Object tables cannot be partitioned.

➤ **OIDINDEX**—Specifies an index on the hidden object identifier column and/or specifies the storage specification for the index. Either index or **storage_specification** must be specified.

➤ **Index**—The name of the index on the hidden object identifier column. If not specified, a name is generated by the system.

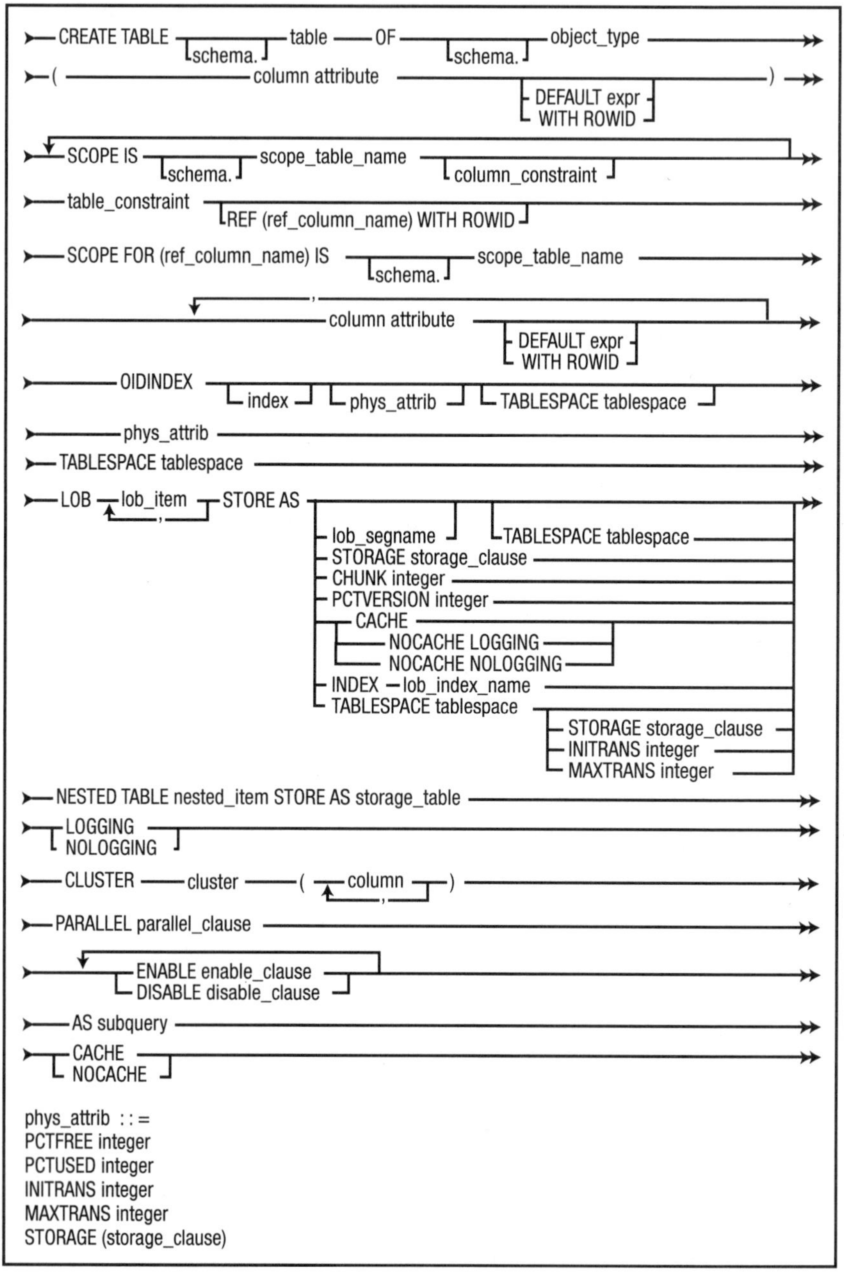

Figure 4.10 The syntax for the **CREATE TABLE** command for object tables.

Practice Questions

Question 1

Evaluate this command:

```
CREATE TABLE sales_items
SELECT id_number, description
FROM inventory
WHERE quantity > 500;
```

Why will this statement cause an error?

○ a. A keyword is missing.

○ b. A clause is missing.

○ c. The **WHERE** clause can't be used for creating a table.

○ d. All of the columns in the inventory table must be included in the subquery.

○ e. The data types in the new table were not defined.

The correct answer is a; the keyword **AS** is missing right before the subquery. Answer b is incorrect because **AS** is a keyword, not a clause. Answer c is incorrect because any valid subquery, including **WHERE** clauses, can be used in a **CREATE TABLE** command. Answer d is incorrect because any portion of a table or set of tables can be selected for use in a new table; you don't have to select all columns. Answer e is incorrect because a table created with a subquery takes on the data types of the selected columns.

Question 2

What is increased when the database contains migrated rows?

○ a. **PCTUSED**

○ b. I/O

○ c. Shared pool size

○ d. **PCTFREE**

The correct answer is b. At first glance, you might be tempted to answer d for this question, but look again. It's not asking how to correct migrated rows (by increasing **PCTFREE** in the affected table); it's asking what's increased in the database when you have migrated rows. Obviously, the correct answer is b—I/O—because multiple reads are required for each migrated row. Answer c is incorrect because migrated rows have nothing whatsoever to do with the shared pool. Answer a is incorrect because, even if the question asked how to correct migrated rows, you'd never increase **PCTUSED** to correct migrated rows.

Question 3

What is the size of the first extent if the storage parameters are **INITIAL 50K**, **NEXT 20K**, and **PCTINCREASE 30**?

○ a. 20K

○ b. 30K

○ c. 50K

○ d. 70K

The correct answer is c. Again, this is a trick question. Exam developers try to confuse you here with too much information. The question asks what is the size of the first extent. The correct answer is c because the **INITIAL** value is set to 50K. The **INITIAL** storage parameter sets the size of the first extent.

Question 4

Which parameter value would you use if your tables will have frequent inserts and deletes?

○ a. Lower **PCTFREE**

○ b. Higher **PCTFREE**

○ c. Lower **PCTUSED**

○ d. Higher **PCTUSED**

The correct answer is c. This is another trick question. Just from scanning the question, you would probably choose b, assuming that an answer dealing with migrated or chained rows was sought. You'd be incorrect because the key word in the question is *deletes*. The parameter that deals directly with deletes is **PCTUSED**, and to allow for inserts and deletes, the value needs to be lowered.

Question 5

> Which two constraints are implicitly defined on a primary key column? [Choose two]
>
> ❑ a. **UNIQUE**
>
> ❑ b. **CHECK**
>
> ❑ c. Foreign key
>
> ❑ d. **NOT NULL**

The correct answers are a and d. A little reasoning and recall about the definition of a primary key will give you the answers. A primary key is a **UNIQUE, NOT NULL** identifier for a table's row.

Question 6

> Which parameter value setting will reserve more room for future updates?
>
> ○ a. Lower **PCTFREE**
>
> ○ b. Higher **PCTFREE**
>
> ○ c. Lower **PCTUSED**
>
> ○ d. Higher **PCTUSED**

The correct answer is b. Given Question 5, you may be tempted to answer c, lower **PCTUSED,** but you'd be wrong. The key to this question is the phrase *future updates*. The only parameter that provides for future updates is **PCTFREE,** so if you want to reserve room for future updates, you'd need to increase **PCTFREE.**

Question 7

What is the size of the third extent if the storage parameters are **INITIAL 50K, NEXT 20K,** and **PCTINCREASE 30**?

○ a. 20K

○ b. 26K

○ c. 30K

○ d. 36K

○ e. 40K

○ f. 100K

The correct answer is b. This is a straightforward calculation. Remember that **NEXT** sets the size for the **NEXT** extent, and **PCTINCREASE** is applied after the **INITIAL** and **NEXT** have been utilized against the value of **NEXT**, so the third extent will be **NEXT + (NEXT * PCTINCREASE/100)** or, in this case, 20 + (20 * 30/100) = 20 + 6 = 26. The other answers are incorrect because they don't equal 26.

Question 8

Which length will be assigned to a **VARCHAR2** column if it's not specified when a table is created?

○ a. 1

○ b. 25

○ c. 255

○ d. 38

○ e. A column length must be specified for a **VARCHAR2** column.

The correct answer is e. Unlike a **CHAR** column, which has a default value of 1, if a length is not specified, the **VARCHAR2** column has no default and must have a length specified.

Question 9

> If a character column will store 266 bytes, how many bytes will the column header entry be?
>
> ○ a. 0
>
> ○ b. 1
>
> ○ c. 2
>
> ○ d. 3
>
> ○ e. 250
>
> ○ f. 266

The correct answer is d. For character data, the data storage is 1 byte per character, so a column that stores 266 bytes will have a length of 266. However, a column that is greater than 256 bytes will have a 3-byte header entry instead of a 1-byte header entry.

Question 10

> Which of the following data types may not appear in an Oracle8 partitioned table? [Choose two]
>
> ❑ a. **VARCHAR2**
>
> ❑ b. **CHAR**
>
> ❑ c. **NUMBER**
>
> ❑ d. **BLOB**
>
> ❑ e. **VARRAY**
>
> ❑ f. **ROWID**

The correct answers are d and e. A partition in Oracle8 cannot contain **VARRAY**s, nested tables, types, **LOB**s, or objects.

Question 11

Which of the following partitioned index types is not permitted in Oracle8?

- ○ a. Local prefixed
- ○ b. Local nonprefixed
- ○ c. Global nonprefixed
- ○ d. Global prefixed

The correct answer is c. A partitioned index cannot be global nonprefixed in Oracle8.

Question 12

Which type of index is always partitioned if its underlying table is partitioned?

- ○ a. Global
- ○ b. Local
- ○ c. Hash
- ○ d. Bitmapped
- ○ e. B-tree

The correct answer is b. A local index is always partitioned exactly as its base table is partitioned. Answer a is incorrect because a global index can be either partitioned or nonpartitioned but doesn't have to be partitioned. Answers c, d, and e are incorrect because hash, bitmapped, and B-tree indexes refer to the types of storage algorithm used but don't pertain to partitioning.

Question 13

If a **TYPE** body contains a **MAP** method, what must it not contain?

○ a. A UDT

○ b. An **ORDER** method

○ c. A **VARRAY**

○ d. A **LONG RAW**

○ e. A **BLOB**

The correct answer is b. A **TYPE** body can contain only a **MAP** method or an **ORDER** method, but not both.

Need To Know More?

 Ault, Michael R. *Oracle8 Administration and Management.* John Wiley & Sons, New York, New York, 1998. ISBN 0-471-19234-1. This book provides a comprehensive look at Oracle8 and Oracle7.x management. Use it for command syntax definitions for all **CREATE** commands.

 Oracle8 Error Messages, Release 8.0.4. Oracle Corporation, Redwood Shores, California, December 1997. Part No. A58312-01. This is the source book for all Oracle errors for version 8. It can be found on the Web at **http://technet.oracle.com**, which has free membership. It is the only place to locate certain limits and restrictions by review of a particular feature's error codes.

 Oracle8 SQL Reference, Release 8.0. Oracle Corporation, Redwood Shores, California, December 1997. Part No. A58225-01. This is the source book for all Oracle SQL for version 8. It can be found on the Web at **http://technet.oracle.com**, which has free membership.

 DBA Pipeline at **www.revealnet.com** is a great place to ask those last-minute questions and to peruse for up-to-the-minute questions, problems, and solutions.

RevealNet Oracle Administrator from RevealNet, Inc. This online reference provides diagrams with hot links to definitions and examples of all DDL commands. It's one of the fastest online searchable references I've come across (even though I might be a bit prejudiced because I'm its principal author). It's more expensive than a book, at around $300 to $400; however, you'll use it long after the books have been put away. It can be downloaded from **www.revealnet.com**.

DDL: Object Manipulation Commands

. . . .

Terms you'll need to understand:

√ DIRECTORY

√ LIBRARY

√ TYPE

√ VARRAY

√ Nested table

√ PROCEDURE

√ PACKAGE

√ INDEX

√ SYNONYM

√ SEQUENCE

√ VIEW

√ ROLLBACK SEGMENT

√ Control file

Techniques you'll need to master:

√ Creating or altering **INDEX**es

√ Creating or altering **SYNONYM**s

√ Creating or altering **VIEW**s

√ Creating or altering **SEQUENCE**s

√ Creating or altering **ROLLBACK SEGMENT**s

√ Creating CONTROL **FILE**s

√ Creating new Oracle8 **DIRECTORY**s

√ Creating new Oracle8 **LIBRARY**s

√ Creating **TYPE**s

The Oracle8 OCP exam for SQL and PL/SQL covers the new types of structures that Oracle8 allows a DBA to create. Types were covered in Chapter 4 as a precursor to object tables. In this chapter, I'll cover the use of the **CREATE** command for nontable items such as indexes, synonyms, and other database objects. In addition, the **DIRECTORY** and **LIBRARY** database structures will be discussed.

Nontable **CREATE** Commands

Without objects in Oracle, the database would be useless. In order to get objects into a database, the **CREATE** commands are used. Chapter 4 covered the **CREATE TABLE** command; in this chapter, I discuss the other **CREATE** commands, starting with **INDEX**es.

The **CREATE** Command For Indexes

Indexes can be created implicitly, as with the specification of unique or primary key constraints, or explicitly with the **CREATE INDEX** command. Only normal, B-tree-type indexes are created implicitly. Normally (except in the case of bitmapped indexes), you should index only a column or set of columns that contain a wide range of values. If a table is small, an index may decrease the speed of a query against it because small tables may be cached in memory or may better be searched with a full table scan. The format for the **CREATE INDEX** command is shown in Figure 5.1.

The Oracle8 **CREATE INDEX** clauses have the following keywords and parameters:

➤ BITMAP—Specifies that the index is to be created as a bitmap, rather than as a B-tree. You cannot use this keyword when you're creating a global partitioned index. This keyword causes the index to be stored as a bitmap and should be used only for low-cardinality data, such as sex, race, and so forth. A bitmap index takes up much less space than other types of indexes.

The option is available only as beta in pre-7.3.2.2 releases (7.3 only) and is bundled with the parallel query option. In earlier versions of Oracle, such as 7.3, several initialization parameters are required to use the option. These include the following parameters to turn on bitmapped indexes (which must be set regardless of version):

➤ COMPATIBLE set to 7.3.2 or higher

➤ V733_PLANS_ENABLED set to TRUE

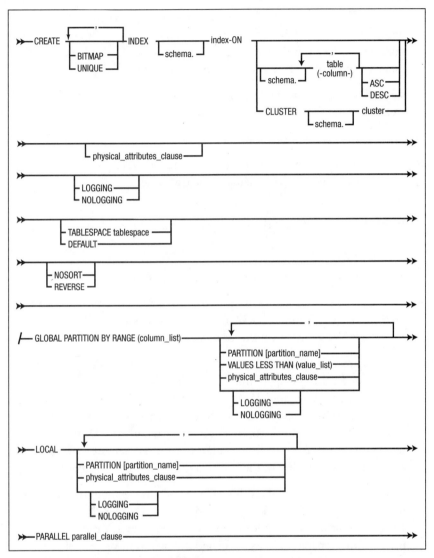

Figure 5.1   The syntax of the **CREATE INDEX** command.

In addition, specific events (commands that turn on specific pieces of code in the Oracle kernel) must be set for bitmapped indexes to work in versions before 7.3.3, as seen here:

➤ event = "10111 trace name context forever"

➤ event = "10112 trace name context forever"

➤ event = "10114 trace name context forever"

➤ UNIQUE—Specifies that the value of the column (or group of columns) in the table to be indexed must be unique. If the index is local nonprefixed (see the **LOCAL** clause, further down in this list), then the index columns must contain the partitioning columns.

➤ schema—The schema to contain the index. If you omit **schema**, Oracle creates the index in your own schema.

➤ index—The name of the index to be created.

➤ table—The name of the table for which the index is to be created. If you do not qualify **table** with **schema**, Oracle assumes that the table is contained in your own schema.

If the index is **LOCAL**, the table must be partitioned.

You cannot create an index on an index-only table.

You can create an index on a nested-table storage table.

➤ column—The name of a column in the table. An index can have up to 16 columns in 7.3 and up to 32 in Oracle8. A data type of **LONG** or **LONG RAW** cannot be used for indexing.

You can create an index on a scalar object (non-**VARRAY**) attribute column or on the system-defined **NESTED_TABLE_ID** column of the nested-table storage table. If an object-attribute column is specified, the column name must be qualified with the table name. If a nested-table column attribute is specified, then it must be qualified with the outermost table name, the containing column name, and all intermediate attribute names leading to the nested-table column attribute.

Column is the name of the column to include in the index, up to a maximum of 16 columns in 7.3 and up to 32 in Oracle8. If more than one column is used, the index is said to be a *composite* or *concatenated* index. Concatenated indexes are generally used to increase performance of a specific query. The order of a concatenated key is important. Only queries that access columns in this order will use the index. For example, table **EXAMPLE** has 16 columns. The first three are used as the concatenated index. Only queries that contain columns 1, 2, 3 or 1, 2 or 1 will use the index.

➤ ASC and DESC—Allowed for DB2 syntax compatibility, although indexes are always created in ascending order. Indexes on character data are created in ascending order of the character values in the database character set.

➤ **CLUSTER schema.cluster**—Specifies the cluster for which a cluster index is to be created. If you do not qualify **cluster** with **schema**, Oracle assumes that the cluster is contained in your current schema. You cannot create a cluster index for a hash cluster.

➤ **physical_attributes_clause**—Contains zero or one or more of the following: **PCTFREE, PCTUSED, INITRANS, MAXTRANS**, or **STORAGE**:

   ➤ **PCTFREE**—The percentage of space to leave free for updates and insertions within each of the nonpartitioned index's data blocks.

   ➤ **PCTUSED**—Establishes the level at which a block will be returned to the free list after deletes.

   ➤ **INITRANS** and **MAXTRANS**—Establish values for these parameters for the index. See the **INITRANS** and **MAXTRANS** parameters of the **CREATE TABLE** command in Chapter 4.

   ➤ **STORAGE**—Establishes the storage characteristics for the index.

➤ **LOGGING**—Specifies that the creation of the index will be logged in the undo (rollback) segments and redo logs, and undo and redo data will be recorded on activity in this index.

   If the index is nonpartitioned, this is the logging attribute of the index.

   If the index is partitioned, this is the default logging attribute of the index partitions created. If index is **LOCAL**, this value is used as the default attribute for index partitions created when new partitions are added to the base table of the index.

   If the **[NO]LOGGING** clause is omitted, the logging attribute of the index defaults to the logging attribute of the tablespace in which it resides.

   If the database is run in **ARCHIVELOG** mode, media recovery from a backup taken before the **LOGGING** operation will re-create the index. However, media recovery from a backup taken before the **NOLOGGING** operation will not recreate the index.

   If the database is run in **ARCHIVELOG** mode, media recovery from a backup will re-create the index.

➤ **NOLOGGING**—Specifies that the creation of the index will not be logged in the undo and redo log file. As a result, media recovery will not re-create the index.

   If the index is nonpartitioned, this is the logging attribute of the index.

If the index is partitioned, this is the default logging attribute of the index partitions created. If index is **LOCAL**, this value is used as the default attribute for index partitions created when new partitions are added to the base table of the index.

If the [NO]LOGGING clause is omitted, the logging attribute of the index defaults to the logging attribute of the tablespace in which it resides.

Using this keyword makes index creation faster than using the **LOG-GING** option because undo and redo log entries are not written.

➤ **TABLESPACE tablespace**—The name of the tablespace to hold the index or index partition. If this option is omitted, Oracle creates the index in the default tablespace of the owner of the schema containing the index. This can cause immediate contention if the table and its index are both contained in the default tablespace of the schema owner.

For a nonpartitioned index, this is the tablespace name.

For a **LOCAL** index, you can specify the keyword **DEFAULT** in place of a tablespace name. New partitions added to the **LOCAL** index will be created in the same tablespace(s) as the corresponding partition(s) of the underlying table.

➤ **NOSORT**—Indicates to Oracle that the rows are stored in the database in ascending order and therefore Oracle does not have to sort the rows when creating the index. You cannot specify **REVERSE** with this option. If the rows are not in ascending order when this clause is used, an ORA-01409 error is returned and no index is created.

➤ **REVERSE**—Stores the bytes of the index block in reverse order, excluding the **ROWID**. You cannot specify **NOSORT** with this option.

➤ **GLOBAL**—Specifies that the partitioning of the index is user-defined and is not equi-partitioned with the underlying table. By default, nonpartitioned indexes are global indexes.

➤ **LOCAL**—Specifies that the index is range-partitioned on the same columns, with the same number of partitions, and with the same partition bounds as the underlying partitioned table. Oracle automatically maintains **LOCAL** index partitioning as the underlying table is repartitioned.

➤ **PARTITION BY RANGE**—Specifies that the global index is partitioned on the ranges of values from the columns specified in **column_list**. You cannot specify this clause for a **LOCAL** index.

➤ **(column_list)**—The name of the column(s) in a table on which the index is partitioned.

The **column_list** must specify a left prefix of the index column list.

The columns cannot contain the **ROWID** pseudo-column or a column of type **ROWID**.

➤ **PARTITION partition_name**—Names the individual partitions. The number of **PARTITION** clauses determines the number of partitions. If the index is local, the number of index partitions must be equal to the number and will correspond to the order of the table partitions.

The **partition_name** is the name of the physical index partition. If **partition_name** is omitted, Oracle punishes you by generating a name with the form SYS_P*n*, where *n* is some arbitrary value from a SYS-maintained sequence. *Name your partitions!*

For **LOCAL** indexes, if **partition_name** is omitted, Oracle generates a name that is consistent with the corresponding table partition. If the name conflicts with an existing index partition name, the form SYS_Pn is used.

➤ **VALUES LESS THAN (value_list)**—Specifies the (noninclusive) upper bound for the current partition in a global index. This means that if the value specified is 10, then everything less than 10, *but not including 10*, will be stored in this partition. The **value_list** is a comma-separated, ordered list of literal values corresponding to **column_list** in the **PARTITION BY RANGE** clause. Always specify **MAXVALUE** as the **value_list** of the last partition. The **MAXVALUE** clause places any values that are greater than the last specified range into this last partition, preventing values from being lost.

You cannot specify this clause for a local index.

➤ **PARALLEL**—Specifies the degree of parallelism for creating the index.

When the **CREATE INDEX** command is used to create a cluster index, an additional type of index known as a *cluster index* can be created. The cluster index is created against the cluster key, which can have a maximum of 32 columns assigned to it. We'll discuss clusters and their peculiarities more in the next section.

The **CREATE** Command For Clusters

A cluster can be used when several tables store a row that's of the same data type and size. First, a cluster index based on the identical data items is created.

If these tables are then clustered, their data values that are part of the cluster index are stored in the same location. A cluster is used when the clustered tables are frequently accessed together. Using a cluster reduces storage requirements and, in some cases, can speed access to data. The major drawback is that—in operations involving updates, inserts, and deletes—performance degradation can occur. The DBA should look at the expected mix of transaction types on the tables to be clustered and cluster only those that are frequently joined and those that don't have numerous updates, inserts, and deletes.

Clusters store shared data values in the same physical blocks (the cluster key values). For tables that are frequently joined, this can speed access; for tables that are frequently accessed separately, clustering is not the answer. An exception is when a single table is clustered. A single-table cluster forces the key values for that table into a single set of blocks; thus, accesses of that table can be sped up. Usually this single-table clustering also uses a hash structure to further improve access times.

Oracle7 added an additional cluster type: the ability to specify a hash cluster. A hash cluster uses a hash form of storage and no index. Hash structures should be used only for static tables. *Hashing* is the process in which a value, either of a unique or a nonunique row, is used to generate a hash value. This hash value is used to place the row into the hashed table. To retrieve the row, the value is simply recalculated. Hashes can be used only for equality operations. The syntax of the **CREATE CLUSTER** command is shown in Figure 5.2.

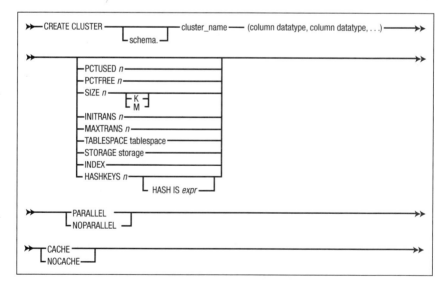

Figure 5.2 The syntax of the **CREATE CLUSTER** command.

The **CREATE CLUSTER** command has the following parameters:

➤ **schema**—Name of the schema where the cluster is stored.

➤ **cluster_name**—Name of the cluster.

➤ **(column datatype, column datatype...)**—List of columns and their data types; this list is called the *cluster key*. The names of the columns do not have to match the table column names, but the data types, lengths, and precisions do have to match.

➤ *n*—An integer (not all of the *n*'s are the same value; *n* is just used for convenience).

➤ **PCTFREE**—Parameter for clusters that applies only to the cluster and not to the individual tables in the cluster.

➤ **SIZE**—Expected size of the average cluster. This is calculated by 19 + (sum of column lengths) + (number of columns).

SIZE should be rounded up to the nearest equal divisor of your block size. For example, if your block size is 2,048 and the cluster length is 223, round up to 256. This, along with **HASHKEYS**, will limit the number of cluster keys stored in a single data block. If **SIZE** is small, then the number of keys that can be assigned to a single block will increase, allowing many keys to be assigned to a single block. If you have very few rows for a cluster key, set **SIZE** to a small value to minimize wasted space in the data block.

Be sure you're familiar with the **SIZE** parameter and information on **HASHKEYS**. Because you may not deal with clusters on a regular basis, be sure to study the sections on clusters and their uses thoroughly.

➤ **STORAGE**—Used as the default for the tables in the cluster. Refer to the **CREATE TABLE** command in Chapter 4 for more details.

➤ **INDEX**—Specifies to create an indexed cluster (default).

➤ **HASHKEYS**—Creates a hash cluster and specifies the number (*n*) of keys. The value is rounded up to the nearest prime number. This value, along with **SIZE**, will limit the number of keys stored in a single data block. The number of hash values generated will be **HASHKEYS+1**.

➤ **HASH IS**—Specifies to create a hash cluster. The specified column must be an integer.

The other parameters are the same as for the **CREATE TABLE** command.

To create a cluster, follow these steps:

1. First, issue the **CREATE CLUSTER** command to create the cluster column definitions.

2. Create the cluster index by using the following syntax:

```
CREATE INDEX index_name ON CLUSTER cluster_name;
```

*Note: You don't specify the columns. The number of columns is taken from the **CREATE CLUSTER** command that was used to create the named cluster.*

3. Create the tables that will be in the cluster. Use the following code:

```
CREATE TABLE cluster_table
(column_list)
CLUSTER cluster_name (cluster column(s))
```

In this instance, *cluster table* is the name for a table that will be a part of the cluster, and *column list* is a list of columns for the table, specified identically to the **CREATE TABLE** command's normal format.

Remember, the cluster columns don't have to have the same name, but must be the same data type, size, and precision, and must be specified in the same order as the columns in the **CREATE CLUSTER** command.

The **CREATE** Command For Sequences

Sequences allow for automatic generation of sequential nonrepeating or, if you desire, repeating integer values for use in keys or wherever numbers of this type should be used. Sequences can be either positive or negative in value and can range from 10e-27 to (10e27)-1 in value. The way in which a sequence increments can be controlled, as can the number of values cached for performance reasons in the shared (or system) global area (SGA) of an instance. The syntax of the **CREATE SEQUENCE** command is shown in Figure 5.3.

The **CREATE SEQUENCE** command has the following parameters:

➤ **schema**—The name of the schema that will own the sequence.

➤ **sequence_name**—The name you want the sequence to have.

➤ **INCREMENT BY**—Tells the system how to increment the sequence. If it's positive, the values are ascending; if it's negative, the values are descending.

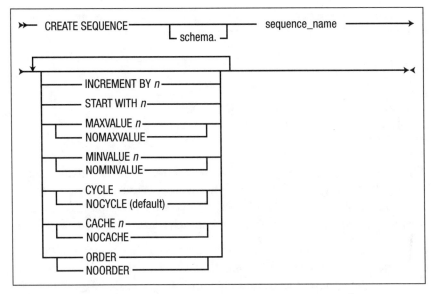

Figure 5.3 The syntax of the **CREATE SEQUENCE** command.

➤ *n*—An integer, positive or negative.

➤ **START WITH**—Tells the system what integer to start with.

➤ **MAXVALUE**—Tells the system the highest value that will be allowed. For ascending sequences, the default is 10e27-1; for descending sequences, the default is 1.

➤ **MINVALUE**—Tells the system how low the sequence can go. For ascending sequences, it defaults to 1; for descending sequences, the default value is 10e27-1.

➤ **CYCLE**—Causes the sequence to automatically re-cycle to **MINVALUE** when **MAXVALUE** is reached for ascending sequences. For descending sequences, it will cause the sequence to re-cycle from **MINVALUE** back to **MAXVALUE**.

➤ **CACHE**—Will cache the specified number of sequence values into the buffers in the SGA. This speeds access, but all cached numbers are lost when the database is shut down. Default value is 20; maximum value is **MAXVALUE-MINVALUE**.

➤ **ORDER**—Forces sequence numbers to be output in order of request. When they are used for time stamping, this may be required. In most cases, the sequence numbers are in order anyway, and **ORDER** is not required.

Sequences avoid the performance problems associated with sequencing numbers generated by application triggers of the form, as seen here:

```
DECLARE
TEMP_NO NUMBER;
BEGIN
LOCK TABLE PO_NUM IN EXCLUSIVE MODE NOWAIT;
SELECT MAX(PO_NUM)+1 INTO TEMP_NO FROM SALES ;
END;
```

If the application requires numbers that are exactly in sequence (that is, 1, 2 , 3, and so on), this trigger may be your only recourse, because if a statement that refers to a sequence is rolled back (canceled), that sequence number is lost. Likewise, any cached sequence numbers are lost each time a database is shut down.

Sequences can't be accessed directly; you can retrieve their values only by using the pseudo-columns **CURRVAL** and **NEXTVAL**. The pseudo-columns can be selected either from **DUAL** into a holding variable in PL/SQL or from the table being inserted (via the **VALUES** clause) into or updated (in the **SET** clause). A value must first be accessed via the **NEXTVAL** pseudo-column before the **CURRVAL** pseudo-column can be accessed.

Uses And Restrictions Of **CURRVAL** And **NEXTVAL**
The pseudo-columns **CURRVAL** and **NEXTVAL** are used:

➤ With the **VALUES** clause of an **INSERT** command

➤ With the **SELECT** subclause of a **SELECT** command

➤ In the **SET** clause of an **UPDATE** command

The pseudo-columns **CURRVAL** and **NEXTVAL** cannot be used:

➤ In a subquery

➤ In a view or snapshot query

➤ With a **DISTINCT** clause

➤ With a **GROUP BY** or **ORDER BY** clause

➤ In a **SELECT** command in combination with another **SELECT** command using **UNION, INTERSECT** or **MINUS** set operators

➤ In the **WHERE** clause of a **SELECT** command

➤ In the **DEFAULT** column value in a **CREATE TABLE** or **ALTER TABLE** command

➤ In the condition of a **CHECK** constraint

The **CREATE** Command For Views

Views are stored queries in Oracle that can be treated as tables. Until fairly recently, views were essentially read-only. Now, with certain caveats, views can be updatable. They're used to hide or to enhance data structures, to make complex queries easier to manage, and to enforce security requirements. Figure 5.4 shows the syntax of the **CREATE VIEW** command.

The **CREATE VIEW** command has the following parameters:

➤ FORCE—Specifies that the view be created even if all permissions or objects it specifies as part of the view aren't available. Before the view can be used, the permissions or objects must be in the database and accessible.

➤ NO FORCE (default)—Means that all objects and permissions must be in place before the view can be created.

➤ view_name—Name of the view.

➤ alias—Valid column name. It doesn't have to be the same as the column it's based on. If aliases aren't used, the names of the columns are used. If a column is modified by an expression, it must be aliased. If four columns are in the query, there must be four aliases.

➤ OF object_type—Explicitly creates an object view of type **object_type**. The columns in the object view are the same as the top-level attributes of the specified **object_type**. Each row will have an assigned **OID**.

➤ WITH OBJECT OID—Specifies the attributes of the row that will be used as a key to uniquely identify each row of the object view. These attributes should correspond to the primary key of the base table. If the base object has an **OID** already, you can specify **DEFAULT**. This is only for Oracle8.

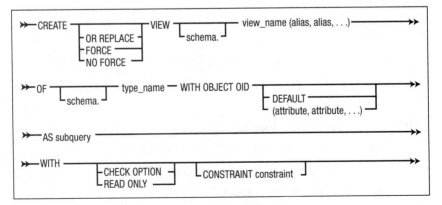

Figure 5.4   The syntax of the **CREATE VIEW** command.

➤ subquery—Any valid **SELECT** statement that doesn't include an **ORDER BY** or **FOR UPDATE** clause. A view can only be based on one or more tables and/or views.

➤ **WITH CHECK OPTION**—Specifies that inserts and updates through the view must be selectable from the view. This can be used in a view based on a view.

➤ **READ ONLY**—Specifies that the view is read-only and can't be changed by using the **INSERT, UPDATE,** or **DELETE** operations.

➤ **CONSTRAINT**—Specifies the name associated with the **CHECK** constraint.

A view can usually be used in the following commands:

➤ COMMENT

➤ DELETE

➤ INSERT

➤ LOCK TABLE

➤ UPDATE

➤ SELECT

A view's **SELECT** statement in the subquery can't select a **CURRVAL** or **NEXTVAL** from a sequence or directly access **ROWID, ROWNUM,** or **LEVEL** pseudo-columns. To use the pseudo-columns for a table, a view select must alias them.

A view is just a window to data; it doesn't store data itself. Views can be used in a SQL statement just like a table can.

You can't update a view if it:

➤ Contains a join

➤ Contains a **GROUP BY, CONNECT BY,** or **START WITH** clause

➤ Contains a **DISTINCT** clause or expressions like **AMOUNT+10** in the column list

➤ Doesn't refer to all **NOT NULL** columns in the table (all **NOT NULLs** must be in the view and assigned a value by the update)

You can update a view that contains pseudo-columns or columns modified by expressions if the update doesn't affect these columns.

You can query the view, **USER_UPDATABLE_COLUMNS**, to find out if the columns in a join view are updatable. Generally speaking, as long as all of the **NOT NULLs** and key columns are included in a join view for a table, that table can be updated through the view.

A join view can have the commands **INSERT**, **UPDATE**, and **DELETE** used against it if:

➤ The DML affects only one of the tables in the join.

➤ For **UPDATE**, all of the columns updated are extracted from a key-preserved table. In addition, if the view has a **CHECK OPTION** constraint, join columns are shielded from update, and so are columns taken from tables that are referred to more than once in the view.

➤ For **DELETE**, there is one and only one key-preserved table in the join, and that table can be present more than once if there is no **CHECK OPTION** constraint on the view.

➤ For **INSERT**, all of the columns are from a key-preserved table, and the views don't have a **CHECK OPTION** constraint. (A table is key-preserved if every key of the table can also be a key of the result of the join. So, a key-preserved table has its keys preserved through a join. It is not necessary that the key or keys of a table be selected for it to be key-preserved. It is sufficient that if the key or keys were selected, then they would also be key(s) of the result of the join.)

As with all stored objects, to create a view, the user must have direct grants on all objects that are a part of the view, including those objects that may be used in views and that are used in the new view. The grants used to create a view can't be from a role; they must be direct grants.

Views can cause poor performance if they're nested too deeply. This can easily occur when they're created against the **DBA_**, **USER_**, or **ALL_** views.

Object Views

To take advantage of the benefits of the new object paradigm in Oracle8, you can make a common relational table into a pseudo-object table by creating what is known as an *object view,* which is directly based on the relational table. The object ID is not system-generated but is based on columns that you specify.

An example using the **EMP** table would be:

```
CREATE TYPE emp_t AS OBJECT (
  empno    NUMBER(5),
  ename    VARCHAR2(20),
```

```
salary    NUMBER(9,2),
job       VARCHAR2(20));

CREATE TABLE emp(
empno     NUMBER(5) CONSTRAINT pk_emp PRIMARY KEY,
ename     VARCHAR2(20),
salary    NUMBER(9,2),
job       VARCHAR2(20));

CREATE VIEW emp_man OF emp_t
 WITH OBJECT IDENTIFIER (empno) AS
  SELECT empno, ename, salary, job
  FROM emp
  WHERE job='MANAGER';
```

This example creates an object view of **EMP_T** (type) objects corresponding to the employees from the **EMP** table who are managers, with **EMPNO**, the primary key of **EMP**, as the object identifier.

The **CREATE** Command For Synonyms

Synonyms are database shorthand notations that allow long, complex combinations of schema, object name, and connection strings to be reduced to a simple alias. Because synonyms remove the requirement to prefix a table, view, or sequence with a schema name, they perform a simple type of data hiding by allowing tables from one or more schemas to appear to be located in the user's schema. The **CREATE SYNONYM** command syntax is shown in Figure 5.5.

The **CREATE SYNONYM** command has the following parameters:

➤ PUBLIC—Creates a public synonym that can be used by all users. Usually only DBAs create public synonyms. By default, synonyms are created as private and can only be used by the user who defines them.

➤ synonym_name—Name or alias that you want the object to assume.

➤ schema—Schema in which the object resides.

➤ object_name—Actual name of the object on which the synonym is being created.

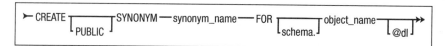

Figure 5.5 The syntax of the **CREATE SYNONYM** command.

➤ **@dl**—Database link that's used only if the object resides in another database.

The **CREATE** Command For Rollback Segments

Rollback segments store system undo data, allowing noncommitted transactions to be rolled back. Rollback segments can be likened to "before image" logs or journals in other database systems. Rollback segments store the before images of changed data. Large transaction failures can usually be attributed to the following rollback-related problems:

➤ Inadequate space in the rollback segment (usually named **RBS**) tablespace for rollback segment expansion

➤ Improper storage specifications for the rollback segment being used, resulting in that segment exceeding its **MAXEXTENTS** value

➤ Improper scheduling, allowing other transactions to cause Snapshot Too Old errors to occur in the transaction (which can also be caused by an improper **INITRANS** setting)

In addition to the **SYSTEM** rollback segment created when the database is built, at least one additional rollback segment must be created. The default **SYSTEM** rollback segment is used strictly to record changes to the data dictionary in the **SYSTEM** tablespace. Usually the number of private rollback segments is determined by determining how many concurrent users will access the database and deciding how many users should be assigned to each rollback segment (by specifying the **MINEXTENTS** value). For example, if you have 100 concurrent users and you want (on the average) 20 users per rollback segment, then the **MINEXTENTS** would be set to 20 for each of 5 rollback segments. For private rollback segments, the calculated ratio of the initialization parameters—**TRANSACTIONS** divided by **TRANSACTIONS_PER_ROLLBACK_SEGMENT**—rounded up to the nearest integer—should be used to determine the number of rollback segments created. The syntax of the **CREATE ROLLBACK SEGMENT** command is shown in Figure 5.6.

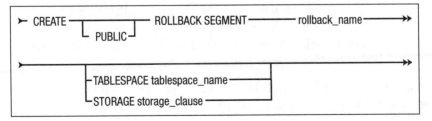

Figure 5.6   The syntax of the **CREATE ROLLBACK SEGMENT** command.

The **CREATE ROLLBACK SEGMENT** command has the following parameters:

➤ **rollback_name**—Name of the rollback segment. Must be unique.

➤ **tablespace_name**—Name of the tablespace in which the segment is to be created. If this name is not specified, the rollback segment is created in the user's default tablespace.

➤ **storage_clause**—Specifies the required storage parameters for the rollback segment. It's strongly suggested that the following guidelines be used:

   ➤ INITIAL = NEXT—**INITIAL** sets the size of the initial segment in a rollback segment. **NEXT** sets the size of the next extent in the rollback segment and subsequent extents, assuming that **PCTINCREASE** is set to zero (it will always be zero for rollback segments in Oracle8 because specification of the parameter results in an error). **NEXT** can be modified after the rollback segment is created.

   ➤ MINEXTENTS = 20 (or your calculated value; 2 is the default on **CREATE ROLLBACK**)—**MINEXTENTS** sets the minimum number of extents that are initially allocated when the rollback segment is created.

   ➤ MAXEXTENTS—A calculated maximum based on the size of the rollback segment tablespace, the size of rollback segments' extents, and the number of rollback segments. If set to **UNLIMITED**, the **MAXEXTENTS** parameter could allow the rollback segment to use up all available free area in the rollback tablespace (disk space allocated to rollback segments). **MAXEXTENTS** can be modified after the rollback segment is created.

   ➤ OPTIMAL—Reflects the size to which the system will restore the rollback segment by deallocating extents after the rollback segment has been increased by a large transaction. **OPTIMAL** should be set to allow your average-sized transaction to complete without wrapping or causing shrinks. **OPTIMAL** and **MINEXTENTS** can be used by the Oracle server to determine the optimal number of extents for rollback segments. **OPTIMAL** can be modified after the rollback segment is created.

After Oracle7.3, **PCTINCREASE** can no longer be set for rollback segments; in earlier versions, it should always be set to zero.

When a rollback segment is created, it's not online. To be used, it must be brought online in one of two ways: by using the **ALTER ROLLBACK SEGMENT rollback_name ONLINE;** command, or by shutting down the database, modifying the INIT.ORA parameter **ROLLBACK_SEGMENTS**, and restarting the database. In any case, the INIT.ORA file parameter should be altered if the rollback segment is to be used permanently, or it won't be acquired when the database is shut down and restarted.

The **CREATE** Command For Control Files

The control file is one of the more important files in the Oracle database system. The control file is a storage location for the names and places of all physical data files for the system. The control file also acts as a database of the SCN and timestamp information that applies to those data files. Without one functional control file (the first one in the list in the **CONTROL_FILES** parameter), the database won't start up.

Sometimes it may be necessary for a DBA to re-create a control file. This option can be used in several situations: when a control file has become damaged and no viable copy is available; when a database name must be changed; and when a fixed limit such as **MAXDATAFILES** has to be altered for a database. If the DBA has good documentation for the database, the **CREATE CONTROLFILE** command can be issued manually; however, it's usually easier to periodically use the **ALTER DATABASE BACKUP CONTROLFILE TO TRACE** command to automatically create a control-file rebuild script.

Additional Data Structure **CREATE** And DDL Commands

In this section, we will cover the new DDL commands for Oracle8 and some additions for external procedures.

LIBRARY Commands

In Oracle8, a *library* is created to refer to an external library of C functions. Coverage of other languages, such as Java, is promised for later releases, but for now only C is available. The external library of C functions must be either a DLL library or a Sun Solaris library. The first command we will cover is the **CREATE** command for libraries.

The **CREATE LIBRARY** Command

The **CREATE LIBRARY** command creates an internal data structure known as a library. A library is a pointer to an external C library of functions. The actual validity (existence) of a library is not verified until access is attempted.

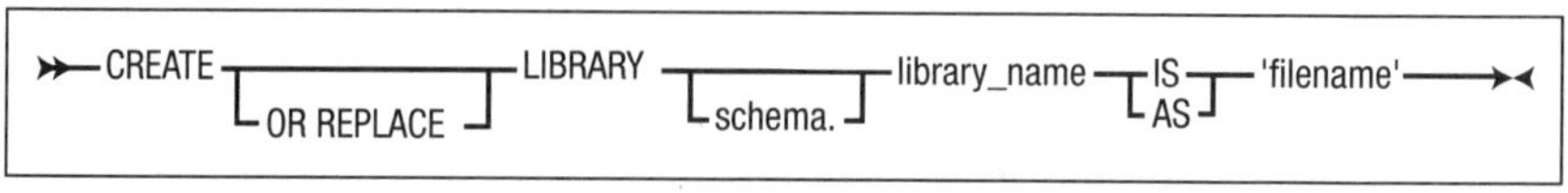

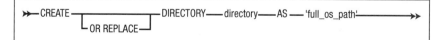

Figure 5.7 The syntax of the **CREATE LIBRARY** command.

The syntax of the **CREATE LIBRARY** command is shown in Figure 5.7.

The **CREATE LIBRARY** command has the following parameters:

➤ **schema**—The schema in which the library is to reside. If not specified, it defaults to the user's default schema.

➤ **library_name**—The name of the library. Must comply with object naming standards.

➤ **filename**—The existing operating-system shared library that is to correspond to the internal library name.

After a library is created, it can be accessed through a **FUNCTION** created to refer to a specific "C" function stored in the external library.

The **DROP LIBRARY** Command

The **DROP LIBRARY** command removes the library alias at only the database level and does not affect the status of the operating system shared library. The syntax of the **DROP LIBRARY** command is shown in Figure 5.8.

DIRECTORY Commands

The *directory* is a new internal object in Oracle8. A directory is a pointer to an external, operating-system directory where **LOB** files are located. A **BFILE** definition must include this internal pointer to the external directory.

The **CREATE DIRECTORY** Command

The syntax of the **CREATE DIRECTORY** command is shown in Figure 5.9.

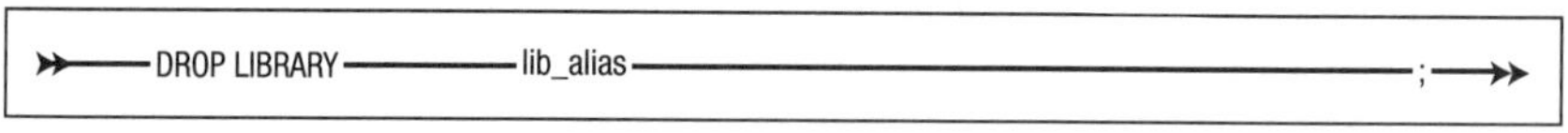

Figure 5.8 The syntax of the **DROP LIBRARY** command.

Figure 5.9 The syntax of the **CREATE DIRECTORY** command.

The **CREATE DIRECTORY** command has the following parameters:

➤ **directory**—This is the name for the internal directory specification; note that no schema is specified.

➤ **full_os_path**—The full operating system path to the directory where the **BFILE**s are located.

The **DROP DIRECTORY** Command

As its name implies, the **DROP DIRECTORY** command drops the specified directory object. The syntax of the **DROP DIRECTORY** command is shown in Figure 5.10.

After a directory is dropped, all **BFILE**s in that directory location become inaccessible. Nothing is done to the actual physical files in the **DIRECTORY** location; in order to drop them, you must use an operating system command.

The **CREATE FUNCTION** Or **PROCEDURE** Command

Functions and procedures are internally stored PL/SQL programs. A *function* must return a single value, and a *procedure* may return zero, one, or several values. A function must be pure; that is, it cannot have any side effects (it cannot change database or process states).

The **CREATE FUNCTION** Command

The syntax of the **CREATE FUNCTION** command and its arguments is shown in Figure 5.11.

The **CREATE FUNCTION** command has the following parameters:

➤ **RETURN datatype**—The **RETURN** clause is used to specify the data type of the single data item that is returned from the **FUNCTION**.

➤ **argument_name**—The name given to the argument. It can be any valid variable name.

➤ **argument_type**—The type of argument: IN, OUT, or IN OUT. Specifies how the argument is to be treated (strictly input, strictly output, or both). This is optional and will default to IN if not specified.

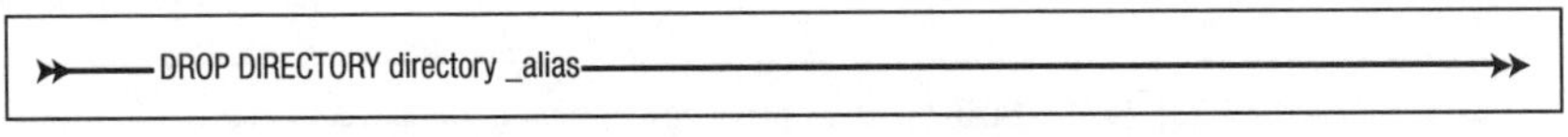

Figure 5.10 The syntax of the **DROP DIRECTORY** command.

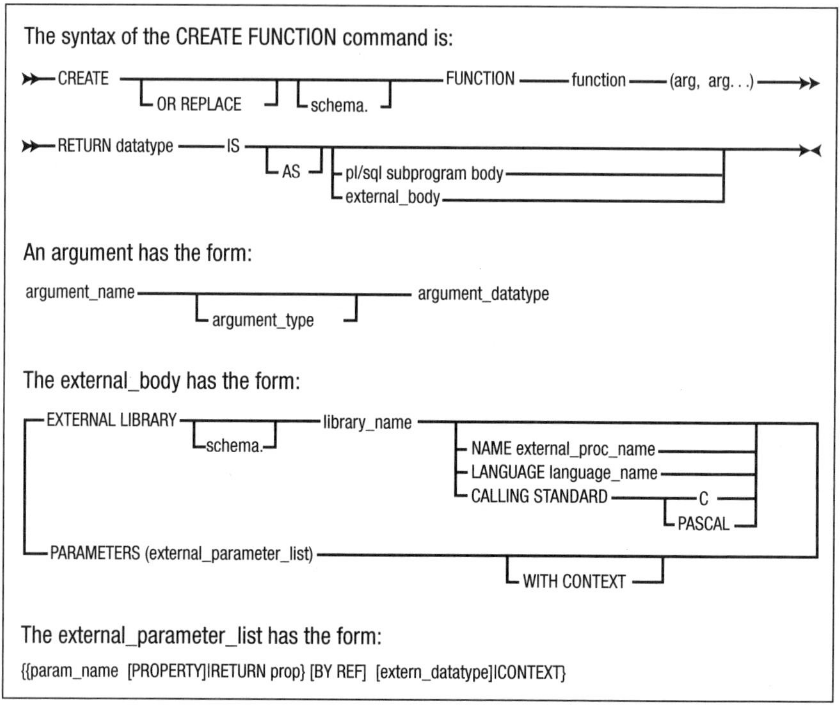

The syntax of the CREATE FUNCTION command is:

An argument has the form:

The external_body has the form:

The external_parameter_list has the form:

{{param_name [PROPERTY]|RETURN prop} [BY REF] [extern_datatype]|CONTEXT}

Figure 5.11 The syntax of the **CREATE FUNCTION** command and some of its arguments and parameters.

➤ argument_datatype—The data type of the argument. It can be any valid scalar data type, such as date, char, varchar2, or number.

➤ external_body—Has the form shown in Figure 5.11.

➤ external_parameter_list—Has the form shown in Figure 5.11, with this code repeated as many times as is needed. The **prop** argument has one of the following values: **INDICATOR, LENGTH, MAXLEN, CHARSETID,** or **CHARSETFORM.**

In order to be usable by **SELECT** and by packaged procedures, a function must have its purity declared if it is placed into a package. You declare a function's purity by including a **PRAGMA RESTRICT_REFERENCES** call for the function after its entry in the package header file. The format is as shown in Figure 5.12.

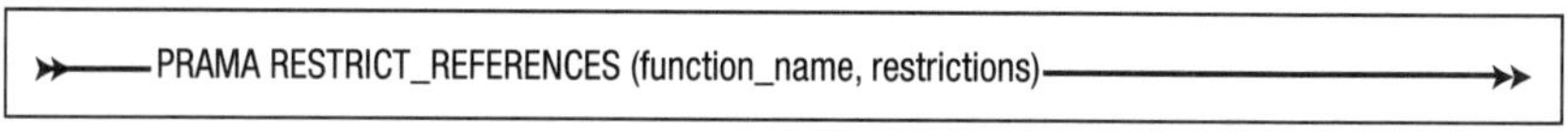

Figure 5.12 A **PRAGMA RESTRICT_REFERENCES** call.

PRAGMA RESTRICT_REFERENCES is a compiler directive that denies member functions read/write access to database tables, packaged variables, or both, and thereby helps to avoid side effects. The arguments for this directive are:

➤ function_name—The name of the function to which the pragma is being applied.

➤ restrictions—A comma-separated list of restrictions that the function meets. These restrictions are taken from the following:

   ➤ WNDS—Specifies that the function writes no database state (does not modify database tables).

   ➤ WNPS—Specifies that the function writes no package state (does not modify packaged variables).

   ➤ RNDS—Specifies that the function reads no database state (does not query database tables).

   ➤ RNPS—Specifies that the function reads no package state (does not refer to packaged variables).

The **CREATE PROCEDURE** Command

A procedure is a stored PL/SQL object. A procedure can have zero, one, or many return values. The syntax of the **CREATE PROCEDURE** command is shown in Figure 5.13.

The **CREATE PROCEDURE** command has the following parameters:

➤ argument_name—The name given to this argument. It can be any valid variable name.

➤ argument_type—The type of argument: IN, OUT, or IN OUT. Specifies how the argument is to be treated (strictly input, strictly output, or both).

➤ argument_datatype—The data type of the argument. It can be any valid scalar data type, such as date, char, or varchar2.

➤ external_body—Has the form shown in Figure 5.13.

➤ external_parameter_list—Has the form shown in Figure 5.13, with this code repeated as many times as is needed. The **prop** argument has one of the following values: **INDICATOR, LENGTH, MAXLEN, CHARSETID,** or **CHARSETFORM.**

For both procedures and functions, the command arguments are as follows:

➤ OR REPLACE—An optional statement specifying that if the procedure or function exists, replace it, and if it doesn't exist, create it.

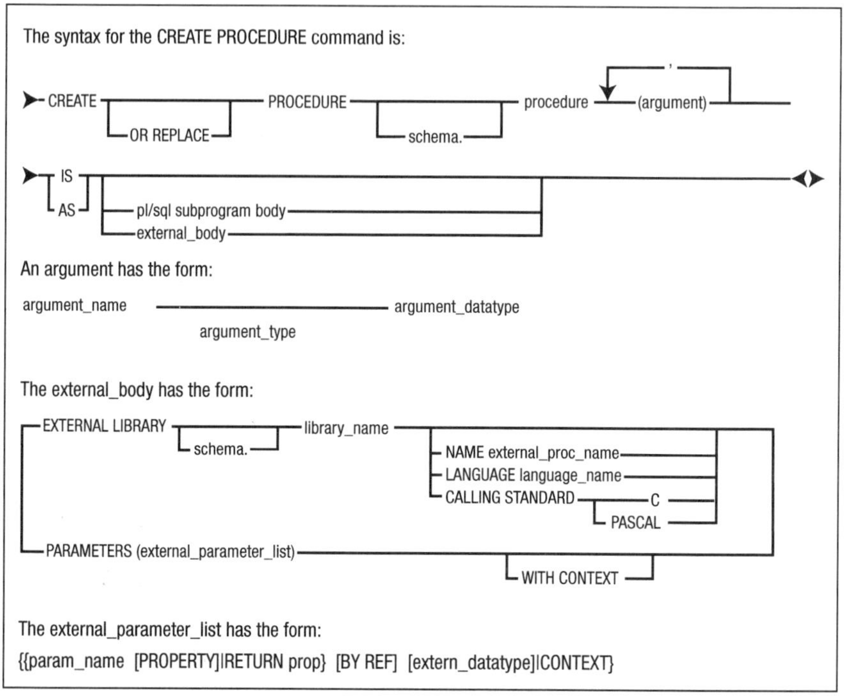

The syntax for the CREATE PROCEDURE command is:

An argument has the form:

The external_body has the form:

The external_parameter_list has the form:

`{{param_name [PROPERTY]|RETURN prop} [BY REF] [extern_datatype]|CONTEXT}`

Figure 5.13 The syntax of the **CREATE PROCEDURE** command and some of its arguments and parameters.

➤ **schema**—The schema in which to place the procedure or function. If this is other than the user's default schema, the user must have the **CREATE ANY PROCEDURE** system privilege.

➤ **procedure** or **function**—The name of the procedure or function being created.

➤ **argument(s)**—The argument of the procedure or function. There can be more than one argument.

➤ **IN**—Specifies that the argument must be specified when the procedure or function is called from SQL, or another procedure or function. For functions, an argument must always be provided.

➤ **OUT**—Specifies that the procedure passes a value for this argument back to the calling object. Not used with functions.

➤ **IN OUT**—Specifies that both the IN and OUT features are in effect for the procedure. Not used with functions.

➤ **datatype**—The data type of the argument. Precision, length, and scale cannot be specified; they are derived from the calling object.

➤ **pl/sql body**—A PL/SQL body of statements.

➤ **IS** or **AS**—The documentation states that these are interchangeable, but one or the other must be specified. However, Oracle didn't tell this to some of its tools, so if you get an error when you're using one, try the other.

The **ALTER FUNCTION** Or **PROCEDURE** Command

If a function or procedure becomes invalid due to problems with objects it depends on—such as other procedures, functions, packages, or underlying tables—it will have to be recompiled. This recompilation is accomplished with the **ALTER** command.

The syntax of the **ALTER** command is shown in Figure 5.14.

The **ALTER FUNCTION** or **PROCEDURE** command has only one argument:

➤ COMPILE—Forces a recompile of the object.

The **DROP FUNCTION** Or **PROCEDURE** Command

To get rid of a function or procedure that is no longer useful, use the **DROP** command. The syntax of the **DROP** command is shown in Figure 5.15.

This command will invalidate any related functions or procedures, so they will have to be recompiled before you can use them via the **ALTER** command.

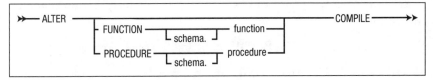

Figure 5.14 The syntax of the **ALTER** command.

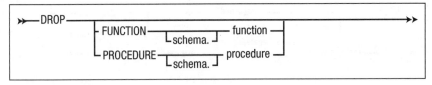

Figure 5.15 The syntax of the **DROP** command.

The **CREATE PACKAGE** Command

A *package* is a compilation of functions, procedures, exceptions, package variables, and cursors that usually form an application or a discrete part of an application. Any time a single subcomponent of a package is referred to, the entire package is brought into memory. A package consists of a *package header* and a *package body*. The command to create a package header follows; this may also be called a *package specification*. The syntax of the **CREATE PACKAGE** command is shown in Figure 5.16.

The **CREATE PACKAGE** command has the following parameters:

➤ OR REPLACE—Used when the user wants to create or replace a package. If the package definition exists, it is replaced; if it doesn't exist, it is created.

➤ schema—The schema in which the package will be created. If this is not specified, the package is created in the user's default schema.

➤ package—The name of the package to be created.

➤ pl/sql package specification—The list of procedures, functions, or variables that make up the package. All components listed are considered to be public.

The **CREATE PACKAGE BODY** Command

After you have specified a package by creating a header, you must create the package body. The package body contains the actual PL/SQL code that the package executes.

The syntax of the **CREATE PACKAGE BODY** command is shown in Figure 5.17.

The **CREATE PACKAGE BODY** command has the following parameters:

➤ OR REPLACE—An optional statement specifying that if the package body exists, it is replaced; if it doesn't exist, it is created.

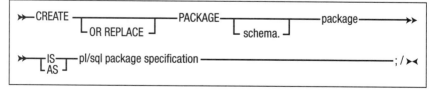

Figure 5.16   The syntax of the **CREATE PACKAGE** command.

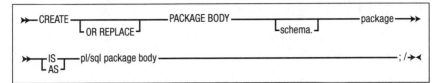

Figure 5.17   The syntax of the **CREATE PACKAGE BODY** command.

➤ **schema**—The schema in which the package will be created. If this is not specified, the package body is created in the user's default schema.

➤ **pl/sql package body**—The collection of all of the SQL and PL/SQL text required to create all of the objects in the package.

The **ALTER PACKAGE** Command

Periodically, a package may become invalid. If a package becomes invalid, you must recompile it by using the **ALTER PACKAGE** command. The syntax of the **ALTER PACKAGE** command is shown in Figure 5.18.

The **ALTER PACKAGE** command has the following parameters:

➤ **schema**—The schema that owns the package

➤ **package**—The package name to be altered

➤ **BODY**—The option to allow the package header to remain while the package body is deleted

The **DROP PACKAGE** Command

When a package is no longer needed, you should drop it by using the **DROP PACKAGE** command. The syntax is shown in Figure 5.19.

Figure 5.18   The syntax of the **ALTER PACKAGE** command.

```
>>─DROP PACKAGE──┬──────┬──┬─────────┬──package───────────────><
                 └BODY ─┘  └schema. ─┘
```

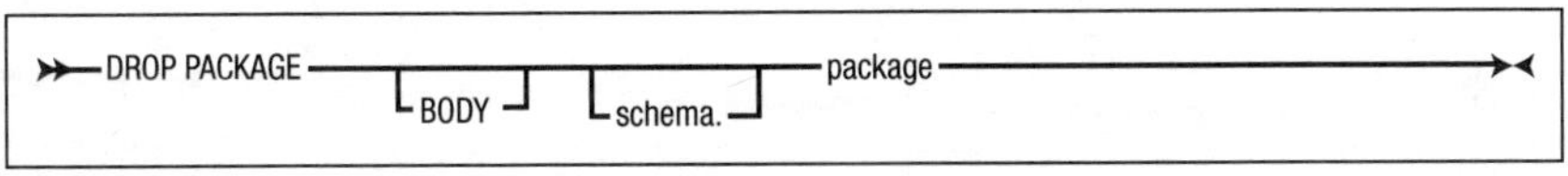

Figure 5.19   The syntax of the **DROP PACKAGE** command.

The **DROP PACKAGE** command has the following parameters:

➤ BODY—The option that allows dropping the body of a package without dropping the header

➤ schema—The schema that owns the package

➤ package—The package to be dropped

If you omit the keyword **BODY**, both the definition and the body are dropped. If you include the keyword **BODY**, just the package body is dropped, leaving the definition intact. When a package is dropped, all dependent objects are invalidated. If the package is not re-created before one of the dependent objects is accessed, Oracle8 tries to recompile the package; this will return an error and cause the command to fail.

Practice Questions

Question 1

In which two statements would you typically use the **CURRVAL** pseudo-column? [Choose two]

- ❑ a. **SET** clause of an **UPDATE** command
- ❑ b. **SELECT** list of a view
- ❑ c. **SELECT** statement with the **HAVING** clause
- ❑ d. Subquery in an **UPDATE** statement
- ❑ e. **VALUES** clause of an **INSERT** statement

The correct answers are a and e. The pseudo-columns CURRVAL and NEXTVAL of a sequence can be used only in the SET clause of an UPDATE command, in the VALUES clause of an INSERT statement, and in the target of an INSERT INTO statement. Answers b, c, and d are incorrect because the pseudo-columns can't be used in a view, in a SELECT using a HAVING clause, or in a subquery. The pseudo-columns also can't be used in a snapshot definition.

Question 2

Which SQL statement creates the **parts_456874_vu** view that contains the ID number, description, and quantity for **manufacturer_id 456874** from the inventory table and does not allow the manufacturer values to be changed through the view?

○ a.
```
CREATE VIEW parts_456874_vu
AS SELECT id_number, description, quantity
FROM inventory
WHERE manufacturer_id = 456874
WITH READ ONLY;
```

○ b.
```
CREATE VIEW parts_456874_vu
AS SELECT id_number, description, quantity
FROM inventory
HAVING manufacturer_id = 456874
WITH READ ONLY;
```

○ c.
```
CREATE VIEW parts_456874_vu
AS SELECT id_number, description, quantity
FROM inventory
WHERE manufacturer_id = 456874
WITH CHECK OPTION;
```

○ d.
```
CREATE VIEW parts_456874_vu
AS SELECT id_number, description, quantity
FROM inventory
WITH CHECK CONSTRAINT;
```

The correct answer is a; it has complete clauses, restricts the view to the proper range of values (those belonging to the **manufacturer_id 456874**), and specifies the proper format **READ ONLY** clause. Answer b won't even compile because it has a **HAVING** clause and no **GROUP BY**; answer c doesn't restrict to **READ ONLY**; and answer d won't compile because there is no **CHECK CONSTRAINT** on views.

Question 3

When you're attempting to control the space allocation and usage of a cluster's data segment, which parameter applies to the cluster and not to the individual tables?

○ a. **PCTFREE**

○ b. **MAXTRANS**

○ c. **INITRANS**

○ d. **SIZE**

○ e. **INITIAL**

The correct answer is a. In **CREATE CLUSTER** statements, the **PCTFREE** applies only to the cluster itself, not to the individual tables. Answer b sets the maximum number of transactions that can access a **TABLE** or **CLUSTER**. Answer c sets the minimum number of transaction entries that is set for a **TABLE** or **CLUSTER**. Answer d sets the **SIZE** for the key for the **CLUSTER** used by all the tables in a **CLUSTER**. Answer e sets the size of the **INITIAL** extent for all tables in the cluster.

Question 4

What is the maximum number of columns in a cluster key?

○ a. 1

○ b. 2

○ c. 4

○ d. 8

○ e. 16

○ f. 32

The correct answer is f. A cluster key can have up to 32 columns.

Question 5

Which of the following is true of a function?

○ a. It can return zero, one, or many values.

○ b. It must return one value.

○ c. It is stored in an external file.

○ d. It may return only one value but doesn't have to.

○ e. It can be used only by pure procedures.

The correct answer is b. A function must return a single value. Answer a is incorrect because it states that zero, one, or many values can be returned. Answer c is incorrect because a function is stored internally to the database. Answer d is incorrect because a function must return a value; it isn't optional. Answer e is incorrect because any procedure can use a properly pure function, not vice versa.

Question 6

According to Oracle training, what should the value of **MINEXTENTS** for a rollback segment be set to?

○ a. 1

○ b. 2

○ c. 20

○ d. 50

The correct answer is c. However, let me stress that this is Oracle training's number, not what you would do in real life. The rollback segment **MINEXTENTS** value should be based on the number of rollback segments and the number of expected DML users, not on some arbitrarily selected value.

Question 7

> You accidentally drop a directory. How will this affect the database?
>
> ○ a. All **BLOB**s stored in the directory are erased.
>
> ○ b. There will be no effect because directories aren't implemented yet.
>
> ○ c. All **BFILE** specifications that use the directory will become invalid.
>
> ○ d. All files stored in the location specified by the directory entry will be erased.

The correct answer is c. A directory is an internal pointer used by **BFILE** entries to locate the external directory where external **LOB** files are stored. Deletion of a directory affects only the **BFILE** entries that point to it. There is no loss of files.

Need To Know More?

Ault, Michael R. *Oracle8 Administration and Management.* John Wiley & Sons, New York, New, York, 1998. ISBN 0-471-19234-1. This book provides a comprehensive look at Oracle8 and Oracle7.x management. Use it for command syntax definitions for all **CREATE** commands.

Oracle8 Error Messages, Release 8.0.4, December 1997, Oracle Corporation, Part No. A58312-01. This is the source book for all Oracle errors for version 8. It is the only place to locate certain limits and restrictions by review of a particular feature's error codes. It can be found on the Web at **http://technet.oracle.com**, which has free membership.

Oracle8 SQL Reference, Release 8.0. Oracle Corporation, Redwood Shores, California, December 1997. Part No. A58225-01. This is the source book for all Oracle SQL for version 8. It can be found on the Web at **http://technet.oracle.com**, which has free membership.

DBA Pipeline at **www.revealnet.com** is a great place to ask those last-minute questions and to peruse for up-to-the-minute questions, problems, and solutions.

RevealNet Oracle Administrator from RevealNet, Inc. This online reference provides diagrams with hot links to definitions and examples of all DDL commands. It's one of the fastest online searchable references I've come across (even though I might be a bit prejudiced because I'm its principal author). It's more expensive than a book, at around $300 to $400; however, you'll use it long after the books have been put away. It can be downloaded from **www.revealnet.com**.

DDL: Using The **ALTER, COMMENT,** And **DROP** Commands

6

Terms you'll need to understand:

√ **ALTER** command

√ **COMMENT** command

√ **DROP** command

√ **TRUNCATE** command

Techniques you'll need to master:

√ Using the **ALTER** command to alter the characteristics of database objects that can be changed

√ Using the **COMMENT** command to document your database objects

√ Using the **DROP** command to remove obsolete objects

This chapter is devoted to the following DDL commands: **ALTER, DROP,** and **COMMENT**. Like **CREATE,** the **ALTER** command has numerous incarnations. Because it is the most complex of the remaining DDL commands, I will cover it first. The **ALTER** command allows changes in various aspects of database objects and allows additions to and removals from existing objects. The **COMMENT** command allows for documentation of database objects. The **DROP** command allows obsolete objects to be removed. All of these commands are important, and database administrators (DBAs) must be familiar with their various aspects.

The **ALTER** Command

The **ALTER** command is used to alter the characteristics of database objects that can be changed. (For the purpose of this chapter, a change is defined as an alteration of structure or characteristics, not simply a recompile.) The **ALTER** command is used with databases, instances, tablespaces, tables, indexes, clusters, and sequences. Procedures, functions, packages, package bodies, triggers, and views can be compiled only through the use of the **ALTER** command, as shown in this code snippet:

```
ALTER object_type schema.object_name COMPILE;
```

One thing to remember about any DDL command—such as **ALTER, DROP,** or **CREATE**—is that it results in an implicit **COMMIT** command. An implicit **COMMIT** command causes any uncommitted changes to be committed to the database, so if you perform **INSERT, UPDATE,** or **DELETE** commands and then issue a **CREATE, ALTER,** or **DROP** command, the previous commands will be committed.

The **ALTER** Command For Databases

Even the best-designed database eventually has to be changed. New log group member files may need to be added, data files may need to be renamed or moved, archive logging status may need to be changed, and so forth. These are all accomplished with the **ALTER DATABASE** command. The syntax for this command is shown in Figure 6.1.

The **ALTER DATABASE** command has the following options and variables:

➤ **database_name**—The database name. It can be a maximum of eight characters long. If the name is not specified, the value in the init.ora file will be used.

```
>>──── ALTER DATABASE [database_name] ──────────────────────────────/

├──── MOUNT [STANDBY|CLONE DATABASE] ─────────────
 ──── CONVERT ───────────────────────
 ──── OPEN [RESETLOGS|NORESETLOGS]──────
 ──── ACTIVATE STANDBY DATABASE ──────────
 ──── ARCHIVELOG|NOARCHIVELOG ────────────
 ──── recover_clause ─────────────────
                                      ,
 ──── ADD LOGFILE [THREAD n] ┴─ [GROUP n]── filespec┘

 ──── ADD LOGFILE MEMBER ┴─ 'filename' [REUSE]┴─ TO
                                                  ── GROUP n ──
                                                            ,
                                                  ─(┴ 'filename'┴)──
                                                  ── 'filename' ──

 ──── DROP LOGFILE ── GROUP n ──
                            ,
                     ─(┴ 'filename'┴)──
                     ── 'filename' ──
 ──── DROP LOGFILE MEMBER 'filename'──────────
                                ,
 ──── CLEAR [UNARCHIVED] LOGFILE              UNRECOVERABLE
                         ── GROUP n ──        DATAFILE
                                 ,
                          ─(┴ 'filename'┴)──
                          ── 'filename' ──
                    ,              ,
 ──── RENAME FILE┴─'filename'┴ TO ┴─'filename'┴
 ──── CREATE STANDBY CONTROLFILE AS 'filename' REUSE ────
 ──── BACKUP CONTROLFILE TO 'filename' REUSE|TO TRACE RESETLOGS|NORESETLOGS ──
                                             ,
 ──── RENAME GLOBAL_NAME TO database ┴ . domain┘
 ──── RESET COMPATABILITY─────────────
 ──── ENABLE [PUBLIC] THREAD n────────
 ──── DISABLE THREAD n───────────
                          ,         ,
 ──── CREATE DATAFILE ┴'filename'┴ [AS ┴filespec┴]
                      ,
 ──── DATAFILE ┴ 'filename'┴
                       ── ONLINE ──
                       ── OFFLINE [DROP] ──
                       ── RESIZE n K|M──
                       ── autoextend clause ──
                       ── END BACKUP ──
```

Figure 6.1   The syntax of the **ALTER DATABASE** command.

➤ **MOUNT**—Indicates that the database is available for some DBA functions but not for normal functions. **MOUNT** has two modes: either exclusive (the default) or **PARALLEL** if the database is part of a shared server and is used with Oracle7. In an Oracle8 database, initialization parameters are used to tell Oracle whether an instance is exclusive or shared. In Oracle8, you can also mount the standby database or a clone database (used in backup and recovery). A mounted database cannot have the **CREATE CONTROLFILE** command issued against it. To use the **RENAME FILE** option in this command, you must mount the database.

➤ STANDBY DATABASE—With version 7.3 and newer, this command operates against a hot-standby database. A *hot-standby database* is one that is left in recovery mode; archive logs are automatically applied against it to keep it current. It's usually located on a second, remote server, and it acts as an automatic failover instance for the current one.

➤ CLONE DATABASE—Oracle8 provides the ability to open and mount a clone database that is used in some recovery scenarios. See *Oracle8 DBA: Backup and Recovery Exam Cram* by Debbie Wong (available April 2000 from The Coriolis Group) for more details.

➤ CONVERT—New in Oracle8, **CONVERT** is used only during an in-place conversion from version 7.x to version 8 of Oracle.

➤ OPEN—Mounts the database and opens it for general use, either with **RESETLOGS** if an incomplete recovery was performed or with **NORESETLOGS** (the default).

➤ ACTIVATE STANDBY DATABASE—Used to activate a standby database.

➤ ARCHIVELOG, NOARCHIVELOG—Turns archive logging on or off.

➤ ADD LOGFILE THREAD—Adds a thread of redo to a Parallel Server instance.

➤ filespec—A file specification in the format of:

```
'file_name' SIZE n K or M REUSE
```

where:

➤ **file_name** is an operating-system-specific full path name.

➤ SIZE n sets the size n in bytes, kilobytes, or megabytes.

➤ K or M is an integer expressed in kilobytes or megabytes.

➤ REUSE specifies to reuse the existing file if there is one. **REUSE** is optional and is used if the file specified already exists and is the proper size. If the file is not the correct size, an error will result.

➤ ADD LOGFILE MEMBER—Adds a log file member to an existing group.

➤ 'filename'—A full path file name.

➤ DROP LOGFILE—Drops an existing log group.

➤ DROP LOGFILE MEMBER—Drops an existing log member.

➤ CLEAR LOGFILE—Reinitializes a specified online redo log and, optionally, does not archive the cleared redo log. **CLEAR LOGFILE** is similar to adding and dropping a redo log except that the command can be issued even if there are only two logs for the thread; it can also be issued for the current redo log of a closed thread. **CLEAR LOGFILE** can't be used to clear a log needed for media recovery. If you have to clear a log containing a redo after the database checkpoint, then incomplete media recovery will be necessary. The current redo log of an open thread can never be cleared. The current log of a closed thread can be cleared by switching logs in the closed thread.

Note: If the CLEAR LOGFILE command is interrupted by a system or instance failure, the database may hang. If this happens, you must reissue the command after you restart the database. If the failure occurred because of I/O errors accessing one member of a log group, that member can be dropped and other members added.

UNARCHIVED must be specified if you want to reuse a redo log that was not archived. Note that specifying **UNARCHIVED** will make backups unusable if the redo log is needed for recovery.

UNRECOVERABLE DATAFILE must be specified if the tablespace has a data file offline and if the unarchived log must be cleared to bring the tablespace online. If this is the case, then the data file and the entire tablespace must be dropped after the **CLEAR LOGFILE** command completes its work.

➤ RENAME—Renames the specified database file. This command is also used when a file must be moved from one location to another because of media failure.

➤ CREATE STANDBY CONTROLFILE AS—Creates a control file for use with the standby database.

➤ BACKUP CONTROLFILE—This can be used in two ways: first, to make a recoverable backup copy of the control file (**TO 'file_name'**), and second, to make a script to rebuild the control file (**TO TRACE**). The **TO TRACE** option can also be used to create a template script that can be used, among other things, to create a database rename script and to show the procedures needed to recover if you have read-only tablespaces in the database.

➤ **RENAME GLOBAL_NAME TO**—Changes the global name of the database. A rename automatically flushes the shared pool but doesn't change data concerning your global name in remote instances, connect strings, or database links.

➤ **RESET COMPATIBILITY**—Marks the database to be reset to an earlier version of Oracle when the database is next restarted. This will render archived redo logs unusable for recovery.

Note: This option will not work unless you have successfully disabled Oracle8 features that affect backward compatibility.

➤ **ENABLE THREAD/DISABLE THREAD**—Allows the enabling and disabling of redo log threads (used only for parallel databases).

➤ **CREATE DATAFILE**—Creates a new data file in place of an old one. You can use this option to re-create a data file that was lost with no backup. The '**file_name**' must identify a file that was once a part of the database. The '**filespec**' specifies the name and size of the new data file. If you omit the **AS** clause, Oracle creates the new file with the same name and size as the file specified by '**file_name**'.

➤ **DATAFILE**—Allows you to perform manipulations—such as resizing, turning autoextend on or off, and setting backup status—against the data files in the instance.

The **ALTER DATABASE** command option that you should be most aware of is the **ALTER DATABASE BACKUP CONTROLFILE** command. Study the difference between when a control file is backed up to trace and when it's physically backed up.

When a control file is backed up to trace, a script file is created that allows the re-creation of the control file. The script created by a **BACKUP TO TRACE** command can also be used to rename an existing database or to document the steps required to recover the database, especially if read-only tablespaces are used. When a **CONTROLFILE** is backed up to a file, it can be used to re-cover the database as a backup copy of the **CONTROLFILE** at that point in time. For more details see *Oracle8 DBA: Backup and Recovery Exam Cram*.

You also need to understand when the **RESETLOGS** option is used with the **ALTER DATABASE OPEN** command. **RESETLOGS** is used only after an incomplete media recovery is performed. Whenever an **OPEN RESTLOGS** is required, you should immediately back up the database because previous archive logs won't be able to be used for future recovery operations.

The **ALTER SYSTEM** Command

A special DDL command, **ALTER SYSTEM**, is used to alter the characteristics of the actual database environment.

> *Note: Although the ALTER SYSTEM command is not actually used to modify data structures, this seems like the logical place to cover the command because it is a derivation of the ALTER command.*

The syntax of the **ALTER SYSTEM** command is shown in Figure 6.2.

The **ALTER SYSTEM** command has the following clauses and options:

➤ **ARCHIVE LOG**—Manually archives redo log files, or enables or disables automatic archiving, depending on the clause specified.

➤ **CHECKPOINT**—Performs either a **GLOBAL** (all open instances on the database) checkpoint or a **LOCAL** (current instance) checkpoint.

➤ **CHECK DATAFILES**—Verifies access to data files. If **GLOBAL** is specified, all data files in all instances accessing the database are verified accessible. If **LOCAL** is specified, only the current instance's data files are verified.

➤ **DISCONNECT SESSION**—Allows a disconnection rather than a kill of a database session.

➤ **ENABLE DISTRIBUTED RECOVERY**—Enables distributed recovery.

➤ **DISABLE DISTRIBUTED RECOVERY**—Disables distributed recovery.

➤ **ENABLE RESTRICTED SESSION**—Allows only those users with the **RESTRICTED SESSION** privilege to log in to the database.

➤ **DISABLE RESTRICTED SESSION**—Allows any user to log on to the instance.

➤ **FLUSH SHARED_POOL**—Forces a flush of nonpinned (objects not currently being used) and nonkept (objects not kept using **DBMS_SHARED_POOL** procedure) objects in the shared pool.

```
>>—— ALTER SYSTEM ——————————————————————————————————————————/
/—————————————————————————————————————————————————————————————>
            ARCHIVE LOG [archive_log_clause] ————————————————————
            CHECKPOINT GLOBALILOCAL——————————————————————
            CHECK DATAFILES GLOBALILOCAL——————————————————
            DISCONNECT SESSION 'n1, n2' POST_TRANSACTION ————————
            ENABLEIDISABLE DISTRIBUTED RECOVERY ————————————
            ENABLEIDISABLE RESTRICTED SESSION —————————————
            FLUSH SHARED_POOL——————————————————————————
            KILL SESSION 'n1, n2'————————————————————————
            SET ——————————————————————————————————————
               ALLOW_PARTIAL_SN_RESULTS=TRUEIFALSE ——————————
               BACKUP_DISK_IO_SLAVES=n DEFERRED ——————————
               BACKUP_TAPE_IO_SLAVES=TRUEIFALSE DEFERRED ——————
               CACHE_INSTANCES=n————————————————————————
               CONTROL_FILE_RECORD_KEEP_TIME=n DEFERRED————————
               DB_BLOCK_CHECKPOINT_BATCH=n————————————————
               DB_BLOCK_CHECKSUM=TRUEIFALSE————————————————
               DB_BLOCK_MAX_DIRTY_TARGET=n————————————————
               DB_FILE_MULTIBLOCK_READ_COUNT=n ————————————
               FIXED_DATE='DD_MM_YYIYYYY_MM_DD_HH24_MI_SS' ——————
               FREEZE_DB_FOR_FAST_INSTANCE_RECOVERY=TRUEIFALSE DEFERRED ——
               GC_DEFER_TIME=n————————————————————————
               GLOBAL_NAMES=TRUEIFALSE——————————————————
               HASH_MULTIBLOCK_IO_COUNT=n ————————————————
               LICENSE_MAX_SESSIONS=n——————————————————
               LICENSE_MAX_USERS=n ——————————————————————
               LICENSE_SESSIONS_WARNING=n ——————————————
               LOG_ARCHIVE_DUPLEX_DEST='text'————————————————
               LOG_ARCHIVE_MIN_SUCCEED_DEST=n ————————————
               LOG_CHECKPOINT_INTERVAL=n ——————————————————
               LOG_CHECKPOINT_TIMEOUT=n —————————————————
               LOG_SMALL_ENTRY_MAX_SIZE=n————————————————
               MAX_DUMP_FILE_SIZE=sizel'UNLIMITED' DEFERRED ——————
               MTS_DISPATCHERS mts_clause ————————————————
               MTS_SERVERS=n ——————————————————————————
               OBJECT_CACHE_MAX_SIZE_PERCENT=n DEFERRED ————————
               OBJECT_CACHE_OPTIMAL_SIZE=n DEFERRED ————————
               OPS_ADMIN_GROUP='text' ————————————————————
               PARALLEL_INSTANCE_GROUP='text' ————————————————
               PARALLEL_TRANSACTION_RESOURCE_TIMEOUT=n ————————
               PLSQL_V2_COMPATABILITY= TRUEIFALSE DEFERRED ————
               REMOTE_DEPENDENCIES_MODE=TIMESTAMPISIGNATURE ——
               RESOURCE_LIMIT=TRUEIFALSE——————————————————
               SCAN_INSTANCES=n DEFERRED ————————————————
               SORT_AREA_SIZE=n DEFERRED ————————————————
               SORT_AREA_RETAINED_SIZE=n DEFERRED ——————————
               SORT_DIRECT_WRITES=AUTOITRUEIFALSE DEFERRED ——————
               SORT_READ_FAC=n DEFERRED ————————————————
               SORT_WRITE_BUFFERS=n DEFERRED ——————————————
               SORT_WRITE_BUFFER_SIZE=n DEFERRED ——————————
               SPIN_COUNT=n DEFERRED ————————————————————
               TEXT_ENABLE=TRUEIFALSE DEFERRED ————————————
               TIMED_STATISTICS=TRUEIFALSE————————————————
               TIMED_OS_STATISTICS=n————————————————————
               TRANSACTION_AUDITING=TRUEIFALSE————————————
               USER_DUMP_DEST='dirname' ————————————————
            SWITCH LOGFILE ——————————————————————————
```

Figure 6.2   The syntax of the **ALTER SYSTEM** command.

➤ **KILL SESSION**—Kills an active database session.

➤ **SET [option]**—The **SET** clause allows many initialization parameters and other setup parameters to be dynamically altered. The following items can be altered:

➤ ALLOW_PARTIAL_SN_RESULTS—Allows partial results when viewing **gv$** internal views.

➤ BACKUP_DISK_IO_SLAVES—Sets the number of backup disk IO slaves.

➤ BACKUP_TAPE_IO_SLAVES—Sets the number of backup tape IO slaves.

➤ CACHE_INSTANCES—In parallel databases, specifies the number of instances that will cache a table.

➤ CONTROL_FILE_RECORD_KEEP_TIME—Sets the time (in days) that records are maintained in the control file before being overwritten.

➤ DB_BLOCK_CHECKPOINT_BATCH—Sets the maximum number of blocks to write in a checkpoint disk write from **DBWR**.

➤ DB_BLOCK_CHECKSUM—Stores the checksum for blocks and checks when doing reads.

➤ DB_BLOCK_MAX_DIRTY_TARGET—Sets the upper limit on the modified buffer's reads/writes during a recovery.

➤ FIXED_DATE—Sets a fixed date in the database for testing. This should not be used; a fixed date should only be used under the guidance of Oracle support.

➤ FREEZE_DB_FOR_FAST_INSTANCE_RECOVERY— Freezes the database during instance recovery to speed the recovery process.

➤ GC_DEFER_TIME—Specifies the time (in hundredths of a second) that the server waits, or defers, before responding to forced-write requests for hot blocks from other instances. Specifying the GC_DEFER_TIME parameter makes it more likely that buffers will be properly cleaned out before being written, thus making them more useful when they are read by other instances.

➤ GLOBAL_NAMES—Turns on or off global name enforcement.

➤ HASH_MULTI_BLOCK_IO_COUNT—Same as **DB_MULTI_ BLOCK_IO_COUNT**, but for hash operations. Sets the number of blocks to read during a hash operation IO to or from disk.

➤ LICENSE_MAX_SESSIONS—Resets the license limit for concurrent sessions.

➤ LICENSE_MAX_USERS—Resets the license limit for named users.

➤ LICENSE_SESSIONS_WARNING—Resets the session's license warning level.

➤ LOG_ARCHIVE_DUPLEX_DEST—Resets the duplexed archive log destination.

➤ LOG_ARCHIVE_MIN_SUCCEED_DEST—Resets the minimum percentage of logs that must reach their archive log locations.

➤ LOG_CHECKPOINT_INTERVAL—Resets the value (in disk blocks) that is used to determine when checkpoints are written.

➤ LOG_CHECKPOINT_TIMEOUT—Resets the value (in seconds) when checkpoints occur.

➤ LOG_SMALL_ENTRY_MAX_SIZE—Resets the redo log small entry maximum size used to determine when a redo entry is switched from a redo copy to an allocation latch.

➤ MAX_DUMP_FILE_SIZE—Sets the maximum server or background process dump file size in OS blocks.

➤ MTS_DISPATCHERS mts_clause—The syntax for the **mts_ clause** is **protocol** n. The *protocol* specifies the network protocol for the dispatcher(s), and the n specifies the number of dispatchers for the specified protocols, up to the value of **MAX_DISPATCHERS** (as a sum of all dispatchers under all protocols).

➤ MTS_SERVERS—The n specifies the number of shared server processes to enable, up to the value of the **MAX_SERVERS** parameter.

➤ OBJECT_CACHE_MAX_SIZE_PERCENT—Sets the percentage over optimal size allowed for a user's objects to still be considered cacheable.

➤ OBJECT_CACHE_OPTIMAL_SIZE—Sets the optimal size for a user's objects in the user's object cache.

➤ OPS_ADMIN_GROUP—Resets the instance's parallel server admin group.

➤ PARALLEL_INSTANCE_GROUP—Resets the instance's parallel instance group specification (its common management group).

➤ PARALLEL_TRANSACTION_RESOURCE_TIMEOUT—
This parameter specifies the maximum amount of time which can
pass before a session; executing a parallel operation times out while
waiting for a resource held by another instance in an incompatible
lock mode. Parameter is specified in seconds.

➤ PLSQL_V2_COMPATIBILITY—Modifies the compile-time
behavior of the PL/SQL compiler to allow the use of constructs that
are illegal in Oracle8 but allowed in earlier releases.

➤ REMOTE_DEPENDENCIES_MODE—Remote-procedure-
call (RPC) dependency mode.

➤ RESOURCE_LIMIT—Turns on or off resource limit checking.

➤ SCAN_INSTANCES—In a parallel database, specifies the number
of instances that participate in parallelized operations.

➤ SORT_AREA_SIZE—Resets the sort area size.

➤ SORT_AREA_RETAINED_SIZE—Resets the sort area
retained size.

➤ SORT_DIRECT_WRITES—For doing sort direct writes to
bypass the buffer cache during disk sort operations; allows you to
turn the option on or off or set it to automatic.

➤ SORT_READ_FAC—Allows you to reset the sort read fac area.

➤ SORT_WRITE_BUFFERS—Allows you to resize the sort buffers
used during sort direct write operations.

➤ SORT_WRITE_BUFFER_SIZE—Allows you to reset the
number of buffers used for sort direct writes.

➤ SPIN_COUNT—Allows you to reset the spin count parameter
used to control latch allocation.

➤ TEXT_ENABLE—Enables or disables text searches.

➤ TIMED_STATISTICS—Turns on or off the collection of statistics
timing information.

➤ TIMED_OS_STATISTICS—Turns on or off the collection of
OS-related timing statistics.

➤ TRANSACTION_AUDITING—Turns on or off the placing of
transaction-related auditing information in the redo log.

➤ USER_DUMP_DEST—Resets the location of the user dump and
trace file.

➤ SWITCH LOGFILE—Switches the active log file groups.

A Detailed Look At **ARCHIVE LOG** Clauses

In Oracle7 and Oracle8, the **ARCHIVE LOG** command is removed from SQLDBA and SVRMGR (except for the pull-down display) and is placed under the **ALTER SYSTEM** command. The new command has additional clauses to handle the more complex archive log scheme in Oracle7 and in Oracle8. The syntax handles the threads and groups associated with the new archive logs. The new syntax is as follows:

```
ALTER SYSTEM ARCHIVE LOG clause;
ARCHIVE LOG clauses:
     [THREAD n]
       [SEQUENCE n] [TO 'location']
       [CHANGE n] [TO 'location']
       [CURRENT] [TO 'location']
       [GROUP n] [TO 'location']
       [LOGFILE 'file_name'] [TO 'location']
       [NEXT] [TO 'location']
       [ALL] [TO 'location']
       [START] [TO 'location']
       [STOP]
```

The **ARCHIVE LOG** command has the following clauses:

➤ THREAD—Specifies the specific redo-log thread to affect. If this isn't specified, then the redo-log thread of the current instance is affected.

➤ SEQUENCE—Archives the redo log group that corresponds to the integer specified by the integer given as the argument.

➤ CHANGE—Corresponds to the System Change Number (SCN) for the transaction you want to archive. It will force archival of the log containing the transaction with the SCN that matches the integer given as the argument in the **CHANGE** argument.

➤ GROUP—Manually archives the redo logs in the specified group. If both **THREAD** and **GROUP** are specified, the group must belong to the specified thread.

➤ CURRENT—Causes all nonarchived redo-log members of the current group to be archived.

➤ LOGFILE—Manually archives the group that contains the file specified by 'filespec'. If a thread is specified, the file must be in a group contained in the thread specified.

➤ NEXT—Forces manual archival of the oldest online redo log that requires it. If no thread is specified, Oracle archives the oldest available unarchived redo-log file group.

➤ ALL—Archives all online archive logs that are part of the current thread and that haven't yet been archived. If no thread is specified, then all unarchived logs from all threads are archived.

➤ START—Starts automatic archiving of redo-log file groups. This applies only to the thread assigned to the current instance. This command also modifies the control file so that the archive status is recorded and used the next time the database is started.

➤ TO—Specifies where to archive the logs. This must be a full path specification.

➤ STOP—Disables automatic archiving of redo-file log groups. This command applies to your current instance.

You should be familiar with the **ALTER SYSTEM** command and its effects on archive logging, so you need to learn these command options backwards and forwards.

The **ALTER** Command For Tablespaces

Tablespaces can be altered to add data files, change online status, change recoverability, change backup status, and change the default storage characteristics for the tablespace. The command to perform these tablespace changes is the **ALTER TABLESPACE** command; its syntax is shown in Figure 6.3.

The **ALTER TABLESPACE** command has the following keywords and parameters:

➤ tablespace_name—Name of the tablespace to be altered.

➤ LOGGING|NOLOGGING—Turns on or off default-level logging for this tablespace. This setting is overridden by any table- or index-level logging settings.

➤ ADD DATAFILE—Adds the data file specified by 'filespec' to the tablespace. (See the syntax description of 'filespec'.) You can add a data file while the tablespace is online or offline, but be sure that the data file is not already in use by another database or the operation will fail. You should back up the control file after any change to the database's physical structure.

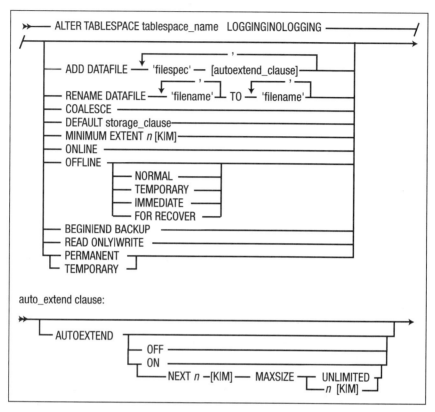

Figure 6.3 The syntax of the **ALTER TABLESPACE** command.

➤ AUTOEXTEND—Enables or disables the autoextending of the size of the data file in the tablespace. The two options for **AUTOEXTEND** are as follows:

➤ OFF—Disables **AUTOEXTEND** if it's turned on. **NEXT** and **MAXSIZE** are set to zero. Values for **NEXT** and **MAXSIZE** must be respecified in further **ALTER TABLESPACE AUTOEXTEND** commands.

➤ ON—Enables **AUTOEXTEND**.

➤ NEXT—Sets the size (in bytes) of the next increment of disk space to be automatically allocated to the data file when more extents are required. You can also use **K** or **M** to specify this size in kilobytes or megabytes. The default is one data block.

➤ MAXSIZE—Sets the maximum disk space allowed for automatic extension of the data file.

➤ UNLIMITED—Sets no limit on allocating disk space to the
   data file.

➤ RENAME DATAFILE—Renames one or more of the tablespace's data
   files. Take the tablespace offline before renaming the data file. Each
   'file_name' must fully specify a data file, using the conventions for file
   names on your operating system. This clause associates the tablespace
   with only the new file rather than the old one. The clause doesn't actually
   change the name of the operating-system file; you must change the name
   of the file through your operating system.

➤ COALESCE—Combines all contiguous free extents into larger contiguous extents for each data file in the tablespace. The space transaction for
   a **COALESCE** will not be committed until eight **ALTER TABLE-
   SPACE** commands have been executed. If **PCTINCREASE** is set to a
   nonzero value, the **SMON** process will perform this operation
   automatically.

Note: COALESCE can't be specified with any other command option.

➤ DEFAULT storage_clause—Specifies the new default storage parameters for objects subsequently created in the tablespace.

➤ MINIMUM EXTENT—Sets the size of the minimum extent for the
   entire tablespace.

➤ ONLINE—Brings the tablespace online.

➤ OFFLINE—Takes the tablespace offline and prevents further access to
   its segments. The options for **OFFLINE** are as follows:

   ➤ NORMAL—Performs a checkpoint for all data files in the
      tablespace. All of these data files must be online. You don't need to
      perform media recovery on this tablespace before bringing it back
      online, but you must use this option if the database is in
      NOARCHIVELOG mode.

   ➤ TEMPORARY—Performs a checkpoint for all online data files in
      the tablespace, but does not ensure that all files can be written. Any
      offline files may require media recovery before you bring the
      tablespace back online.

   ➤ IMMEDIATE—Does not ensure that tablespace files are available
      and does not perform a checkpoint. You must perform recovery on
      the tablespace before bringing it back online.

➤ **FOR RECOVER**—Takes offline the production database tablespaces in the recovery set. Use this option when one or more data files in the tablespace are unavailable.

The default is **NORMAL**. If you're taking a tablespace offline for a long time, you may want to reassign any users who have been assigned to the tablespace (as either a default or a temporary tablespace) to some other tablespace. Users can't allocate space for objects or sort areas in the tablespaces that are offline. You can reassign users to new default and temporary tablespaces with the **ALTER USER** command.

➤ **BEGIN BACKUP**—Signifies that an online backup is to be performed on the data files that compose this tablespace. This option doesn't prevent users from accessing the tablespace. You must use this option before beginning an online backup. You don't need to use this option on a read-only tablespace. **BEGIN BACKUP** can be used only in **ARCHIVELOG** mode. The **BEGIN BACKUP** command suspends updates to the header block of the data files for the referenced tablespace, and changes to any block for the tablespace cause the entire block to be written to the redo log the first time it is changed, and then change vectors are written from then on.

While the backup is in progress, you can't:

➤ Take the tablespace offline normally.

➤ Shut down the instance.

➤ Begin another backup of the tablespace.

➤ **END BACKUP**—Signifies that an online backup of the tablespace is complete. Use this option as soon as possible after completing an online backup. If a tablespace is left in **BACKUP** mode, the database will think it needs recovery the next time the database is shut down and started, and you might not be able to recover. You don't need to use this option on a read-only tablespace, and this option can't be specified unless the database is in **ARCHIVELOG** mode.

➤ **READ ONLY**—Signifies that no further write operations are allowed on the tablespace. Read-only tablespaces provide two benefits: After the initial data backup, the data no longer has to be backed up, and no redo or rollback is generated in the use of read-only tablespaces.

➤ **READ WRITE**—Signifies that write operations are allowed on a previously read-only tablespace.

➤ PERMANENT—Specifies that the tablespace is to be converted from a temporary one to a permanent one. A permanent tablespace is one in which permanent database objects are stored. This is the default when a tablespace is created.

➤ TEMPORARY—Specifies that the tablespace is to be converted from a permanent to a temporary one. A temporary tablespace is one in which no permanent database objects can be stored.

At least one of the lines following the **ALTER TABLESPACE** command must be supplied. The definitions for most of the arguments are the same as those for the **CREATE** command.

The **COALESCE** clause, for those tablespaces in which **SMON** doesn't clean up free space (that is, any tablespace with a default storage option **PCTINCREASE** of zero), forces a scavenge of free segments.

The **ALTER** Command For Tables

Tables can be altered to add columns; change column types and lengths; or add, change, or drop column or table constraints. A table's storage characteristics can also be altered (for subsequent extents or data blocks only). The syntax of the **ALTER TABLE** command is shown in Figure 6.4.

The **ALTER TABLE** command has the following parameters:

➤ add_column_options—Allows you to add a column or constraint to a table or cluster table. You cannot add columns to a nested table.

➤ modify_column_options—Allows you to modify the definition of an existing column. You cannot modify columns of an index-only table.

➤ physical_attributes_clause—Allows you to modify the following physical attributes: **PCTFREE, PCTUSED, PCTINCREASE, MAXEXTENTS, INITRANS, MAXTRANS,** and **NEXT**. Changes to any of these affect only new blocks, not existing blocks, in a table.

➤ LOGGING|NOLOGGING—Allows you to reset the logging attribute of the table.

➤ LOB_storage_clause—Allows you to modify the **LOB** storage associated with the table.

➤ nested_table_storage_clause—Allows you to reset the nested storage table storage for a nested table.

➤ drop_clause—used to drop an integrity constraint.

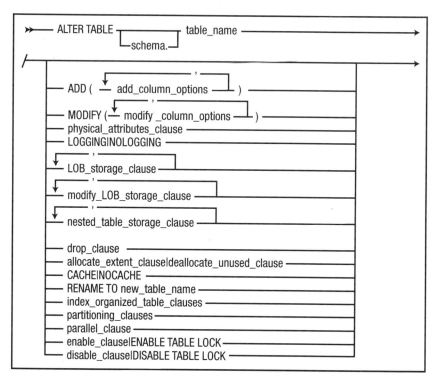

Figure 6.4 The syntax of the **ALTER TABLE** command.

➤ **allocate_extent_clause**—Allows you to force the allocation of a new table extent and to specify its location.

➤ **deallocate_unused_clause**—Used to deallocate unused extents from a table.

➤ **CACHE|NOCACHE**—When set to **CACHE**, causes the table to be maintained in the most recently used side of the LRU list.

➤ **RENAME**—Takes the place of the **RENAME** command in previous releases and allows renaming of the table.

➤ **index_organized_table_clauses**—Allows you to specify that this table is an index-only table.

➤ **partitioning_clauses**—Allows you to modify the table's partitions, if it has any.

➤ **parallel_clause**—Allows you to turn on and off parallel activities on the table, and allows you to set the degree of parallelism for the table. The **parallel_clause** has the syntax shown in Figure 6.5.

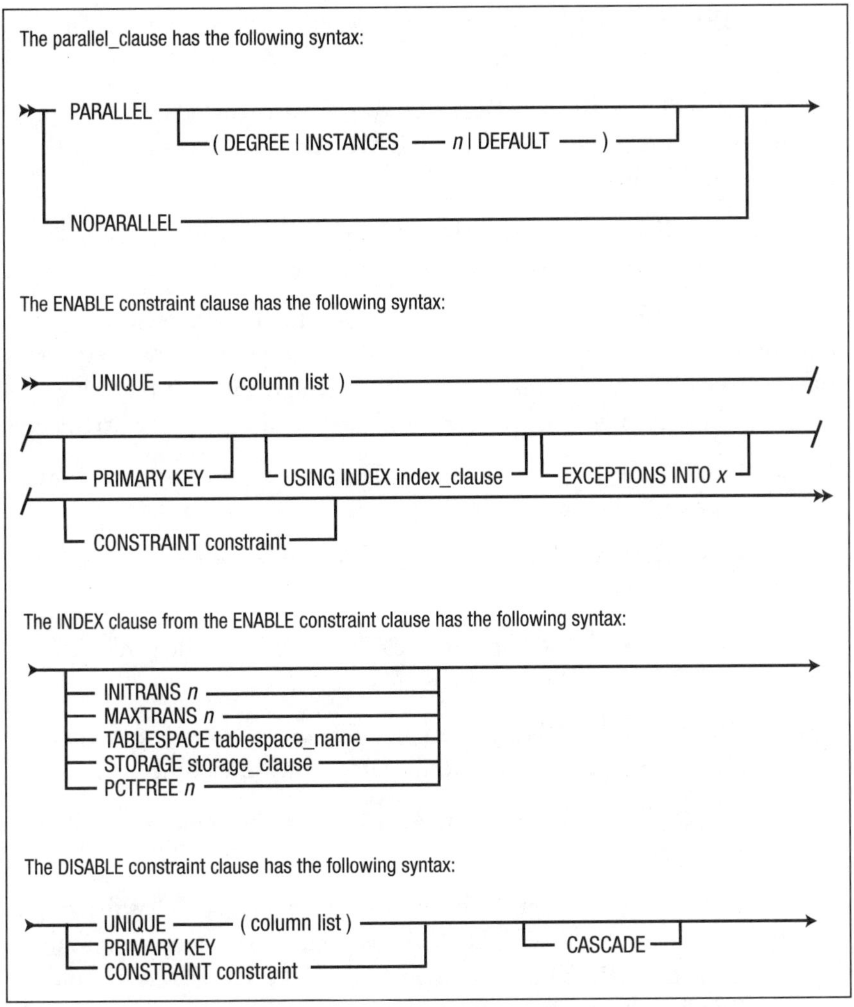

The parallel_clause has the following syntax:

The ENABLE constraint clause has the following syntax:

The INDEX clause from the ENABLE constraint clause has the following syntax:

The DISABLE constraint clause has the following syntax:

Figure 6.5   The syntax of some of the **ALTER TABLE** command's clauses.

The **PARALLEL** clause has the following parameters:

➤ **DEGREE**—Specifies that this is a parallel query operation. The n, an integer value, tells the number of parallel query slaves to allocate for a single level of parallel operations on this object. Note that multiples of this value may be used if the operation involves sorting.

➤ **INSTANCES**—Specifies this is a parallel server object where n (an integer) specifies the number of parallel instances to use to cache the object.

➤ DEFAULT—Specifies to use the default settings for degree of parallel for the instance.

➤ ENABLE/DISABLE TABLE LOCK—Clauses that allow you to turn on and off the capability of placing DML and DDL locks in a parallel server environment.

The **ENABLE** constraint clause of the **ALTER TABLE** command has the syntax shown in Figure 6.5.

The **ENABLE** clause is used to enable constraints. When enabling a primary key or unique key, always specify the **index_clause** and especially the **TABLESPACE** clause to prevent the required index from being created in the table's tablespace. The clause has the following parameters:

➤ UNIQUE—Enables the column list as a unique constraint creating the required index.

➤ PRIMARY KEY—Enables the primary key constraint (if any) defined on the table.

➤ USING INDEX—Used to specify the index-specific parameters for **UNIQUE** and **PRIMARY KEY** indexes.

➤ EXCEPTIONS INTO *x*—Sends data on any rows not meeting the constraint requirements into the table represented by *x*.

➤ CONSTRAINT constraint—Enables the constraint named by the clause.

The **INDEX** clause from the **ENABLE** constraint clause has the syntax shown in Figure 6.5. The **INDEX** clause parameters are the same as those defined in the **CREATE TABLE** and **CREATE INDEX** commands. The **DISABLE** constraint clause has the syntax shown in Figure 6.5

Specifying the **CASCADE** option with either **DISABLE** or **DROP** allows Oracle to cascade the operation to all dependent integrity constraints. **DISABLE** turns a constraint off (note that for **UNIQUE** and **PRIMARY KEY** constraints, this also drops the related indexes). **ENABLE** or **ADD** turns a constraint on or creates it. For **UNIQUE** or **PRIMARY KEY** constraints, an index will be created. If the index clause is not specified, the index is created in the default tablespace of the creator with the default storage characteristics of that tablespace.

ALTER TABLE Specifics

The following are tasks you can accomplish with the **ALTER TABLE** command:

➤ Use the **ADD** clause to add columns that have null values to any table.

➤ Use the **MODIFY** clause to increase the size of columns or to change the precision of numeric columns.

➤ Use the **MODIFY** clause to change columns with all null values so that the columns are shorter or have a different data type.

➤ Alter the **PCTFREE, PCTUSED, INITRANS,** or **MAXTRANS** values for any table.

➤ Use the **STORAGE** clause to alter the storage parameters for any table.

➤ Use the **PARALLEL** clause to change or remove the parallelism of a table.

➤ Use **CACHE** or **NOCACHE** to specify whether a table is to be cached or not.

➤ Use the **DROP** clause to remove a constraint.

➤ Use the **DEFAULT** value clause to add a default value to any column.

➤ Use the **DISABLE** clause to disable a constraint. (This is the only way to disable a constraint.) When the **CASCADE** option is specified with **DISABLE,** it also disables all dependent integrity constraints.

➤ Use the **DEALLOCATE UNUSED** clause to deallocate space that is not being used. (You can use the **KEEP** option to specify a safety margin above the high-water mark.)

➤ Use the **ENABLE** clause to enable a constraint that was created as disabled. (The **ENABLE** clause can be used only in **CREATE** and **ALTER TABLE** commands.)

➤ Use the **ADD CONSTRAINT** clause to add a primary, not null, check, or foreign key constraint to an existing table.

The things you can't do with the **ALTER TABLE** command include:

➤ Modify a column that has values to be shorter or to be a different data type than it already is.

➤ Add a **NOT NULL** column to a table that has rows in a single step operation with only the **ALTER TABLE** command.

➤ Alter a column to **NOT NULL** if it has rows with null values in that column.

➤ Rename a column.

➤ Drop a column.

➤ Change a column's data type to an incompatible data type.

The **ALTER TABLE** command also allows the allocation of new extents with specification of size and placement (in different tablespaces, if desired) and deallocation of unused extents. When you deallocate unused extents, the bytes reserved for future inserts above the high-water mark are set using the **KEEP** clause of the **DEALLOCATE** clause.

If a table will grow at a rate that makes calculation of exact sizing difficult, increase the value of the **PCTINCREASE** parameter. Usually I suggest doing space calculations as accurately as possible, applying a 50 percent fudge factor to allocate enough space, and setting **PCTINCREASE** to zero. However, in some situations, the only way to handle extreme table growth is to use a high **PCTINCREASE**.

In this chapter, I've covered the clauses that it's most important that you know. For details on clauses that haven't been covered in detail, see the references at the end of the chapter.

The **ALTER** Command For Clusters

Clusters are altered with the **ALTER CLUSTER** command. With this command, you can change only the sizing and storage parameters; you cannot add or remove columns. The syntax of the command is shown in Figure 6.6.

The definitions for the **ALTER CLUSTER** parameters are the same as those for the **CREATE TABLE, CREATE CLUSTER,** and storage clause parameters.

You need to know only how these parameters relate to tables.

The **ALTER** Command For Indexes

Indexes are altered with the **ALTER INDEX** command. Indexes can have their physical storage clauses altered, and they can be rebuilt. You can't add, modify, or remove columns from an existing index by using the **ALTER INDEX**

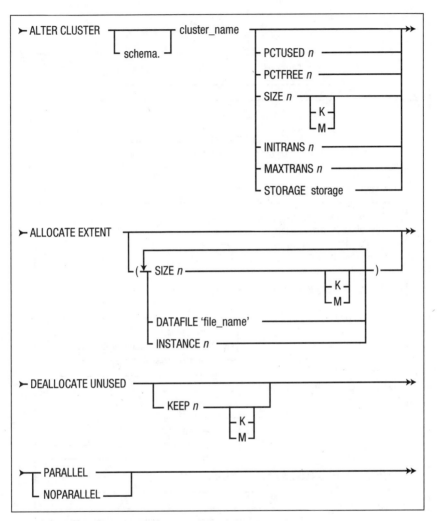

Figure 6.6   The syntax of the **ALTER CLUSTER** command.

command. To change an index's columns, you must drop and re-create the index. The syntax of the **ALTER INDEX** command is shown in Figure 6.7.

The parameters for the **index_physical_attributes_clause** are zero or one or more of the following:

➤ **PCTFREE** *n*

➤ **INITRANS** *n*

➤ **MAXTRANS** *n*

➤ **STORAGE** *storage_clause*

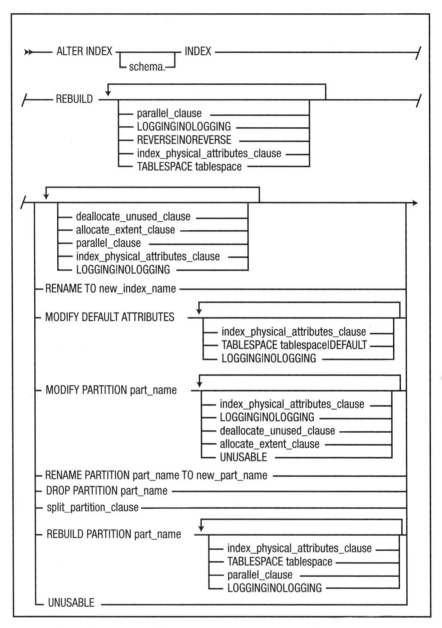

Figure 6.7 The syntax of the **ALTER INDEX** command.

For the **ALTER INDEX** command, the parameters are the same as those for the **CREATE TABLE** command, with the exception of the **REBUILD** clause. The **REBUILD** clause allows the specified index to be rebuilt on the fly in versions 7.3.x and newer databases.

The major uses of the **ALTER INDEX** command are to deallocate oversized index space, to change the storage characteristics of an existing index, or to rebuild existing indexes. Notice that you can use the **TABLESPACE** clause to move an index from its existing location to a new location.

 It's not important for you to know the partition-related additions to the **ALTER INDEX** command (including the **UNUSABLE** clause), so they're not discussed here. For details on clauses that haven't been covered in detail, see the references at the end of the chapter.

The **ALTER** Command For Sequences

Sequences can be altered to change minimum, maximum, caching, and increment values. The syntax of the **ALTER SEQUENCE** command is shown in Figure 6.8.

Only future sequence numbers are affected by the **ALTER SEQUENCE** command. To alter the **START WITH** clause, you must drop and re-create the sequence. For ascending sequences, the **MAXVALUE** can't be less than the current sequence value. For descending sequences, the **MINVALUE** can't be greater than the current sequence value.

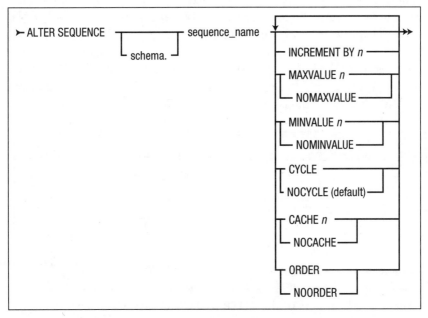

Figure 6.8 The syntax of the **ALTER SEQUENCE** command.

The **ALTER** Command For Rollback Segments

The only items that can be altered for a rollback segment are the items that deal with storage characteristics or rollback-segment status and size. Rollback segments can be altered to affect the **NEXT**, **OPTIMAL**, and **MAXEXTENTS** storage parameters. Rollback segments can be taken offline or placed online. Using the **SHRINK** clause, you can shrink rollback segments either to a specified size or to the value of **OPTIMAL** if the size isn't specified. The syntax of the **ALTER ROLLBACK SEGMENT** command is shown in Figure 6.9.

Although you can't change a view by using an **ALTER** command, you can re-create it without loss of privilege grants by using the **CREATE OR REPLACE** command. So, to alter a view, you must redefine the entire specification for the view by using the **CREATE OR REPLACE** command. Using this command removes the need to first drop the view and then re-create it and regrant privileges.

The **COMMENT** Command

Although the **COMMENT** command may not be a true DDL command, it fits in with the **ALTER** commands, so I'll cover it here. The **COMMENT** command adds comments—at the table, view, or column levels—to the data dictionary. The comments entered with the **COMMENT** command can be seen by using the **DBA_TAB_COMMENTS** and **DBA_COL_COMMENTS** views or their related **USER_** and **ALL_** series of views. The syntax of the **COMMENT** command is shown in Figure 6.10.

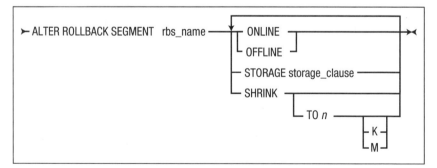

Figure 6.9 The syntax of the **ALTER ROLLBACK SEGMENT** command.

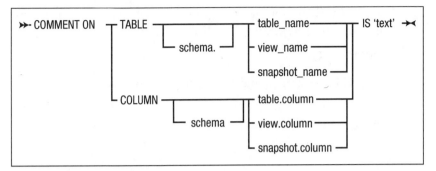

Figure 6.10   The syntax of the **COMMENT** command.

Using the **COMMENT** command is an excellent way to document your application tables, views, snapshots, and columns internally, so a simple query using the **DBA_, USER_,** or **ALL_** views will produce documentation concerning the purpose of a table, view, snapshot, or individual column.

The **DROP** Command

The only way to drop an object (other than an index explicitly tied to a constraint) is to use the **DROP** command. The **DROP** command is used to remove tables, indexes, clusters, tablespaces, sequences, stored objects, and synonyms. Any command that frees up space—such as a **DROP** command, a **TRUNCATE** command, or an **ALTER** command with a **DEALLOCATE** clause—can result in tablespace fragmentation. The general syntax of a **DROP** command is shown in Figure 6.11.

The **DROP** command has the following options:

➤ **object_type**—Type of object to drop. Accepted object types are:

   ➤ TABLE (can use **CASCADE CONSTRAINTS**)

   ➤ TABLESPACE (can use **INCLUDING CONTENTS**)

   ➤ USER (can use **CASCADE**)

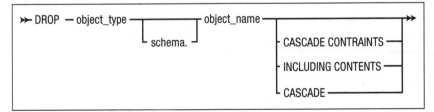

Figure 6.11   General syntax of the **DROP** command.

➤ PACKAGE (only entire packages or package bodies; you can't drop individual package items)

➤ PROCEDURE

➤ FUNCTION (only standalone; you can't drop individual package items)

➤ TRIGGER

➤ SYNONYM

➤ DATABASE LINK

➤ VIEW

➤ TYPE

➤ schema—Owner of the object to be dropped (usually required only if you are not the owner; then, you must have adequate **DROP** privileges against the object or have been granted the privilege database wide with the **DROP ANY...** type privilege).

➤ object_name—Name of the object to be dropped.

➤ CASCADE CONSTRAINTS—Tells Oracle to drop any related foreign key constraint for a parent table. If **ON DELETE CASCADE** is in effect, all related rows will also be dropped from child tables.

➤ INCLUDING CONTENTS—Forces a drop for tablespaces and their objects, even if the tablespace still contains objects.

➤ CASCADE—Allows users who still have objects in the database to be dropped. This option drops the users' objects along with the users.

A **DROP** command is a DDL command and can't be rolled back. Any dropped object must be re-created if the **DROP** command was issued in error. If you find yourself frequently dropping and creating the same table, consider making the table permanent and just issuing **TRUNCATE** commands. If a table that is frequently created and dropped is shared among several users, add a trigger to populate a session identifier (**sessionid**) column and then just delete the rows from that user when the user is finished.

Practice Questions

Question 1

> Which SQL command syntax would you use to remove the view **parts_vu**?
>
> ○ a. **DELETE VIEW parts_vu;**
>
> ○ b. **DELETE parts_vu;**
>
> ○ c. **DROP parts_vu;**
>
> ○ d. **DROP VIEW parts_vu;**

The correct answer is d; it's the only one of the listed commands that uses the correct syntax. Answer a has incorrect syntax. Answer b will delete the data contained in the underlying tables for view **parts_vu** if the criteria allowing deletion are fulfilled. Answer c doesn't supply the **object_type** required by the syntax for the **DROP** command.

Question 2

> Evaluate this SQL command:
>
> ```
> ALTER TABLESPACE users COALESCE;
> ```
>
> Which background process performs the same task?
>
> ○ a. **PMON**
>
> ○ b. **SMON**
>
> ○ c. **DBWR**
>
> ○ d. **LGWR**

The correct answer is b, **SMON**. **SMON** performs space management as part of its system monitoring tasks. Answer a is incorrect because **PMON** cleans up process-related areas and does no space management at the system level. Answer c, **DBWR**, is incorrect because **DBWR** performs dirty buffer writes and does no space management functions at all. Answer d, **LGWR**, is incorrect because **LGWR** writes out the log buffer and checkpoint data but performs no space management functions.

Question 3

> Which two parameters are storage parameters for rollback segments and can be altered? [Choose two]
>
> ❑ a. **NEXT**
> ❑ b. **PCTINCREASE**
> ❑ c. **OPTIMAL**
> ❑ d. **FREELISTS**
> ❑ e. **ROLLBACK_SEGMENTS**

The correct answers are a, **NEXT**, and c, **OPTIMAL**. Answer b is incorrect because since Oracle7.3, **PCTINCREASE** is no longer a modifiable parameter for rollback segments; it's set to zero and can't be changed. Answer d is incorrect because **FREELISTS** aren't set for rollback segments. Answer e is incorrect because **ROLLBACK_SEGMENTS** is an initialization parameter for the instance, not a storage parameter for rollback segments.

Question 4

> When you're altering a table, which parameter indicates the number of bytes above the high-water mark that the table will have after space deallocation?
>
> ○ a. **ENABLE**
> ○ b. **DEALLOCATE UNUSED**
> ○ c. **KEEP**
> ○ d. **ALLOCATE EXTENT SIZE**

The correct answer is c, **KEEP**. Answer a is incorrect because **ENABLE** is used to enable constraints or triggers and has nothing to do with space management. Answer b, although dealing with space management, has nothing to do with the amount of space retained above the high-water mark. Answer d concerns extent allocation, not deallocation, so it, too, is incorrect.

Question 5

> A change to which storage parameter will affect only subsequently added data blocks?
>
> ○ a. **INITRANS**
>
> ○ b. **MAXTRANS**
>
> ○ c. **INITIAL**
>
> ○ d. **MINEXTENTS**

The correct answer is a, **INITRANS**. Answer b, **MAXTRANS**, will apply to all extents, not just subsequently added ones. Answers c and d, **INITIAL** and **MINEXTENTS**, are set when the object is created; they can't be changed unless the object is dropped and re-created.

Question 6

> Which clause would you use in an **ALTER TABLE** command to drop a column from a table?
>
> ○ a. **REMOVE**
>
> ○ b. **DROP**
>
> ○ c. **DELETE**
>
> ○ d. **ALTER**
>
> ○ e. A column can't be dropped from a table.

The proper answer is e because you can't drop a column from a table. This is a trick question that is actually testing whether you know what can and can't be done to a table. Answers a through d are all incorrect because you can't drop a column from a table, but also for the following reasons: answer a is incorrect because there's no **REMOVE** clause in an **ALTER TABLE** command; answer b is incorrect because **DROP** is used only to drop a constraint; answer c is incorrect because there's no **DELETE** option for the **ALTER TABLE** command; and answer d is incorrect because there's no **ALTER** clause for the **ALTER TABLE** command.

Question 7

You alter the database with this command:

```
ALTER TABLE inventory
MODIFY (price NUMBER(8,2) DEFAULT 0);
```

Which task was accomplished? [Choose the best answer]

○ a. A new column was added to the table.

○ b. A column constraint was added to the table.

○ c. A column was altered.

○ d. A default value was added to a column.

The correct answer is d. This is also a trick question because from common understandings (or perhaps I should say, misunderstandings), there are several correct answers. However, only d is the right answer. Answer a is incorrect because the code uses a **MODIFY** clause, which works only on existing columns. Answer b may be considered correct in some circles because the default value is considered a constraint in some references and is viewed with the same views as other constraints, but this answer is not technically correct. Answer c might also be correct, but because we don't have an exhibit to compare the **NUMBER(8,2)** with, we can't be sure, so we must assume that this answer is also incorrect. The only answer that is 100 percent correct is answer d.

Question 8

> Which **ALTER** statement would you use to add a primary key constraint on the **manufacturer_id** column of the inventory table?
>
> ○ a.
> ```
> ALTER TABLE INVENTORY
> MODIFY manuacturer_id CONSTRAINT PRIMARY KEY;
> ```
> ○ b.
> ```
> ALTER TABLE inventory
> MODIFY CONSTRAINT PRIMARY KEY manufacturer_id;
> ```
> ○ c.
> ```
> ALTER TABLE inventory
> ADD CONSTRAINT PRIMARY KEY (manufacturer_id);
> ```
> ○ d.
> ```
> ALTER TABLE inventory
> ADD CONSTRAINT manufacturer_id PRIMARY KEY;
> ```

The correct answer is c. Answer a is incorrect because it uses the incorrect syntax. Only a **NOT NULL** constraint can be added or removed by using a column constraint syntax in an **ALTER TABLE** command. Answer b is incorrect because you can't modify a constraint. Besides, looking at the question, it says to *add* a primary key. Answer d is incorrect because it doesn't specify the column with **PRIMARY KEY**. If a column had been specified in answer d, a primary key constraint named **manufacturer_id** would have been created.

Question 9

> You logged on to the database to update the inventory table. After your session began, you issued three **UPDATE** commands; then, you issued an **ALTER TABLE** command to add a column constraint. You were just about to issue a **COMMIT** command when the system crashed. Which changes were made to the inventory table?
>
> ○ a. Only the **UPDATE** commands
>
> ○ b. Only the **ALTER TABLE** command
>
> ○ c. Both the **UPDATE** commands and the **ALTER TABLE** command
>
> ○ d. None

The correct answer is c. This is almost a trick question because the question is checking whether or not you understand that an implicit commit is issued before and after each DDL command. Answer a is incorrect because we know that the **UPDATE** preceded the **ALTER TABLE**, and the **ALTER TABLE** does an implicit commit, committing both sets of operations. Answer b is incorrect because we know that the **UPDATE** commands that preceded the **ALTER TABLE** command were covered by its implicit commit. Answer d is incorrect because we know that a DDL command always does an implicit commit, so both sets of operations were committed.

Question 10

You issue this command:

```
ALTER TABLESPACE
ADD DATAFILE 'e:\oracle5\data\ortest1\data02.dbf'
    SIZE 10m;
```

What is the result of this command on the database?

○ a. There is none.

○ b. A tablespace is added.

○ c. The physical database configuration is altered.

○ d. The logical database configuration is altered.

The correct answer is c. Answer a is incorrect because the database is affected. Answer b is incorrect because the code is altering an existing tablespace, not adding a new one. Answer d is incorrect because the code is altering an existing tablespace's physical configuration, not changing its logical one.

Question 11

What does the **COMMENT ON TABLE** command do?

○ a. Assigns a table alias.

○ b. Adds a comment column to a table.

○ c. Adds a comment about a column to the data dictionary.

○ d. Adds a comment about a table to the data dictionary.

The correct answer is d. Answer a is incorrect because alias assignment is done only in DML, not DDL, statements. Answer b is incorrect because a column can be added to a table only by using the **ALTER TABLE** command. Answer c is incorrect because the **COMMENT ON COLUMN** command, not the **COMMENT ON TABLE** command, is used to insert column comments into the database data dictionary.

Need To Know More?

Ault, Michael R. *Oracle8 Administration and Management.* John Wiley & Sons, New York, New York, 1998. ISBN 0-471-19234-1. This book provides a comprehensive look at Oracle8 and Oracle7.x management. Use it for command syntax definitions for all **CREATE** commands. The book also contains numerous examples for partitions, index-only tables, and nested tables, as well as for the new object features.

Ault, Michael R. *Oracle8 Black Book.* The Coriolis Group, Scottsdale, Arizona, 1998. ISBN 1-57610-187-8. This how-to book on Oracle8's new features provides extensive examples using all features of Oracle8, including LOBs and JAVA.

Honour, Dalberth, and Mehta Kaplan. *Oracle8 How-To.* Waite Group Press, Corte Madera, California, 1998. ISBN 1-57169-123-5. An excellent book for how-to information on all aspects of Oracle8.

Oracle8 Server SQL Reference, Release 8.0, Volumes 1 and 2. Oracle Corporation, Redwood Shores, California, June 1997. Part No. A54648-01 and A54649-01. This is the source book for all Oracle SQL for version 8. All Oracle documentation is available online at **http://technet.oracle.com**. Membership is free.

DCL Commands

Terms you'll need to understand:

√ Grants

√ System privileges

√ Object privileges

√ Roles

√ Profiles

Techniques you'll need to master:

√ Creation and management of users

√ Granting system and object privileges

√ Revoking grants

√ The use of roles

√ Understanding the use of profiles for password and resource management

Database access begins with the creation of user records. The users are then assigned—either directly or through roles—specific rights to perform actions. The rights to perform actions are called *system* and *object privileges*. System privileges are rights to perform actions in the database. Object privileges are access rights to an object (table, index, synonym, procedure, and so on) within the database, including the columns within tables.

In this chapter, I'll explain how you use object and system privileges, along with roles, to manage users and objects. In the process of explaining the use of the Data Control Language (DCL) commands, I will also cover the creation, alteration, and dropping of users. Although this will involve some inclusion of DDL commands, I believe this will not be catastrophic because the DDL involved is central to the DCL commands discussed.

Users

For a user to access your database, an account must be created in the Oracle database for the user. The exceptions to this are the SYS and SYSTEM users that are created by Oracle when the database is created. In the sections that follow, I will discuss the creation, alteration, and dropping of users for the Oracle database.

Creating Users

To create a user, you must have the **CREATE USER** privilege. You can create users with Server Manager or at the command line in SQL*Plus. The command syntax for creating a user is illustrated in Figure 7.1.

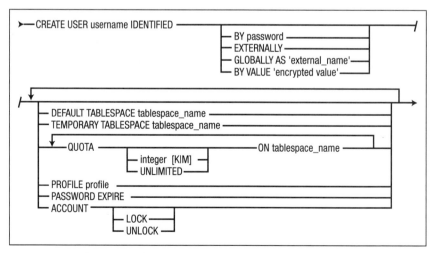

Figure 7.1   The syntax for creating a user.

Here is an example:

```
CREATE USER  james  IDENTIFIED BY    abc1
DEFAULT TABLESPACE  users
TEMPORARY TABLESPACE  temp
PASSWORD EXPIRE
QUOTA  1M ON  users
PROFILE  enduser  ;
```

You need to assign each new user a password or indicate that operating system authentication will be used. Passwords are stored in the database in encrypted format and cannot be read by any user. The use of operating system authentication means that once a user has logged in at the operating system level, no username or password will be required when that user logs in to the Oracle database. Users who are not assigned an Oracle password are designated as **IDENTIFIED EXTERNALLY**. Oracle depends on the operating system for authentication of the user. To use external authentication with other than the default username prefix of "OPS$", you must set the **OS_AUTHENT_PREFIX** in the database parameter file. In Oracle8, you can also create the user in a locked state or with a pre-expired password. The **BY VALUE** clause allows you to reset a user's password to a previous encrypted value; this clause is used when you're transferring a user manually from one database to another.

Password expiry options are set using a **PROFILE**, which I will discuss later.

The **IDENTIFIED GLOBALLY** clause is used to tell Oracle that the user authentication is obtained from a central authority, such as the Oracle Security Server.

When you create a user, you can designate a specific tablespace to be the *default tablespace* for that user. The designation of a default tablespace means that all the objects created by that user will be placed in that tablespace unless the user specifically indicates that the database object be placed in another tablespace. If no default tablespace is indicated for a user, the system tablespace will be the default for that user.

When you create a user, you can also designate a specific tablespace to be the *temporary tablespace*. The temporary tablespace is used for any database actions that require the use of a workspace for storing intermediate results of actions such as sorting.

If no temporary tablespace is indicated for a user, the system tablespace will be used. When you designate a default tablespace, a temporary tablespace, or a quota on a tablespace, this does not implicitly grant any system or object privileges on the default tablespace, but the user is granted unlimited quota on the designated temporary tablespace. You can use the **QUOTA** clause to give a user permission to create objects in tablespaces.

> *Note: I suggest that the only users who are left with the system tablespace as their default tablespace are users—such as SYS and DBSNMP—that are created and maintained internally by Oracle processes. All users should have an explicitly assigned temporary tablespace to prevent sorting from occurring in the system tablespace.*

As the database administrator (DBA), you can access the **DBA_USERS** view for information on all users. Each user can access the **USER_USERS** view (which is the same as the **DBA_USERS** view except it leaves out the password field) for information related to them. Table 7.1 shows the data stored in the **DBA_USERS** view.

To enable a user to create objects in a tablespace, you need to specify a quota for that user on that tablespace. The tablespace quota can be limited to a specific number of kilobytes or megabytes, or can be designated as unlimited. An unlimited quota indicates that the user can have any portion of a tablespace that is not already in use by another user. If the user is not assigned the **UNLIMITED TABLESPACE** system privilege and the assigned limit is reached, the user will no longer be able to create additional objects or insert rows into any objects he owns in that tablespace. One thing to remember is that the

Table 7.1 Data dictionary views for user data.	
Column	Definition
DBA_USERS	
username	Oracle login name for the user
user_id	Oracle unique user id number
password	An encrypted password or **IDENTIFIED EXTERNALLY**
account_status	The account status when password expiry functions are used
lock_date	Date that the expiry function locked the account
expiry_date	Date that the password will expire if expiry parameters are set
default_tablespace	Tablespace assigned as the default for the user
temporary_tablespace	Tablespace assigned for actions requiring a workspace
created	Date that the user was created within the Oracle database

RESOURCE and DBA roles automatically grant **UNLIMITED TABLE-SPACE,** so use them only when they're absolutely required.

The **DBA_TS_QUOTAS** view provides tablespace quota information for all users in the database. The **USER_TS_QUOTAS** view provides tablespace quota information for the current user and contains the same information without user name, because it is restricted to the user who queries the view. When you query **DBA_TS_QUOTAS** or **USER_TS_QUOTAS,** a designation of −1 in the **max_bytes** and **max_blocks** columns indicates that the user has unlimited quota on that tablespace. Table 7.2 shows the data dictionary views associated with quotas.

Altering Users

To change a user record, you must have the **ALTER USER** privilege. You can alter users with Oracle Enterprise Manager (OEM) or at the command line in SQL*Plus or svrmgrl. The command line syntax for altering a user is shown in Figure 7.2.

Here is an example:

```
ALTER  USER bill IDENTIFIED BY  xyz2
DEFAULT TABLESPACE  users
TEMPORARY TABLESPACE temp
QUOTA  1M  ON  users
PROFILE  enduser
DEFAULT ROLE ALL
ACCOUNT UNLOCK;
```

Table 7.2 Data dictionary view **DBA_TS_QUOTAS.**	
Column	**Definition**
DBA_TS_QUOTAS	
tablespace_name	Name of the tablespace
username	Name of the user
bytes	Number of bytes assigned to that user
blocks	Number of blocks assigned to that user
max_bytes	Maximum number of bytes allowed for the user, or -1 for unlimited
max_blocks	Maximum number of blocks allowed for the user, or -1 for unlimited

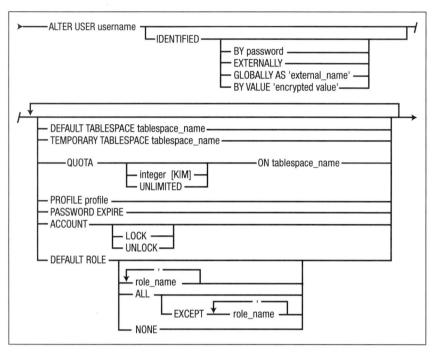

Figure 7.2   The syntax for altering a user.

After a user is created, the only thing that a person with **ALTER USER** privilege cannot alter for that user is the username. The password, default tablespace, temporary tablespace, quota on a tablespace, profile, locked state, global name, password expiration state, and default role can all be altered by someone with the **ALTER USER** system privilege.

Each user can alter the Oracle password you initially assigned to that user record when you created it, provided that the user is not identified externally (via the operating system). In addition to the end user, users with the **ALTER USER** system privilege can issue the **ALTER USER** command to change any user's password. The use of operating system authentication can also be changed by a user with the **ALTER USER** system privilege. Any changes to the password will take effect the next time that user logs in to Oracle.

When you change the default tablespace for a user, all future objects created by that user will be created in the new default tablespace you designated (unless otherwise specified by the user when the object is created). Remember that the user must have a quota in the tablespace to create new objects in that tablespace. If a user reaches the maximum number of bytes assigned (specified in the quota), then only a user with the **ALTER USER** system privileges will be able to increase the quota limit for the user.

Dropping Users

To drop a user, you must have the **DROP USER** system privilege. You can drop users with Server Manager or at the command line in SQL*Plus. The command line syntax for dropping a user is illustrated in Figure 7.3.

Here is an example:

```
DROP  USER  edward  CASCADE;
```

If a user owns any database objects, you can drop that user only by including the **CASCADE** keyword in the **DROP USER** command. The **DROP USER** command with the **CASCADE** keyword drops the user and all objects owned by that user. If you are using Server Manager to drop a user, you need to indicate that the associated schema objects be included in the command to drop the user. If a user owns objects and you fail to include **CASCADE**, you will receive an error message, and the user will not be dropped. If a user is currently connected to the database, you cannot drop that user until he exits. After a user is dropped, all information on that user and all objects owned by that user are removed from the database.

After you have issued the command to drop a user, you cannot perform a rollback to re-create the user and his objects. **DROP USER** is a DDL command, which cannot be rolled back.

If you need the objects created by a user you want to drop, you can revoke the **CREATE SESSION** system privilege to prevent the user from logging on, instead of dropping the user. You can also copy the objects to another user by importing the objects from an export made before you drop the user. To prevent the problem of dropping a user without losing your application tables, all application tables should be owned by a separate application schema instead of by an actual database user schema.

Grants

Two types of privileges can be granted:

➤ System privileges

➤ Object privileges

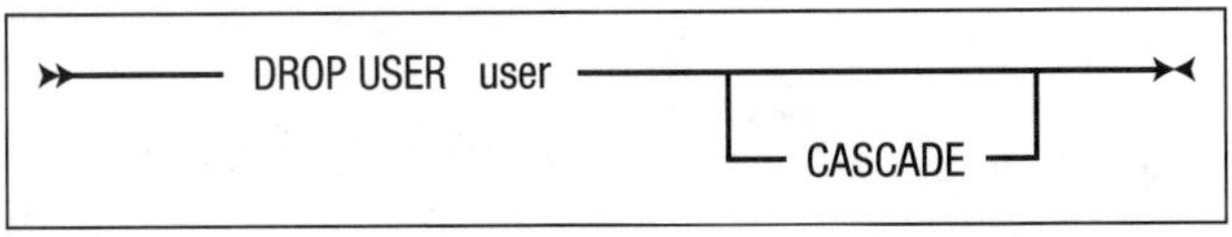

Figure 7.3   The syntax for the **DROP USER** command.

System privileges enable a user to perform a particular system-wide action or to perform a particular action on a particular type of object. For example, the privilege to create a table (**CREATE TABLE**) or to insert rows into any table (**INSERT ANY TABLE**) are system privileges.

Object privileges enable a user to perform a particular action on a specific object, including tables, views, sequences, procedures, functions, and packages. For example, the privilege to insert rows into a particular table is an object privilege. Object privilege grants always include the name of the object for which the privilege is granted. Object privileges extend down to the level of individual columns in a table. These privileges are discussed in the following sections.

System Privileges

All users require the **CREATE SESSION** privilege to access the database. This privilege is automatically granted to all users in the **CONNECT** role grant when you use Oracle Enterprise Manager to create the users. If you create the user in command-line mode, you must remember to explicitly grant each user the **CREATE SESSION** system privilege either directly or through a role. Figure 7.4 shows the syntax for the **GRANT** command. Here is an example of the command used to grant **CREATE SESSION** and **CREATE TABLE** privileges:

```
GRANT  create session, create table
TO  annie
WITH ADMIN OPTION;
```

Rules about system privilege grants also include the granting of roles that have been created.

System privileges can be granted to other users when the initial grant made includes **WITH ADMIN OPTION**.

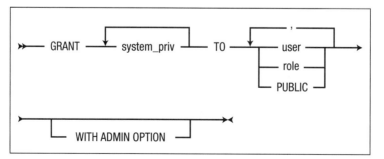

Figure 7.4 The syntax for the **GRANT** command.

There are more than 80 distinct privileges. Most of these are self-explanatory. Table 7.3 lists all the system privileges, as listed in RevealNet's Oracle Administration product (used with its permission).

Table 7.3	Oracle database system privileges.
System Privilege	**Allows Grantee To . . .**
For Clusters:	
CREATE CLUSTER	Create clusters in grantee's schema.
CREATE ANY CLUSTER	Create a cluster in any schema except SYS. Behaves similarly to **CREATE ANY TABLE**.
ALTER ANY CLUSTER	Alter clusters in any schema except SYS.
DROP ANY CLUSTER	Drop clusters in any schema except SYS.
For Contexts:	
CREATE ANY CONTEXT	Create any context namespace.
DROP ANY CONTEXT	Drop any context namespace.
For Databases:	
ALTER DATABASE	Alter the database.
ALTER SYSTEM	Issue **ALTER SYSTEM** statements.
AUDIT SYSTEM	Issue **AUDIT sql_statements** statements.
For Database Links:	
CREATE DATABASE LINK	Create private database links in grantee's schema.
CREATE PUBLIC DATABASE LINK	Create public database links.
DROP PUBLIC DATABASE LINK	Drop public database links.
For Directories:	
CREATE ANY DIRECTORY	Create directory database objects.
DROP ANY DIRECTORY	Drop directory database objects.
For Indexes:	
CREATE INDEX	In the grantee's schema, create an index on any table in the grantee's schema, or create a domain index.

(continued)

Table 7.3 Oracle database system privileges (continued).

System Privilege	Allows Grantee To . . .
CREATE ANY INDEX	In any schema except SYS, create a domain index or create an index on any table.
ALTER ANY INDEX	Alter indexes in any schema except SYS.
DROP ANY INDEX	Drop indexes in any schema except SYS.
For Libraries:	
CREATE LIBRARY	Create external procedure/function libraries in grantee's schema.
CREATE ANY LIBRARY	Create external procedure/function libraries in any schema except SYS.
DROP LIBRARY	Drop external procedure/function libraries in the grantee's schema.
DROP ANY LIBRARY	Drop external procedure/function libraries in any schema except SYS.
For Procedures:	
CREATE PROCEDURE	Create stored procedures, functions, and packages in grantee's schema.
CREATE ANY PROCEDURE	Create stored procedures, functions, and packages in any schema except SYS.
ALTER ANY PROCEDURE	Alter stored procedures, functions, or packages in any schema except SYS.
DROP ANY PROCEDURE	Drop stored procedures, functions, or packages in any schema except SYS.
EXECUTE ANY PROCEDURE	Execute procedures or functions (stand-alone or packaged). Refer to public package variables in any schema except SYS.
For Profiles:	
CREATE PROFILE	Create profiles.
ALTER PROFILE	Alter profiles.
DROP PROFILE	Drop profiles.
For Roles:	
CREATE ROLE	Create roles.

(continued)

Table 7.3   Oracle database system privileges (continued).

System Privilege	Allows Grantee To ...
ALTER ANY ROLE	Alter any role in the database.
DROP ANY ROLE	Drop roles.
GRANT ANY ROLE	Grant any role in the database.
For Rollback Segments:	
CREATE ROLLBACK SEGMENT	Create rollback segments.
ALTER ROLLBACK SEGMENT	Alter rollback segments.
DROP ROLLBACK SEGMENT	Drop rollback segments.
For Sequences:	
CREATE SEQUENCE	Create sequences in grantee's schema.
CREATE ANY SEQUENCE	Create sequences in any schema except SYS.
ALTER ANY SEQUENCE	Alter any sequence in the database.
DROP ANY SEQUENCE	Drop sequences in any schema except SYS.
SELECT ANY SEQUENCE	Refer to sequences in any schema except SYS.
For Sessions:	
CREATE SESSION	Connect to the database.
ALTER RESOURCE COST	Set costs for session resources.
ALTER SESSION	Issue **ALTER SESSION** statements.
RESTRICTED SESSION	Log on after the instance is started using the SQL*Plus **STARTUP RESTRICT** statement.
For Snapshots:	
CREATE SNAPSHOT	Create snapshots in grantee's schema.
CREATE ANY SNAPSHOT	Create snapshots in any schema except SYS.
ALTER ANY SNAPSHOT	Alter any snapshot in the database.
DROP ANY SNAPSHOT	Drop snapshots in any schema except SYS.
For Synonyms:	
CREATE SYNONYM	Create synonyms in grantee's schema.

(continued)

Table 7.3 Oracle database system privileges (continued).

System Privilege	Allows Grantee To . . .
CREATE ANY SYNONYM	Create private synonyms in any schema except SYS.
CREATE PUBLIC SYNONYM	Create public synonyms.
DROP ANY SYNONYM	Drop private synonyms in any schema except SYS.
DROP PUBLIC SYNONYM	Drop public synonyms.
For Tables:	
CREATE ANY TABLE	Create tables in any schema except SYS. The owner of the schema containing the table must have space quota on the tablespace to contain the table.
ALTER ANY TABLE	Alter any table or view in the schema.
BACKUP ANY TABLE	Use the Export utility to incrementally export objects from the schema of other users.
DELETE ANY TABLE	Delete rows from tables, table partitions, or views in any schema except SYS.
DROP ANY TABLE	Drop or truncate tables or table partitions in any schema except SYS.
INSERT ANY TABLE	Insert rows into tables and views in any schema except SYS.
LOCK ANY TABLE	Lock tables and views in any schema except SYS.
UPDATE ANY TABLE	Update rows in tables and views in any schema except SYS.
SELECT ANY TABLE	Query tables, views, or snapshots in any schema except SYS.
For Tablespaces:	
CREATE TABLESPACE	Create tablespaces.
ALTER TABLESPACE	Alter tablespaces.
DROP TABLESPACE	Drop tablespaces.
MANAGE TABLESPACE	Take tablespaces offline and online, and begin and end tablespace backups.

(continued)

Table 7.3 Oracle database system privileges (continued).

System Privilege	Allows Grantee To ...
UNLIMITED TABLESPACE	Use an unlimited amount of any table-space. This privilege overrides any specific quotas assigned. If you revoke this privilege from a user, the user's schema objects remain but further tablespace allocation is denied unless authorized by specific tablespace quotas. You cannot grant this system privilege to roles.

For Triggers:

CREATE TRIGGER	Create a database trigger in grantee's schema.
CREATE ANY TRIGGER	Create database triggers in any schema except SYS.
ALTER ANY TRIGGER	Enable, disable, or compile database triggers in any schema except SYS.
DROP ANY TRIGGER	Drop database triggers in any schema except SYS.
ADMINISTER DATABASE TRIGGER	Create a trigger on **DATABASE**. (You must also have the **CREATE TRIGGER** or **CREATE ANY TRIGGER** privilege.)

For Types:

CREATE TYPE	Create object types and object type bodies in grantee's schema.
CREATE ANY TYPE	Create object types and object type bodies in any schema except SYS.
ALTER ANY TYPE	Alter object types in any schema except SYS.
DROP ANY TYPE	Drop object types and object type bodies in any schema except SYS.
EXECUTE ANY TYPE	Use and refer to object types and collection types in any schema except SYS, and invoke methods of an object type in any schema if you make the grant to a specific user. If you grant **EXECUTE ANY TYPE** to a role, users holding the enabled role will not be able to invoke methods of an object type in any schema.

(continued)

Table 7.3 Oracle database system privileges (continued).

System Privilege	Allows Grantee To ...
For Users:	
CREATE USER	Create users. This privilege also allows the creator to assign quotas on any tablespace, set default and temporary tablespaces, and assign a profile as part of a **CREATE USER** statement.
ALTER USER	Alter any user. This privilege authorizes the grantee to change another user's password or authentication method, assign quotas on any tablespace, set default and temporary tablespaces, and assign a profile and default roles.
BECOME USER	Become another user. (Required by any user performing a full database import.)
DROP USER	Drop users.
For Views:	
CREATE VIEW	Create views in grantee's schema.
CREATE ANY VIEW	Create views in any schema except SYS.
DROP ANY VIEW	Drop views in any schema except SYS.
Miscellaneous Privileges:	
ANALYZE ANY	Analyze any table, cluster, or index in any schema except SYS.
AUDIT ANY	Audit any object in any schema except SYS by using **AUDIT schema_objects** statements.
COMMENT ANY TABLE	Comment on any table, view, or column in any schema except SYS.
FORCE ANY TRANSACTION	Force the commit or rollback of any in-doubt distributed transaction in the local database. Induce the failure of a distributed transaction.
FORCE TRANSACTION	Force the commit or rollback of grantee's in-doubt distributed transactions in the local database.
GRANT ANY PRIVILEGE	Grant any system privilege.

(continued)

Table 7.3 Oracle database system privileges (continued).	
System Privilege	**Allows Grantee To . . .**
SYSDBA	Perform **STARTUP, SHUTDOWN, ALTER DATABASE** (open, mount, back up, or change character set), **CREATE DATABASE ARCHIVELOG**, and **RECOVERY** operations. Includes the **RESTRICTED SESSION** privilege.
SYSOPER	Perform **STARTUP, SHUTDOWN, ALTER DATABASE OPEN/MOUNT/BACKUP, ARCHIVELOG**, and **RECOVERY** operations. Includes the **RESTRICTED SESSION** privilege.

As the DBA, you can access the **DBA_SYS_PRIVS** view for information on the system privileges granted to users. The format of this view is shown in Table 7.4.

Users can see information related to them by accessing the corresponding user view: **USER_SYS_PRIVS**.

Object Privileges

Object privileges define a user's rights on existing database objects. All grants on objects take effect immediately.

To grant an object privilege, you must be the owner of the object, have been granted **WITH GRANT OPTION** on that object for that privilege, or have the system privilege **GRANT ANY PRIVILEGE**. You can also grant access to all users by granting the privilege to **PUBLIC**. Figure 7.5 shows the syntax for the **GRANT** command used to grant a table-level object privilege.

Table 7.4 Contents of the **DBA_SYS_PRIVS** data dictionary view.	
Column	**Definition**
grantee	Oracle login name or role that received the privilege.
privilege	The system privilege granted to the user or role.
admin_option	Indicates **YES** if the grantee can pass along the privilege, or **NO** if the grantee cannot pass along the system privilege.

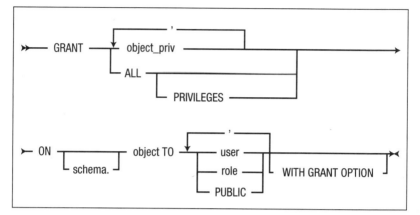

Figure 7.5 The syntax for the **GRANT** command used for a table-level or snapshot-level grant.

Here is an example:

```
GRANT select
ON   bob.emp
TO   derek;
```

As the DBA, you can access the **DBA_TAB_PRIVS** view for information on the object privileges granted to users. You should note that although it is named **DBA_TAB_PRIVS**, this view also includes information on views and sequences, as well as tables. Table 7.5 shows the contents of this view.

By accessing the corresponding user view **USER_TAB_PRIVS**, users can see information on objects for which they are the owner, grantor, or grantee. By using the **ALL_TAB_PRIVS** view, users can see information for all objects for which **PUBLIC** or those users are the grantees.

Table 7.5   Contents of the DBA_TAB_PRIVS data dictionary view.

Column	Definition
grantee	Oracle login name or role that received the privilege
owner	Owner of the table
table_name	Name of the table, view, or sequence
grantor	Oracle login name of the person granting the privilege
privilege	System privilege granted to the user
grantable	Indicates **YES** if the grantee can pass along the privilege, or **NO** if the grantee cannot pass along the system privilege

A table owner can grant the following object privileges to other users:

➤ ALTER

➤ DELETE

➤ INDEX

➤ INSERT

➤ REFERENCES

➤ SELECT

➤ UPDATE

➤ EXECUTE (for stored functions, procedures, and packages)

All grants on objects and the revoking of those grants are valid immediately, even if a user is currently logged in to the database. The **SELECT** privilege can be granted only on tables, views, and snapshots. The **EXECUTE** privilege is used for packages, procedures, and functions. Remember that packages, procedures, and functions are always executed with the permissions of the owner of that package, procedure, or function.

By granting other users **INSERT, UPDATE, DELETE,** and **SELECT** privileges on your table, you allow them to perform that action on the table. By granting users the **ALTER** privilege, you allow them to modify the structure of your table or create a trigger on your table. By granting users the **INDEX** privilege, you allow them to create indexes on your table.

The **REFERENCES** privilege differs from the other privileges in that it does not actually grant the capability to change the table or data contained in the table. The **REFERENCES** privilege allows users to create foreign key constraints that refer to your table.

A user can access the **USER_TAB_PRIVS_RECD** view for information on table privileges where that user is the grantee. The corresponding **ALL_TAB_PRIVS_RECD** view includes all grants on objects where that user or **PUBLIC** is the grantee. Table 7.6 shows the contents of the **USER_TAB_PRIVS_RECD** view.

A user can access the **USER_TAB_PRIVS_MADE** view for information on table privileges that he or she has granted to others. The corresponding **ALL_TAB_PRIVS_MADE** view includes information on all the grants that user has made, as well as grants by others on that user's objects. Table 7.7 shows the contents of the **USER_TAB_PRIVS_MADE** view.

Table 7.6	Contents of the **USER_TAB_PRIVS_RECD** data dictionary view.
Column	**Definition**
owner	Owner of the table
table_name	Name of the table, view, or sequence
grantor	Oracle login name of the person granting the privilege
privilege	System privilege granted to the user
grantable	Indicates **YES** if the grantee can pass along the privilege, or **NO** if the grantee cannot pass along the object privilege

Table 7.7	Contents of the **USER_TAB_PRIVS_MADE** data dictionary view.
Column	**Definition**
grantee	Oracle user granted the privilege
table_name	Name of the table, view, or sequence
grantor	Oracle login name of the person granting the privilege
privilege	System privilege granted to the user
grantable	Indicates **YES** if the grantee can pass along the privilege, or **NO** if the grantee cannot pass along the object privilege

Column Privileges

Only **INSERT, UPDATE,** and **REFERENCES** privileges can be granted at the column level. When granting **INSERT** at the column level, you must include all the **NOT NULL** columns in the row. Figure 7.6 shows the syntax for granting object privileges at the column level.

Here is an example:

```
GRANT  update(emp_name)
ON  edwin.emp
TO  joan;
```

As the DBA, you can access the **DBA_COL_PRIVS** view for information on the column-level object privileges granted to users. Table 7.8 shows the contents of the **DBA_COL_PRIVS** view.

Users can access the **USER_COL_PRIVS_RECD** view for information on column-level object privileges that have been granted to them. The

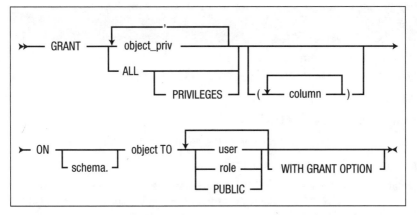

Figure 7.6 The syntax for the **GRANT** command used for column-level privilege grants.

Table 7.8   Contents of the DBA_COL_PRIVS data dictionary view.

Column	Definition
grantee	Oracle login name or role that received the privilege
owner	Owner of the table
table_name	Name of the table
column_name	Name of the column
grantor	Oracle login name of the person granting the privilege
privilege	System privilege granted to the user
grantable	Indicates **YES** if the grantee can pass along the privilege, or **NO** if the grantee cannot pass along the object privilege

ALL_COL_PRIVS_RECD view includes information on all column privileges that have been granted to them or to **PUBLIC**. The format of the **USER_COL_PRIVS_RECD** view is shown in Table 7.9.

Users can access the **USER_COL_PRIVS_MADE** view for information on column privileges that they have granted to others. The corresponding **ALL_COL_PRIVS_MADE** view includes information on all columns where the user is the owner or the grantor. The contents of the **USER_COL_PRIVS_MADE** view are shown in Table 7.10.

Users can access information on all columns where they are the grantor, grantee, or owner, or where access has been granted to **PUBLIC** with the corresponding **ALL_TAB_PRIVS_MADE** and **ALL_TAB_PRIVS_RECD** views.

Table 7.9	Contents of the **USER_COL_PRIVS_RECD** data dictionary view.
Column	**Definition**
owner	Oracle user (schema) that owns the table
table_name	Name of the table
column_name	Name of the column
grantor	Oracle login name of the person granting the privilege
privilege	System privilege granted to the user
grantable	Indicates **YES** if the grantee can pass along the privilege, or **NO** if the grantee cannot pass along the column-level object privilege

Table 7.10	Contents of the **USER_COL_PRIVS_MADE** data dictionary view.
Column	**Definition**
grantee	Oracle user granted the privilege
table_name	Name of the table
column_name	Name of the column
grantor	Oracle login name of the person granting the privilege
privilege	System privilege granted to the user
grantable	Indicates **YES** if the grantee can pass along the privilege, or **NO** if the grantee cannot pass along the column-level object privilege

View Grants

Views can have the **SELECT, INSERT, UPDATE,** and **DELETE** grants issued against them. To perform **SELECT, INSERT, UPDATE,** or **DELETE** operations against views (where it is allowed), you must grant the privileges for the underlying tables to the users you want to have these privileges.

The information on grants made to views is located in the same views as for tables.

Other Grants

The only allowed grant for sequences is **SELECT**. For procedures, functions, packages, libraries, and User-Defined Types, you may only grant **EXECUTE** privileges. The only allowed grant for a directory is **READ**, and it is the only object that has a **READ** grant.

Revoking Grants

When you use **WITH ADMIN OPTION** to pass system privileges to others, revoking the system privileges from the original user will cause them to not cascade. The system privileges granted to others must be revoked directly. In contrast, when you use **WITH ADMIN OPTION** to pass object privileges to others, the object privileges are revoked when the grantor's privileges are revoked.

 It is important to note that only object privileges will cascade when revoked; system privileges will not.

When the **WITH ADMIN OPTION** or **WITH GRANT OPTION** has been included in a grant to another user, the privilege cannot be revoked directly. You must revoke the privilege and then issue another grant without **WITH ADMIN OPTION** or **WITH GRANT OPTION**.

The command-line syntax for revoking a system privilege is shown in Figure 7.7.

In this format, roles are counted the same as system privileges and are grouped with users.

Here are some examples:

```
REVOKE   create table
FROM   judy;

REVOKE create table
FROM developer_role;

REVOKE dba
FROM monitor_role;
```

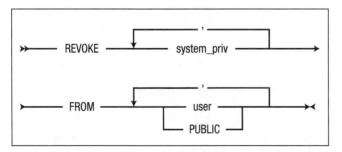

Figure 7.7   The syntax for revoking a system privilege.

To revoke an object privilege, you must be the owner of the object, have used the **WITH GRANT OPTION** privilege to grant that privilege to that user, or have the **GRANT ANY PRIVILEGE** system privilege.

You can revoke object and system privileges with Server Manager or at the command line in SQL*Plus. The command-line syntax for revoking an object privilege is shown in Figure 7.8.

Here is an example:

```
REVOKE select
ON mike.emp
FROM stan;
```

When the object privilege **REFERENCES** has been granted, you must specify **CASCADE CONSTRAINTS** to drop the foreign key constraints that were created.

Roles

Using roles has several benefits, including:

➤ Reducing the number of grants and thereby making it easier to manage security

➤ Dynamically changing the privileges for many users with a single grant or revoke

➤ Selectively enabling or disabling privileges and grants, depending on the application

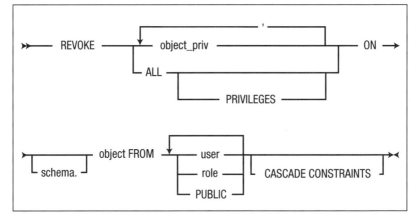

Figure 7.8 The syntax for revoking an object privilege.

Roles can be used for granting most system and object privileges. Privileges granted through a role cannot be used for creating objects (views, packages, procedures, and functions). You need to grant privileges directly to the user for this.

Creating Roles

A *role* is a collection of grants, privileges, and other roles that can be granted as a unit to users or other roles. In order to use a role, you need to create the role first and then grant system and object privileges to that role. When you create the role, you have three password options:

➤ No authentication

➤ Operating system authentication

➤ Password authentication

You can set operating system authentication either when you create the role or by using the database initialization parameters **OS_ROLES=TRUE** and **REMOTE_OS_ROLES=TRUE**. If you are using the multithreaded server option, you cannot use operating system authentication for roles.

To create a role, you must have the **CREATE ROLE** system privilege. You can create roles with Oracle Enterprise Manager or at the command line in SQL*Plus or svrmgrl. The command-line syntax for creating a role is shown in Figure 7.9.

You can also identify a role globally by using the **GLOBALLY** keyword in the **IDENTIFIED** clause. This means that the role will be authenticated by the Oracle Security Server.

Here is an example:

```
CREATE  ROLE    appusers
NOT  IDENTIFIED;
```

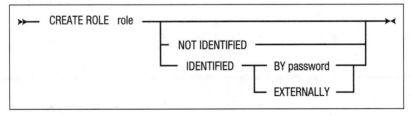

Figure 7.9 The syntax for creating a role.

To alter a role, you must have the **ALTER ANY ROLE** system privilege or have been granted the role with **WITH ADMIN OPTION**. The creator of any role automatically has the **WITH ADMIN OPTION** for that role.

Granting Roles To Users And Privileges To Roles

To grant a role to a user, you must either be the creator of that role or have the **GRANT ANY ROLE** privilege. You can grant roles to users by using Oracle Enterprise Manager or at the command line in SQL*Plus or svrmgrl. Grants to roles will not take effect for a user if that user is currently logged in to the database with that role. When the user exits or sets another role, the changes will take effect. After roles have been granted to a user, they can be enabled and disabled.

Figure 7.10 shows the syntax for granting roles to users.

Here is an example:

```
GRANT  enduser
TO  patrick;
```

The command-line syntax for granting privileges to a role is the same as the syntax for granting privileges to a user. Figure 7.11 shows the syntax for granting system privileges to roles.

Here is an example:

```
GRANT  create  session
TO  enduser;
```

Figure 7.12 shows the syntax for granting object privileges to roles.

Figure 7.10 The syntax for granting roles to users.

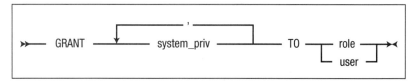

Figure 7.11 The syntax for granting system privileges to roles.

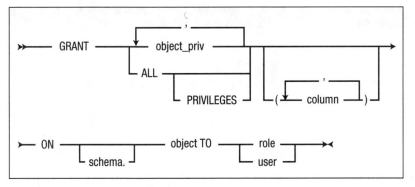

Figure 7.12   The syntax for granting object privileges to roles.

Here is an example:

```
GRANT  select
ON   john.emp
TO   enduser;
```

The only system privilege that cannot be granted to a role is the **UNLIM-ITED TABLESPACE** grant; however, it is implicitly granted whenever the **DBA** or **RESOURCE** role grant is made to a user. Grants on objects can be passed to other users or to roles if the grantee has been given the **WITH GRANT OPTION** privilege. However, you cannot assign to a role a privilege that includes the **WITH GRANT OPTION** privilege. The **INDEX** and **REFERENCES** privileges cannot be granted to a role; they must be granted only to a user. You can grant that role to a user or to another role. However, you cannot grant a role to itself even indirectly.

You can look at the data dictionary tables shown in Table 7.11 for information on the views for reviewing a roles system and object privileges.

Table 7.11 Data dictionary views for roles.	
Column	**Definition**
DBA_ROLES	
role	Name of the role
password_required	Yes, No, Global, or—for operating system authentication—External
DBA_ROLE_PRIVS	
grantee	Name of the user or role receiving the grant

(continued)

Table 7.11	Data dictionary views for roles (continued).
Column	Definition
granted_role	Name of the role
admin_option	Y if it was granted with the admin option
default_role	Y if this is the grantee's default role
ROLE_ROLE_PRIVS	
role	Name of the role receiving the role grant
granted_role	Name of the different role granted to the role listed in this row
admin_option	Indicates that the role was granted with the admin option
ROLE_SYS_PRIVS	
role	Name of the role receiving the system privilege
privilege	System privilege being granted
admin_option	Indicates that the grant was given with the admin option

The ROLE_TAB_PRIVS view shown in Table 7.12 provides information on tables and column grants to roles.

Setting Roles

When a user is created, the default for active roles is set to **ALL**. The default **ALL** means that all the roles granted to a user are active. The DBA can change the default with an **ALTER USER** command. A user can enable multiple

Table 7.12	Contents of the **ROLE_TAB_PRIVS** data dictionary view.
Column	Definition
role	Name of the role
owner	Owner of the table, view, or sequence
table_name	Name of the table, view, or sequence
column_name	Name of the column within the table, if applicable
privilege	Object privilege granted to that role
grantable	**YES** if it was granted with the admin option; **NO** otherwise

roles at one time and then either use the **SET ROLE** command to switch between roles or use the **SET ROLE ALL** command to activate all roles. The **SET ROLE ALL** command will not work if any of the roles assigned to that user require either a password or operating system authentication.

The command-line syntax for setting roles is shown in Figure 7.13.

Here is an example of setting a role:

```
SET ROLE master_dba IDENTIFIED BY dba2000;
```

Users can look at the **SESSION_ROLES** view to find the roles that are currently enabled for them. Users can look at the **SESSION_PRIVS** view to see the privileges available to their session.

If you determine that all control of roles will be at the operating system level, you can set the database initialization parameter **OS_ROLES** equal to **TRUE**. All roles must still be created first in the database. Any grants you previously made using the database command line or Server Manager are still listed in the data dictionary, but they cannot be used and are not in effect. If the use of roles is determined at the operating system level, the multithreaded server option cannot be used.

You can use the **MAX_ENABLED_ROLES** parameter in the database initialization file to set the number of roles that you will allow any user to have enabled at one time.

Special Roles

When you install the Oracle executables, Oracle creates the following two roles:

➤ OSOPER

➤ OSDBA

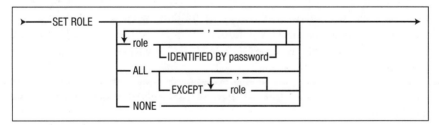

Figure 7.13 The syntax for setting roles.

When you create the database, Oracle creates the following three roles:

➤ CONNECT

➤ RESOURCE

➤ DBA

When you execute the sql.bsq script, Oracle creates the following two roles:

➤ EXP_FULL_DATABASE

➤ IMP_FULL_DATABASE

When the views and packages for Recovery Manager are created, Oracle creates the following five roles:

➤ SELECT_CATALOG_ROLE

➤ EXECUTE_CATALOG_ROLE

➤ DELETE_CATALOG_ROLE

➤ RECOVER_CATALOG_ROLE

➤ RECOVERY_CATALOG_OWNER

Finally, with the addition of the advanced queuing option, Oracle creates the following two roles:

➤ AQ_ADMINISTRATOR_ROLE

➤ AQ_USER_ROLE

Next, I'll explain these special roles and how they are used for database maintenance.

OSOPER And OSDBA

The **OSOPER** and **OSDBA** roles are created at the operating system level when Oracle is installed. They cannot be granted. The **OSOPER** and **OSDBA** roles are needed to perform database operations when the database is not mounted and therefore the data dictionary is not accessible. You use **OSOPER** and **OSDBA** roles when you use **CONNECT INTERNAL** to connect to the database using Server Manager.

Users with the **OSOPER** role can perform the following database management commands:

➤ STARTUP

➤ SHUTDOWN

➤ ALTER DATABASE OPEN/MOUNT

➤ ALTER DATABASE BACKUP CONTROLFILE

➤ ALTER TABLESPACE BEGIN/END BACKUP

➤ ARCHIVE LOG

➤ RECOVER

The **OSDBA** role has all of the privileges of the **OSOPER** role. In addition, the **OSDBA** role has all system privileges granted with **WITH ADMIN OPTION** to allow whoever has it to grant system privileges to other users. The **OSDBA** role is used to create the database and for time-based recovery processes. Both the **OSOPER** and **OSDBA** roles include the **RESTRICTED SESSION** system privilege.

If you intend to allow remote users to **CONNECT INTERNAL,** you need to set the **REMOTE_LOGIN_PASSWORDFILE** option in your database parameter file to either **EXCLUSIVE** or **SHARED.** The user will then connect in Server Manager with the **AS SYSDBA** or **AS SYSOPER** clause at the end of the **CONNECT** command (**CONNECT SYS AS SYSDBA**). The privileges assigned to **SYSDBA** correspond to those for **OSDBA.** The privileges assigned to **SYSOPER** correspond to **OSOPER.** Using an external operating system file, the operating system verifies the password provided. This external file is generated using the **ORAPWD** utility. When the password for the **SYS,** and indirectly the **INTERNAL,** accounts is changed with the **ALTER USER** command, the changes are mapped to the operating system password file.

CONNECT, RESOURCE, And DBA Roles

The **CONNECT, RESOURCE,** and **DBA** roles are predefined roles that are available for backward compatibility. These are created by Oracle when the database is created. When you create a user with Oracle Enterprise Manager, the **CONNECT** role is automatically granted to that user.

The following system privileges are granted to the **CONNECT** role:

➤ ALTER SESSION

➤ CREATE CLUSTER

➤ CREATE DATABASE LINK

➤ CREATE SEQUENCE

➤ CREATE SESSION

➤ CREATE SYNONYM

➤ CREATE TABLE

➤ CREATE VIEW

When you grant a user the **RESOURCE** role, that user is granted the **UNLIMITED TABLESPACE** system privilege as well. The following system privileges are granted to the **RESOURCE** role:

➤ CREATE CLUSTER

➤ CREATE PROCEDURE

➤ CREATE SEQUENCE

➤ CREATE TABLE

➤ CREATE TRIGGER

➤ CREATE TYPE

The **DBA** role includes all system privileges (95 separate grants), the capability to grant those system privileges to others, and **UNLIMITED TABLESPACE**. If the **EXP_FULL_DATABASE** and **IMP_FULL_DATABASE** roles have been created, they are granted implicitly with the **DBA** role, as are the **DELETE**, **EXECUTE**, and **SELECT_CATALOG_ROLE** roles.

You can grant additional privileges to or revoke privileges from the **CONNECT**, **RESOURCE**, and **DBA** roles, just as you would with any other role that you created.

Export And Import Roles

Oracle provides a script named catexp.sql. This script creates the **EXP_FULL_DATABASE** and **IMP_FULL_DATABASE** roles. You can grant these roles to a user who will be executing the Export and Import utilities.

The **EXP_FULL_DATABASE** role has the **SELECT ANY TABLE** and **BACKUP ANY TABLE** system privileges. In addition, this role has **INSERT**, **DELETE**, and **UPDATE** privileges on the **SYS.INCVID**, **SYS.INCFIL**, and **SYS.INCEXP** tables.

The **IMP_FULL_DATABASE** role has the **BECOME USER** system privilege.

Profiles

Profiles are a named set of resource limits. By setting up profiles with defined limits on resources, you can set limits on the system resources used. Profiles are very useful in large, complex organizations with many users. By creating and assigning profiles to users, you can regulate the amount of resources used by each database user. In Oracle8, password attributes were added into profiles.

Creating Profiles

By default, when you create users, they are given the default profile. The default profile provides unlimited use of all resources.

The syntax to create a profile is shown in Figure 7.14.

Possible values for the **resource_parameters** specifications in Figure 7.14 (you can specify multiple parameters per command) are as follows:

```
[SESSIONS_PER_USER n|UNLIMITED|DEFAULT]
[CPU_PER_SESSION n|UNLIMITED|DEFAULT]
[CPU_PER_CALL n|UNLIMITED|DEFAULT]
[CONNECT_TIME               n|UNLIMITED|DEFAULT]
[IDLE_TIME                  n|UNLIMITED|DEFAULT]
[LOGICAL_READS_PER_SESSION  n|UNLIMITED|DEFAULT]
[LOGICAL_READS_PER_CALL     n|UNLIMITED|DEFAULT]
[COMPOSITE_LIMIT            n|UNLIMITED|DEFAULT]
[PRIVATE_SGA                n [K|M]|UNLIMITED|DEFAULT]
```

Where:

➤ **SESSIONS_PER_USER**—Used to limit the number of open database sessions a user can have concurrently.

➤ **CPU_PER_SESSION**—Used to limit the total CPU resource used by a single session. This value is not additive across parallel query slaves.

➤ **CPU_PER_CALL**—Used to limit the total CPU used in a single call from a single session.

➤ **CONNECT_TIME**—Used to limit the total time a session can stay connected to the database.

➤ **IDLE_TIME**—Used to limit the amount of time an inactive session will remain logged in to the database.

➤ **LOGICAL_READS_PER_SESSION**—Used to limit the number of logical reads a single session can perform. This limit is not additive across parallel query slaves.

➤ CREATE PROFILE profile LIMIT resource_parameters I password_parameters ——; ——➤

Figure 7.14 The syntax to create a profile.

➤ LOGICAL_READS_PER_CALL—Used to limit the number of logical reads in a single call from a single process.

Possible values for the **password_parameters** specifications in Figure 7.14 (Oracle8 and above) are as follows:

```
[FAILED_LOGIN_ATTEMPTS expr|UNLIMITED|DEFAULT]
[PASSWORD_LIFE_TIME     expr|UNLIMITED|DEFAULT]
[PASSWORD_REUSE_TIME    expr|UNLIMITED|DEFAULT]
[PASSWORD_REUSE_MAX     expr|UNLIMITED|DEFAULT]
[PASSWORD_LOCK_TIME     expr|UNLIMITED|DEFAULT]
[PASSWORD_GRACE_TIME    expr|UNLIMITED|DEFAULT]
[PASSWORD_VERIFY_FUNCTION function_name|NULL|DEFAULT]
```

Where:

➤ FAILED_LOGIN_ATTEMPTS—Used to set the number of times a user can enter an improper password before the account is locked.

➤ PASSWORD_LIFE_TIME—Used to set the period of time in days that a password is valid.

➤ PASSWORD_REUSE_TIME—Used to set the minimum period of time in days before a password can be reused.

➤ PASSWORD_REUSE_MAX—Used to set the number of times a password may be reused.

➤ PASSWORD_LOCK_TIME—Used to set the amount of time an account will be locked once FAILED_LOGIN_ATTEMPTS has been exceeded.

➤ PASSWORD_GRACE_TIME—Used to set the time in days that a user has to reset their password once PASSWORD_LIFE_TIME has been exceeded.

➤ PASSWORD_VERIFY_FUNCTION—Used to name the function used to verify that a password is complex enough.

Password parameters have the following restrictions:

➤ Expr must resolve to either an integer value or an integer number of days.

➤ If PASSWORD_REUSE_TIME is set to an integer value, PASSWORD_REUSE_MAX must be set to UNLIMITED.

➤ If PASSWORD_REUSE_MAX is set to an integer value, PASSWORD_REUSE_TIME must be set to UNLIMITED.

➤ If both **PASSWORD_REUSE_TIME** and **PASSWORD_REUSE_MAX** are set to **UNLIMITED,** Oracle uses neither of these password resources.

➤ If **PASSWORD_REUSE_MAX** is set to **DEFAULT** and **PASSWORD_REUSE_TIME** is set to **UNLIMITED,** Oracle uses the **PASSWORD_REUSE_MAX** value defined in the **DEFAULT** profile.

➤ If **PASSWORD_REUSE_TIME** is set to **DEFAULT** and **PASSWORD_REUSE_MAX** is set to **UNLIMITED,** Oracle uses the **PASSWORD_REUSE_TIME** value defined in the **DEFAULT** profile.

➤ If both **PASSWORD_REUSE_TIME** and **PASSWORD_REUSE_MAX** are set to **DEFAULT,** Oracle uses whichever value is defined in the **DEFAULT** profile.

For example:

```
CREATE PROFILE   enduser   LIMIT
CPU_PER_SESSION                60000
LOGICAL_READS_PER_SESSION   1000
CONNECT_TIME                   30
PRIVATE_SGA                    102400
CPU_PER_CALL                   UNLIMITED
COMPOSITE LIMIT                60000000
FAILED_LOGIN_ATTEMPTS       3
PASSWORD_LIFE_TIME          90
PASSWORD_REUSE_TIME         180
PASSWORD_LOCK_TIME          3
PASSWORD_GRACE_TIME         3
PASSWORD_VERIFY_FUNCTION Verify_function_one;
```

You can assign a profile to a user when you create the user or by altering the user. The syntax to alter the profile for a user is:

```
ALTER USER PROFILE profile;
```

For example:

```
ALTER USER scott
PROFILE appuser;
```

You must have the **CREATE PROFILE** system privilege to create a profile. To alter a profile, you must be the creator of the profile or have the **ALTER**

PROFILE system privilege. To assign a profile to a user, you must have the CREATE USER or ALTER USER system privilege.

Profiles And Resource Limits

The default cost assigned to a resource is unlimited. By setting resource limits, you can prevent users from performing operations that will tie up the system and prevent other users from performing operations. You can use resource limits for security to ensure that users log off the system and do not leave the session connected for long periods of time. You can also assign a composite cost to each profile. The system resource limits can be enforced at the session level, at the call level, or both.

The *session level* restrictions are from the time the user logs into the database until the user exits. The *call level* restrictions are for each SQL command issued. Session-level limits are enforced for each connection. When a session-level limit is exceeded, only the last SQL command issued is rolled back, and no further work can be performed until a commit, a rollback, or an exit is performed. Table 7.13 lists the system resources that can be regulated at the session level.

One thing to note if you use parallel query option (PQO) is that the resources are applied to each new session, not accumulated over all of the sessions that a parallel operation uses.

You can combine the CPU_PER_SESSION, LOGICAL_READS_PER_SESSION, CONNECT_TIME, and PRIVATE_SGA system resources to create a COMPOSITE LIMIT.

Table 7.13 Resources regulated at the session level.	
System Resource	**Definition**
CPU_PER_SESSION	Total CPU time; expressed in hundreds of seconds
SESSIONS_PER_USER	Number of concurrent sessions allowed for a user
CONNECT_TIME	Allowed connection time; expressed in minutes
IDLE_TIME	Inactive time allowed on the server; expressed in minutes
LOGICAL_READS_PER_SESSION	Number of data blocks read, including both physical and logical reads from memory and disk
PRIVATE_SGA	Bytes of SGA used in a database with the multithreaded server; expressed in K or MB

Call-level limits are enforced during the execution of each SQL statement. When a call-level limit is exceeded, the last SQL command issued is rolled back. All the previous statements issued are still valid, and the user can continue to execute other SQL statements. The following system resources can be regulated at the call level:

➤ **CPU_PER_CALL**—For the CPU time allowed for the SQL statement.

➤ **LOGICAL_READS_PER_CALL**—For the number of data blocks read for the SQL statement.

You can assign a cost to a resource by using the **ALTER RESOURCE COST** command. Resource limits that you set explicitly for a user take precedence over the resource costs in an assigned profile. The command-line syntax for this command is shown in Figure 7.15.

For example:

```
ALTER RESOURCE COST CONNECT_TIME 100;
```

The **ALTER RESOURCE COST** command specifies the weights Oracle uses to calculate the total resource cost used for a session. Oracle calculates the total resource cost by multiplying the amount of each resource used in the session by the resource's weight and summing the results for all four resources. Both the products and the total cost are expressed in units called *service units*.

Although Oracle monitors the use of other resources, only the four specified in Figure 7.15 contribute to the total resource cost for a session.

The weight that you assign to each resource in Figure 7.15 determines how much the use of that resource contributes to the total resource cost. Using a resource with a lower weight contributes less to the cost than using a resource with a higher weight. If you do not assign a weight to a resource, the weight defaults to 0 and use of the resource does not contribute to the cost. The weights you assign apply to all subsequent sessions in the database.

Once you have specified a formula for the total resource cost, you can limit this cost for a session with the **COMPOSITE_LIMIT** parameter of the **CREATE PROFILE** command. If a session's cost exceeds the limit, Oracle aborts the

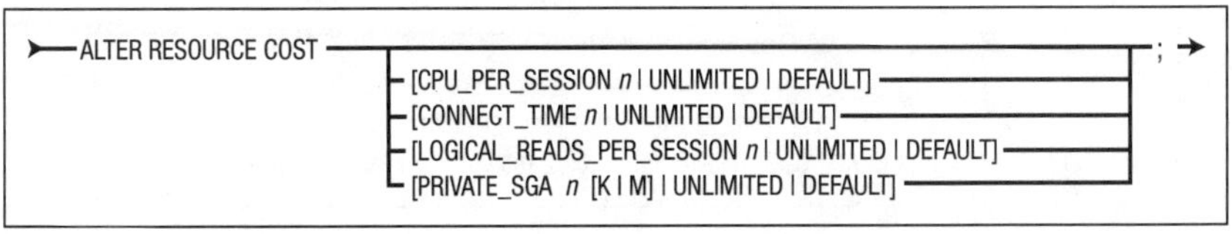

Figure 7.15 The syntax of the **ALTER RESOURCE COST** command.

session and returns an error. If you use the **ALTER RESOURCE COST** command to change the weight assigned to each resource, Oracle uses these new weights to calculate the total resource cost for all current and subsequent sessions.

Use of resource limits is set in the database initialization parameter **RESOURCE_LIMIT=TRUE**. By default, this parameter is set to false. This parameter can be changed interactively with an **ALTER SYSTEM** command.

The **DBA_PROFILES** view provides information on all the profiles and the resource limits for each profile. The **RESOURCE_COST** view shows the unit cost associated with each resource. Each user can find information on his resources and limits in the **USER_RESOURCE_LIMITS** view. Table 7.14 describes these data dictionary views.

Altering Profiles

If you have the **CREATE PROFILE** or **ALTER PROFILE** system privilege, you can alter any profile, including the Oracle-created **DEFAULT** profile. You can alter a profile to change the cost assigned to each resource. The syntax to alter a profile is shown in Figure 7.16.

Table 7.14   Data dictionary views for resources.

Column	Definition
DBA_PROFILES	
Profile	The name given to the profile.
Resource_name	The name of the resource assigned to the profile.
Limit	The limit placed on the profile.
RESOURCE_COST	
Resource_name	The name of the resource.
Unit_cost	The cost assigned.
USER_RESOURCE_LIMITS	
Resource_name	The name of the resource.
Limit	The limit placed on the user.

>—ALTER PROFILE profile LIMIT resource_parameters I password_parameters——; →

Figure 7.16   The syntax to alter a profile.

The possible values for the **resource_parameters** specifications are:

```
[SESSIONS_PER_USER  n|UNLIMITED|DEFAULT]
[CPU_PER_SESSION    n|UNLIMITED|DEFAULT]
[CPU_PER_CALL       n|UNLIMITED|DEFAULT]
[CONNECT_TIME       n|UNLIMITED|DEFAULT]
[IDLE_TIME          n|UNLIMITED|DEFAULT]
[LOGICAL_READS_PER_SESSION n|UNLIMITED|DEFAULT]
[LOGICAL_READS_PER_CALL    n|UNLIMITED|DEFAULT]
[COMPOSITE_LIMIT           n|UNLIMITED|DEFAULT]
[PRIVATE_SGA               n [K|M|UNLIMITED|DEFAULT]]
```

The possible values for the **password_parameters** specifications are:

```
[FAILED_LOGIN_ATTEMPTS expr|UNLIMITED|DEFAULT]
[PASSWORD_LIFE_TIME     expr|UNLIMITED|DEFAULT]
[PASSWORD_REUSE_TIME    expr|UNLIMITED|DEFAULT]
[PASSWORD_REUSE_MAX     expr|UNLIMITED|DEFAULT]
[PASSWORD_LOCK_TIME     expr|UNLIMITED|DEFAULT]
[PASSWORD_GRACE_TIME    expr|UNLIMITED|DEFAULT]
[PASSWORD_VERIFY_FUNCTION function_name|NULL|DEFAULT]
```

For example:

```
ALTER PROFILE enduser LIMIT
CPU_PER_SESSION 60000
LOGICAL_READS_PER_SESSION 1000
CONNECT_TIME 60
PRIVATE_SGA 102400
CPU_PER_CALL UNLIMITED
COMPOSITE LIMIT 60000000;
```

To disable a profile during a session, you must have the **ALTER SYSTEM** privilege. A limit that you set for the session overrides the previous limit set by the profile. To reset the profile to the limit originally set by the database, set the limit to **DEFAULT**. The following code shows how the resource limit checking can be turned on (using **TRUE**) or off (using **FALSE**) through use of the **ALTER SYSTEM** command:

```
ALTER SYSTEM SET RESOURCE_LIMIT = TRUE|FALSE;
```

For example:

```
ALTER SYSTEM SET RESOURCE_LIMIT = TRUE ;
```

Profiles And Passwords

A new feature in Oracle8 is the ability to control password expiry and password complexity and validity. You use profiles to control passwords. Table 7.15 lists the password control attributes in a profile and their definitions.

Oracle also provides a template PL/SQL procedure for use in creating your own password complexity and verification function. The example PL/SQL procedure is located in $ORACLE_HOME/rdbms/admin/utlpwdmg.sql on Unix and in %ORACLE_HOME%\rdbms80\admin\utlpwdmg.sql on NT. Other than the required input and return variables, the password verification function can be as simple, or as complex, as you want it to be.

Table 7.15 Password control attributes in a profile.	
Attribute	**Description**
FAILED_LOGIN_ATTEMPTS	Specifies the number of failed attempts to log into the user account allowed before the account is locked.
PASSWORD_LIFE_TIME	Limits the number of days the same password can be used for authentication. The password expires if it is not changed within this period, and further connections are rejected.
PASSWORD_REUSE_TIME	Specifies the number of days that the current password can be reused. If you set **PASSWORD_REUSE_TIME** to an integer value, you must set **PASSWORD_REUSE_MAX** to **UNLIMITED**.
PASSWORD_REUSE_MAX	Specifies the number of password changes required before the current password can be reused. If you set **PASSWORD_REUSE_MAX** to an integer value, you must set **PASSWORD_REUSE_TIME** to UNLIMITED.
PASSWORD_LOCK_TIME	Specifies the number of days an account will be locked after the specified number of consecutive failed login attempts.
PASSWORD_GRACE_TIME	Specifies the length of a grace period: the number of days in which a warning is issued and login is allowed. If the password is not changed during the grace period, the password expires.

(continued)

Table 7.15   Password control attributes in a profile (continued).

Attribute	Description
PASSWORD_VERIFY_FUNCTION	Allows a PL/SQL password-complexity verification script to be passed as an argument to the **CREATE PROFILE** statement. Oracle provides a default script, but you can create your own routine or use third-party software instead. **FUNCTION** is the name of the password-complexity verification routine. **NULL** indicates that no password verification is performed and is the default value.

Practice Questions

Question 1

> What is displayed when you query **USER_USERS**?
>
> ○ a. Information about all users of the database
>
> ○ b. Information about the current user
>
> ○ c. Tablespace quotas for all users
>
> ○ d. Tablespace quotas for the current user

The correct answer is b. Views prefixed with **USER** will give information relevant to the current user only, which explains why answer a and c are incorrect. Answer d is incorrect because quota information is not contained in the USER_USERS view.

Question 2

> Which keyword, when added to a **DROP USER** command, will remove all objects contained in a user's schema?
>
> ○ a. **DEFAULT**
>
> ○ b. **QUOTA**
>
> ○ c. **CASCADE**
>
> ○ d. **EXCEPT**

The correct answer is c. If a user owns objects, he cannot be dropped unless you explicitly include the **CASCADE** option in the **DROP USER** command. It is not possible to drop a user and keep the user's objects in the database. You can export the user's objects and import them into another user record, or another user can use his **SELECT** privileges on the objects to copy them before the first user is dropped. After a **DROP USER** statement is issued, it cannot be rolled back.

Question 3

> Which view would you query to display the number of bytes charged to each user?
>
> ○ a. **USER_USERS**
>
> ○ b. **ALL_USERS**
>
> ○ c. **DBA_USERS**
>
> ○ d. **USER_TS_QUOTAS**
>
> ○ e. **DBA_TS_QUOTAS**

The correct answer is e. The **DBA_TS_QUOTAS** view lists the number of bytes for each user. This view also includes the maximum bytes as set by the quota assigned to the user. Note the wording of this question. It asks how you would obtain tablespace usage information for each user. You can eliminate **USER_TS_QUOTAS**, answer d, because it will give tablespace usage information on the current user only. Answers a, b, and c are incorrect since the **USER** series of views do not give quota information. Pay special attention to whether the question asks for statistics on the current user or all users.

Question 4

> Evaluate this command:
>
> ```
> ALTER USER jennifer
> QUOTA 0 ON SYSTEM;
> ```
>
> Which task will this command accomplish?
>
> ○ a. Remove user Jennifer.
>
> ○ b. Drop user Jennifer's objects from **SYSTEM** tablespace.
>
> ○ c. Revoke user Jennifer's tablespace quota on **SYSTEM** tablespace.
>
> ○ d. Allocate tablespace to user Jennifer.

The correct answer is c. Jennifer may have quotas on several tablespaces, and this command will revoke Jennifer's usage on only the **SYSTEM** tablespace. A process of elimination is used. The command in this question will not remove or drop the user Jennifer (answers a and b). It will not allocate tablespace to Jennifer (answer d). The only applicable answer is c.

Question 5

> When you're creating a user, which step can be skipped if the user will not be creating any objects?
>
> ○ a. Assign a username and password.
>
> ○ b. Assign a default tablespace.
>
> ○ c. Assign a tablespace for temporary tables.
>
> ○ d. Assign a default profile.

The correct answer is b. Be sure to read this question carefully. Notice the words "will not be creating any objects." If a default tablespace is not explicitly assigned, the **SYSTEM** tablespace will be the implicit default. However, if a user will not be creating objects, he will not actually be placing anything in the **SYSTEM** tablespace. It is also true that if a profile is not created, the default profile is implicitly assigned; but that is true regardless of whether the user is going to create objects. However, it's not a good practice to leave general users assigned to the **SYSTEM** tablespace as their default for temporary assignments.

Question 6

> Who needs a DBA assigned usage quota?
>
> ○ a. The owner of an object that is read-only.
>
> ○ b. A user who is about to create a table.
>
> ○ c. A user who only reads data from an object owned by another user.
>
> ○ d. A user who is inserting data into an object owned by another user.

The correct answer is b. Inserting data into an object owned by another user will use the quota of the user who owns the object. Answer a is incorrect because if the object is read-only, no quota is assigned. Answer c is incorrect because if a user only reads information, that user doesn't need quota, because the only space used for a read is temporary (if a sort is required), and temporary tablespace quota is assigned automatically. Answer d is incorrect because data inserted into another user's object uses their quota.

Question 7

What does the option **EXTERNALLY** do when you're using the **CREATE USER** command to create a user?

- ○ a. Allow the user remote access.
- ○ b. Allow the user network access.
- ○ c. Allow the user to access the database without a password.
- ○ d. Requires that the user's password be verified by the operating system.

The correct answer is d. When you create a user with **IDENTIFIED EX-TERNALLY**, you do not specify a password. The username and password are verified by the operating system.

Question 8

Jennifer used **WITH GRANT OPTION** to grant a privilege to Sharon. Sharon granted the privilege to Jacob. If Jennifer's privilege is revoked, who else will lose privileges?

- ○ a. Only Sharon
- ○ b. Only Jacob
- ○ c. Both Sharon and Jacob
- ○ d. No one else will lose privileges

The correct answer is c. **WITH GRANT OPTION** indicates that an object privilege was granted. Remember that when an object privilege is revoked, the revocation cascades to all the users who received the privilege from that user.

Question 9

Jennifer used **WITH ADMIN OPTION** to grant a privilege to Sharon. Sharon granted the privilege to Jacob. If Jennifer's privileges are revoked, who else will lose privileges?

○ a. Only Sharon

○ b. Only Jacob

○ c. Both Sharon and Jacob

○ d. No one else will lose privileges

The correct answer is d. **WITH ADMIN OPTION** indicates that a system privilege was granted. Revoking system privileges from a user does not cascade to others.

Question 10

Which characteristic describes a role?

○ a. Can only consist of object privileges.

○ b. Is owned by the DBA.

○ c. May be granted to any role except itself.

○ d. May be granted to itself.

The correct answer is c. Both system and object privileges can be granted to a role, and a role can be granted to another user. However, recursive grants of a role to itself are not allowed.

Question 11

Which command could you use to set a default role for a user?

○ a. **CREATE ROLE**

○ b. **ALTER USER**

○ c. **CREATE USER**

○ d. **SET ROLE**

The correct answer is b. It is correct that you can set a default role for a user when the user is created. However, the question implies that the user and role are already created. Answer a, **CREATE ROLE**, is used to create a role initially, not change an existing user. Answer c, **CREATE USER,** is used to create a user, not alter a user's properties, such as default roles. Answer d, **SET ROLE,** is used to turn on a nondefault role that a user may have assigned to them.

Need To Know More?

 Ault, Mike. *Oracle 8i Administration and Management.* John Wiley and Sons, New York, New York, 1999. ISBN 0-47-35453-8. Chapter 9 discusses objects, privileges, and user administration.

 Honour, Dalberth, and Mehta Kaplan. *Oracle8 How-To.* Waite Group Press, Corte Madera, California, 1998. ISBN 1-57169-123-5. Chapters 3 and 8 discuss users and security.

 Oracle8 Server SQL Reference, Release 8.0, Volumes 1 and 2. Oracle Corporation, Redwood Shores, California, June 1997. Part No. A54648-01 and A54649-01. This is the source book for all Oracle SQL for version 8.

Oracle8 Server Administrator's Guide, Release 8.0. Oracle Corporation, Redwood Shores, California, June 1997. Part No. A32535-1.

All Oracle documentation is available online at **http://technet.oracle.com**. Membership is free.

The Oracle Data Dictionary

. . . .

Terms you'll need to understand:

√ Data dictionary

√ Metadata

√ Virtual table

√ Dynamic performance table (DPT)

√ Dynamic performance view (DPV)

√ View

√ Packages

√ Procedures

√ Functions

√ SQL

Techniques you'll need to master:

√ Mining the data dictionary

√ Structuring the data dictionary

In Chapter 7, you learned about database access through the use of system and object privileges. In this chapter, we'll look at the guts of the Oracle system: the data dictionary.

Overview Of The Oracle Data Dictionary

The Oracle data dictionary stores the information required for the Oracle system to operate. This information includes all the details about the structures that make up the items we think of as being in a database. The data dictionary is *data about data*, or, as it is more popularly called, *metadata*. Metadata details data types, lengths, precesions, and what data items are contained in which objects. All details of tables, indexes, synonyms, views, grants, roles, and so forth are contained in the data dictionary. An expert with a few minutes' access to your data dictionary will know more about your database than you could have told him in the same amount of time. This is one reason why the **SYS** and **SYSTEM** user passwords should be instantly changed and jealously guarded after installation is complete.

Oracle sets the **SYSTEM** and **SYS** passwords to **MANAGER** and **CHANGE_ON_INSTALL**, respectively; you should always reset them.

Oracle C Structs And V$ Views

It may surprise some of you to learn that Oracle is written in C. However, the main structures (called *structs*) are actually C struct blocks. These normally aren't visible to users; indeed, you have to define a view against them to even be able to describe them. Listing 8.1 is a partial list of the major C structs, commonly called the X$ tables.

Listing 8.1 Partial list of **X$** tables.

```
NAME
-------------------------------

X$KQFTA
X$KQFVI
X$KQFVT
X$KQFDT
X$KQFCO
X$KCVFHONL
X$KCVFHMRR
```

```
X$KGLTABLE
X$KGLBODY
X$KGLTRIGGER
X$KGLINDEX
X$KGLCLUSTER
X$KGLCURSOR
```

Until recently, these structs were only documented internally, and little documentation about them was available. Now, by detective work in the virtual performance view structures documented in the virtual view **V$FIXED_VIEW_DEFINITION**, we can see their names (from a query against the SYS-owned virtual table, **V$FIXED_TABLE**) and get an idea of what each struct is used for.

You probably don't need to be concerned with the base C structs, but you should study the virtual views (the **V$** views) that use them extensively; these are called *dynamic performance tables (DPTs)* or *dynamic performance views (DPVs)*.

 I must stress the importance of knowing all you can about all of the **V$** views; they make your life as an Oracle DBA much easier.

An example of a DPT from a query against the **V$FIXED_VIEW_DEFINITION** table is shown in Listing 8.2. In Oracle8, the base views' names are changed to **GV$**, and an instance number is added to each. For simplicity's sake, however, I am showing the view as it would appear if the **V$** view were the top level (99 percent of you will never use parallel servers, where the instance number is important).

Listing 8.2   Example **V$** table and its definition.

```
VIEW_NAME           VIEW_DEFINITION
-------------------  ---------------------------------------------
V$DATAFILE          select
                    fe.indx+1,decode(bitand(fe.festa,19),0,
                    'OFFLINE',1,'SYSOFF',
                    2,'ONLINE',3,'SYSTEM',16,'RECOVER',18,
                    'RECOVER','UNKNOWN'),
                    decode(bitand(fe.festa, 12),
                    0,'DISABLED',4,'READ ONLY',12,
                    'READ WRITE','UNKNOWN'),
                    to_number(fe.fecps),fh.fhfsz*fe.febsz,
                    fe.fecsz*fe.febsz,fn.fnnam from x$kccfe
                    fe,x$kccfn fn, x$kcvfh fh where
```

```
fe.fedup!=0 and fe.indx+1=fn.fnfno  and
fn.fntyp=3 and fh.hxfil=fn.fnfno and
fn.fnnam is not null
```

The X$ tables generally won't be used by the DBA, and for the most part, other than those mentioned below, they will not be covered on the test. The X$ tables sometimes change dramatically between releases, so don't depend on the above list being the same as you would get from your instance.

Generally speaking, the V$ tables are used to show transitory performance information based on the underlying C structs, known as the X$ tables. These DPTs are the only views in Oracle where the data will change almost every time you select from them. This dynamism is why they are called *dynamic* performance tables or views. Because they are based on C structs that are an integral part of the kernel of Oracle, they're also available in a mounted but not open database. Except for a few special DPTs built by optional scripts as needed, the V$ DPTs are created by internalized procedures when the database is built.

Two important X$ tables are **X$KCBCHB** and **X$KCBRHB**. These tables are used to determine the performance characteristics of the SGA db block buffers. Both tables contain a **COUNT** column and an **INDX** column. The **INDX** column corresponds to a single buffer in the db block buffers. The **COUNT** column corresponds to the number of cache hits either gained or lost from the addition or removal of buffers. One row exists for each block monitored, as determined by the least recently used (LRU) block statistics initialization parameters. If you remember that the "R" in **X$KCBRHB** stands for *raise* and the central C in **X$KCBCHB** stands for *chop*, it'll help you keep track of which table tracks raises (increases) and which table tracks chops (decreases) in the database block buffers. In Oracle version 8.1.5, these tables are replaced by a single view.

The only data-structure information contained in the X$ and V$ objects is information that would be used in recovery, and the only information needed for recovery concerns the physical data files (**V$DBFILE**) and the redo logs (**V$LOGHIST** and **V$LOGFILE**). Other than these few views, the others concern performance statistics. The actual metadata is stored in database tables identical in structure to the tables and objects they document.

General database users usually don't need to access the V$ DPTs. Some DPTs, like the **V$DATABASE** view, do contain useful information, such as the Oracle version and database name, for general users. I usually grant select permission to the public user for this view and verify that a public synonym is available.

You should know the following V$ DPTs:

➤ **V$RECOVERY_STATUS**—This view was added to version 7.3 to allow the DBA to track the status of media recovery.

➤ **V$RECOVERY_FILE_STATUS**—This view was added to version 7.3 to allow the DBA to query the status of media recovery.

➤ **V$DB_OBJECT_CACHE**—This view provides information on the amount of sharable memory used by a cached PL/SQL object.

➤ **V$SYSSTAT**—This view has a plethora of system-level statistics. Statistics such as **sorts (memory)** tell how many times a particular type of operation has been performed since startup. Generally speaking, sort location tracking is vital for most applications, and sorts should be done in memory whenever possible, especially for Online Transaction Processing (OLTP) applications. This view is also used to monitor client/server traffic statistics. When tuning the system global area (SGA), you can use this view with the **X$KCBRBH** table to evaluate the effect of an increase or decrease in the size of the database buffer cache.

➤ **V$LATCH**—This view contains information on latches and locks. The **SLEEPS** column indicates the number of times that a process waited for a latch. For example, information on the requests for latches that were willing to wait (**WILLING_TO_WAIT** column) is contained in the **MISSES** and **GETS** columns of this view. If you suspect that latch contention is happening, issue a query against this view's **SLEEPS** column to display the number of times a process has waited for a particular latch.

➤ **V$CACHE**—This view is normally used only in parallel-server installations. However, it's useful in more situations than that because you can use it to analyze the database buffer cache in both exclusive and shared server modes. The view shows only objects currently being cached. This view is created by the catparr.sql script, which must be run in addition to the standard catproc.sql script for it to be created.

➤ **V$SYSTEM_EVENT**—This view contains information on system-wide events and is used by the utlbstat and utlestat scripts as a source of statistics. System status, such as the need to increase the redo log buffer size (**LOG_BUFFER**), can be ascertained by looking at the system events (in this case, "log buffer space") listed in this view. Another system event that DBAs should watch for is the "buffer busy waits" event, which indicates contention for the database buffer cache. The total number of event waits for each category is shown in this view.

➤ **V$TRANSACTION**—This view contains information on all transactions in the database. Along with the **V$SESSION** view, **V$TRANSACTION** can be used to get details about a specific user transaction.

➤ **V$SESSION**—This view documents all sessions currently attached to the database. It contains columns that indicate if the session is causing lock contention and, if so, in which row. Because their values are required by the **ALTER SYSTEM KILL SESSION** command, the **SERIAL#** and **SID** columns are useful if you need to kill a user session.

➤ **V$SESSION_EVENT**—This view contains information on session-level events and is used by the utlbstat/utlestat scripts as a source of statistics. It's also useful for determining whether there's I/O contention for the redo log files. Information such as system-wide waits per session are here as well.

➤ **V$LOGFILE**—This view contains the list of all redo log files and their locations. When used with the **V$DBFILE** view, its output is used to provide input to the **CREATE CONTROLFILE** command.

➤ **V$DBFILE**—This view contains the names and locations of all database data files. When used with the **V$LOGFILE** view, it provides the data for input to the **CREATE CONTROLFILE** command. It also provides information used to generate the commands used during a backup operation to back up the physical database data files. This information is also contained in the **DBA_DATA_FILES** view.

➤ **V$LIBRARYCACHE**—This view documents activity in the shared pool library caches. The ratio of **RELOADS** to **PINS** for a specific type of cache should always be less than 1 percent in a properly tuned database. The **RELOADS** column represents the number of object definitions that have been aged out of the library cache for lack of space. The **PINS** column represents the executions of an item in the library cache. The **GETHITRATIO** column should always show a value of greater than 0.9 in an ideally tuned database.

➤ **V$SESSION_WAIT**—This view contains information on session waits and is used by the utlbstat/utlestat scripts as a source of statistics. The wait times, indicated in the **WAIT_TIME** column, record a session's last wait time if the initialization parameter **TIMED_STATISTICS** is set to **TRUE** or **ALTER SYSTEM** is used to reset the parameter to **TRUE**.

➤ **V$SORT_SEGMENT**—This view is a map to the sort extent pool (SEP); it contains such items as the total extents for the **TEMP** tablespace areas, and it's used to monitor sort segments in the **TEMP** tablespace. Each time an unused extent is found in the SEP, the column **EXTENT_HITS** is incremented by one.

➤ V$WAITSTAT—This view contains information on wait statistics, such as high free-list contention. Entries greater than zero in the **VALUE** column indicate possible contention for that resource if the initialization parameter **TIMED_STATISTICS** is set to **TRUE** or **ALTER SYSTEM** is used to reset the parameter to **TRUE**.

For some reason, Oracle likes to refer to rollback segments by the term *undo*, so any references to undo headers or blocks are referring to rollback segments.

The Oracle $ (Dollar) Tables

The final level of the Oracle internals (other than the views based upon them) is collectively known as the *$ tables* or *dollar tables*. Oracle sometimes refers to them as the *base data dictionary tables*. They're called dollar tables because, initially, all of them ended with a dollar sign (for example, **COL$**, **TAB$**, **IND$**). But lately, Oracle has moved away from this standard, so it can often be difficult to identify the actual data dictionary tables. (This is a good reason not to place anything in the **SYSTEM** tablespace that isn't a part of the data dictionary or that doesn't belong to the SYS user.) The dollar tables are built by the sql.bsq script, which until recently was a hands-off item. Oracle has finally allowed us to edit the sql.bsq script to improve storage parameters for the dollar tables and indexes (in early Oracle7 releases, this was done by experienced DBAs but not supported by Oracle itself). I suggest that you look over the sql.bsq script because it has some interesting internal documentation that shines light into Oracle's data dictionary. Most of the tables created by the sql.bsq script contain comments on each of the table attributes (columns) detailing the column's purpose. Table 8.1 shows the names and descriptions of the dollar tables for a version 8.0.5 Oracle database.

Generally speaking, access to dollar tables should be restricted to DBA personnel. Users, however, can use the next set of views I'll discuss: the DBA_, USER_, and ALL_ set of data dictionary views.

The Data Dictionary User Views: **DBA_, USER_, And ALL_**

Usually the view hierarchy flows from the C structs to the V$ DPTs and from the dollar tables to the **DBA_, USER_**, and **ALL_** views. Sometimes shortcuts are taken and the C structs and dollar tables are both used, but rarely. Generally, the **DBA_** and other views of their type are based on the dollar tables.

Table 8.1 Dollar tables and their descriptions.

Table Name	Description
ACCESS$	Access table for database objects.
ARGUMENT$	Procedure argument table; describes procedural arguments.
ATEMPTAB$	A temporary table used by Oracle8; don't mess with it.
ATTRCOL$	Oracle8 table that stores information about User-Defined Type (UDT) attributes used in columns.
ATTRIBUTE$	Oracle8 table that stores details about UDT attributes.
AUD$	Audit trail table, which contains entries for all audited actions.
AUDIT$	Audit options table, which tracks auditing actions activated.
AUDIT_ACTIONS	Contains descriptions of auditable actions.
BOOTSTRAP$	Table used during instance startup.
CCOL$	Table of all constraint columns for the database.
CDEF$	Table of all constraint definitions in the database.
CLU$	Table of all clusters in the database.
COL$	Contains descriptions of all columns used in the database.
COLLECTION$	Contains information about collection types (**VARRAY**s and nested tables).
COLTYPE$	Contains information on columns that contain types rather than regular data types.
COM$	Contains all object and column comments for the database.
CON$	Contains all constraint names in the database.
DBMS_ALERT_INFO	Contains data on user-defined alerts created by **DBMS_ALERT**.
DBMS_LOCK_ALLOCATED	Contains information about locks allocated with **DBMS_LOCK**.
DEFROLE$	Shows all default roles assigned to users in the database.

(continued)

Table 8.1   Dollar tables and their descriptions (continued).

Table Name	Description
DEPENDENCY$	Shows all interobject dependencies in the database.
DIR$	Contains information about directories.
DUAL	Single-column, single-value table used for nondirected selects.
DUC$	Table for procedure tracking in the database.
ERROR$	Shows current errors for all users in the database.
EXPACT$	Shows functions to run against tables during export.
FET$	Shows all free extents in the database.
FILE$	Shows all files for the database tablespaces.
HISTGRM$	Shows specifications for histograms used in the database.
HIST_HEAD$	Contains all database histogram header data.
ICOL$	Contains all database index columns.
IDL_CHAR$	IDL table for character pieces.
IDL_SB4$	IDL table for SB4 pieces.
IDL_UB1$	IDL table for UB1 pieces.
IDL_UB2$	IDL table for UB2 pieces.
ID_GENS$	Contains a number that corresponds to the number of identification generators in an Oracle8 database.
INCEXP	Incremental export support table.
INCFIL	Shows incremental export file names and users.
INCVID	Contains the identifier for the last valid incremental export.
IND$	Shows all database indexes.
INDPART$	Shows all index partitions in the database.
JOB$	Contains all database-defined jobs.
KOPM$	Oracle8 metadata table.
LAB$	Contains all database-defined labels.

(continued)

Table 8.1 Dollar tables and their descriptions (continued).

Table Name	Description
LIBRARY$	Contains **LIBRARY** definitions for an Oracle8 database.
LINK$	Shows all database links.
LOB$	Shows Oracle8 **LOB** definitions.
METHOD$	Shows UDT method definitions for Oracle8.
MIGRATE$	Used during Oracle7-to-Oracle8 migration.
MLOG$	Shows all snapshot local master tables.
MLOG_REFCOL$	Tracks filter columns for snapshot logs.
NOEXP$	Contains a list of tables that will not be exported.
NTAB$	Contains information on all nested tables in the database.
OBJ$	Shows all database objects.
OBJAUTH$	Shows table authorizations.
OBJPRIV$	Shows privileges granted to objects in the database.
OID$	Contains all object identifiers in the database (Oracle8 only).
PARAMETER$	Tracks all parameters for methods in UDTs.
PARTCOL$	Tracks partition key columns for partitioned tables.
PARTOBJ$	Tracks all partitioned objects; has a one-to-many relationship with **PARTCOL$**.
PENDING_SESSIONS$	Child table for **PENDING_TRANS$**.
PENDING_SUB_SESSIONS$	Child table for **PENDING_SESSIONS$**.
PENDING_TRANS$	Table of pending or in-doubt transactions.
PROCEDURE$	Table of database procedures.
PROFILE$	Table of database profile resource mappings.
PROFNAME$	Table of database profile names.
PROPS$	Table of database fixed properties.
PSTUBTBL	Table created by the diutl.sql routine, used to generate stubs for procedures and functions.

(continued)

Table 8.1   Dollar tables and their descriptions (continued).

Table Name	Description
REFCON$	Contains **REF** constraint information.
REG_SNAP$	Contains information on registered snapshots.
RESOURCE_COST$	Table of resource costs used with profiles.
RESOURCE_MAP	Maps resource numbers to resource names.
RESULTS$	Maps result sets for UDT methods.
RGCHILD$	Table of all refresh group children.
RGROUP$	Table of all refresh groups.
SEG$	Maps all database segments.
SEQ$	Shows all database sequences.
SLOG$	Shows all snapshots on local masters.
SNAP$	Shows all local snapshots.
SNAP_COLMAP$	Contains snapshot aliasing information.
SNAP_REFOP$	Contains data on fast refresh operations for snapshots.
SNAP_REFTIME$	Contains the last refresh time for all snapshots.
SOURCE$	Stores source code for all stored objects in the database.
STMT_AUDIT_OPTION_MAP	Maps audit actions to audit-action names.
SYN$	Shows all synonyms in the database.
SYSAUTH$	Shows all system privilege grants for the database.
SYSTEM_PRIVILEGE_MAP	Maps system privilege numbers to privilege names.
TAB$	Table of all database tables.
TABLE_PRIVILEGE_MAP	Maps table privilege numbers to table privilege names.
TABPART$	Contains information on all table partitions.
TRIGGER$	Contains all trigger definitions for the database.
TRIGGERCOL$	Maps triggers to the columns they work against.
TRUSTED_LIST$	Lists trusted users for trusted DB links in Trusted Oracle.

(continued)

Table 8.1 Dollar tables and their descriptions (continued).

Table Name	Description
TS$	Shows all tablespaces for the database.
TSQ$	Shows all tablespace quota grants in the database.
TYPE$	Contains data on all **TYPE**s (UDTs) defined in the database.
TYPED_VIEW$	Contains information on typed views (used to map relational tables into object-oriented structures).
TYPE_MISC$	Table of miscellaneous type data (UDT).
UET$	Shows all used extents in the database.
UGROUP$	Contains information on rollback segment groups.
UNDO$	Shows all rollback segments for the database.
USER$	Shows all user definitions for the database.
USER_ASTATUS_MAP	Used with the password management utility to show user status.
USER_HISTORY$	Used with the password usage tracking feature in Oracle8.
VIEW$	Shows all view definitions for the database.
_default_auditing_options_	Maps all default auditing option numbers to names.

The **DBA_** views are the DBA's windows into the data dictionary. These views contain the condensed versions of the dollar tables in readable format. The **USER_** views provide a window into the user-owned object details in the data dictionary, and the **ALL_** views contain information on every object that the user has access to or has the privilege of using. In most cases, the views in the different hierarchies are identical except that a nonmeaningful column (such as **OWNER** in the **USER_** views) may be excluded.

You usually keep the **DBA_** views from users by not declaring public synonyms against them. However, a knowledgeable user, if he or she wants or needs to, can get information from the views with a query, using the SYS schema prefix.

For the purpose of the exam, you can safely assume the views to be identical (unless the question is on how they differ!) and apply information gleaned about the **DBA_** views to the others.

In this section, we'll limit our discussion to the **DBA_** views. Table 8.2 lists these and their purposes.

For the most part, the names of the views are self-explanatory. For example, the **DBA_TABLES** view shows the details of all tables in the database. However, although some may have accurate names, they still may confuse inexperienced DBAs. For example, views with the word "RESOURCE" in them apply to database profiles because resources are the part and parcel of profiles.

Table 8.2 DBA views and their descriptions.	
View Name	**Description**
DBA_2PC_NEIGHBORS	Contains information about incoming and outgoing connections for pending transactions.
DBA_2PC_PENDING	Contains information about distributed transactions awaiting recovery.
DBA_ANALYZE_OBJECTS	Contains information about analyzed objects in the database.
DBA_AUDIT_EXISTS	Lists audit-trail entries produced by **AUDIT NOT EXISTS** and **AUDIT EXISTS**.
DBA_AUDIT_OBJECT	Contains audit-trail records for statements concerning objects—specifically: tables, clusters, views, indexes, sequences, [public] database links, [public] synonyms, procedures, triggers, rollback segments, tablespaces, roles, and users.
DBA_AUDIT_SESSION	Contains all audit-trail records concerning **CONNECT** and **DISCONNECT**.
DBA_AUDIT_STATEMENT	Contains audit-trail records concerning **GRANT, REVOKE, AUDIT, NO AUDIT,** and **ALTER SYSTEM**.
DBA_AUDIT_TRAIL	Contains all audit-trail entries.
DBA_BLOCKERS	Contains information on all sessions that are blocking other sessions. Built by the catblock.sql script.
DBA_CATALOG	Shows all database tables, views, synonyms, and sequences.
DBA_CLUSTERS	Shows descriptions of all clusters in the database.
DBA_CLUSTER_HASH_ EXPRESSIONS	Shows hash functions for all clusters.

(continued)

Table 8.2 DBA views and their descriptions (continued).

View Name	Description
DBA_CLU_COLUMNS	Maps table columns to cluster columns.
DBA_COL_COMMENTS	Lists all entered column comments for all tables and views.
DBA_COL_DESCRIPTION	Shows descriptions of columns of all tables and views.
DBA_COL_PRIVS	Shows all grants on columns in the database.
DBA_COLL_TYPES	Contains information on all collection types, such as nested tables and **VARRAY**s.
DBA_CONSTRAINTS	Shows constraint definitions on all tables.
DBA_CONS_COLUMNS	Contains information about accessible columns in constraint definitions.
DBA_DATA_FILES	Contains information about database files.
DBA_DB_LINKS	Shows all database links in the database.
DBA_DDL_LOCKS	Contains information on all database DDL locks. Built by the catblock.sql script.
DBA_DML_LOCKS	Contains information on all database DML locks. Built by the catblock.sql script.
DBA_DEPENDENCIES	Shows dependencies to and from objects.
DBA_DIRECTORIES	Contains information on all **DIRECTORY** objects.
DBA_ERRORS	Shows current errors on all stored objects in the database.
DBA_EXP_FILES	Shows descriptions of export files.
DBA_EXP_OBJECTS	Shows objects that have been incrementally exported.
DBA_EXP_VERSION	Shows the version number of the last export session.
DBA_EXTENTS	Shows extents composing all segments in the database.
DBA_FREE_SPACE	Shows free extents in all tablespaces.
DBA_FREE_SPACE_COALESCED	Shows statistics on coalesced space in tablespaces.
DBA_FREE_SPACE_COALESCED_TMP1	Shows coalesced free extents for all tablespaces.

(continued)

Table 8.2   DBA views and their descriptions (continued).

View Name	Description
DBA_FREE_SPACE_ COALESCED_TMP2	Shows free extents in tablespaces.
DBA_HISTOGRAMS	Contains histograms on columns of all tables. This view is obsolete in Oracle8 and will probably be eliminated eventually in favor of **DBA_TAB_HISTOGRAMS**.
DBA_INDEXES	Shows descriptions of all indexes in the database.
DBA_IND_COLUMNS	Shows columns composing indexes on all tables and clusters.
DBA_IND_PARTITIONS	Contains information on all index partitions in the database.
DBA_JOBS	Shows all jobs in the database.
DBA_JOBS_RUNNING	Shows all jobs in the database that are currently running. Joins **V$LOCK** and **JOB$**.
DBA_KEEPSIZES	Used by the **DBMS_SHARED_POOL** package to temporarily store shared pool object sizes.
DBA_LGLLOCK	Contains information on internal KGL locks. Built by the catblock.sql script.
DBA_LIBRARIES	Contains information on all **LIBRARY** objects.
DBA_LOBS	Contains information on all database **LOB**s (Large Objects, such as **BLOB**, **CLOB**, and **NCLOB** data types).
DBA_LOCK	Contains information on all locks or latches and all outstanding requests for locks or latches in the database. Created by catblock.sql.
DBA_LOCK_INTERNAL	Contains information on all database internal locks. Built by the catblock.sql script.
DBA_METHOD_PARAMS	Contains information on all of the parameters for all of the UDT methods in the database.
DBA_METHOD_RESULTS	Contains information on all of the UDT method result types in the database.
DBA_NESTED_TABLES	Contains information on all nested table objects.
DBA_OBJECTS	Shows all objects in the database.
DBA_OBJECT_SIZE	Shows sizes, in bytes, of various PL/SQL objects.

(continued)

Table 8.2 DBA views and their descriptions (continued).

View Name	Description
DBA_OBJ_AUDIT_OPTS	Shows auditing options for all tables and views.
DBA_PART_COL_STATISTICS	Contains information on all the partition key columns in the database, as well as their histogram information.
DBA_PART_HISTOGRAMS	Contains information on all partitioned table histograms.
DBA_PART_INDEXES	Contains information on all partitioned indexes in the database.
DBA_PART_KEY_COLUMNS	Contains information on all partition keys in the database.
DBA_PART_TABLES	Contains information on all partitioned tables in the database.
DBA_PENDING_ TRANSACTIONS	Contains information on pending transactions for a distributed environment; shows prepared but not executed transactions.
DBA_PRIV_AUDIT_OPTS	Shows descriptions of current system privileges being audited across the system and by users.
DBA_PROFILES	Displays all profiles and their limits.
DBA_QUEUES	Contains information on the advanced queuing options queues.
DBA_QUEUE_TABLES	Contains information on all of the advanced queuing options queue tables.
DBA_QTABLE_SORT	Contains information on how the advanced queuing options queue messages are stored.
DBA_RCHILD	Shows all the children in any refresh group. This view is not a join.
DBA_REFRESH	Shows all the refresh groups.
DBA_REFRESH_CHILDREN	Shows all the objects in refresh groups.
DBA_REFS	Contains information on all **REF** columns in the database.
DBA_REGISTERED_ SNAPSHOTS	Contains information on remote snapshots on local tables.
DBA_REPAUDIT_ATTRIBUTE	Contains information about attributes automatically maintained for replication.
DBA_REPAUDIT_COLUMN	Contains information about columns in all shadow tables for all replicated tables in the database.

(continued)

Table 8.2   DBA views and their descriptions (continued).

View Name	Description
DBA_REPCAT	Contains information about replicated objects in the database.
DBA_REPCATLOG	Contains information about asynchronous administration requests.
DBA_REPCOLUMN_GROUP	Shows all column groups of replicated tables in the database.
DBA_REPCONFLICT	Shows all conflicts for which users have specified resolutions in the database.
DBA_REPDDL	Shows arguments that do not fit in a single replicated log record.
DBA_REPGENERATED	Shows objects generated to support replication.
DBA_REPGROUP	Contains information about all replicated object groups.
DBA_REPGROUPED_ COLUMN	Shows columns in all the column groups of replicated tables in the database.
DBA_REPKEY_COLUMNS	Shows primary columns for a table using column-level replication.
DBA_REPOBJECT	Contains information about replicated objects.
DBA_REPPARAMETER_ COLUMN	Shows all columns used for resolving conflicts in the database.
DBA_REPPRIORITY	Shows values and their corresponding priorities in all priority groups in the database.
DBA_REPPRIORITY_GROUP	Contains information about all priority groups in the database.
DBA_REPPROP	Shows propagation information about replicated objects.
DBA_REPRESOLUTION	Shows descriptions of all conflict resolutions in the database.
DBA_REPRESOLUTION_ METHOD	Shows all conflict resolution methods in the database.
DBA_REPRESOLUTION_ STATISTICS	Shows statistics for conflict resolutions for all replicated tables in the database.
DBA_REPRESOL_STATS_ CONTROL	Contains information about statistics collection for conflict resolutions for all replicated tables in the database.

(continued)

Table 8.2 DBA views and their descriptions (continued).

View Name	Description
DBA_REPSCHEMA	Shows n-way replication information.
DBA_REPSITES	Shows n-way replication information.
DBA_RGROUP	Shows all refresh groups. This view is not a join.
DBA_ROLES	Shows all roles that exist in the database.
DBA_ROLE_PRIVS	Shows roles granted to users and roles.
DBA_ROLLBACK_SEGS	Shows descriptions of rollback segments.
DBA_SEGMENTS	Shows storage allocated for all database segments.
DBA_SEQUENCES	Shows descriptions of all sequences in the database.
DBA_SNAPSHOTS	Shows all snapshots in the database.
DBA_SNAPSHOT_LOG_FILTER_COLS	Contains an entry for each column used as a snapshot filter column.
DBA_SNAPSHOT_LOGS	Shows all snapshot logs in the database.
DBA_SNAPSHOT_REFRESH_TIMES	Contains information on the refresh times for all snapshots in the database.
DBA_SOURCE	Shows the source of all stored objects in the database.
DBA_STMT_AUDIT_OPTS	Shows descriptions of current system-auditing options across the system and by user.
DBA_SYNONYMS	Shows all synonyms in the database.
DBA_SYS_PRIVS	Shows system privileges granted to users and roles.
DBA_TABLES	Shows descriptions of all tables in the database.
DBA_TABLESPACES	Shows descriptions of all tablespaces.
DBA_TAB_COLUMNS	Shows columns of user's tables, views, and clusters.
DBA_TAB_COL_STATISTICS	Contains statistical data for each column in each table in the database.
DBA_TAB_COMMENTS	Contains all table-level comments for the database.
DBA_TAB_DESCRIPTION	Shows descriptions of all tables and views in the database.

(continued)

Table 8.2 DBA views and their descriptions (continued).	
View Name	**Description**
DBA_TAB_HISTOGRAMS	Contains a row for each table that is using a histogram in the database.
DBA_TAB_PARTITIONS	Contains information on all partitions for all partitioned tables in the database.
DBA_TAB_PRIVS	Shows all grants on objects in the database.
DBA_TRIGGERS	Shows all triggers in the database.
DBA_TRIGGER_COLS	Shows column usage in all triggers.
DBA_TS_QUOTAS	Shows tablespace quotas for all users.
DBA_TYPES	Contains information on all UDTs in the database.
DBA_TYPE_ATTRS	Contains information on all attributes for all types in the database.
DBA_TYPE_METHODS	Contains information on all UDT methods defined in the database.
DBA_UPDATABLE_ COLUMNS	Shows descriptions of database updatable columns.
DBA_USERS	Contains information about all users of the database.
DBA_VIEWS	Shows text of all views in the database.
DBA_WAITERS	Contains information on all sessions that are waiting on a lock, as well as the session they are waiting on. Built by the catblock.sql script.

Oracle Add-On Tables And Utility Scripts

Numerous scripts are housed in the $ORACLE_HOME/rdbms/admin directory on Unix and in the %ORACLE_HOME%\rdbms80\Admin directories on Windows 98 and Windows NT. Many scripts are automatically run by the catalog.sql and catproc.sql scripts during automated database builds or must be run manually during a manual build; others are optional. The optional scripts provide help in tuning the database, checking lock problems, and adding useful tables that a DBA should know about.

The catalog.sql script creates all of the commonly used data dictionary views. Scripts such as cataudit.sql (which creates the audit tables and is run by catproc.sql) have their antiscripts; for example, the antiscript for cataudit.sql is catnoaud.sql. Generally, an antiscript will have "no" embedded in its name and will be used to undo whatever its opposite script performed.

The catproc.sql script also runs virtually all of the dbms*.sql and prvt*.plb scripts, including dbmsutil.sql, which builds the **DBMS_APPLICATION_INFO** package and other useful utilities. The scripts that are considered extra but that are extremely useful are:

➤ *utlchain.sql*—This script creates the default table for storing the output of the **ANALYZE... LIST CHAINED ROWS** command.

➤ *utldidxs.sql*—This procedure has two parameters to allow DBAs to specify which statistics should be extracted from **INDEX$INDEX_STATS** and **INDEX$BADNESS_STATS**.

➤ *utldtree.sql*—This procedure, view, and temporary table allows you to see all objects that are (recursively) dependent on the given object. Note that you'll see only objects for which you have permission.

➤ *utlbstat.sql and utlestat.sql*—These are companion scripts. The utlestat.sql script generates the delta statistics based on the initial statistics loaded using utlbstat.sql. These scripts are used to generate the report.txt output file of statistics used for tuning.

➤ *utlexcpt.sql*—This script creates the **EXCEPTIONS** table used to hold table-entry information that causes conflicts when you're creating constraints. The row ID, table name, owner, and violated constraints are listed.

➤ *utllockt.sql*—This script generates a simple lock wait-for graph. This script prints the sessions in the system that are waiting for locks and the locks that they are waiting for. The printout is tree structured. If a session ID is printed immediately below and to the right of another session, it's waiting for that session. The session IDs printed on the left side of the page are the ones everyone is waiting for.

➤ *dbmspool.sql and prvtpool.plb*—These scripts build the **DBMS_SHARED_POOL** package of procedures for managing the shared pool. This package contains procedures for monitoring and pinning objects such as large packages or procedures in the shared pool.

➤ *utloidxs.sql*—This procedure is used to find information about the selectivity of columns. Use it to:

   ➤ Identify prospective columns for new indexes.

   ➤ Determine how selective a current index is.

   ➤ Determine whether or not a current index is useful.

➤ *utlsidxs.sql*—This script uses the utloidxs.sql script to analyze all indexes in a schema for usefulness.

➤ *utltkprf.sql*—This script grants public access to all views used by **TKPROF** with the **verbose=y** option, and it creates the **TKPROFER** role.

➤ *utlxplan.sql*—This script creates the table (**PLAN_TABLE**) that is used by the **EXPLAIN PLAN** statement. The **EXPLAIN** statement used in the **SET AUTOTRACE ON** command in SQL*Plus requires the presence of this table to store the descriptions of the row sources. The data in **PLAN_TABLE** is used to query and evaluate SQL statements using the **EXPLAIN** clause with the **AUTOTRACE** command, without using tracing or **TKPROF**.

➤ *catblock.sql*—This script creates many useful views about database locks. These views are:

> ➤ DBA_KGLLOCK

> ➤ DBA_LOCK (with synonym DBA_LOCKS)

> ➤ DBA_LOCK_INTERNAL

> ➤ DBA_DML_LOCKS

> ➤ DBA_DDL_LOCKS

> ➤ DBA_WAITERS

> ➤ DBA_BLOCKERS

The creation of a database is not complete until several scripts have been run. These scripts create the data dictionary views and install the procedure options and utilities. The catalog.sql script creates the most commonly used data dictionary views. The catproc.sql script creates the procedural options and utilities (**DBMS_** packages). In addition to these "must have" scripts, you should also run the catblock.sql, the dbmspool.sql, and the prvtpool.plb scripts. I also suggest that the catparr.sql script, which installs the parallel server views, be run because some of these views are useful for tuning purposes.

Exam questions about the data dictionary and Oracle internals will mostly be in the realm of tuning and monitoring. Your biggest problem will be that you'll tend to outsmart yourself. You'll say, "Naw, the answer can't be that, that's too easy." Remember, the data dictionary was designed to be easy to use (at least at the higher levels), so objects are named for the items they contain.

An example of what I'm talking about is the use of the **DBA_** views. If you review you'll notice a trend: **DBA_TABLES** monitors all tables, **USER_TABLES** monitors a single user's tables, and **ALL_TABLES** monitors all tables that a user has access to. Likewise, the **V$** views are named for the functions they perform; the **V$DBFILES** view shows database data files, **V$INSTANCE** gives instance-specific values, **V$SESSION** monitors sessions, and so forth. With a little experience, and by keeping your head, you can derive most of the answers from the questions.

Practice Questions

Question 1

> If you query the **X$KCBRHB** virtual table, which value will the **COUNT** column display?
>
> ○ a. The number of blocks in the database buffer cache.
>
> ○ b. The number of additional cache hits gained by adding additional cache blocks.
>
> ○ c. The number of reads in the database buffer cache.
>
> ○ d. The number of buffers added to the database buffer cache.

The correct answer is b. The **COUNT** column corresponds to the number of cache hits either gained or lost from the addition or removal of buffers. One row exists for each block monitored as determined by the least recently used (LRU) block statistics initialization parameters. If you remember that the "R" in **X$KCBRHB** stands for *raise* and the central "C" in **X$KCBCHB** stands for *chop*, it'll help you keep track of which table tracks raises (increases) and which table tracks chops (decreases) in the database block buffers.

Question 2

> Which data dictionary view would you query to display information related to profiles?
>
> ○ a. **RESOURCE_COST**
>
> ○ b. **USER_USERS**
>
> ○ c. **DBA_CONSTRAINTS**
>
> ○ d. **USER_CONSTRAINTS**

Trick! question

The correct answer is a. This is a trick question because it involves one of the few tables that doesn't reflect its true purpose, even though its name is accurate. To answer this question, you need to know what a profile is and know that it uses values called resources. Once you know that a profile has resources assigned to it, there's only one possible answer and that's a, **RESOURCE_COST**.

Question 3

> Which view could you query to display users with **CREATE PROCEDURE** privileges?
>
> ○ a. **DBA_USER_PRIVS**
>
> ○ b. **DBA_SYS_PRIVS**
>
> ○ c. **DBA_COL_PRIVS**
>
> ○ d. **USER_TAB_PRIVS_RECEIVED**

The correct answer is b. If you know that **CREATE PROCEDURE** is a SYS-TEM-level privilege, you should know that you'll query the **DBA_SYS_PRIVS** view. This question can be considered a trick question. A quick glance and a general knowledge of how Oracle names work might lead you to choose answer a, **DBA_USER_PRIVS**. However, this view doesn't exist. Once you eliminate a, you can also quickly eliminate answers c and d because they deal with column (**COL**) and table (**TAB**) privileges.

Question 4

> Which category of data dictionary views does not have an **OWNER** column?
>
> ○ a. **USER_**
>
> ○ b. **DBA_**
>
> ○ c. **ALL_**
>
> ○ d. All categories of data dictionary views have an **OWNER** column.

The correct answer is a, **USER_**. Because the **USER_** views are for objects in which the user is the owner, there's no need for an **OWNER** column. Answer b is incorrect because **DBA_** views show all objects for which they were created, and an **OWNER** column would be mandatory. Likewise, because the **ALL_** views show all objects for which a user has access, an **OWNER** column is required in this type of view as well. Therefore, answer c is incorrect. You should know that answer d is incorrect.

Question 5

> Which data dictionary view could a user query to display the number of bytes charged to his or her user name?
>
> ○ a. **ALL_USERS**
>
> ○ b. **USER_USERS**
>
> ○ c. **DBA_TS_QUOTAS**
>
> ○ d. **USER_TS_QUOTAS**
>
> ○ e. Only the DBA can display the number of bytes charged to a user.

The correct answer is d. This question refers to a quota. Once you understand this, you can apply the naming convention rules. The question asks what data dictionary view can a *user* query. This means that we're looking for a **USER_** view. Quotas are placed on tablespaces, so we're looking for a view for tablespaces (**TS_**) and a view about quotas. The only view name that meets the above criteria is answer d, **USER_TS_QUOTAS**.

Question 6

> Which view would you query to display the users who have been granted **SYSDBA** and **SYSOPER** system privileges?
>
> ○ a. **USER_USERS**
>
> ○ b. **ALL_USERS**
>
> ○ c. **V$PWFILE_USERS**
>
> ○ d. **DBA_USERS**

The correct answer is c, **V$PWFILE_USERS**. This view is used only to identify users who've been granted **SYSDBA** and **SYSOPER**. If you know the **DBA_USERS** view, you know that it contains a user name, default and **TEMP** tablespaces, a profile assignment, and other user-related data, but it contains no privilege information or grant information. Therefore, any views related to the **DBA_** view (**USER_USERS** or **ALL_USERS**) won't have any privilege or grant information. With these two tidbits, we've eliminated three of four answers. In this case, we are left with answer c.

Question 7

Which script file creates the base data dictionary tables?

○ a. utlmontr.sql

○ b. catexp.sql

○ c. sql.bsq

○ d. cataud.sql

○ e. catproc.sql

The correct answer is c, sql.bsq. Again, if you don't know the answer right off, with a little name sleuthing, you can eliminate the incorrect answers. You should realize that the utlmontr.sql script is probably for utilities and concerns monitoring, not data dictionary base tables. The catexp.sql script is probably about catalogs (that is, views or tables) and exports. Again, this is not a data dictionary base table type of item. The cataud.sql script deals with a catalog and probably auditing. Finally, you could venture an educated guess that the catproc.sql script concerns catalogs and procedures, not a base-level item. This leaves the sql.bsq script, answer c. One way to remember that sql.bsq is about data dictionary base tables is to equate the "b" in bsq with base.

Question 8

Which package can you use to pin large objects in the library cache?

○ a. **STANDARD**

○ b. **DBMS_STANDARD**

○ c. **DIUTL**

○ d. **DBMS_SHARED_POOL**

The correct answer is d. This question requires you to remember that the library cache is another name for the shared pool. The only answer that concerns the shared pool is d, **DBMS_SHARED_POOL**.

Question 9

Which Oracle version 7.3 fixed view can you query to get the status of media recovery?

○ a. **V$CONTROLFILE**

○ b. **V$RECOVERY_FILE_STATUS**

○ c. **V$DATAFILE**

○ d. **V$RECOVERY_STATUS**

The correct answer is d. The **V$RECOVERY_STATUS** view shows the status of media recovery. In this question, you have to answer the question exactly. Both **V$RECOVERY_FILE_STATUS** and **V$RECOVERY_STATUS** show recovery status, so we can eliminate the other **V$** DPTs shown by using name conventions. However, **V$RECOVERY_FILE_STATUS** shows the status of the database's data files during recovery, so that answer is incorrect.

Need To Know More?

Ault, Michael R. *Oracle8 Administration and Management.* John Wiley & Sons, New York, New York, 1998. ISBN 0-471-19234-1. This book provides a comprehensive look at Oracle8 and Oracle7.x management. Use it for the definitions of all **DBA_**, **V$**, and data-dictionary related topics.

Gurry, Mark and Peter Corrigan. *Oracle Performance Tuning, 2nd Edition.* O'Reilly & Associates, Sebastopol, California, 1996. ISBN 1-056592-237-9. This is a must-have for tuning Oracle databases. This book covers all aspects of Oracle database tuning and any tuning related questions are covered inside this volume. A must have for any DBA's bookshelf.

Oracle8 Reference, Release 8.0. Oracle Corporation, Redwood Shores, California, December 1997. Part Number A58242-01. This Oracle manual provides information about the **V$** views and the **DBA_** views and their uses.

Database Design
And Modeling

Terms you'll need to understand:

√ Strategy

√ Analysis

√ Design

√ Build

√ Transition

√ Production

√ Entity

√ Relationship

√ Entity relationship diagram (ERD)

√ Function hierarchy diagram (FHD)

√ Attribute

√ Column

√ Unique identifier (UID)

√ Primary key

√ Foreign key

√ Referential integrity

√ Rules of normalization

Techniques you'll need to master:

√ Applying the five-step system development cycle

√ Reading an entity relationship diagram (ERD)

√ Understanding the process of normalization

√ Converting from an ERD to tables, relations, and constraints

Ninety percent of any field is learning the jargon—the language specific to that field. The other 10 percent is applying techniques. With Oracle, the jargon is that of relational databases. Much of this jargon can be attributed to Dr. E.F. (Ted) Codd, who formulated the rules called *normal forms* for data. He also formulated the relational algebra upon which relational databases are designed. If you're preparing to take the OCP exams, you should already be familiar with the relational-database jargon. This chapter is designed to be only a refresher. If you're not familiar with the jargon, there's a comprehensive list of references in the "Need To Know More?" section at the end of this chapter. Applying the techniques in the field is what experience is all about, and if you know the jargon, the techniques are easy to learn.

The Five-Step System Development Cycle

You may see the five-step process or the seven-step process (depending on the granularity of each step) used in many books on systems and software design. Figure 9.1 shows the Oracle interpretation of the steps as a five-step process.

The five-step system development cycle consists of:

1. Strategy and analysis

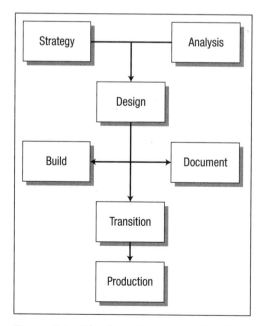

Figure 9.1 The five-step system development cycle.

2. Design

3. Build and document

4. Transition

5. Production

Each of the steps is important, and adherence to this type of methodology has been shown to produce systems that are easy to maintain. Oracle computer-aided design and engineering tools (CASE), such as Designer 2000 and Developer 2000, use this methodology.

Step 1: Strategy And Analysis

In the strategy and analysis step, the user and system requirements are gathered and analyzed. The expected deliverable from this stage would be a set of requirements (in the form of documents) that specify the *whats* of the system, not the *hows*. A project plan and development time frame may also be specified at this time, with the understanding that if the design cycle shows problems with the time lines, they'll be adjusted. At this point, the documents are high level and provide the big picture.

Step 2: Design

In the design step, the user requirements and system specifications are applied to create a design document consisting of an entity relationship diagram (ERD), flow charts, function decompositions, module descriptions, data flow diagrams, and so forth. (The ERD is discussed further in the "Database Design" section later in this chapter.) The purpose of the design step is to convey the *hows* of the application; programming languages, database systems, coding, and naming standards are specified here.

Step 3: Build And Document

In the build and document step, the design is converted from specifications and diagrams to actual executables and database structures. During this step, the as-built documents are written; these documents instruct users how to use the system and instruct production support how to support the application. ERDs are mapped to tables, columns, and relations; function decompositions are mapped to stored procedures; and 3GL executables and module descriptions are mapped to GUIs, screens, and executables. The build and document step also incorporates unit testing and system test functions. The database layout (physical placement) is optimized and application (or statement) tuning is performed.

Step 4: Transition

In the transition step, the application is put through user-acceptance testing. Final procedures are developed and turnover packages are prepared. Database memory usage and IO balance, as well as contention tuning, occurs at this time because true user load can't usually be tested without users.

Step 5: Production

In the production step, the application is passed off to production support and moves into a maintenance mode in which code is locked down and database changes are minimized. Once a system is in production, the activities around it move into the support and maintenance arena. Strict change control is the rule under production-level applications, and no ad hoc changes to structure or code are allowed.

Database Design

Tables, tuples, and attributes have already been discussed throughout this book, and we've also touched on relationships. Now, let's look at relationships more closely and see how they apply to relational databases. Stop for a moment and consider the company where you work or perhaps for whom you're consulting. The company has employees or, let's say, the company employs workers. The reverse is also true; a worker is employed by a company. This is a *relationship*—a logical tie between information that's contained in entities. In this case, the information is from the entities: the company and the workers. Notice that a relationship must make sense from both directions. If a relationship doesn't work both ways, it isn't a proper relationship, and you should re-evaluate it.

Can a worker have more than one job? Of course. Can a company have more than one worker? Yes. So let's restate the relationship. A company can employ one or more workers. A worker may be employed by one or more companies.

This is called a *many-to-many* relationship. Of course, other types of relationships exist. Within a company, a worker usually works for only one department at a time, though a department may have many workers. This is called a *one-to-many relationship*. Generally speaking, most many-to-many relationships can be broken down into one-to-many relationships; and one-to-many relationships form a majority of the relationships in a relational database. A relationship occurs between two *entities*. In the earlier example, *worker* and *company* are entities. An entity is always singular in nature, and in most cases, an entity will map into a table. A diagram showing the logical structure of a relational database is called an *entity relationship diagram*, or ERD for short (see Figure 9.2).

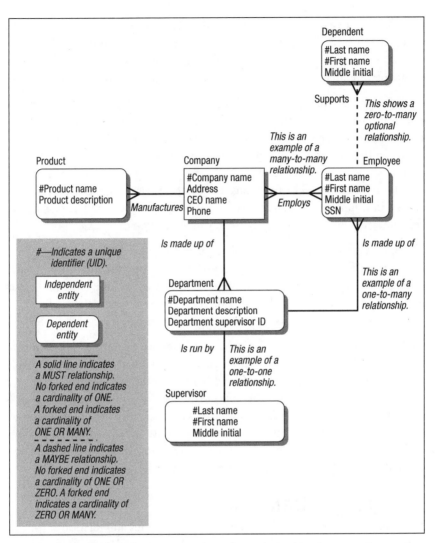

Figure 9.2   Example of a simple entity relationship diagram.

 Study Figure 9.2 carefully. You should be able to identify what the symbols mean (such as the pound sign indicating UID and the various line types indicating different types of relationships).

Another aspect of a relational database is its functions. Don't be confused. In this case, a *function* is a reason for a database feature, not a stored PL/SQL program. Without functions, a database would have no purpose for being. Functions start at a high level, such as providing a means to track and report the work history of employees. Functions can be broken down or, if you wish, decomposed, until they are atomic—that is, until they reach the smallest possible unit. A purist would break down a function until it consisted of operations involving individual attributes, such as adds, deletes, updates, or retrieves.

For example, say we wished to retrieve a record (or tuple) from a table, update one of its columns (or attributes), and then return the row to the table. In one light, this operation could be considered one function: the update of attribute *x*. In a different light, it could be decomposed into the individual retrieves, modifies, and updates of the columns. In most cases, going into great and gory detail is not required. The functions that a database is designed to perform are shown in a function hierarchy diagram (FHD). Entities (hence, tables) and relations map into functions. Figure 9.3 shows a simple FHD.

The final aspect of a relational database is its modules. A *module* may perform one or more functions and may map into a form, a report, a menu, or a procedure. For example, a single module representing a form can handle numerous atomic functions, such as adding, updating, retrieving, and deleting tables or even a group of tables or data records.

Let's summarize. A relational database is made up of entities consisting of attributes. These entities and attributes can be mapped into tables and columns. Each occurrence of an entity adds a row to the table it maps to. These rows are called tuples. Each entity links to one or more other entities by means of relationships. A relationship is defined as a named association between two things of significance (entities). Relationships must be valid in both directions and must have degree, such as one-to-many or many-to-many. Relationships must also show *optionality*, such as *may be* or *must be*.

Designing A Database

Functions are used to tell what's done with the entities and relationships. Entities and relationships map into functions. Modules implement functions and map into forms, reports, menus, or procedures. The normal sequence of database design is:

1. Perform entity and attribute analysis.

2. Normalize entity and attribute structure to at least third normal form (discussed in the next section).

3. Identify unique identifiers (UIDs) for each entity.

4. Define entity relationships.

5. Map entities to tables.

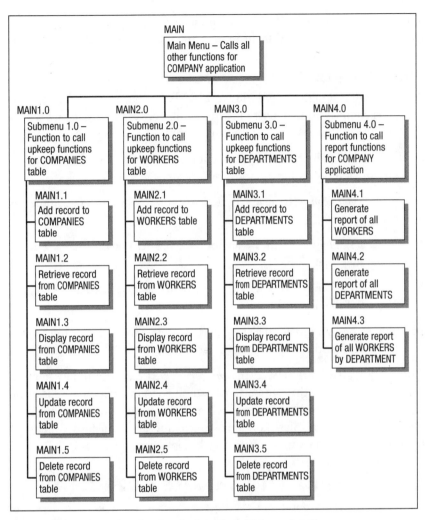

Figure 9.3 Example of a simple functional hierarchy diagram.

6. Map attributes to columns.

7. Map UIDs to primary keys.

8. Map relationships to foreign keys.

This logical movement from the abstract to the concrete allows for a properly designed database. Primary-key and foreign-key relationships are collectively termed *referential integrity*. Other constraints, such as user-defined or column constraints, are also available. User-defined constraints are usually specified to enforce business rules. Column constraints generally enforce typing rules (for example, a character field that can use only numbers and that has a constraint to enforce this value rule), validate input, or enforce a **NOT NULL** restriction.

Normalization

All of relational design depends on Dr. E.F. (Ted) Codd's rules. The entire set of rules is complex and, to most of us, rather obscure at times. Luckily, they've been used to produce the rules of normalization. These, simply stated, are:

➤ *Precursor*—Each occurrence of an entity is uniquely identifiable by a combination of attributes and/or relationships.

➤ *First normal form*—Remove repeated attributes or groups of attributes to their own entity.

➤ *Second normal form*—Remove attributes dependent on only part of the unique identifier.

➤ *Third normal form*—Remove attributes dependent on attributes that are not part of the unique identifier.

In short, to be in third normal form, all attributes in an entity must relate directly to the identifier and only to the identifier.

This unique identifier is called the *primary key*. It can be a unique number (such as a Social Security number) or a combination of attributes called a *concatenated key* or a *combination key* (such as a last name and a date of birth). Generally speaking, primary keys are used to enforce relationships by mapping the keys into related entities, where they become *foreign keys*.

Oracle And The Object Paradigm

For years, Oracle Corporation has been one of the major contenders, if not the major contender, in the relational database arena. Now with Oracle8, Oracle Corporation enters full force into the object-relational-database world. With this new object-orientation for Oracle comes a new bag of jargon that developers and database administrators (DBAs) have to get a grip upon.

> *Note: I regret to say that none of the material from here to the practice questions is on the SQL/PLSQL exam, but I am including it here for completeness because the object-oriented features of Oracle8 are some of the major changes in this version. You can skip this section if you like, but if you want to be ready to use the new features, I suggest that you read on. In addition, it is anticipated that the 8i exam will be broadened to cover objects and object design.*

Object-Oriented Terms

Here are a few object-oriented terms to ease the transition into the object paradigm:

➤ *Encapsulation*—The feature of an object-oriented program that means it is completely standalone—that is, it is not dependent on another object, nor is another object dependent on it for its function. Because an encapsulated object is passed attributes and returns attributes with no other external communication required (i.e., no global or public variables, and no external calls to other objects or methods), it is said to implement *data hiding* or *binding*.

➤ *Polymorphism*—Allows a single method to be used by multiple classes or objects. An example would be overloading an Oracle PL/SQL function to handle multiple data types. An overloaded function (or procedure) in PL/SQL has several functions or procedures with the same name and argument structure, except that one of the passed arguments is a different data type. The user has no idea that multiple functions or procedures exist; he or she simply calls the function or procedure and gets the results back.

➤ *Inheritance*—Is just what it appears to be. We have touched on the concept of classes; well, classes can be subdivided into superclasses and subclasses. Inheritance allows subclasses to inherit behaviors from their superclass. Generally speaking, a superclass will be a general class of generic functions with subclasses that exhibit more and more specialized behavior. Oracle8 will not support inheritance until release 8.2 at the earliest.

➤ *Persistence*—Allows for object data to be available across executions.

➤ *Passive database*—A database that does not store the implementations of the methods defined for a class. The database must provide implementation of methods in their application code.

➤ *Active database*—A database that stores implementations of the methods for its classes, so the methods are stored and retrieved with the objects. An active database by its very nature is more robust and flexible than a passive database.

Oracle-Specific Object Terms

The Oracle object-oriented extensions have Oracle8-specific definitions. These extensions involve how Oracle uses object technology. Let's look at some of these Oracle-specific definitions to complete this discussion of object-oriented jargon:

➤ *Object type*—An object type (called *abstract data type* in early-release documentation) is a data type that defines Oracle objects. An Oracle object is one instance of an Oracle object type. Oracle objects can be persistent (such as tables or views) or transient (such as a memory construct in PL/SQL). The **CREATE TYPE** command is used to create an Oracle object type. Persistent object types will have an object identifier (OID), and nonpersistent object types will not. These object types are sometimes referred to as complex objects.

➤ *Object table*—An object table is a table of Oracle object types. If a pre-Oracle8 table is ported to Oracle8, it doesn't automatically become an object table. To get a relational table to behave as if it were an object table, you must make it part of an object view. Only objects represented by true object tables have OIDs. Object tables were referred to as *extent tables* or *typed tables* in early-release Oracle8 documents.

➤ *Object identifier (OID)*—As I said before, only objects stored in an object table have an OID. The OID is guaranteed to be globally unique, and it consists of a 128-byte hexadecimal value. By itself, an OID cannot be used to locate an object instance; only a **REF** that contains location data can be used for locating an object instance. The OID is used to enforce object identity.

➤ *Object*—An object is a single instance of an object data type; an object may or may not have an associated OID. If the object is from an object table, it will have an OID; if it is from Oracle Call Interface variables or PL/SQL variables, it will not.

➤ *Nested object*—An object is said to be nested if its object type is used to specify a single column in an object table.

➤ *Nested table*—The **CREATE TYPE** command can be used to create a type that is actually a table. This table type can then be used to create a table of that type. This table can be used as a column in a second object table, resulting in a nested table.

➤ *Data types*—There are three types of data type in Oracle8: built-in, library, or user-defined. Built-in types are the standard **NUMBER, DATE, VARCHAR2, LONG, LONG RAW, BLOB,** etc. User-Defined Types (UDTs) are specialized types built by users or **VAR**s. Library types are types built by a third party and supplied to the user. (Library types are generally a specialized form of the user-defined data type.) User-Defined Types with methods provide enforcement of classes. UDTs are made of the atomic data types or attributes and methods.

➤ *Methods*—Methods are stored procedures—written in PL/SQL and stored in the UDT—that perform operations on types. Methods enforce object behaviors.

➤ *LOBs*—New in Oracle8 is extended coverage for Large Objects (**LOBs**). There are several types of **LOBs**: character **LOB** (**CLOB**), Binary **LOB** (**BLOB**), National Character **LOB** (**NCLOB**), and a **LOB** stored externally to the database. This **LOB** is a **BFILE**, which is generally to be used for long binary files such as digitized movies or audio tracks.

➤ *External procedures*—Another new Oracle8 feature is the ability to call procedures from PL/SQL that don't reside in the database. By procedures I mean a 3GL program. Currently (version 8.0.5), only C is supported, but more languages will be available later. External procedures are also referred to as *3GL callouts*. One problem with these is that for each process that makes a 3GL callout, a new callout process is created, and because they don't yet work with MTS, this effectively doubles the number of operating system processes required in an environment that uses callouts.

➤ *Constructor*—This is an Oracle-kernel-generated method used to instantiate an instance of an Oracle object type. A constructor is differentiated from a user-created method in two ways: a constructor is system created, and it's automatically applied when a call is made to an object type or when an object type is needed and it doesn't have an implicit or explicit **SELF** parameter (to use a bit of object-speak).

➤ *Forward Type Definition*—I prefer to call this a *type-in-type*. Essentially it means that you can define an object type and then use that type in any number of subsequent type definitions. In this special case, both types refer to each other in their definitions. This involves the use of an incomplete type. For you C programmers, this is identical to forward declaration.

➤ *Object view*—An object view allows normal relational tables to be referred to like objects in an object relational database. The object view process supplies synthesized OIDs for relational rows.

➤ *Encapsulation*—Encapsulation is the process by which attributes and behaviors are stored together. Oracle's new type specifications allow attributes and methods to be stored together in the database.

➤ *Persistence*—Oracle allows both persistent and nonpersistent data structures. Persistent structures are tables, object tables, clusters, and so on, and nonpersistent structures are PL/SQL types.

These terms might appear to be varnish-overs of current technology. Maybe this is the case, or maybe not; either way, the new kid on the block is object oriented, and we all have to follow wherever he leads.

In many cases, object-oriented design and implementation will be more difficult until a base of objects and development techniques is established. This is
what is known as the bleeding edge, and we are it. Other than Oracle, there are
several other database systems that are, or claim to be, object databases.

Principles And Goals Of Object-Oriented Programming

Object-oriented programming has both principles and goals. Here are nine
principles that govern object-oriented programming:

➤ *Principle 1*—Actions in object-oriented programming are initiated by
transmission of a message to an agent (i.e., an object) responsible for the
action.

➤ *Principle 2*—Messages in object-oriented programming encode the
request for action and are accompanied by any arguments (information)
needed by the agent to carry out the action.

➤ *Principle 3*—If an object accepts a message, it accepts the responsibility
to carry out the action. The action is carried out via a method.

➤ *Principle 4*—All objects can be considered instances of a specific class. A
class is a grouping of similar objects. Objects exhibit both *state* (values)
and *behavior* (methods).

➤ *Principle 5*—All objects of a specific class use the same method in
response to similar messages. Classes may exhibit relationships to
subclasses and superclasses.

➤ *Principle 6*—All subclasses inherit attributes and perhaps methods from
their superclasses.

➤ *Principle 7*—The class hierarchy (subclass—class—superclass tree) is
walked up from whatever class is initially referred to until the appropriate method is found to deal with a message. If no method is found, an
error is issued. This principle is known as *method binding*.

➤ *Principle 8*—The issuer of a message doesn't need to know how the
message action is carried out; the issuer needs to know only that if the
message is accepted by an object, the action will be carried out. This
principle is called *information hiding*.

➤ *Principle 9*—A subclass can exhibit different behaviors than its superclass
does; that is, a subclass can override the behaviors by applying exceptions. Often the method used will have the same name. Therefore,

multiple subclasses will have the same method but will arrive at the required action by different routes. This principle is called *polymorphism*.

The goals of object-oriented programming are simple: provide jobs for all of those C++, Visual Basic, and Visual C++ programmers out there. Seriously, though, object-oriented programming has some definite goals:

➤ *Make code reusable*—Ultimately the top goal of object-oriented programming is to develop a full set of off-the-shelf reusable components that can be used universally to develop software, just as a set of boards is used to assemble a modern computer.

➤ *Separate form and function*—Because of data hiding, encapsulation, and polymorphism, you no longer have to worry about the "hows"—you can worry only about the "whats." (Once someone writes fully reusable "hows," that is...)

➤ *Make programming more engineering and less art*—By using a standard set of reusable components, software engineers can concentrate on building applications instead of on building tools to build applications.

Characteristics Of An Object-Oriented System

So, what are the characteristics of object-oriented systems? Essentially, object-oriented systems are those systems in which code units (objects) have been pushed down into the same area as the data that they act upon. In other words, data units and code units are indistinguishable. This situation produces objects that can be readily reused and that behave in an object-oriented manner.

From the perspective of the users of object-oriented systems, users should see a consistent look and feel as they move throughout the application. This consistent look and feel is brought about by the reuse of screen and interface objects throughout the application.

From the maintenance programmer's viewpoint, an object-oriented system will consist of a series of objects that—as long as the maintenance programmer doesn't change the messages that the object understands—the programmer can alter at will with the assurance that the object will still function within the application framework. In addition, modifications to objects will be transferred throughout the structure of the application—that is, modifications to type primitives will promulgate to wherever they are used in the system.

The drawback of the object-oriented system is that executables are much larger. This is a result of several factors: the pairing of data and behaviors; the required code to ensure inheritance, polymorphism, and encapsulation; and the use of shared class libraries. Another factor is the use of generalized coding practices instead of the pinpoint solution coding that's used in non–object-oriented-applications. This increase in size of object-oriented applications will also result in slower applications. However, any losses in speed will (hopefully) be regained in better, more robust, more easily maintained applications.

Benefits Of The Object-Oriented Approach

So, what are benefits of the object-oriented approach to application development? There are several:

➤ *Code reusability*—If the application is done right, it will produce multiple objects—such as screen handlers, printer objects, and IO objects—that will be reusable in other projects and in multiple sections of the application.

➤ *Ease of maintenance*—The object-oriented approach allows individual objects to be upgraded, refined, and replaced without touching any of the rest of the code base. This isolation of object code should speed maintenance and, as long as the maintenance programmer follows the object interface rules, allow maintenance to be done at the single object level.

➤ *Standardization of application interfaces*—If all applications use the same interface objects, then all of your applications will have the same look and feel for your users. This standardization reduces the learning time for new applications and reduces operator errors.

Oracle8 And The Object-Oriented Paradigm

So what does all of this mean in relation to Oracle8? (No pun intended.) How does Oracle8 measure up to the standards for object-oriented applications? Let's answer these questions before we go on.

To be object oriented, a database system has to exhibit at least some of the characteristics of an object-oriented system. Does Oracle8 meet these criteria? Let's start by seeing what Oracle8 does to enforce the principles of object orientation.

➤ *Principle 1*—Actions in object-oriented programming are initiated by transmission of a message to an agent (i.e., an object) responsible for the action.

How Oracle implements this principle—The use of methods in types allows messages to be sent to objects built from these types. The action (method) is then carried out on the data stored in the type.

➤ *Principle 2*—Messages in object-oriented programming encode the request for action and are accompanied by any arguments (information) needed by the agent to carry out the action.

How Oracle implements this principle—Messages, in the form of method calls, are sent to objects built of Oracle types. Arguments may be passed with these method calls. Based on the contents of a message, Oracle types implement the appropriate methods on the data contained in the type.

➤ *Principle 3*—If an object accepts a message, it accepts the responsibility to carry out the action. The action is carried out via a method.

How Oracle implements this principle—If a method doesn't exist in a specific type, an error is returned.

➤ *Principle 4*—All objects can be considered instances of a specific class. A class is a grouping of similar objects. Objects exhibit both state (values) and behavior (methods).

How Oracle implements this principle—Types can be used to build objects, or they can be used in other types that can then be used in objects. Types have attributes which, when used to build objects, exhibit state (values). Each type can incorporate methods to enforce behavior for that type.

➤ *Principle 5*—All objects of a specific class use the same method in response to similar messages. Classes may exhibit relationships to subclasses and superclasses.

How Oracle implements this principle—If a type containing a method is used in an object, the method will be used no matter what object the type is used to build. If a type contains a subtype, the subtype's methods are available to the supertype when it's dealing with the subtype.

➤ *Principle 6*—All subclasses inherit attributes and perhaps methods from their superclasses.

How Oracle implements this principle—Oracle doesn't use inheritance until the late 8.1 or 8.2 release. All methods are local to the type they inhabit and aren't inherited up or down the type-subtype chain for an object.

➤ *Principle 7*—The class hierarchy (subclass—class—superclass tree) is walked up from whatever class is initially referred to until the appropriate method is found to deal with a message. If no method is found, an error is issued. This principle is known as *method binding*.

How Oracle implements this principle—Oracle8 type methods are local to the type they inhabit (until later releases of Oracle). Unless the method is in the specific type being addressed, an error is returned. There is no walking of the class hierarchy.

➤ *Principle 8*—The issuer of a message doesn't need to know how the message action is carried out; the issuer needs to know only that if the message is accepted by an object, the action will be carried out. This principle is called *information hiding*.

How Oracle implements this principle—Oracle type methods are fully compliant with this principle. The issuer of a call to a method doesn't have to concern itself with how it is carried out by the Oracle type method. If a method exists (i.e., the message is accepted), then the action will be carried out.

➤ *Principle 9*—A subclass can exhibit different behaviors than its superclass does—that is, a subclass can override the behaviors by applying exceptions. Often the method used will have the same name. Therefore, multiple subclasses will have the same method but will arrive at the required action by different routes. This principle is called *polymorphism*.

How Oracle implements this principle—Pseudo-polymorphism can be built into Oracle by the use of overloading in type methods, stored functions, or procedures, or with trigger logic. I say this is pseudo-polymorphism because it cannot be directly implemented at the type/subtype level until later releases of Oracle8.

So, how does Oracle measure up? Other than lacking inheritance and having only pseudo-polymorphism, pretty good. Although it is not 100 percent compliant with object orientation, it is much closer than many people think. When full inheritance is established, along with polymorphism, Oracle will be fully compliant. This is being promised for later releases of Oracle8 or possibly in Oracle9.

Developing A Type Hierarchy

One of the first steps in beginning an object-oriented development project is to develop a type hierarchy. The type hierarchy will determine inheritance characteristics for a set of classes, subclasses, and superclasses. You might question whether or not this step is important for Oracle8 because Oracle8 doesn't yet support inheritance. I suggest that an ounce of prevention is worth a pound of cure. If you design your types in Oracle so that they will easily map into the predefined type structure, then you will be miles ahead when Oracle does support inheritance.

In any object-oriented class structure, there are four general classes of types (taken from *An Introduction to Object Oriented Programming*, by Timothy Budd, Addison-Wesley Publishing, 1991). These are:

➤ *Data Manager, Data, or State classes*—Classes that maintain data or state information.

➤ *Data Sinks or Data Sources*—Classes that generate data (a source) or accept data for processing (a sink).

➤ *View or Observer classes*—Classes that allow data objects to be viewed, displayed, or printed. They generate user-viewed instances of other objects.

➤ *Facilitator or Helper classes*—Classes that maintain no state information themselves but facilitate complex processing. A synonym for these types would be a *catalyst type*.

How do these classes relate to Oracle8 development? Oracle8 provides the Data Manager class, which maintains data and the state of objects. Using Oracle development tools, you construct classes that perform the functions of View or Observer classes. Using PL/SQL, C++, Visual Basic, or other tools, you build the Facilitator and Helper classes. Data Sources are usually pre-existent, but they can be built with any of the tools already mentioned. Data Sinks are constructed in the same fashion as Data Sources.

Types generally move from the abstract to the concrete. For example, a superclass for all objects that move people and goods could be called "VEHICLE." A VEHICLE has the property that it moves people or goods by physical means. (If we want to include matter transports, à la Star Trek, then we would call the class "TRANSPORTERS.") Physical means are defined as using road, track, sea, or air. This is a pretty loose class; notice a distressing lack of attributes. However, we can now add subtypes to our class (or type) hierarchy. We shall add AUTOMOBILE, TRUCK, TRAIN, and AIRPLANE. We can further enhance our type structure by adding attributes to each of the subtypes now defined.

You'll notice that a type hierarchy generally has one supertype, and several types and subtypes and attributes. The best way to determine something's status in a type hierarchy is to apply the "HAS-A, IS-A" test. This test is simply a semantic one. If you can say that something "IS-A" something else, then it is a subtype of that something else; for example, a wife is a female, and a husband is a male. A woman is a female; a man is a male. Therefore, "wife" and "woman" are two subtypes of "female," and "man" and "husband" are subtypes of "male." As long as you can "IS-A" up a hierarchy, then you haven't reached the ultimate supertype. For example: Husband is a man is a male is a human is a primate is an animal is a living creature.

So, in our example type hierarchy, the generalized "living creature" is the ultimate supertype for a husband or wife.

Determining attributes can sometimes be difficult. For example, a husband HAS-A wife, and a wife HAS-A husband, so are wife and husband attributes or types? I'll leave this for you to decide! Anyway, a general test is that if an object HAS-A something, then that something is probably an attribute and not a subtype.

This doesn't mean that attributes can't be types in their own right. A company HAS-AN employee, but an employee HAS-A job. If an object has "HAS-A"s associated with it, then it is most likely a separate object that may have a reference back to the first object. This is how we resolve the husband/wife tangle from the previous example: by saying that a wife is married to a husband (notice the singular usage, at least in most Western cultures). Another example would be an automobile type and its attribute list. An automobile HAS-A tire (more than one, hopefully), but a tire HAS-A size, HAS-AN inflation limit, HAS-A tread type, and HAS-A manufacturer. It is the same with virtually every other part of an automobile as well.

You should identify the least granular type levels and start there in your application. For example, if you are building an automobile-rental-tracking application, you don't need to walk the type hierarchy back up to the vehicle level or allow for trains, planes, ships, or trucks, so you can start at the automobile and track down the chain. Start at the top level that applies to your application and work on the type dependency chain from there.

Defining Type Methods (Behaviors)

Type methods in Oracle8 define type behaviors. When a type is created, Oracle8 automatically builds constructor, modifier, and destructor methods. Special behaviors—such as computing total price, determining status from value (or state, if you prefer), defining order of return when selected—can be built into an Oracle8 type.

After a type hierarchy is established and you have a list of types, dependent types, and attributes, you need to create a list of type behaviors. These behaviors can be brought about by external action requests via messages, or by internal actions required by changes of state. Methods are probably most useful for change-of-state actions. For example, a method could be defined to automatically update a Purchase Order object's Total attribute when a line item is added, updated, or deleted. A method could be defined to notify a second object via a message (called an *alert*) that, upon completion of the Purchase Order object, initiates an action to order more of whatever is on the purchase order.

You must decide what types will have what behaviors and then translate these behaviors into methods. A method should never attempt to update, add, or delete another type's attribute state. A method can send a message that causes the messaged type to initiate an action, but it cannot do the action itself. A sure sign that a type may have to be broken into multiple subtypes is that you find yourself giving it to many behaviors. Behaviors should be atomic in nature. If a behavior affects multiple attributes in a type, it should be externalized into a Helper class object (such as a PL/SQL function, procedure, or trigger).

What are some fatal design flaws when you're defining methods? Here are several:

➤ *A type with too many methods*—Shows that there are dependent types hidden within the type's structure that should be placed into their own type.

➤ *A type with no methods*—Shows that the type probably isn't a type and can be deleted or absorbed into another type.

➤ *Types with methods that will never be used*—Often the result of a development team's communication problems. Usually the result of not understanding the type's true function in the type structure or hierarchy.

➤ *A type with disconnected methods*—Usually happens to the last types or first types defined. A result of thinking, "We know we need this behavior, but we don't know where." If a type's assigned methods don't directly affect the type or its attributes, those methods don't belong there.

➤ *Multiple types with the same method*—Usually happens to types that are actually subtypes of a common supertype. In Oracle8, this method should be moved to an external procedure until true inheritance becomes available. When Oracle8 offers true inheritance, you can create a supertype and place a common method there.

Relationships And Objects
In Oracle8, relationships are shown by the use of **REF** statements. **REF** relationships are one-to-one.

For dependent entities whose behavior is limited to a fixed number of occurrences per parent record, Oracle suggests the use of **VARRAY**s, which are stored in line with the parent records in RAW format. However, in tests it appears that this wastes space, and a nested table may be more efficient. For multiple relationships where the ultimate number is unknown or is extremely high, or where the size of the resulting RAW would be too long (like any time in early releases), I suggest using a nested table. For related one-to-one data, I suggest using a type specification.

Rules For Using Types

Here are some rules for using types:

➤ A VARRAY or nested table cannot contain a **VARRAY** or nested table as an attribute.

➤ When using nested tables, you must specify a store table in which to store their records.

➤ Store tables inherit the physical attributes of their parent table.

➤ Default values cannot be specified for **VARRAY**s.

➤ Constraints (even **NOT NULL**) cannot be used in type definitions (they must be specified using an **ALTER TABLE** command).

➤ A table column specified as a **VARRAY** cannot be indexed.

➤ A table using **VARRAY**s or nested tables cannot be partitioned.

➤ **VARRAY**s cannot be directly compared in SQL.

➤ An incomplete type (forward typing) is allowed, but an incomplete type cannot be used in a **CREATE TABLE** command until it is complete.

➤ The scalar parts of a type can be indexed directly in the parent-table object.

➤ **VARRAY** and nested table subattributes cannot be indexed directly on a parent-table object.

➤ A nested table's store table attributes can be indexed.

Converting From Oracle7 To Oracle8 Using Types

Here are a few conversion guidelines:

➤ Attribute sets that are related one-to-one with the main object should be placed in a **TYPE** definition and used directly.

➤ Attribute sets that have a low, fixed number of occurrences should be placed into **VARRAY**s. (This may not be true if constraints or direct comparisons are required.)

➤ Attribute sets with many occurrences or those that require constraints and value-to-value comparison should be placed in nested tables.

➤ If a type is to be used in a **REF**able object, the object must be created with the **AS OBJECT** clause.

➤ **REF** clauses in a **TYPE** declaration must be finished via an **ALTER TABLE** command on the final object table if scoping or **ROWID** storage are required.

➤ Use of **WITH ROWID** and **OIDINDEX** clauses should be encouraged to speed access and, in some cases, to reduce storage requirements.

➤ Analysis of dependencies is critical to success.

Oracle8 will require a great deal more front-end analysis in order to prevent recoding. Oracle8 is a new view of the programming world, and you will have to change your perception of how the database works to fully utilize the provided features.

Practice Questions

Question 1

> Which symbol indicates a UID?
>
> ○ a. *
>
> ○ b. o
>
> ○ c. #
>
> ○ d. &
>
> ○ e. $

The correct answer is c; the pound sign (#) indicates a unique identifier. Answer a is incorrect because the asterisk (*) is used to denote a primary key value. Answer b is incorrect because the lowercase "o" is used to indicate a candidate key. Answer d is incorrect because the ampersand (&) isn't used in CASE nomenclature. Answer e is incorrect because the dollar sign ($) isn't used in CASE nomenclature.

Question 2

> What does a single solid line between two entities represent?
>
> ○ a. Optional
>
> ○ b. Mandatory
>
> ○ c. One or more
>
> ○ d. One and only one

The correct answer is d, a one and only one relationship. Answer a is incorrect because an optional relationship is shown by a dotted line. Answer b, though partially correct in that a solid line represents a mandatory relationship, doesn't completely answer the question. Answer c is incorrect because a one-or-more relationship is shown with a crow's-foot symbol on the "many" end of the relationship line.

Question 3

> Which statement shows a many-to-one relationship?
>
> ○ a. Each street may have one and only one sign.
>
> ○ b. Many signs may be on one and only one street.
>
> ○ c. Many signs may be on many streets.

The correct answer is b. In this case, the answer is contained in the wording "Many signs may be on one and only one street." Even though the normal wording is reversed (usually it would be "each street may have one or more signs"), this statement still denotes a one-to-many relationship. Answer a is incorrect because it clearly denotes a one-to-one relationship. Answer c is incorrect because it's clearly not a many-to-many relationship.

Question 4

> Which type of constraint is used to enforce business rules?
>
> ○ a. Column
>
> ○ b. Referential
>
> ○ c. Entity
>
> ○ d. User-defined

The correct answer is d. By definition, a user-defined constraint is used to enforce business rules. Answer a is incorrect because column constraints are used to enforce validity, value, and **NULL** and **NOT NULL** constraints only. Answer b is incorrect because referential constraints are used for data concurrency only. Answer c is incorrect because there's no such thing as an entity constraint.

Question 5

> Which type of integrity constraint exists if only a number value can be in-
> serted into a column?
>
> ○ a. Column
>
> ○ b. Referential
>
> ○ c. Entity
>
> ○ d. User-defined

The correct answer is a. The constraint described is used to enforce typing;
only column constraints are used to enforce typing. Answer b is incorrect because referential constraints are used for data concurrency only. Answer c is
incorrect because there are no entity constraints. Answer d is incorrect because
user-defined constraints are used for business rules, not for data validity.

Question 6

> Which component of an entity relationship diagram is a named association
> between two things of significance?
>
> ○ a. Entity
>
> ○ b. Attribute
>
> ○ c. Relationship

The correct answer is c because the question is actually stating the definition of
a relationship. Answer a is incorrect because an entity is a thing of significance,
such as a car or person, so the question is actually asking "Which component
of an entity relationship diagram is a named association between two entities?"
A named association is a relationship. Answer b is incorrect because an attribute is part of an entity.

Question 7

When you're designing a database, which step comes first?

- ○ a. Map attributes to columns.
- ○ b. Map entities to tables.
- ○ c. Map UIDs to primary keys.
- ○ d. Map relationships to foreign keys.

The correct answer is b. You must first map the entities into tables, or you won't have anything in which to place the attributes when you map them into columns. If you don't have columns, you can't specify primary keys; and if you don't have primary keys, you can't map out the relationships to other tables by using primary-key/foreign-key relationships. Answer a is incorrect because you can't map attributes to columns until you've mapped entities to tables. Answer c is incorrect because you can't map UIDs to primary keys until attributes are mapped to columns. Answer d is incorrect because relationships can't be mapped to foreign keys until UIDs are mapped to primary keys.

Question 8

In which stage of the system development cycle should you complete user acceptance testing?

- ○ a. Strategy and analysis
- ○ b. Design
- ○ c. Build and document
- ○ d. Transition
- ○ e. Production

The correct answer is d. The process of user acceptance testing is done during the transition phase, and it would not make sense to try to do user testing before a complete system is available. Answer a is incorrect because strategy and analysis constitute the first step of the cycle, and there's nothing to test yet. Answer b is incorrect because at the design step, there's nothing to test yet. Answer c is incorrect because, at this step, we build and document, so although there are things that can be tested, they aren't ready for users until all modules are ready. Answer e is incorrect because by the time you reach the production step, you had better have tested and let the users test the application.

Question 9

Which integrity constraint type states that foreign key values must match a primary key or be null?

○ a. Entity

○ b. Referential

○ c. Column

○ d. User-defined

The correct answer is b because the question is actually stating the definition of a referential integrity constraint. Answer a is incorrect because there are no entity constraints. Answer c is incorrect because column constraints enforce validity, value, or null status. Answer d is incorrect because user-defined constraints are used to enforce business rules.

Question 10

What is the first stage of the system development cycle?

○ a. Build and document

○ b. Design

○ c. Transition

○ d. Strategy and analysis

○ e. Production

The correct answer is d. The first stage is strategy and analysis. You can't design a system until you understand it. The strategy and analysis stage provides understanding used to design the system. The five steps of the development cycle should occur in this order:

1. Strategy and analysis

2. Design

3. Build and document

4. Transition

5. Production

Question 11

In which stage of the system development cycle should you involve the user community?

○ a. Strategy and analysis

○ b. Design

○ c. Build and document

○ d. Transition

○ e. Production

○ f. All of the above

For a properly developed system, the only answer that is correct is f. Users must be involved at all stages of application development.

Need To Know More?

Anstey, David A. *Oracle8 Object-Oriented Design.* The Coriolis Group, Scottsdale, Arizona, 1998. ISBN 1-57610-186-X. The entire book provides a good foundation for utilizing the object-related features of Oracle8.

Atre, Shaku. *Data Base: Structured Techniques for Design, Performance, and Management.* John Wiley & Sons, New York, New York, 1988. ISBN 0-47185-251-1. This book provides a complete overview of databases from their beginnings to relational databases, and it provides insights on proper normalization techniques and the *whys* behind the *hows*. Although it is now out of print, some online bookstores offer to search for a copy.

Ault, Michael R. *Oracle8 Administration and Management.* John Wiley & Sons, New York, New York, 1998. ISBN 0-47119-234-1. The introduction chapter reviews relational theory, entity relational modeling, and normalization.

Ault, Michael R. *Oracle8 Black Book.* The Coriolis Group, Scottsdale, Arizona, 1998. ISBN 1-57610-187-8. Chapters 1 through 6 provide a thorough grounding in object-related features of Oracle8.

Barker, Richard. *CASE*METHOD: Entity Relationship Modeling.* Addison-Wesley Publishing Co., Inc., Reading, Massachusetts, 1990. ISBN 0-20141-696-4. This book was written to follow Oracle's CASE methodology, so it is an excellent look at Oracle's CASE structure and implementation.

Barker, Richard. *CASE*METHOD: Tasks and Deliverables.* Addison-Wesley Publishing Co., Inc., Reading, Massachusetts, 1990. ISBN 0-20141-697-2. Together, this book and the other two *CASE*METHOD* books in this list detail all of Oracle's development methodologies and cover the system development cycle, entity relationship diagramming, and conversion of interviews into attributes, entities, and so forth.

Barker, Richard and Cliff Longman. *CASE*METHOD: Function and Process Modeling.* Addison-Wesley Publishing Co., Inc., Reading, Massachusetts, 1992. ISBN 0-20156-525-0. This book provides real-world examples to guide you through the process of function and process modeling.

Brathwaite, Kenmore S. *Relational Databases: Concepts, Design and Administration*. McGraw-Hill, Inc., New York, New York, 1991. ISBN 0-07007-252-3. Another excellent book covering relational database design and structure.

Date, Christopher J. *Introduction to Database Systems Vol. 2, 4th Edition*. Addison-Wesley Publishing Co., Inc., Reading, Massachusetts, 1982. ISBN 0-20114-474-3. Date's book may be a bit much for those not acquainted with relational theory, but it will give you all the great and gory details of relational theory.

PL/SQL

Terms you'll need to understand:

√ Anonymous PL/SQL block

√ Procedure

√ Function

√ Package header

√ Package body

√ Implicit cursor

√ Explicit cursor

√ Flow control

Techniques you'll need to master:

√ Creating anonymous PL/SQL blocks

√ Creating procedures

√ Creating functions

√ Using implicit and explicit cursors

√ Using flow control statements

One of the most important additions to Oracle has been PL/SQL. In normal SQL, you deal with single- or multiple-value sets only. In SQL, there's no way to conditionally insert, update, or select values based on multiple-condition sets (for example, if value A is 6, then make B equal currentcount+1, or if A is 7, make B equal currentcount-1). There's also no way to do single-line processing of a set of values in SQL. All of this functionality—conditional processing, flow control, and single-line set processing—came along when Oracle added PL/SQL. Both SQL and PL/SQL directly support DML commands, but special Oracle-provided packages must be employed to use DDL commands in PL/SQL. Unlike SQL, PL/SQL also allows for exception handling routines.

The PL/SQL Engine

The PL/SQL engine processes PL/SQL blocks submitted from the user program or interface. The PL/SQL blocks are parsed into the procedural statements and SQL statements. These parsed statements are processed by passing the procedural statements to the Procedural Statement Executor inside the engine. The Procedural Statement Executor also processes data that is local to the application and then passes the SQL statements, as needed, to the Oracle8 server SQL Statement Executor.

Memory Use And PL/SQL

A time-saving feature of PL/SQL is that it allows a correctly written, parsed program to be used many times. A PL/SQL package, function, procedure, and trigger used once will remain in memory until it's no longer frequently accessed. PL/SQL objects are stored both in unparsed and parsed forms in the database, hence, PL/SQL objects are collectively known as *stored objects*. In addition, PL/SQL uses the advantageous block structure that allows programs to be compartmentalized by function. By wrapping many SQL lines into one PL/SQL program, client/server applications reduce network traffic because a PL/SQL program is sent to the database as one transaction, not as multiple smaller transactions. The PL/SQL engine can also be incorporated into other program sets, such as those involving forms and reports, thereby reducing transaction processing in these programs as well. A PL/SQL subprogram must contain a header, an executable section, and an **END** command.

PL/SQL Basics

PL/SQL uses the block concept contained within a **BEGIN...END;** construct. An unnamed PL/SQL block that's used either as a standalone block in SQL*Plus or as part of a trigger is known as an *anonymous PL/SQL block*. These anonymous blocks can be used in all Oracle environments. The **BEGIN...END;** construct, usually called the *executable section*, is the only required part of a PL/SQL program; it must begin with the keyword **BEGIN** and end with the keyword **END** followed by a semicolon. All **BEGIN...END;** keywords must be balanced.

A *database trigger* is a PL/SQL program (actually an anonymous PL/SQL block) that's associated with a table and is executed (or fired) automatically based on a predefined action, such as **INSERT, UPDATE,** or **DELETE,** against the table.

A complete PL/SQL program consists of the following:

➤ *A declaration section*—Where variables, cursors, and constants are defined

➤ *An executable section*—Where the program logic is performed

➤ *An exception handling section*—Where errors are handled

An anonymous PL/SQL program can consist of any of the following:

➤ Just a **BEGIN...END;** block

➤ A **DECLARE** section and a **BEGIN...END;** block

➤ A **DECLARE, BEGIN...END;,** and **EXCEPTION** section

Anonymous PL/SQL programs can be as short as a single line or span dozens of pages and be as complex as any procedure, function, or trigger. For a block to be valid, the **BEGIN...END;** statements must contain an executable statement. The most simple anonymous PL/SQL block would be:

```
BEGIN
    NULL;
END;
```

Of course, this block doesn't do anything. (In PL/SQL, **NULL** is an executable statement; it is used to fill in when you don't have any processing to do but must have a PL/SQL block, such as in some **EXCEPTION** situations.)

By definition, any stored PL/SQL block (that is, the PL/SQL program is stored in the data dictionary tables and doesn't need to be read from an external file) is a named PL/SQL block. A named PL/SQL block can be a procedure or a function. Beginning with Oracle7.3, trigger definitions are now stored objects even though they contain anonymous PL/SQL blocks. The most simple PL/SQL named object (hence, a stored object) would be:

```
PROCEDURE start_it IS
BEGIN
NULL;
END start_it;
```

Although the purpose of such a stored object isn't really clear right now, I'll show you what it can be used for in a little bit.

Related PL/SQL procedures and functions can be combined into stored structures called *packages*. PL/SQL packages consist of a *header section*, which declares all publicly available contents of the package and their variables, and the *package body*, which contains the actual package definitions and any private objects, not usable outside of the package. When any publicly available part of a package is used, the entire package is read into memory and made available.

In some cases, a package may be used by multiple users who access the same application. In this situation, the package should be read into memory and *pinned* (removed from the aging algorithm) to keep it in memory. To prevent shared-pool fragmentation, this preloading of packages should be done before any *ad hoc* SQL generation occurs. To this end, a procedure similar to the **start_it** procedure shown in the earlier snippet should be included in all packages, so a simple call to the **start_it** procedure inside the package loads the entire package into memory, where it can be pinned using the **DBMS_SHARED_POOL** package.

PL/SQL Procedures

PL/SQL procedures are stored, named objects that can return zero, one, or many values to the calling process. However, only one row of values can be returned from a single procedure call. Procedure variables used for sending variables into the program and for receiving values from the program are specified at the start of the program. These procedure variables are designated as **IN** (input variables only that can't have their values altered by the program, so they're treated as constants), **OUT** (output variables that are set by the program during execution), and **IN OUT** (variables that are used for both input and output of values).

When you're creating procedures, the next line after the end of the procedure definition must be a forward slash (/) to tell Oracle to compile the procedure. The last statement of a PL/SQL procedure must end with a semicolon.

As was demonstrated with the **start_it** procedure, neither input nor output is required in a procedure. A procedure also doesn't require a declarative section. In fact, the only required part of a procedure is the **PROCEDURE** line and the executable block.

Procedures are created using the **CREATE PROCEDURE** command. The syntax for the **CREATE PROCEDURE** command is shown in Figure 10.1.

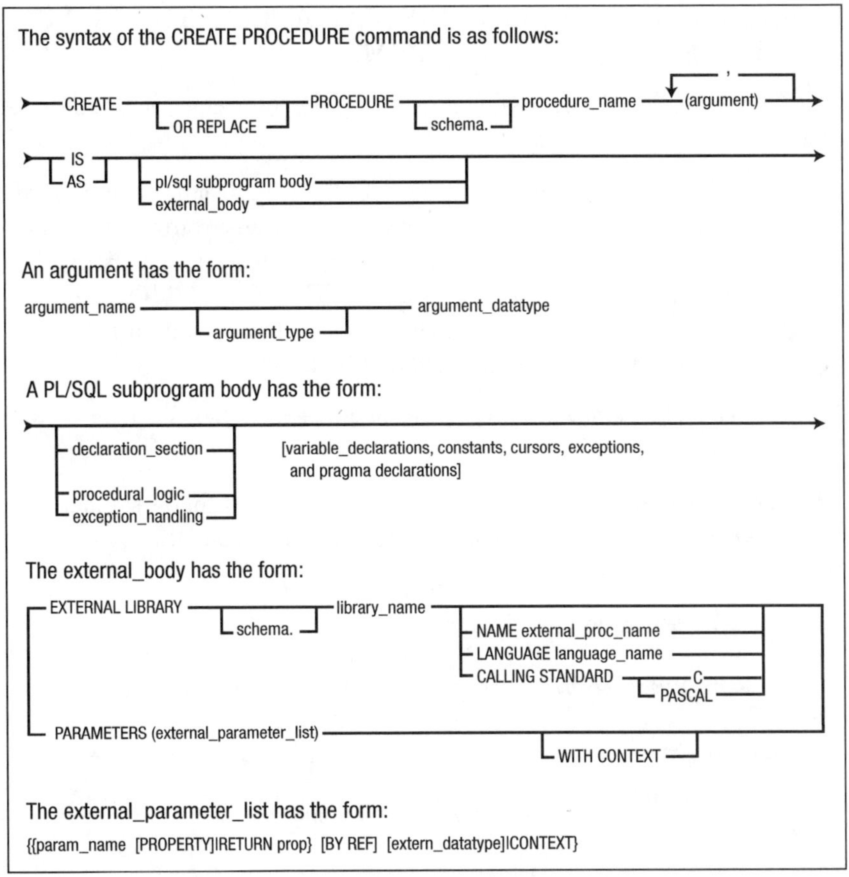

The syntax of the CREATE PROCEDURE command is as follows:

An argument has the form:

A PL/SQL subprogram body has the form:

The external_body has the form:

The external_parameter_list has the form:

`{{param_name [PROPERTY]|RETURN prop} [BY REF] [extern_datatype]|CONTEXT}`

Figure 10.1   Syntax for the **CREATE PROCEDURE** command and some of its arguments, parameters, and subprograms.

The **CREATE PROCEDURE** command has the following parameters:

➤ **argument_name**—The name given to this argument. It can be any valid variable name.

➤ **argument_type**—The type of argument: **IN, OUT,** or **IN OUT.** It specifies how the argument is to be treated (strictly input, strictly output, or both).

➤ **argument_datatype**—The data type of the argument. It can be any valid scalar data type.

➤ **external_body** argument—Has the form shown in Figure 10.1.

➤ **external_parameter_list** argument—Has the form shown in Figure 10.1, with this code repeated as many times as is needed. The **prop** argument has one of the following values: **INDICATOR, LENGTH, MAXLEN, CHARSETID,** or **CHARSETFORM.**

The **CREATE PROCEDURE** command has the following clauses and variables:

➤ **CREATE [OR REPLACE]**—Causes SQL to create a procedure. If **OR REPLACE** is not used and the procedure exists, an error will result. The **OR REPLACE** allows for in-place altering of a procedure without affecting any of its grants or dependencies. The **CREATE [OR REPLACE]** clause must be at the beginning of the statement for the procedure to be created or replaced in SQL*Plus.

➤ **schema**—The name of the owner of the procedure. Defaults to current user.

➤ **procedure_name**—The name of the procedure (must follow standard table naming conventions, which are covered in Chapter 4).

➤ **argument**—Argument declarations in a comma-separated list. An argument declaration has the format:

```
argument_name  argument_characteristic argument_type
```

For example:

```
(role_name IN VARCHAR2, newpass IN VARCHAR2)
```

Notice that no size information is specified—only the data type of the argument is specified—and that each argument is declared independently. Multiple declarations can't be attached to a single type specification; each argument must have its own type of specification. The *argument_characteristic* is **IN, OUT,** or **IN OUT.** An **IN** argument acts as a constant and can be an expression. An **OUT** argument can only be written to and is used to return a value to the calling process. An **IN OUT** argument is used to pass in a value and then, after the value has been changed, return it to the calling process. The *argument_type* must be specified or an error will result. If the argument characteristic isn't defined, it defaults to **IN.**

➤ **IS** or **AS**—Some tools will balk at using **IS,** some will balk at using **AS,** and some don't care, so be watchful when you're using coding tools. One of these keywords must be specified or an error will result.

➤ **variable_declaration**—A variable declaration of the form:

```
variable_name  datatype;
```

Variable names must follow the rules for table names, with only one variable name per data type declaration. The data type is any allowed PL/SQL data type. The declaration must end with a semicolon. For example:

```
Test_date    DATE;
Test_score   NUMBER;
Retest_date  DATE;
```

Multiple variable declarations for a single data-type line are not allowed. For example:

```
Test_date, retest_date    DATE:
```

is not allowed.

➤ **CONSTANT**—Similar to a variable definition except that the keyword **CONSTANT** must be used. A constant's value can't be changed after it is set unless it's redeclared inside a subsequent block. A constant declaration looks like this:

```
passing_score CONSTANT NUMBER := 68;
```

In this example, the variable **passing_score** is assigned the value of **68** as a numeric data type. The := compound symbol in PL/SQL is used to show assignment, and the = sign is used to show equality only.

➤ **CURSOR**—If a SQL statement will retrieve multiple values, you should set it as a cursor by using a cursor declaration. The cursor declaration has the form:

```
CURSOR cursor_name (input_variables) IS executable_sql_statement;
```

For example:

```
CURSOR get_stat(stat IN VARCHAR2) IS
       SELECT name,value
       FROM v$sysstat
       WHERE name = stat;
```

The input variables for a cursor can't have a dimension specified. **CHAR, VARCHAR2,** and **NUMBER** are allowed, but **CHAR(2), VARCHAR2(20),** or **NUMBER(10,2)** would be rejected with a format error if you tried to use them.

➤ **exception_declaration**—An *exception* is an error-handling routine. Numerous predefined exceptions don't need to be declared in your program, but any user-defined exceptions must be declared in this section. An exception declaration looks like this:

```
exception_name EXCEPTION;
```

The exception name follows the naming guidelines. User-defined exceptions must be explicitly called using the **RAISE** command. Implicit exceptions are invoked automatically when they occur.

➤ **PRAGMA** declaration—A **PRAGMA EXCEPTION_INIT** declaration usually goes hand in hand with the exception declaration. A *pragma* is a PL/SQL interpreter directive that remaps standard Oracle errors into user-defined errors. The **PRAGMA** call is formatted like this:

```
PRAGMA EXCEPTION_INIT(exception_name, error_number)
```

For example:

```
PRAGMA EXCEPTION_INIT(table_not_found, -904);
```

➤ **procedural_logic**—The procedural logic (also known as the executable section) is the collection of SQL and PL/SQL statements used to manipulate data wrapped in **BEGIN...END;** blocks in the database. These blocks can be nested to any depth up to the maximum allowed size of a stored procedure. (On some systems, there is a limit of 32K to 64K for a single stored procedure.) The **RAISE** command for use in exceptions can be used only in the procedural logic or executable section of a PL/SQL program. Remember that the last line of any PL/SQL program must end in a semicolon.

➤ **exception_handling**—In the final section of a PL/SQL procedure (or an individual block), you process exceptions. The exception handling, although a good practice, isn't required. The exception section of a procedure performs error trapping. All user-defined exceptions must be defined in the declaration section of the procedure before they can be raised or used. An exception processing section is formatted like this:

```
EXCEPTION
      WHEN exception_name THEN
      Error_handling_code
END;
```

For example:

```
EXCEPTION
WHEN table_not_found THEN
   INSERT INTO error_log
      VALUES (sysdate,'Table '||table_name||' not found');
END;
```

Procedures allow complex processing to be reduced to a single procedure call statement. Procedures also enforce uniform processing techniques and ensure that good standards are followed. The use of procedures encourages code reuse and allows reuse of stored code from the shared pool, thus improving performance. In a client/server environment, use of procedures forces processing to the server and reduces network traffic.

The new external procedure format available in Oracle8 allows reference to an external C sharable library function. The C function must be in a DLL or shared library module that is referred to by a **LIBRARY** definition internal to Oracle.

PL/SQL Functions

PL/SQL functions allow multiple inputs and must return a single value. This characteristic of functions—that they must return a value—is the major difference between a function and a procedure. Functions can either be standalone or be placed in packages. If a function is to be used outside of its package, the function must have its purity defined to the Oracle system through use of the **PRAGMA RESTRICT_REFERENCES** call in the package header right after the function's declaration. The **CREATE FUNCTION** command syntax is shown in Figure 10.2.

The **CREATE FUNCTION** command has the following parameters:

➤ **argument_name**—The name given to this argument. It can be any valid variable name.

➤ **argument_type**—The type of argument: **IN, OUT,** or **IN OUT.** It specifies how the argument is to be treated (strictly input, strictly output, or both). This is optional and will default to **IN** if not specified.

The syntax of the CREATE FUNCTION command is as follows:

```
>>─CREATE ───────────────────────────── FUNCTION ──── function ──┬─(argument) ──┬──>>
          └─ OR REPLACE ─┘ └─ schema. ─┘                         └──────────────┘

>>─RETURN datatype ──┬─ IS ─┬──────────────────────────────────────────────────><
                     └─ AS ─┘  ├─ pl/sql subprogram body ─────────┤
                               └─ external_body ─────────┘

>>─RETURN expr; ──────────────────────────────────────────────────────────────>

>>─END ──┬──────────┬─────────────────────────────────────────────────────────>
         └─ function ─┘
```

An argument has the form:

```
argument_name ──┬──────────────────┬── argument_datatype
                └─ argument_type ─┘
```

A PL/SQL subprogram body has the form:

```
>─────────────────────────────────────────────────────────────>
  ┌─ declaration_section ────┐   [variable_declarations, constants, cursors, exceptions,
  ├─ functional_logic ───────┤      and pragma declarations]
  └─ exception_handling──────┘
```

The external_body argument has the form:

```
┌─EXTERNAL LIBRARY ─────────────┬─ library_name ─┐
│                  └─ schema. ─┘                 ├─ NAME external_proc_name ──────┐
│                                                ├─ LANGUAGE language_name ───────┤
│                                                └─ CALLING STANDARD ──────┬─ C ─┐
│                                                                          └─ PASCAL ─┘
└─ PARAMETERS (external_parameter_list) ────────────────┐
                                         └─ WITH CONTEXT ─┘
```

The external_parameter_list argument has the form:

{{param_name [PROPERTY]|RETURN prop} [BY REF] [extern_datatype]|CONTEXT}

Figure 10.2 Syntax of the **CREATE FUNCTION** command and some of its arguments, parameters, and subprograms.

➤ **argument_datatype**—The data type of the argument. It can be any valid scalar data type. The **datatype** specification must not have a dimension specified; for example, it should be **CHAR**, not **CHAR(3)**.

➤ **external_body** argument—Has the form shown in Figure 10.2.

➤ **external_parameter_list** argument—Has the form shown in Figure 10.2, with this code repeated as many times as is needed. The **prop** argument has one of the following values: **INDICATOR, LENGTH, MAXLEN, CHARSETID,** or **CHARSETFORM**.

The **CREATE FUNCTION** command has the following clauses and variables:

➤ **schema**—Name of the function owner.

➤ **declaration_section**—Any locally defined variables, constants, exceptions, or cursors.

➤ **functional_logic**—Contains code used for processing in the function.

➤ **exception_handling**—Exception handling code for the function.

➤ *expr*—Expression to be returned to the calling user. The expression can be as simple as a local variable name or as complex as a mathematical equation that returns a value calculated from input values.

➤ **function**—Same as the name specified for the function.

Functions are used to manipulate data and return a single value. Functions by definition can't alter a package's, program's, or data item's state. This means that functions can't be used to write data or to change the state of the system or database. This nonaltering of system items is referred to as a function's *purity* (covered in Chapter 5). A function must contain a **RETURN** statement.

Creating Anonymous PL/SQL Blocks

Anonymous PL/SQL blocks are used inside SQL routines, inside triggers, or directly from operating system files. Anonymous PL/SQL blocks can be used to do virtually anything that procedures and functions can, with the exception that they aren't stored in the database. An anonymous PL/SQL block has the general form:

```
DECLARE
    Declarations
BEGIN
    Executable section
EXCEPTION
    Exception handlers
END;
```

The only required portion of an anonymous PL/SQL block is the **BEGIN...END;** block with the executable section. Notice that there's no **CREATE OR REPLACE** command; anonymous blocks are built directly in SQL*Plus or directly as a text file by using a system editor.

 Anonymous PL/SQL blocks can be called from any of Oracle's executable environments. The blocks are executed by reading them into the SQL*Plus buffer with a **GET** command and then executing a **RUN**, *R*, or backslash (/) command followed by an

Enter or Return keystroke. Anonymous PL/SQL is especially useful in SQL*Plus scripts in which complex processing is required but the frequency of use doesn't warrant a stored procedure or function. Triggers are built using anonymous PL/SQL blocks.

Exception Handling

By using proper coding techniques, such as exception processing, you can eliminate application hangs due to errors. Any user-defined exception or error must be implicitly invoked with the **RAISE** command. For example:

```
BEGIN
    ---- processing ----
    IF inventory_count < min_stocking_value THEN
        RAISE need_to_reorder;
    END IF;
    ---- processing ----
END;
```

A special form of exception is known as the **OTHERS** exception. The **OTHERS** exception should be a part of any set of exceptions. It traps any nonspecific error that happens so you can exit gracefully from your routine. The **WHEN OTHERS** clause is allowed only in an exception section of a procedure, function, or anonymous PL/SQL block.

Using Cursors

Cursors are predefined DML statements, usually **SELECT**s. Cursors can be explicit or implicit in nature. All cursors have attributes that are used to determine cursor status.

Explicit Cursors

Explicit cursors are predefined SQL statements that can return more than one row. Cursors are processed explicitly through the use of **OPEN, FETCH,** and **CLOSE** commands or through the use of cursor loops. An **OPEN** command parses the cursor code and calls the rows identified by the query. **FETCH** processes the cursor code to retrieve one row from the selected set of rows, and the values are inserted into a record or a set of variables specified with an **INTO** clause. **CLOSE** closes the cursor, releasing any memory assigned to the cursor. A cursor loop has the format:

```
FOR rec_id IN cursor_id LOOP
---- processing ----
END LOOP;
```

One advantage of the cursor **FOR** loop is that no **OPEN, FETCH,** or **CLOSE** commands are required for cursor control. That's all handled by the loop logic.

The *rec_id* must be a suitably defined record structure or a properly typed variable to hold what is returned from the cursor. The *cursor_id* is the name of the cursor. The effect of issuing this type of command is to open and parse, and then fetch rows from the cursor until no more records are found, at which time the cursor loop ends.

Implicit Cursors

An implicit cursor is automatically defined when any SQL statement is issued. An implicit cursor will result in two fetches against the database: one to determine whether more than one row will be returned (if there is, you get an implicit exception raised), and the next to actually get the row. Implicit cursors can be used to process only one row at a time.

Cursor Attributes

Explicit and implicit cursors have built-in attributes that allow tracking of their status. For explicit cursors, these cursor attributes are:

➤ **Cursor_name%FOUND**—Before the first fetch on an opened cursor, this is **NULL**. If the latest fetch is successful, **%FOUND** becomes **TRUE**. This attribute shouldn't be checked until after a fetch has executed.

➤ **Cursor_name%ISOPEN**—Before a cursor is opened, this is **FALSE**. If the cursor has been opened and if it's still open, this is **TRUE**.

➤ **Cursor_name%NOTFOUND**—If the last fetch yields a row, this is **FALSE**. If the last fetch was unsuccessful, this is **TRUE**.

➤ **Cursor_name%ROWCOUNT**—Returns the count for the number of rows fetched thus far. Before a cursor is opened, this yields a **NULL**. Before the first fetch, this yields zero. If **%ROWCOUNT** is checked before a cursor is opened, it will raise the **INVALID_CURSOR** exception. Until a cursor is closed, the **%ROWCOUNT** will contain the last valid count of records fetched.

You can use cursor attributes with the most current SQL statement (implicit cursor) by appending "SQL" to the front of their names instead of the names of the cursors. With the exception that no **OPEN** or **FETCH** logic is needed, the attributes work the same with an implicit or explicit cursor.

Controlling Flow In PL/SQL

Flow control—the use of loops and logic control such as **IF...THEN...ELSE**—was the primary reason PL/SQL was created. SQL, though great for set processing, was found lacking when it came to procedural structure. Indeed, it wasn't designed to be structured to process individual records like a procedural language, only groups or sets of records.

PL/SQL loop control is executed through several types of loop control statements; the easiest is the **LOOP...END LOOP;** statement. This simple structure is augmented through additional control clauses, such as **WHILE, EXIT,** and **EXIT WHEN.** PL/SQL also supports the **FOR...LOOP...END LOOP;** construct that allows iteration control, as well as the **WHILE...LOOP...END LOOP;** construct for conditional control.

IF...THEN...ELSE Structures

The **IF...THEN...ELSE** structure allows a single-pass conditional statement to be created. The conditions are always evaluated against the Boolean **TRUE** to determine if processing should be done or if control should pass to the next section. The full syntax for the **IF..THEN...ELSE** construct is:

```
IF condition1 THEN
    Sequence of statements
ELSIF condition2 THEN
    Sequence of statements
ELSE
    Final sequence of statements
END IF;
```

The condition statements can be simple or complex equalities or Boolean values. If the condition in the statement yields a **TRUE**, the following sequence of statements is executed. If the condition is **FALSE**, the processing passes down the decision tree of **ELSIF**s to the final **ELSE** and **END IF**. The only required part of the structure is the **IF...END IF;**. Be sure that the **END IF** is two separate words, or an error will result. Notice also that the term is **ELSIF**, not **ELSEIF**. Finally, the final **ELSE**, if present, has no condition associated with it; it shows the final decision in the decision tree if all others are **FALSE**. If the **ELSE** isn't present, the control passes back into the program body.

A Simple LOOP...END LOOP; Construct

The most simple loop structure is the **LOOP...END LOOP;**. Note that unless control is passed from an **EXIT, EXIT WHEN,** or exception generation, a **LOOP...END LOOP;** is an infinite loop. Never depend on an exception to throw you out of a loop. The actual structure of a **LOOP...END LOOP;** looks like the following:

```
<<label_name>>
LOOP
    Sequence of statements
END LOOP label_name;
```

The *label_name* is not required, but for a nested loop structure, its use makes debugging easier.

If you use the **EXIT** command, simple loops become more controllable, as seen here:

```
<<label_name>>
LOOP
    Sequence of statements
    IF condition THEN EXIT label_name;
END LOOP label_name;
```

The condition can also be built into the **EXIT** by using the **WHEN** statement:

```
<<label_name>>
LOOP
    Sequence of statements
    EXIT label_name WHEN condition;
END LOOP label_name;
```

Alternate forms of the **EXIT** and **WHEN** statements can be used, such as:

```
WHEN condition EXIT;
```

The **WHILE...END LOOP;** Loop

Another useful form of the loop is the **WHILE** loop. The **WHILE** loop allows you to specify a condition at the start of the loop; until the condition is met, the loop executes. Unlike an **IF** statement, which processes its set of statements only if the condition it tests is **TRUE**, a **WHILE** loop will execute its contained statements until its limiting condition is **FALSE**. The **WHILE** loop should be used when an exact count of items to be processed is not available, which means that the loop must continue until finished. A **WHILE** loop doesn't contain an **EXIT** statement. The form for a **WHILE** loop is:

```
WHILE condition LOOP
    Sequence of statements
END LOOP;
```

Always be sure that the limiting condition will be reached. A statement inside the **WHILE** loop must itself initiate the setting of the Boolean condition, or you've created an infinite loop. Note that you can also use the **WHILE NOT** condition **LOOP** form.

The **FOR** Loop

The **FOR** loop is used to process a specific number of iterations. The order of iteration can be set to either the default ascending order (1, 2, 3) or the reverse order (3, 2, 1). A specialized form of the **FOR** loop is the cursor loop that we've already discussed. The format of the **FOR** loop is:

```
FOR index IN [REVERSE] lower_bound..higher_bound LOOP
    Sequence of statements
END LOOP;
```

Notice that there's no **STEP** command as there is in some languages that allow alteration of the iteration interval. In PL/SQL, the iteration interval is always one. To use intervals, you can use the **MOD(m,n)** command within an **IF...END IF** structure or some other means of iteration control implemented. The lower or upper bounds can be replaced with variables. Note that the **EXIT** command and its alternative structures using **WHEN** can be used inside the **FOR** loop structure to force a premature exit from the loop.

The **GOTO** And **NULL** Statements

The **GOTO** statement is also present in PL/SQL. Luckily, it's seldom used and it's not a crucial statement. A **GOTO** statement is an unconditional branch. A **GOTO** cannot branch into an **IF** construct, **LOOP** construct, or sub-block. A **GOTO** can branch to another location inside the current block or to a location inside an enclosing block, but not into an exception handler. You can also use **GOTO** to branch out of an **IF** or **LOOP**, but that construct's context is closed and must be re-entered from the beginning.

The **NULL** statement is the only executable command that doesn't do anything. In fact, not doing anything is its purpose. I already showed you one possible use of **NULL** in the **start_it** procedure. You can also use **NULL** for testing and for placement inside an exception block where you want to handle an exception that's been raised but, other than exiting the block, you don't want to take any other action. A common use of **NULL** is in a **WHEN OTHERS** exception block.

DML And PL/SQL

All of the flow control, structure, and other PL/SQL features are useless unless they can be used in the processing of data. PL/SQL uses Data Manipulation Language (DML) statements just like standard SQL to process the data in the database. Some functions or highly specialized procedures may contain no DML, but this is the exception rather than the rule. In general, four DML statements are used in PL/SQL: INSERT, UPDATE, DELETE, and **SELECT**.

Use Of **INSERT** In PL/SQL

The **INSERT** command is used in PL/SQL the same way it's used in normal DML processing in SQL sessions. However, you can also use **INSERT** with user-defined storage types created using the **%TYPE** and **%ROWTYPE** calls against the database or from the **TYPE** declarations in the declaration section. The **SQL%ROWCOUNT, SQL%FOUND**, and **SQL%NOTFOUND** attributes can be used after an **INSERT** statement to determine the status of the insert operation. If the transaction is successful (that is, rows are inserted), **%FOUND** will be **TRUE, %NOTFOUND** will be **FALSE**, and **%ROWCOUNT** will show the number of rows inserted. If the transaction is unsuccessful (that is, no rows are inserted), **%FOUND** will be **FALSE, %NOTFOUND** will be **TRUE**, and **%ROWCOUNT** will be zero.

Use Of **UPDATE** In PL/SQL

The **UPDATE** command is used in PL/SQL the same way it's used in normal DML processing in SQL sessions. However, you can also use **UPDATE** with user-defined storage types created using the **%TYPE** and **%ROWTYPE** calls against the database or from the **TYPE** declarations in the declaration section. The **SQL%ROWCOUNT, SQL%FOUND**, and **SQL%NOTFOUND** attributes can be used after an **UPDATE** statement to determine the status of the update operation. If the transaction is successful (that is, rows are updated), **%FOUND** will be **TRUE, %NOTFOUND** will be **FALSE**, and **%ROWCOUNT** will show the number of rows updated. If the transaction is unsuccessful (that is, no rows are updated), **%FOUND** will be **FALSE, %NOTFOUND** will be **TRUE**, and **%ROWCOUNT** will be zero.

The only addition to standard SQL for the **UPDATE** command is the **WHERE CURRENT OF** clause. This clause is used to specify the name of a cursor whose **SELECT** statement includes the **FOR UPDATE** qualifier.

Use Of **DELETE** In PL/SQL

The **DELETE** command is used in PL/SQL the same way it's used in normal DML processing in SQL sessions. However, you can also use **DELETE** with user-defined storage types created using the **%TYPE** and **%ROWTYPE** calls against the database or from the **TYPE** declarations in the declaration section. The **SQL%ROWCOUNT, SQL%FOUND**, and **SQL%NOTFOUND** attributes can be used after a **DELETE** statement to determine the status of the delete operation. If the transaction is successful (that is, rows are deleted), **%FOUND** will be **TRUE, %NOTFOUND** will be **FALSE**, and

%ROWCOUNT will show the number of rows deleted. If the transaction is unsuccessful (that is, no rows are deleted), **%FOUND** will be **FALSE**, **%NOTFOUND** will be **TRUE**, and **%ROWCOUNT** will be zero.

The only addition to standard SQL for the **DELETE** command is the **WHERE CURRENT OF** clause. This clause is used to specify the name of a cursor whose **SELECT** statement includes the **FOR UPDATE** qualifier.

Use Of **SELECT** In PL/SQL

Of the four commands (**INSERT, UPDATE, DELETE,** and **SELECT**), **SELECT** has the most differences between how it's used in PL/SQL and how it's used in SQL. In SQL, a **SELECT** command is expected to return sets of rows that satisfy a specified condition from one or more tables. In PL/SQL, the command must return only one row unless the command is placed in a cursor. The format for a **SELECT** statement that's not in a cursor adds the **INTO** keyword and requires a list of variables or types into which the retrieved row is to be inserted. For example, the following code would generate an error:

```
SELECT ename FROM emp WHERE emp_number = 1;
```

whereas the following code is perfectly acceptable (assuming that **my_ename** has been declared):

```
SELECT ename INTO my_ename FROM emp WHERE emp_number = 1;
```

If a **SELECT** statement returns more than one row, the statement must be placed in a cursor to be used in PL/SQL, as seen here:

```
CURSOR get_ename IS
   SELECT ename FROM emp;
```

To use a **SELECT** statement placed inside a cursor, either use the **OPEN**, **FETCH**, and **CLOSE** set of commands, or use a cursor loop to process the return sets of data, as seen here:

```
BEGIN
   ---- processing ----
   OPEN get_ename;
   FETCH get_ename INTO my_ename;
   WHILE get_ename%FOUND LOOP
   ---- processing ----
      FETCH get_ename INTO my_ename;
   END LOOP;
   CLOSE get_ename;
```

```
    ---- more processing ----
END;
```

or with a cursor loop, as seen here:

```
BEGIN
    ---- processing ----
    FOR my_ename IN get_ename LOOP
    ---- processing ----
    END LOOP;
    ---- more processing ----
END;
```

In either case, the SQL **SELECT** statement returning multiple rows must be inside a cursor. Remember that for every item in the **SELECT** list, there must be a corresponding item in the **INTO** list. A record specification or a type specification can be used as the target for the **INTO** clause. A type is specified using **%TYPE**. A record is either implicitly created in the **FOR** loop or explicitly created using the **%ROWTYPE** or **TYPE** and **RECORD** declarations.

The **SQL%FOUND, SQL%NOTFOUND,** and **SQL%ROWCOUNT** attributes can be used to determine the status of a noncursor **SELECT** statement. If the transaction is successful (that is, a row is selected), **%FOUND** will be **TRUE**, **%NOTFOUND** will be **FALSE**, and **%ROWCOUNT** will show a value of 1. If the transaction is unsuccessful (that is, no row is selected), **%FOUND** will be **FALSE, %NOTFOUND** will be **TRUE**, and **%ROWCOUNT** will be zero.

To allow for update or deletion, you can add the **FOR UPDATE** clause to the **SELECT** command to lock the row or rows selected.

COMMIT And ROLLBACK In PL/SQL

PL/SQL is transaction-based. Just as in SQL, a transaction can be *committed* (made permanent) using **COMMIT**, or *rolled back* (removed) using **ROLLBACK**. When a **COMMIT** is issued inside a PL/SQL block, all pending transactions inside the block are committed and made permanent, ending the current transaction. Similarly, if a **ROLLBACK** is issued, all pending transactions are rolled back and forgotten, also ending the current transaction. A **ROLLBACK** can also be used to roll back to a **SAVEPOINT** to preserve a portion of a large, complex transaction.

ALTER And DROP Commands

The only option allowed for an **ALTER** command used for packages, package bodies, procedures, and functions is the **COMPILE** option. The **COMPILE** option forces a recompilation of the object and is used to recompile packages that may have been made invalid by temporary unavailability of something it was dependent upon. To alter an object's contents, use the **CREATE OR REPLACE** command.

The **DROP** command removes the specified object from the database. A procedure or function inside a package can't be dropped. You must use the **CREATE OR REPLACE** command to rebuild the package itself without the object.

Changes For Oracle8

Oracle8 includes changes to allow external procedure calls (documented in the syntax sections earlier in this chapter), the ability to use object types (UDTs) in PL/SQL, the ability to use collections such as **VARRAY**s or nested tables, the capability of using **LOB** data types (**BLOB, CLOB, NCLOB, BFILE**), and an expansion of the NLS parts of PL/SQL.

External Procedures

PL/SQL now provides an interface to call external procedures and functions written in the C programming language. The procedures and functions must be stored in a shared library external to Oracle. Internally, Oracle developers will use a **LIBRARY** definition to tell Oracle where the sharable library is located. After a **LIBRARY** has been defined, the call to the external code is made through an external body definition in either a **PROCEDURE** wrapper or a **FUNCTION** wrapper.

Object Types

The new object-oriented features of Oracle8 use User-Defined Types (UDTs) to model real-world objects in abstract terms. This allows complex objects to be handled *in toto* instead of as individual code pieces. A UDT combines data, in the form of attributes, and programs, in the form of methods, to create objects.

A UDT can have methods associated with it. Methods can be general, map, or order. A general method manipulates data values and may update other values inside the type, or even inside a different type, based on values specified. A **MAP** or **ORDER** method returns information used to compare or arrange the values stored inside the UDT, providing a means to say that one UDT is greater than, less than, or equal to another.

UDTs are populated through constructor methods. A constructor method is automatically created whenever a UDT is created. A constructor method is named the same as its UDT and must be called explicitly; constructors are never called implicitly.

Attributes inside a UDT are accessed via the dot type notation. An example would be a type called ADDRESS that contains STREET, POBOX, SUITE, CITY, STATE, and ZIP attributes. The ZIP attribute would be called by use of ADDRESS.ZIP nomenclature.

A UDT can be related to a second UDT via a reference; this reference is called a **REF** value. A **REF** always goes from the child to the parent because **REF** values are strictly 1:1 in nature. When UDTs are related by **REF** values, you can delete a parent value without deleting the child. When this type of orphan record occurs between a parent and child UDT, the child is said to have a **DANGLING REF**. This **DANGLING REF** condition can result in crashes of the server in early Oracle8 releases and statement failure in all Oracle8 versions unless the **DANGLING** clause is used whenever a **DANGLING REF** might be present.

Collection Types

Oracle8 allows the use of **VARRAY**s and nested tables. **VARRAY**s (short for variable-arrays) and nested tables act like arrays in third-generation languages. A nested table is used identically to an index-by table from PL/SQL version 2. These objects can be declared and used inside PL/SQL programs. The collection types also have built-in collection methods that determine minimum (**FIRST**) and maximum (**LAST**) occupied values, as well as the total number of values present (**COUNT**) or allowed (**LIMIT**) in a given collection.

Methods are also provided to determine whether a particular site in a nested table is filled (**EXISTS**) and to allow extension of **VARRAY**s (**EXTEND**). You can also determine the previous index value (**PRIOR**) and next index value (**NEXT**). Also provided is a way to trim a single value from the end of a collection (**TRIM**) or trim a set of values from the end of a collection (**TRIM(n)**). Finally, a method to remove specific records from a collection (**DELETE**) is also available.

LOB Data Types

Oracle8 provides the DBMS_LOB package to allow manipulation of **LOB** values. The DBMS_LOB package contains procedures and functions to load, parse, delete, get the length of, and compare **LOB** values and **BFILE** values.

NLS And Oracle8

NLS data types, prefaced by N (**NCHAR, NVARCHAR2, NCLOB**), allow users to interact with the database in their own language. In addition, you can create the database in one language by using the **NLS_CHARACTER_SET** setting and store the data in another language by using the **NLS_NATIONAL_CHARACTER_SET** setting.

Practice Questions

Question 1

What does the Procedural Statement Executor within the PL/SQL engine do?

- ○ a. Separates the SQL statements and sends them to the SQL Statement Executor.
- ○ b. Processes server-side data.
- ○ c. Processes data that is local to the application.
- ○ d. Passes blocks of PL/SQL to the Oracle8 server.

The correct answer is c. The Procedural Statement Executor within the PL/SQL engine processes data that is local to the application. Answer a is incorrect because this is a function of the PL/SQL engine but not of the Procedural Statement Executor inside the engine. Answer b is incorrect because the server-side data is processed by the Oracle8 server, not by the Procedural Statement Executor. Answer d is incorrect because this is a function of the user process, such as SQL*Plus or Server Manager, not of the PL/SQL engine or its subcomponent, the Procedural Statement Executor.

Question 2

Evaluate this procedure:

```
PROCEDURE price_increase
    (v_quote    IN BOOLEAN,
     v_stock    IN BOOLEAN,
     v_approval    IN OUT BOOLEAN)
IS
BEGIN
    V_approval:=v_quota AND v_stock;
END;
```

If **v_quota** equals **NULL** and **v_stock** equals **NULL**, which value is assigned to **v_approval**?

O a. **TRUE**

O b. **FALSE**

O c. **NULL**

O d. None of the above

The correct answer is c, because any combination involving a **NULL** results in a **NULL**. Answer a is incorrect because to evaluate to **TRUE**, both values would have to be **TRUE**. Answer b is incorrect because to evaluate to **FALSE**, one value would have to be **TRUE** and the other **FALSE**, or both would have to be **FALSE**. Answer d is incorrect because a Boolean value is allowed to be only **TRUE, FALSE,** or **NULL**.

Question 3

In which section of a PL/SQL block is a **WHEN OTHERS** clause allowed?

O a. Header

O b. Declarative

O c. Executable

O d. Exception

O e. None of the above

The correct answer is d. The **WHEN OTHERS** clause is an exception-handling clause. Answers a, b, and c are incorrect because the **WHEN OTHERS** clause is allowed only in an exception section and is used to process implicit exceptions that aren't specifically covered by **WHEN** statements in the exception section.

Question 4

Evaluate this cursor statement:

```
DECLARE
    CURSOR price_cursor
         (v_price NUMBER(8,2)) IS
      SELECT id_number, description,
      manufacturer_id
      FROM inventory
      WHERE price > v_price;
```

Why will this statement cause an error?

- O a. A parameter isn't defined.
- O b. The size of the variable can't be specified.
- O c. A **WHERE** clause can't be used in a cursor statement.
- O d. The **SELECT** statement is missing the **INTO** clause.

The correct answer is b, because only a variable's type, not its size, is specified in the input variable section. Answer a is incorrect because all required parameters are specified. Answer c is incorrect because a **WHERE** clause is allowed in cursor statements. Answer d is incorrect because, in a cursor statement, the **INTO** clause must *not* be specified. The **INTO** clause is specified only in a **SELECT** statement used as an implicit cursor in PL/SQL; this is an explicit cursor.

Question 5

> When will a **SELECT** statement in a PL/SQL block raise an exception?
>
> ○ a. When it retrieves only one row.
>
> ○ b. When it retrieves more than one row.
>
> ○ c. When the data types within the **SELECT** statement are inconsistent.
>
> ○ d. When the **SELECT** statement is missing a required clause.

The correct answer is b. An exception will be raised if an implicit cursor retrieves more than one row. Answer a is incorrect because an implicit cursor (a **SELECT** statement in a PL/SQL block) by definition is allowed to return only a single row. Answers c and d are incorrect because this type of error will not allow the PL/SQL program unit to be successfully compiled. If you can't compile the code, it can't execute, and if it can't execute, it can't raise an exception.

Question 6

> Which type of commands are supported by PL/SQL?
>
> ○ a. DDL
>
> ○ b. DCL
>
> ○ c. DML
>
> ○ d. No commands are supported by PL/SQL

The correct answer is c, DML (Data Manipulation Language). Answer a, DDL, is incorrect because Data Definition Language is not directly supported in PL/SQL. To use DDL, you must use one of the special support packages, such as DBMS_SQL or DBMS_UTILITY. Answer b, DCL, is incorrect. DCL (Data Control Language) commands cannot be executed directly in PL/SQL. Answer d is incorrect because answer c is correct.

Question 7

Which PL/SQL program construct must return a value?

- ○ a. Anonymous block
- ○ b. Stored function
- ○ c. Stored procedure
- ○ d. Database trigger
- ○ e. Application trigger

The correct answer is b, stored function. Answer a is incorrect because an anonymous PL/SQL block is incapable of returning a value; there's no syntax for it. Answer c is incorrect because the major difference between a function and a procedure is that a function must return a value, whereas a procedure doesn't have to. Answers d and e are incorrect because, again, the syntax and functionality of a trigger don't permit the return of values.

Question 8

Which three PL/SQL subprogram components are required?

- ❑ a. Header
- ❑ b. Declarative
- ❑ c. Executable
- ❑ d. Exception handling
- ❑ e. End

The correct answers are a, c, and e. Answer b is incorrect because a declarative section is not required. Answer d is incorrect because you aren't required to put exception handling into your application (even though it's a good idea). Remember, our simplest procedure would be:

```
CREATE PROCEDURE start_it AS    < This is the header
BEGIN
    NULL;
END;        < From the BEGIN to the END is the
            executable section. Every block
            must have a BEGIN and END.
```

Question 9

Using SQL*Plus, you attempt to create this procedure:

```
    PROCEDURE price_increase
    (v_precent_increase    NUMBER)
IS
BEGIN
    UPDATE inventory
    SET price = price * v_percent_increase;
    COMMIT;
END;
```

Why does this command cause an error?

○ a. A parameter mode was not declared.

○ b. The procedure does not return a value.

○ c. The **CREATE OR REPLACE** clause is missing.

○ d. A data type is not specified.

The correct answer is c. This is a trick question because many people will not understand what the question is asking. Remember, if it isn't shown in the question, then it isn't there. In this case, the **CREATE OR REPLACE** command line is not shown. Answer a is incorrect because the mode will default to **IN** if not specified. Answer b is incorrect because procedures don't have to return values; only functions have to return values. Answer d is incorrect because a data type (**NUMBER**) is clearly specified.

Question 10

Which PL/SQL program construct is associated with a database table and is fired automatically?

○ a. Anonymous block

○ b. Stored function

○ c. Stored procedure

○ d. Database trigger

○ e. Application trigger

○ f. Application procedure

The correct answer is d. Answer a is incorrect because an anonymous block, although used to create the code in a trigger, can't by itself be invoked by an action taken against a database table. Answers b and c are incorrect because a stored function or stored procedure must be explicitly called from another program unit or from the command line; it can't be tied to a table to happen automatically. Answer e is incorrect because an application trigger is fired by an application action, not by a table action. Answer f is incorrect because an application procedure must be explicitly called from an application.

Question 11

Which clause is required in a **SELECT** statement within a PL/SQL block?

- ○ a. **WHERE**
- ○ b. **INTO**
- ○ c. **GROUP BY**
- ○ d. **HAVING**
- ○ e. **ORDER BY**

The correct answer is b, **INTO**. Answer a is incorrect because a **WHERE** clause isn't required for a **SELECT** statement. Answer c is incorrect because the **GROUP BY** clause isn't allowed in an implicit cursor (a PL/SQL **SELECT** statement) because a **SELECT** statement inside PL/SQL returns only one value by definition. Answer d is incorrect because a **SELECT** statement inside PL/SQL returns only one value by definition, and the **HAVING** clause is used with the **GROUP BY** clause, which is used for a multivalue return. Answer e is incorrect because by definition a **SELECT** statement inside a PL/SQL block returns only one value.

Question 12

Using SQL*Plus, you create this procedure:

```
CREATE OR REPLACE PROCEDURE price_increase
    (v_manufacturer_id IN NUMBER,
     v_percent_increase IN NUMBER)
IS
    v_rows_update BOOLEAN;
BEGIN
    UPDATE inventory
           SET price = price * v_percent_increase
           WHERE manufacturer_id = v_manufacturer_id;
    v_rows_updated:=SQL%NOTFOUND;
END;
```

What value will be assigned to **v_rows_updated**?

○ a. **TRUE**, if any prices were changed

○ b. **TRUE**, if no prices were changed

○ c. **FALSE**, if no prices were changed

○ d. **NULL**

The correct answer is b. Answer a is incorrect because **%NOTFOUND** will evaluate to TRUE only if no prices were changed. Answer c is incorrect because if prices weren't changed, the value would be TRUE. Answer d is incorrect because **%NOTFOUND** will be set to either TRUE or FALSE, based on the results of the **UPDATE** command that precedes it.

Question 13

What causes a PL/SQL **WHILE** loop to terminate?

○ a. A Boolean variable or expression evaluates to **TRUE**.

○ b. A Boolean variable or expression evaluates to **FALSE**.

○ c. A Boolean variable or expression evaluates to **NULL**.

○ d. Control is passed to the **EXIT** statement.

○ e. The specified number of iterations have been performed.

The correct answer is b. Answers a and c are incorrect because a **WHILE** condition must evaluate to **FALSE** for the loop to terminate. Answer d is incorrect because a **WHILE** loop doesn't have an **EXIT** statement. Answer e is incorrect because only a **FOR** loop terminates on a specified number of iterations, and the question is talking about a **WHILE** loop.

Question 14

Evaluate this incomplete loop:

```
LOOP
    INSERT INTO inventory (id_number,
                           description)
        VALUES (v_id_number, v_description);
    V_counter := v_counter +1;
```

Which statement needs to be added to conditionally stop the execution of the loop?

○ a. **END LOOP**

○ b. **EXIT**

○ c. **EXIT WHEN**

○ d. **END**

○ e. No statement is needed

The correct answer is c. Answer a is incorrect because although **END LOOP** ends the loop structure, it doesn't end loop processing. Answer b is incorrect because although **EXIT** will terminate loop processing, it won't do so conditionally unless paired with **WHEN**. Answer d is incorrect because just placing an **END** at this point without an **END LOOP** will cause a syntax error. Answer e is incorrect because an **EXIT WHEN** is required.

Need To Know More?

Ault, Michael R. *Oracle8 Black Book*. Coriolis Group Books, Scottsdale, Arizona, 1998. ISBN 1-57610-187-8. This book tells you how to use all of the new Oracle8 features, including LOBs, collections, and UDTs.

Feuerstein, Steven. *Oracle PL/SQL Programming*. O'Reilly & Associates, Sebastopol, California, 1995. ISBN 1-56592-335-9. This book is considered one of the seminal references on PL/SQL. Although the advanced edition of this book is also a must-have for any serious PL/SQL developer, as far as studying for the OCP-DBA exam, this earlier edition is probably the better choice because the advanced version uses more PL/SQL to build PL/SQL instead of covering PL/SQL at a lower level.

Owens, Kevin. *Building Intelligent Databases With Oracle PL/SQL, Triggers, and Stored Procedures*. Prentice-Hall PTR, Upper Saddle River, New Jersey, 1996. ISBN 0-13-443631-8. An excellent reference for all phases of PL/SQL use and development.

Urman, Scott and Tim Smith. *Oracle PL/SQL Programming*. Osborne-McGraw Hill, New York, New York, 1996. ISBN 0-07882-176-2. This is a good Oracle PL/SQL reference from Oracle Press.

Oracle8 Server SQL Reference, Release 8.0, Volumes 1 and 2. Oracle Corporation, Redwood Shores, California, June 1997. Part No. A54649-01. This is the source book for all Oracle SQL and Embedded SQL, including SQL for use in PL/SQL. It can be found on the Web at **http://technet.oracle.com**, which has free membership.

Oracle8 Server Application Developer's Guide, Release 8.0. Oracle Corporation, Redwood Shores, California, June 1997. Part No. A54642-01. This book discusses how the various parts of Oracle SQL, PL/SQL, and the database engine function together and how to use PL/SQL to develop applications. It can be found on the Web at **http://technet.oracle.com**, which has free membership.

PL/SQL User's Guide and Reference, Release 8.0. Oracle Corporation, Redwood Shores, California, June 1997. Part No. A54654-01. This book discusses the flow and logic control statements for use in PL/SQL, as well as how to build and use anonymous blocks, functions, procedures, packages, and triggers. It can be found on the Web at **http://technet.oracle.com**, which has free membership.

 PL/SQL Knowledge Base, Online Reference, Version 99.2, 1999, RevealNet, Inc., available from **www.revealnet.com**. This online knowledge base provides instant lookup of information on topics, examples, syntax, and good practices.

Sample Test

This chapter provides pointers to help you develop a successful test-taking strategy. This chapter discusses how to choose proper answers, how to decode ambiguity, how to work within the Oracle framework, how to decide what to memorize, and how to prepare for the test. Finally, I provide a number of questions that cover the subject matter likely to appear on Test 1 of the Oracle Certified Database Administrator track, "Introduction to Oracle: SQL and PL/SQL." In Chapter 12, you'll find the answer key to this test. Good luck!

Questions, Questions, Questions

Each exam in the DBA test series consists of 55 to 75 questions. You are allotted 90 minutes for each of the DBA exams. The questions on the exam will be of two types:

➤ Multiple choice with a single answer

➤ Multiple choice with multiple answers

Always take the time to read the question twice before selecting an answer. Not every question has only one answer. Some questions will have multiple answers; in this case, the questions will state how many answers you should select. There is no partial credit given for incomplete answers; if the question asks for two answers, you have to give two answers, or the entire question is counted as incorrect.

When taking the test, always read all of the answers, and never assume that a question can't be as easy as it looks. In some cases, questions really are easy, and second guessing the question is one of the biggest problems with taking this type of test.

Picking Correct Answers

Obviously, the only way to pass any exam is to select enough of the right answers to obtain a passing score. Unfortunately, exams are written by human beings. Tests like the SAT and GRE have been run through batteries of test experts and have been standardized; the Oracle Certified Professional exams have not. Although a question might make perfect sense to the person who wrote it, the wording can be ambiguous, diabolical, or convoluted to just about anyone else. In other cases, the question may be so poorly written—or worse, have an opinion rather than a hard fact as an answer—that unless you have an inside track, you just can't divine the correct answer from your knowledge base. When you have no idea what the answer is, you can almost always eliminate one or more answers because:

➤ The answer doesn't apply to the situation.

➤ The answer describes a nonexistent issue.

➤ The answer is already eliminated by the question text.

After you have eliminated obviously wrong answers, you must rely on your retained knowledge to eliminate further answers. Look for what are called *distracters*. These are answers that sound perfectly plausible but refer to actions, commands, or features not present or not available in the described situation.

If you have eliminated all the answers you can through logic and knowledge and you are left with more than one choice, I suggest using *question inversion*. Question inversion is the process where you rephrase the question in terms of each remaining answer, seeking the premise of the existing question as the answer. Here is an example:

The color of a clear daytime sky is blue because:

○ a. Dust particles in the atmosphere scatter the blue components of light.

○ b. The sun puts out a great deal of light in the blue spectrum.

○ c. Oxygen absorbs most of the other spectral elements.

○ d. The Van Allen belt absorbs much of the ultraviolet spectrum, thus allowing only the blue components to reach us.

Now, say you have reduced the possible choices to answers a and c. Try rephrasing the question: "The dust in the atmosphere, scattering the blue components of light, causes the daytime sky to be _____ in color." Or: "Oxygen-absorbing spectral elements cause the daytime sky to be _____ in color."

Sometimes this rephrasing will jog your memory to produce the correct answer. (By the way, the correct answer is a.) Answer d is an example of a distracter: It sounds logical on the surface, unless you know that the Van Allen belt absorbs and deflects charged particle radiation, but light passes straight through (the ozone layer takes care of the ultraviolet).

Finally, if you just can't decide between two (or more) answers, guess! An unanswered question is always wrong, and at least with an educated guess you have some chance of getting the question correct.

Decoding Ambiguity

Tests are not designed to ensure that everyone passes. Tests are designed to test knowledge on a given topic. A properly designed test has a bell-curve distribution for the target qualified audience where a certain percent will fail. A problem with the Oracle tests is that they have been tailored to Oracle's training materials, even though some of the material in the training is hearsay, some consists of old-DBA tales, and some is just incorrect. In the previous chapters, I have tried to point out the obvious errors. For example, I have noticed that for a numeric type question, the correct answer is generally the highest number if the highest is the most conservative way to go, or the lowest number if that is the most conservative. Some examples would be: Oracle's insistence that the percent increase for a temporary tablespace should be 50 percent and that to be properly tuned, a rollback segment should have 20 extents as a minimum. Normally, **PCTINCREASE** will be set at zero or at the expected growth rate for the object and you set up for four users per rollback segment, which indicates 4 extents.

The only way to overcome some of the test's limitations is to be prepared. You will discover that many exam questions test your knowledge of things not directly related to the issue raised by the questions. This means that the answers offered to you, even the incorrect ones, are as much a part of the skill assessment as are the questions. If you don't know all the aspects of the test topic cold, you won't be able to eliminate answers that are obviously wrong because they relate to a different aspect of the topic than the one addressed by the question.

Questions may give away the answers, especially questions dealing with commands and data dictionary topics. Read a question and evaluate the answers in light of common terms, names, and structure.

Another problem is that Oracle uses some terminology in its training materials that is found nowhere else in its documentation sets. An example would be the use of sort extent pools (SEPs) and other training-specific terminology.

Working Within The Framework

The exam questions are presented to you in a random order. A question on SQL may follow a question on PL/SQL, followed by one on database design. However, this randomness can work to your advantage because a future question may unwittingly answer the question you are puzzling over. You will find that the incorrect answer to one question may be the correct answer to one further down the line. Take the time to read all of the answers for each question, even if you spot the correct one immediately (or should I say, especially if you spot the correct one immediately?). Also, the exam format enables you to mark questions that you want to revisit or mark those you feel may give you insight into other questions—even if you know you have answered them correctly.

Deciding What To Memorize

The amount of memorization you will have to do depends on whether you are a visual learner. If you can see the command structure diagrams in your head, you won't need to memorize as much as if you can't. The test will stretch your recollection skills through command syntax and operational command sequences used within the Oracle environment, testing not only when you should use a feature, but also when you shouldn't.

The important types of information to memorize are:

➤ The parts of procedures, functions, and packages

➤ Commands and their uses

➤ Use of anonymous PL/SQL blocks

➤ Restrictions on command use (such as with joins in **SELECT**)

➤ Use of SQL*Plus

➤ Database design and implementation topics (normalization, ERDs, and so on)

I recommend working your way through this book while sitting in front of an Oracle database so you can try out commands, test the questions' answers, and play with unfamiliar features. If you do so, you should have no problem understanding the questions when they appear on the exam.

Preparing For The Test

If one is to excel in any endeavor, one must practice. The perfect musical performance looks easy, but you don't see the hours, days, and weeks of practice it took to make it look that way. Taking tests and passing them is the same. Without practice to identify your weak areas, you go into a test with blinders on and are easily broadsided. I've included a practice exam in this chapter. You should give yourself 90 uninterrupted minutes (use the honor system—you will gain no benefit from cheating). The idea is to see where you are weak and need further study, not to answer 100 percent of the questions correctly by looking up the answers. After your time is up or you finish, you can check your answers in Chapter 12. It might even be easier to make a copy of the sample test so you can take it multiple times.

If you want additional practice, other sample exams are available on Oracle's education and certification site (**http://education.oracle.com/certification**) or inside RevealNet's Oracle Administrator Knowledgebase (**www.revealnet.com**).

Taking The Test

Once you are sitting in front of the testing computer, there is nothing more you can do to increase your knowledge or preparation, so relax. Take a deep breath, stretch, and attack the first question.

Don't rush; there is plenty of time to complete each question and to return to skipped questions. If you read a question twice and are still clueless, mark it for revisiting and move on. Easy and hard questions are randomly distributed, so don't take too long on hard questions or you may cheat yourself of the chance to answer some end-of-test easy questions. Hard and easy questions have the same number of points, so take care of the easy ones *first* and revisit the hard ones after answering everything that you can.

As you answer each question that you have marked to revisit, remove the mark and go on. If a question is still impossible, go on to the next one you marked. On your final pass (just before time is called), guess on those that you are completely clueless on. Remember, if a question isn't answered, it is always counted wrong, but a guess just may be correct.

That's it for pointers. Here are some questions for you to practice on.

Sample Test

Question 1

Which two characters require the **ESCAPE** option to be used as literals?

❑ a. _

❑ b. $

❑ c. /

❑ d. %

Question 2

You attempt to create a view with this command:

```
CREATE VIEW parts_view
AS SELECT id_number, description, sum(quantity)
FROM inventory
WHERE id_number = 1234
GROUP BY id_number;
```

Which clause causes an error?

○ a. **CREATE VIEW parts_view**

○ b. **AS SELECT id_number, description, sum(quantity)**

○ c. **FROM inventory**

○ d. **WHERE id_number = 1234**

○ e. **GROUP BY id_number;**

Question 3

What is one of the purposes of a column constraint?

○ a. Enforce relationships between tables.

○ b. Ensure that a column value is numeric rather than character.

○ c. Enforce entity rules.

○ d. Enforce business rules.

Question 4

Based on Table 11.1, evaluate this **UPDATE** statement:

```
UPDATE inventory
SET description = 'Sold Out'
WHERE id_number = 'A12345'
AND quantity = 0;
```

Which clause will cause an error?

○ a. **UPDATE inventory**

○ b. **SET description = 'Sold Out'**

○ c. **WHERE id_number = 'A12345'**

○ d. **AND quantity = 0;**

○ e. None of the above

Table 11.1   Instance chart for table INVENTORY.

Column Name:	ID_NUMBER	DESCRIPTION	MANUFACTURER_ID	QUANTITY	PRICE
Key Type:	PK		FK		
Nulls/Unique:	NN, U	NN	NN		
FK Table:			MANUFACTURER		
FK Column:			ID_NUMBER		
Data Type:	NUM	VARCHAR2	VARCHAR2	NUM	NUM
Length:	9	26	25	9	8,2

Question 5

The PL/SQL executable section contains which type of statements?

○ a. PL/SQL and SQL statements to manipulate data in the database

○ b. The procedure or function name and input/output variable definitions

○ c. The definition of program variables, constants, exceptions, and cursors

○ d. Statements to deal with error handling

Question 6

What is the purpose of the **IN** operator?

- ○ a. Compare two similar values.
- ○ b. Perform an equality comparison.
- ○ c. Evaluate a range of values.
- ○ d. Restrict results to a specified list of values.

Question 7

Evaluate this command:

```
ALTER TABLE customer
DISABLE CONSTRAINT pk_customer CASCADE;
```

Which task would this command accomplish?

- ○ a. Delete only the primary key values.
- ○ b. Disable all dependent integrity constraints.
- ○ c. Disable only the primary key constraint.
- ○ d. Alter all dependent integrity constraint values.

Question 8

When can an index be placed on a view?

- ○ a. When you only **SELECT** from the view
- ○ b. When you only **DELETE** from the view
- ○ c. When there is a **WITH CHECK OPTION** used to create the view
- ○ d. When you can **UPDATE** using the view
- ○ e. Never

Question 9

You query the database with this command:

```
SELECT manufacturer_desc
FROM manufacturer
WHERE manufacturer_id LIKE '%F\%B\%I\_%' ESCAPE '\'
/
```

For which character pattern will the **LIKE** operator be searching?

○ a. **F%B%I_**

○ b. **FBI_**

○ c. **F\%B\%I%_**

○ d. **F\B\I_**

Question 10

In the executable section of a PL/SQL block, you include this statement:

```
Product.max_inventory1 := 30;
```

Which task will this accomplish?

○ a. A composite variable will be assigned a value.

○ b. A constant will be assigned a value.

○ c. An index identifier will be assigned a value.

○ d. A record will be assigned a value.

Question 11

Using Table 11.2, evaluate the following query:

```
SELECT TO_CHAR(price, '$099999.99')
FROM inventory;
```

How is the price value 0.50 displayed?

○ a. .50

○ b. $.50

○ c. $000000.50

○ d. $0.50

Table 11.2   Instance chart for table INVENTORY.

Column Name:	ID_NUMBER	DESCRIPTION	MANUFACTURER_ID	QUANTITY	PRICE
Key Type:	PK		FK		
Nulls/Unique:	NN, U	NN	NN		
FK Table:			MANUFACTURER		
FK Column:			ID_NUMBER		
Data Type:	NUM	VARCHAR2	VARCHAR2	NUM	NUM
Length:	9	26	25	9	8,2

Question 12

Evaluate this function created with SQL*Plus:

```
CREATE OR REPLACE FUNCTION raise_price
    (start_value IN NUMBER)
RETURN number
IS
BEGIN
    RETURN (start_value * 1.75);
END lower_price;
```

Why will this function cause an error?

○ a. A clause is missing.

○ b. The **END** clause is incorrect.

○ c. A keyword is missing.

○ d. The parameter mode should not be specified.

○ e. The **CREATE OR REPLACE** statement is invalid.

Question 13

What is the purpose of the **USER_** set of data dictionary views?

○ a. List all objects, of the specific type, that the user has created.

○ b. List all objects, of the specific type, that the user has been granted rights on.

○ c. List all objects, of the specific type, in the database.

○ d. List all dynamic data, of the specific type, about the database.

Question 14

You have entered a three-line command in the command buffer of a SQL*Plus session. You press the Enter key twice. At the SQL prompt, you enter the following command followed by a carriage return (the Enter key):

```
DEL
```

What is the state of the buffer?

○ a. The buffer is cleared of all lines.

○ b. The buffer is holding the command **DEL**.

○ c. The buffer is holding the first two lines of the original text.

○ d. The buffer is holding the last two lines of the original text.

Question 15

Using Table 11.3, evaluate this command:

```
SELECT id_number
FROM inventory
WHERE price IN (0.25, 2.21);
```

Which value would be displayed?

○ a. 36025

○ b. 36023

○ c. 43081

○ d. 36028

Table 11.3   Contents of the INVENTORY table.

ID_NUMBER	DESCRIPTION	MANUFACTURER_ID	QUANTITY	PRICE	ORDER_DATE
36025	Spike 1 in	acme0525	234	2.45	12-May-97
36027	Nail 3/8	smith0626	134	0.25	15-Oct-97
36023	Chain	Jones0426	245	8.25	20-Jun-97
36028	Canvas	packy0122	1245	2.21	26-Oct-97
43081	Rubber Sheets	rubberrus0804	334	28.31	02-Feb-98

Question 16

When you're designing an application, which step comes first?

- ○ a. Map attributes to columns.
- ○ b. Map entities to tables.
- ○ c. Normalize ERD.
- ○ d. Map UID to primary keys.
- ○ e. Map relationships to foreign keys.

Question 17

Evaluate this statement:

```
SELECT a.isotope, b.gamma_energy
FROM chart_n a, g_energy b
WHERE a.isotope ='IODINE'
AND a.isotope = b.isotope
AND a.mass_no='131'
```

Which type of join is shown?

- ○ a. Equijoin
- ○ b. Nonequijoin
- ○ c. Self-join
- ○ d. Outer join

Question 18

What is the third stage of the system development cycle?

- ○ a. Build and document
- ○ b. Design
- ○ c. Transition
- ○ d. Strategy and analysis
- ○ e. Production

Question 19

When will a PL/SQL block not compile? [Choose two]

- ❑ a. When an implicit cursor retrieves only one row
- ❑ b. When an implicit cursor retrieves more than one row
- ❑ c. When the data types within a **SELECT** statement are inconsistent
- ❑ d. When an embedded **SELECT** statement is missing a required clause

Question 20

What is the purpose of the SQL*Plus command **GET**?

- ○ a. Get the contents of a previously saved operating system file into the buffer.
- ○ b. Get a printer assignment.
- ○ c. Get the contents of the buffer for editing.
- ○ d. Return a storage location for the buffer contents.

Question 21

What is the purpose of a referential integrity constraint?

- ○ a. Enforce business rules.
- ○ b. Ensure that entities are internally consistent.
- ○ c. Validate data entries of a specified type.
- ○ d. Enforce the rule that a child foreign key must have a valid parent primary key.

Question 22

Which two operators cannot be used in an outer join condition? [Choose two]

- ❑ a. =
- ❑ b. **IN**
- ❑ c. **AND**
- ❑ d. **OR**

Question 23

Which of the following is executed automatically?

○ a. Anonymous PL/SQL block

○ b. Function

○ c. Procedure

○ d. Trigger

Question 24

What is the default length of a **CHAR** column?

○ a. 38

○ b. 255

○ c. 4000

○ d. 1

Question 25

Which of the following activities would take place in the production phase of the system development cycle?

○ a. Interview users.

○ b. Develop ERDs.

○ c. Perform normal routine maintenance.

○ d. Code all program modules.

○ e. Test the system for user acceptance.

Question 26

Which of the following would contain the list of tables from which to retrieve data?

○ a. **SELECT** list

○ b. **ORDER BY** clause

○ c. **FROM** clause

○ d. **GROUP BY** clause

Question 27

What function would you use to convert a numeric value into a **VARCHAR2**?

○ a. **TO_CHAR**

○ b. **TO_NUM**

○ c. **TO_DATE**

○ d. **TO_VARCHAR**

Question 28

Which section of a PL/SQL routine contains functions for error trapping?

○ a. Declarative

○ b. Definition

○ c. Exception

○ d. Executable

Question 29

You query the database with this command:

```
SELECT
CONCAT(LOWER(SUBSTR(description,10)),
LENGTH(product_name)) "Product ID"
FROM inventory;
```

Which function is evaluated second?

○ a. **CONCAT()**

○ b. **LENGTH()**

○ c. **LOWER()**

Question 30

You query the database with this command:

```
SELECT
    isotope, group_id,mass_no,
    DISTINCT(atomic_weight)
FROM chart_n;
```

What values are displayed?

○ a. Distinct combinations of **isotope**, **group_id**, **mass_no**, and **atomic_weight**.

○ b. **isotope** and distinct combinations of **group_id**, **mass_no**, and **atomic_weight**.

○ c. **isotope**, **group_id**, **mass_no**, and distinct values of **atomic_weight**.

○ d. No values will be displayed because the statement will fail.

Question 31

For which of the following would you use the **ALTER TABLE...MODIFY** option?

○ a. Add a column to the table.

○ b. Disable a table constraint.

○ c. Drop a table column.

○ d. Increase the precision of a numeric column.

Question 32

Evaluate this command:

```
SELECT group_id, isotope, AVG(atomic_weight)
FROM char_n
WHERE AVG(atomic_weight) > 89.00
GROUP BY group_id, isotope
ORDER BY AVG(atomic_weight);
```

Which clause will cause an error?

○ a.
```
SELECT group_id, isotope, AVG(atomic_weight)
```
○ b.
```
WHERE AVG(atomic_weight) > 89.00
```
○ c.
```
GROUP BY group_id, isotope
```
○ d.
```
ORDER BY AVG(atomic_weight);
```

Question 33

Which type of PL/SQL statement would you use to increase the price values by 10 percent for items with more than 2,000 in stock and by 20 percent for items with fewer than 500 in stock?

○ a. An **IF...THEN...ELSE** statement

○ b. A simple **INSERT** loop

○ c. A simple **UPDATE** statement

○ d. A **WHILE** loop

Question 34

You query the database with this command:

```
SELECT id_number, (quantity - 100 / 0.15 - 35 + 20)
FROM inventory;
```

Which expression is evaluated first?

○ a. **quantity - 100**

○ b. **0.15 - 35**

○ c. **35 + 20**

○ d. **100 / 0.15**

Question 35

In light of Table 11.4, you attempt to query the database with this command:

```
SELECT NVL(100/efficiency, 'none')
FROM calibrations;
```

Why does this statement cause an error when the efficiency values are null?

○ a. The expression attempts to divide a **NULL** value.

○ b. The character string **none** is not a valid value for the **NVL** substitution.

○ c. A **NULL** value cannot be converted into a string value with any function.

○ d. A **NULL** value used in an expression cannot be converted to an actual value.

Table 11.4 Table calibrations.			
Column Name:	INSTRUMENT_ID	EFFICIENCY	CAL_DATE
Key Type:	PK		
Nulls/Unique:	NN, U		
FK Table:			
FK Column:			
Data Type:	NUM	NUM	DATE
Length:			

Question 36

What is the purpose of the PL/SQL **FETCH** command?

○ a. To define a cursor to be used later

○ b. To retrieve values from the active set into local variables

○ c. To call the rows identified by a cursor query into the active set

○ d. To release the memory used by the cursor

Question 37

After reviewing Table 11.5, and assuming that the 'RR' value is the default date format, evaluate this command:

```
DELETE FROM inventory
WHERE
order_date>TO_DATE('11.30.1999',
                   'MM.DD.YYYY');
```

Which of the listed **ID_NUMBER** values would be deleted?

○ a. 43081

○ b. 36023

○ c. 36027

○ d. None would be deleted because the statement will fail

Table 11.5   Contents of the INVENTORY table.

ID_NUMBER	DESCRIPTION	MANUFACTURER_ID	QUANTITY	PRICE	ORDER_DATE
36025	Spike 1 in	acme0525	234	2.45	12-May-99
36027	Nail 3/8	smith0626	134	0.25	15-Oct-99
36023	Chain	Jones0426	245	8.25	20-Jun-99
36028	Canvas	packy0122	1245	2.21	26-Oct-99
43081	Rubber Sheets	rubberrus0804	334	28.31	02-Feb-00

Question 38

Which privilege can be granted only on a **DIRECTORY**?

○ a. **ALTER**

○ b. **DELETE**

○ c. **READ**

○ d. **INSERT**

Question 39

Evaluate this procedure:

```
CREATE OR REPLACE FUNCTION found_isotope
   (v_energy_line IN BOOLEAN,
    v_proper_ratio IN BOOLEAN)
RETURN NUMBER
IS
Ret_val NUMBER;
BEGIN
   IF (v_energy_line AND v_proper_ratio)
   THEN
       ret_val:=1;
   ELSIF NOT (v_energy_line AND v_proper_ratio)
   THEN
       ret_val:=2;
   ELSIF (v_energy_line AND v_proper_ratio) IS NULL
   THEN
       ret_val:=-1;
   END IF;
   RETURN ret_val;
END;
```

If **v_energy_line** equals **TRUE**, and **v_proper_ratio** equals **NULL**, which value is assigned to **ret_val**?

○ a. 1

○ b. 2

○ c. −1

○ d. None of the above

Question 40

In a **SELECT** statement, which character is used to pass in a value at runtime?

○ a. \

○ b. %

○ c. &

○ d. _ (underscore)

Question 41

Evaluate this command:

```
SELECT i.isotope, g.calibration
FROM chart_n i, gamma_calibrations g
WHERE i.energy = g.energy;
```

What type of join is the command?

○ a. Equijoin

○ b. Nonequijoin

○ c. Self-join

○ d. The statement is not a join query

Question 42

What is the purpose of the **SUBSTR** string function?

○ a. To insert a capital letter for each new word in the string

○ b. To return a specified substring from the string

○ c. To return the number of characters in the string

○ d. To substitute a non-null string for any null values returned

Question 43

What will the following operation return? [Choose two]

```
SELECT TO_DATE('01-jan-00') - TO_DATE('01-dec-99')
FROM dual;
```

❑ a. 365 if the **NLS_DATE_FORMAT** is set to 'DD-mon-RR'

❑ b. A **VARCHAR2** value

❑ c. An error; you can't do this with dates

❑ d. −36493 if the **NLS_DATE_FORMAT** is set to the default value

Question 44

You query the database with this command:

```
SELECT atomic_weight
FROM chart_n
WHERE (atomic_weight BETWEEN 1 AND 50
OR atomic_weight IN (25, 70, 95))
AND atomic_weight BETWEEN (25 AND 75)
```

Which of the following values could the statement retrieve?

○ a. 51

○ b. 95

○ c. 30

○ d. 75

Question 45

In the executable section of a PL/SQL block, you include these statements:

```
Isotope_record.isotope := 'XENON';
Isotope_record.group := 'NOBLE GAS';
```

Which task will be accomplished?

○ a. A record field will be assigned a character string value.

○ b. A record field will be created based on the **isotope** table.

○ c. A constant will be initialized.

○ d. A constant will be created.

Question 46

Which of the following best describes a relationship?

○ a. A thing of significance

○ b. A distinct characteristic of a thing of significance

○ c. A named association between two things of significance

○ d. A description of the way that data flows

Question 47

Which statement is true about the **TRUNCATE TABLE** command?

○ a. It disables constraints in the target table.

○ b. It removes the target table from the database.

○ c. It can reset the highwater mark for a table.

○ d. Data removed is recoverable via the **ROLLBACK** command.

Question 48

Which of the following is a use of the **TO_NUMBER** function?

○ a. Convert a **VARCHAR2** value into a **DATE** value.

○ b. Convert a **DATE** value into a **VARCHAR2** value using a specified format.

○ c. Convert a **VARCHAR2** value into a **NUMBER** value.

○ d. Convert a specified **VARCHAR2** value into a **CHAR** value.

Question 49

Evaluate this command:

```
CREATE TABLE purchase_items
    (id_number        NUMBER(9),
     description      VARCHAR2(25))
AS
SELECT id_number, description
FROM inventory
WHERE quantity < 10;
```

Why will this statement cause an error?

○ a. A clause is missing.

○ b. A keyword is missing.

○ c. The **WHERE** clause cannot be used when you're creating a table.

○ d. The data types in the new table must not be defined.

Question 50

What is a characteristic of only PL/SQL?

○ a. Accepts input of variables.

○ b. Allows shutdown of the database.

○ c. Allows use of exception handling routines based on error numbers.

○ d. None of the above.

Question 51

Examine Table 11.6. Which value is displayed if you query the database with the following command?

```
SELECT COUNT(DISTINCT(description))
FROM inventory;
```

○ a. 8

○ b. 1

○ c. 4

○ d. **COUNT** returns an error if it is not run against a primary key

Table 11.6   Contents of the **INVENTORY** table.

ID_NUMBER	DESCRIPTION	MANUFACTURER_ID	QUANTITY	PRICE	ORDER_DATE
36025	Spike 1 in	acme0525	234	2.45	12-May-97
36027	Nail 3/8	smith0626	134	0.25	15-Oct-97
36023	Chain	Jones0426	245	8.25	20-Jun-97
36028	Chain	packy0122	1245	2.21	26-Oct-97
43081	Rubber Sheets	rubberrus0804	334	28.31	02-Feb-98

Question 52

Evaluate this command:

```
CREATE FORCE VIEW isotope_groups
AS SELECT element, group_id, count(*) isotopes
FROM chart_n
WHERE atomic_weight>50
GROUP BY element,group_id
ORDER BY atomic_weight;
```

Which clause will cause an error?

O a.
```
AS SELECT isotope, group_id
```
O b.
```
FROM chart_n
```
O c.
```
WHERE atomic_weight>50
```
O d.
```
ORDER BY atomic_weight;
```

Question 53

You write a **SELECT** statement with two join conditions. What is the maximum number of tables you have joined together without generating a Cartesian product?

O a. 0

O b. 4

O c. 2

O d. 3

Question 54

Which of the following is a purpose of the user-defined constraint?

○ a. To enforce not-null restrictions

○ b. To enforce referential integrity

○ c. To enforce business rules

○ d. To take action based on insertions, updates, or deletions in the base
       table

Question 55

Which character can be used in a table name if the name is not placed inside
double quotes?

○ a. %

○ b. *

○ c. #

○ d. @

Question 56

Which command would you use to remove all the rows from the **isotope**
table and not allow rollback?

○ a. **DROP TABLE isotope;**

○ b. **DELETE isotope;**

○ c. **TRUNCATE TABLE isotope;**

○ d. There is no way to remove all rows and not allow rollback

Question 57

Use Tables 11.7 and 11.8 to evaluate this command:

```
INSERT INTO inventory (id_number,
                       manufacturer_id)
VALUES (56023,'beth104ss');
```

Which type of constraint will be violated?

O a. Check

O b. Not null

O c. Primary key

O d. Foreign key

Table 11.7 Instance chart for table INVENTORY.

Column Name:	ID_NUMBER	DESCRIPTION	MANUFACTURER_ID	QUANTITY	PRICE
Key Type:	PK		FK		
Nulls/Unique:	NN, U	NN	NN		
FK Table:			MANUFACTURER		
FK Column:			ID_NUMBER		
Data Type:	NUM	VARCHAR2	VARCHAR2	NUM	NUM
Length:	9	26	25	9	8,2

Table 11.8 Contents of the INVENTORY table.

ID_NUMBER	DESCRIPTION	MANUFACTURER_ID	QUANTITY	PRICE	ORDER_DATE
36025	Spike 1 in	acme0525	234	2.45	12-May-97
36027	Nail 3/8	smith0626	134	0.25	15-Oct-97
36023	Chain	Jones0426	245	8.25	20-Jun-97
36028	Canvas	packy0122	1245	2.21	26-Oct-97
43081	Rubber Sheets	rubberrus0804	334	28.31	02-Feb-98

Question 58

What is the advantage of using the **%TYPE** attribute to declare a PL/SQL type?

○ a. The name of an unused column in the underlying table may change.

○ b. The data types or data type sizes of the underlying table columns may change by runtime.

○ c. The **%TYPE** attribute forces the data type of the underlying database table column to be what you specify.

○ d. All column constraints are applied to the variables declared using **%TYPE**.

Question 59

Which statement would you use to query the database for the quantity and description of each item that was ordered before June 1, 1999, and whose price is less than 0.25 or greater than 10.00?

○ a.
```
SELECT quantity, description FROM inventory
    WHERE price BETWEEN 0.25 and 10.00 OR
    order_date < '01-jun-1999';
```

○ b.
```
SELECT quantity, description FROM inventory
    WHERE ( price < 0.25 OR price > 10.00) AND
    order_date<'01-jun-1999';
```

○ c.
```
SELECT quantity, description FROM inventory
    WHERE price < 0.25 OR
    price > 10.00 AND
    order_date > '01-jun-1999';
```

○ d.
```
SELECT quantity, description FROM inventory
    WHERE price IN (0.25, 10.00) OR
    order_date < '01-jun-1999';
```

Question 60

Evaluate the following command:

```
CREATE TABLE customer
(
customer_id NUMBER CONSTRAINT pk_customer PRIMARY
    KEY
USING INDEX TABLESPACE customer_index,
Customer_entry_date DATE,
customer_addresses address_nt,
customer_phones phone_v
)
NESTED TABLE customer_addresses STORE AS addresses
        PCTFREE 10
        PCTUSED 80
        INITRANS 5
        MAXTRANS 255
        TABLESPACE tele_data
        STORAGE (
                INITIAL 20m
                NEXT 10m
                MINEXTENTS 1
                MAXEXTENTS 10
                PCTINCREASE 0
        )
PARTITION BY RANGE (customer_id)
(PARTITION before_2000
  VALUES LESS THAN (2000)
TABLESPACE data1,
PARTITION before_400
  VALUES LESS than (3000)
TABLESPACE data2,
PARTITION greater_than_3000
  VALUES LESS THAN (MAXVALUE)
TABLESPACE data3)
/
```

Question 60 (continued)

Assuming that **address_nt** is a valid nested table type and **phone_v** is a valid **VARRAY** type, and all tablespaces are valid, which portion of the above command will fail?

○ a. The **CREATE TABLE** portion

○ b. The specifications for the **NESTED STORAGE**

○ c. The way the types are referred to

○ d. The partitioning clause

Answer Key

1. a, d	21. d	41. a
2. e	22. b, d	42. b
3. b	23. d	43. a, d
4. c	24. d	44. c
5. a	25. c	45. a
6. d	26. c	46. c
7. b	27. a	47. c
8. e	28. c	48. c
9. a	29. c	49. d
10. d	30. d	50. c
11. c	31. d	51. c
12. b	32. b	52. d
13. a	33. a	53. d
14. c	34. d	54. c
15. d	35. b	55. c
16. c	36. b	56. c
17. a	37. a	57. b
18. a	38. c	58. b
19. c, d	39. b	59. b
20. a	40. c	60. d

Question 1

The correct answers are a and d. The underscore (_) is used as a single-character wildcard, and the percent sign (%) is used as a multicharacter wildcard; both must be escaped to be used as literals in a **LIKE** clause. The dollar sign ($), answer b, and the forward slash (/), answer c, can be used as literals, so they do not have to be escaped.

Question 2

The correct answer is e. The **GROUP BY** clause will cause an error because it doesn't include the **DESCRIPTION** column. All of the other lines are syntactically correct, so all the other answers are incorrect.

Question 3

The correct answer is b. Column constraints are used to verify values and enforce uniqueness as well as not-null. Answer a is incorrect because referential constraints are used to ensure data integrity between tables. Answer c is incorrect because there is no such thing as an entity constraint (as far as I know) to enforce entity rules. Finally, answer d is incorrect because user-defined constraints are used to enforce business rules and have nothing to do with data validation rules.

Question 4

The correct answer is c. The **WHERE** clause will cause an error. After examining the exhibit, you should notice that the **ID_NUMBER** column is a **NUMBER** data-type column. Attempting to compare this with 'A12345' would result in an error because the letter "A" cannot be implicitly converted to a number. The other lines have the correct syntax, so answers a, b, and d are incorrect. Answer e ("none of the above") is incorrect because answer c is correct.

Question 5

The correct answer is a. This answer comes directly from the definition of the executable section. Answer b is the definition of the header section; the executable section never contains the definitions for variables, nor does it provide the name of the procedure. Answer c is incorrect because this is the function of the declarative section of a PL/SQL program. Answer d is incorrect because this is the definition of the exception section of a PL/SQL block and not the executable section.

Question 6

The correct answer is d. The **IN** operator is used to compare a value or expression to a list of values. Answer a is incorrect because the **LIKE** operator is used to compare a wildcard search value against a column or expression that contains or yields similar values. Answer b is incorrect because the equal sign (=) is used to show equality, as in an equijoin, not to check a list of values. Answer c is incorrect because **BETWEEN** is used to compare a value or expression to a range of values, not to a list of values.

Question 7

The correct answer is b. The command disables the primary key constraint and cascades this to disable all dependent constraints. Answer a is incorrect because no data is deleted by this statement. Answer c is incorrect because this command disables the primary key and all dependent constraints. Answer d is incorrect because, once again, no values are altered; only constraints are altered.

Question 8

The correct answer is e. You cannot index a view. Whether you **SELECT**, **DELETE**, or **UPDATE** a view, index creation is not allowed, even with a **WITH CHECK OPTION** clause.

Question 9

The correct answer is a. The backslashes are used to escape the percent signs and the underscore, thus allowing them to be treated as literals. Answer b is incorrect because it doesn't include the percent signs (%) that have been escaped. Answer c is incorrect because the backslashes (\) would be ignored. Answer d is incorrect because the backslashes would be ignored and the percent signs (%) would be shown instead.

Question 10

The correct answer is d. The format of the declaration shows that you're dealing with a record because dot notation indicates that a record type is being used. Answer a is incorrect because the statement does not contain a composite variable. Answer b is incorrect because nowhere do you see the keyword **CONSTANT** in the declaration. Answer c is incorrect because you are not dealing with an index identifier.

Question 11

The correct answer is c, $000000.50. The leading $ and zero in the format statement tell Oracle to format the number such that if the leading numbers before the decimal are all zero, show a zero for each format character to the left of the decimal. (Because there is no answer that says, "The query will fail," you don't really need an exhibit to answer this question. You can safely assume that the **PRICE** column is numeric.) Answer a is incorrect because no leading zero or dollar sign is displayed. Answer b is incorrect because no leading zeros to the left of the decimal are displayed. Answer d is incorrect because this answer would be generated by the format $0.99, not the one shown.

Question 12

The correct answer is b. The **END** clause specifies a function name of **lower_price**, but the **CREATE OR REPLACE** command specifies it to be **raise_price**. All the other lines are syntactically correct, so all the other answers are incorrect.

Question 13

The correct answer is a. The purpose of the **USER_** set of data dictionary views is to list all objects, of the specific type, that the user has created. Answer b is incorrect because this describes the **ALL_** views and not the **USER_** views. Answer c is incorrect because this describes the **DBA_** views. Answer d is incorrect because this describes the **V$** views.

Question 14

The correct answer is c. The buffer is holding the first three lines of the original text. Entering the **DEL** (delete) command in SQL*Plus removes the current line (in this case, the last line) from the buffer. Because you have three lines in the buffer, if you remove one, you have two left. Answer a is incorrect because you deleted only one line, not all lines. Answer b is incorrect because the editing commands and **DEL** are not placed in the buffer. Answer d is incorrect because you deleted only the current line, thus leaving the first two lines still in the buffer.

Question 15

The correct answer is d. The key to evaluating the **SELECT** statement is to look at the **IN** clause. The command will return a value only if the price is either 0.25 or 2.21. Records 36027 and 36028 both meet these criteria, but the only record listed is 36028 (answer d). None of the other answers has a price value that is in the list of values specified in the **IN** clause.

Question 16

The correct answer is c, normalize ERD (entity relationship diagram). When designing an application, the order of the steps is as follows:

1. Normalize ERD.

2. Map entities to tables.

3. Map attributes to columns.

4. Map UID to primary keys.

5. Map relationships to foreign keys.

Question 17

The correct answer is a. An equijoin occurs when an equality condition is used to join a table to one or more other tables. Notice that two tables are joined using an equal condition, making this an equijoin. Answer b is incorrect because the statement is an equijoin, not a nonequijoin. Answer c is incorrect because the statement is an equijoin of two tables, not a self-join of one table to itself. Answer d is incorrect because the outer join symbol (+) has not been used.

Question 18

The correct answer is a. The build and document step is the third stage of the system development cycle. The following is the order of the stages of the system development cycle:

1. Strategy and analysis

2. Design

3. Build and document

4. Transition

5. Production

Question 19

The correct answers are c and d. An error in the **SELECT** statement format for a cursor will result in a syntax error, prohibiting the build of the PL/SQL block. Answer a is incorrect because retrieving only one row is the correct behavior for an implicit cursor; thus, it wouldn't raise an exception or prohibit a block from being built internally. Answer b is incorrect because returning multiple rows to an implicit cursor will raise an exception when the block is executed, but it won't cause a compilation error.

Question 20

The correct answer is a. The purpose of the SQL*Plus **GET** command is to get the contents of a previously saved operating system file into the buffer. Answer b is incorrect because getting a printer assignment is the purpose of the **SPOOL** command. Answer c is incorrect because getting the contents of the buffer for editing is the purpose of the **LIST** command. Answer d is incorrect because returning a storage location for the buffer contents is not a function of any SQL*Plus command.

Question 21

The correct answer is d. Answer d—enforce the rule that a child foreign key must have a valid parent primary key—is actually the definition of a referential integrity constraint. Answer a is incorrect because a user-defined constraint is used to enforce business rules. Answer b is incorrect because entity constraints don't exist. Answer c is incorrect because a column constraint is used to validate data entry.

Question 22

The correct answers are b and d. The **IN** operator and the **OR** operator cannot be used in an outer join. Answer a is incorrect because an equal sign (=) can be used in an outer join. Answer c is incorrect because an **AND** operator can also be used in an outer join.

Question 23

The correct answer is d. Triggers are associated with tables and are automatically fired on specified actions against the table. Answer a is incorrect because an anonymous PL/SQL block must be called into the command buffer and executed; it is not executed automatically. Answer b is incorrect because functions must be implicitly called by a user, procedure, trigger, or other function, so they are not executed automatically. Answer c is incorrect because procedures must be implicitly called by a user, procedure, trigger, or other function, so they are not executed automatically.

Question 24

The correct answer is d. The default length of a **CHAR** column is 1.

Question 25

The correct answer is c. In the production stage, only normal maintenance functions are performed. Answer a is incorrect because users are interviewed in the strategy and analysis phase. Answer b is incorrect because ERDs (entity relationship diagrams) are developed in the build and document phase. Answer d is incorrect because all program modules are coded in the build and document phase. Answer e is incorrect because testing the system for user acceptance is part of the transition phase.

Question 26

The correct answer is c. The **FROM** clause contains the list of tables from which to select data. Answer a is incorrect because a **SELECT** clause contains a list of items to retrieve from a table. Answer b is incorrect because an **ORDER BY** clause contains a list of columns or expressions used to determine sort order for the result set. Answer d is incorrect because the **GROUP BY** clause contains a specified column list to group the returned data.

Question 27

The correct answer is a. The **TO_CHAR** function is the only function used to convert a numeric data item into a **VARCHAR2** format. Answer b is incorrect because the **TO_NUM** function is used to convert a **VARCHAR2** into a **NUMBER**, not the other way around. Answer c is incorrect because **TO_DATE** is used to convert a **CHAR, VARCHAR2,** or **NUMBER** into a **DATE** value. Answer d is incorrect because **TO_VARCHAR** is not a valid Oracle8 function.

Question 28

The correct answer is c. The exception section is used specifically to trap errors. Answer a is incorrect because the declarative section of a PL/SQL routine is used to define variables, cursors, and exceptions. Answer b is incorrect because the definition section specifies the PL/SQL object type, its name, and the input and/or output variables. Answer d is incorrect because the executable section contains the procedural logic and performs the processing for the PL/SQL object; although it may **RAISE** exceptions, it doesn't process them.

Question 29

The correct answer is c. The **LOWER()** function is evaluated second. The statement inside the parentheses is evaluated first. In this case, we have nested parentheses, so the inner and then the outer parenthetical functions will be executed, in that order. Answer a is incorrect because **CONCAT()** is outside the parentheses. Answer b is incorrect because **LENGTH()** is also outside the parentheses.

Question 30

The correct answer is d. No values will be displayed because the statement is syntactically incorrect and will fail. A **DISTINCT** operator cannot be used in this manner. Answers a, b, and c are incorrect due to the **DISTINCT** operator's improper placement, which will cause the entire statement to fail.

Question 31

The correct answer is d. The **MODIFY** option of the **ALTER TABLE** command is used only to change the characteristics or the data type of a column. Answer a is incorrect because adding a column to the table must be done with an **ADD** clause. Answer b is incorrect because disabling a table constraint is not allowed in this version of Oracle. Answer c is incorrect because dropping a table column is not allowed.

Question 32

The correct answer is b. You cannot use a grouping function such as **AVG** in a **WHERE** clause. The rest of the clauses are syntactically correct and thus are incorrect.

Question 33

The correct answer is a. In this question, you are asked to perform conditional tests and take action based on the results of the test. The only PL/SQL structure capable of this is the **IF...THEN...ELSE** statement. Answer b is incorrect because a simple **INSERT** loop wouldn't use a condition complex enough to handle the conditions specified. Answer c is incorrect because a simple **UPDATE** statement couldn't do a conditional update as specified. Answer d is incorrect because a **WHILE** loop wouldn't properly handle the update specified.

Question 34

The correct answer is d because multiplication (*) and division (/) are evaluated first in the hierarchy of operations. The other two operators shown (+ and -) are below division in the hierarchy of operations.

Question 35

The correct answer is b. The character string 'none' cannot be substituted for a NULL value using the NVL function. For the NVL command to be used, the value being tested for NULL and the substitution value have to be of the same data type. In this example, we are attempting to substitute a character string for a numeric value, so this will generate an error. Answer a is incorrect because the division will return a NULL value, which the NVL command should be able to handle. Answer c is incorrect because you can replace a NULL value with a string using the DECODE function. Answer d is incorrect because converting a NULL value in an expression to an actual value is the purpose of the NVL function.

Question 36

The correct answer is b. The FETCH command retrieves values returned by the cursor from the active set into the local variables. Answer a is incorrect because defining a cursor to be used later is the function of the CURSOR command. Answer c is incorrect because calling the rows identified by a cursor query into the active set is the function of the OPEN command. Answer d is incorrect because releasing memory used by the cursor is the function of the CLOSE command.

Question 37

The correct answer is a. Of the values available in the table, only 43081 is in the answer set, so it is the correct answer. Its order_date is the only one greater than 30 Nov. 1999. Answers b and c are incorrect because they don't meet the selection criteria. Answer d is incorrect because the value in answer a would be deleted.

Question 38

The correct answer is c. The only allowed grant on a DIRECTORY is READ. Answers a, b, and d are incorrect because these privileges cannot be granted on a DIRECTORY.

Question 39

The correct answer is b. A combination of **NULL** and **TRUE** or of **NULL** and **FALSE** will result in a **FALSE** (a value of 2 in our function); a combination of **TRUE** and **TRUE** will result in a **TRUE**; and a combination of **FALSE** and **FALSE** will result in a **FALSE**. A combination of **TRUE** and **FALSE** also results in a **FALSE**. Answer a is incorrect because both conditions would have to be **TRUE** for the result to be **TRUE** (corresponding to 1 in our function). Answer c is incorrect because both conditions would have to be **NULL** for the answer to be −1, which corresponds to a **NULL** value. Answer d is incorrect because answer b is correct.

Question 40

The correct answer is c. The ampersand character (&), either by itself or with a second ampersand, denotes substitution at runtime. Answer a is incorrect because the backslash (\) is used to escape the percent (%) and underscore (_) characters, unless something else is specified with the **ESCAPE** keyword. Answer b is incorrect because the percent sign (%) is the multicharacter wildcard. Answer d is incorrect because the underscore (_) is used as the single-character wildcard.

Question 41

The correct answer is a. Because the **SELECT** statement is using an equality test (using an equal sign), this is an equijoin operation. Answer b is incorrect because this is not a not-equal (!=, <>) type of join. Answer c is incorrect because a self-join is a table joined to itself, and this statement has two tables being joined. Answer d is incorrect because answer a is correct.

Question 42

The correct answer is b. The entire purpose of the **SUBSTR** function is to return a substring from a character value. Answer a is incorrect because inserting a capital letter for each new word in the string is the purpose of the **INITCAP** function. Answer c is incorrect because returning the number of characters in the string is the purpose of the **LENGTH** function. Answer d is incorrect because substituting a non-null string for any null values returned is the purpose of the **NVL** function.

Question 43

The correct answers are a and d. When two dates are subtracted, you receive a numeric value that corresponds to the number of days between the dates—either positive if the first date is greater than the second, or negative if the first date is less than the second. Depending on the value of the **NLS_DATE_ FORMAT**, the 00 will be either 1900 (default of dd-mon-yy) or 2000 (if set to dd-mon-rr), so both 365 and −36493 could result. Answer b is incorrect because date arithmetic returns a date or a number, not a **VARCHAR2** value. Answer c is incorrect because answers a and d are correct.

Question 44

The correct answer is c, 30. Answer a (51) is excluded by the **BETWEEN 1 AND 50 OR atomic_weight IN (25, 70, 95)** clause. Answer b (95) is excluded by the **AND atomic_weight BETWEEN (25 AND 75)** clause. Answer d (75) is excluded by the **atomic_weight (BETWEEN 1 AND 50) OR atomic_weight IN (25, 70, 95)** clause.

Question 45

The correct answer is a. A record field will be assigned a character string value. Answer b is incorrect because you aren't using a **%ROWTYPE**, which is used to create a record based on a complete table row. Answers c and d are incorrect because you aren't using the keyword **CONSTANT**.

Question 46

The correct answer is c. A relationship is a named association between two items of significance; this is the definition of a relationship. Answer a is incorrect because it describes an entity. Answer b is incorrect because it describes an attribute. Answer d is incorrect because it describes a data flow diagram.

Question 47

The correct answer is c. The **TRUNCATE TABLE** command can reset the highwater mark for a table if the **REUSE STORAGE** clause is not used. Answer a is incorrect because **TRUNCATE** doesn't disable constraints and can't be used with active constraints in place. Answer b is incorrect because **TRUN-CATE** removes data, not tables. Answer d is incorrect because **TRUNCATE** is a DDL statement and can't be rolled back with a **ROLLBACK** command.

Question 48

The correct answer is c. Converting a **VARCHAR2** value into a **NUMBER** value is a use of the **TO_NUMBER** function. Answer a is incorrect because this describes the **TO_DATE** function. Answer b is incorrect because this describes the **TO_CHAR** function. Answer d is incorrect because this is an implicit conversion and doesn't require a function.

Question 49

The correct answer is d. The data types in the new table must not be defined. Answers a and b are incorrect because the statements outside of the column definitions are syntactically correct. Answer c is incorrect because a **WHERE** clause can be used in a **CREATE TABLE** subselect.

Question 50

The correct answer is c. Only PL/SQL allows the use of exception handling routines based on error numbers. Answer a is incorrect because SQL allows input of variables, but no exception processing based on error numbers. Answer b is incorrect because PL/SQL cannot be used to shut down the database. Answer d is incorrect because answer c is correct.

Question 51

The correct answer is c. Four rows in the table are returned by the query. Answer a is incorrect because there aren't eight rows in the table. Answer b is incorrect because there is more than one row in the table with a unique description. Answer d is incorrect because you can count on any column in a table.

Question 52

The correct answer is d because you cannot use **ORDER BY** in a view. Answers a, b, and c are incorrect because they are syntactically correct.

Question 53

The correct answer is d. You can determine the minimum number of joins based on the formula $n-1$, where n is the number of tables to be joined. Therefore, with two join conditions, the maximum number of tables that could be joined is three. Answer a is incorrect because a zero-table join is not possible.

Answer b is incorrect because a four-table join would require three join conditions. Answer c is incorrect because, although you could use two join conditions to join two tables, the question specifically asks for the maximum number that could be joined without causing a Cartesian product.

Question 54

The correct answer is c. User-defined constraints are used to enforce business rules. Answer a is incorrect because enforcing not-null restrictions is the purpose of a column constraint. Answer b is incorrect because enforcing referential integrity is the purpose of a referential integrity constraint. Answer d is incorrect because taking action based on insertions, updates, or deletions in the base table is the purpose of a trigger.

Question 55

The correct answer is c because the only character that can be used is the pound sign (#). Answer a is incorrect because the percent sign (%) is a restricted character used for multicharacter wildcards. Answer b is incorrect because the asterisk (*) is used to denote multiplication and thus is a reserved character. Answer d is incorrect because the at sign (@) is used as a special character in SQL*Plus and thus is a reserved character.

Question 56

The correct answer is c. The **TRUNCATE** command removes all of the rows from a table. Because it is a DDL command, it does implicit commits, thus not allowing rollback operations. Answer a is incorrect because the **DROP** command would remove the entire table. Answer b is incorrect because the **DELETE** command, which can delete rows, allows rollback because it is not a DDL command. Answer d is incorrect because answer b is correct.

Question 57

The correct answer is b. The not-null constraint will be violated. Notice that the **DESCRIPTION** column is missing from the **INSERT** statement. **DESCRIPTION** has a not-null constraint, so you must include it in any **INSERT** activity on the table. Answer a is incorrect because none of the table items show a **CHECK** constraint as being assigned. Answer c is incorrect because the primary key is being inserted. Answer d is incorrect because a value for the foreign key column **MANUFACTURER_ID** is specified; also, because the exhibits don't show that the value exists in the **MANUFACTURER** table, you have to assume that it does.

Question 58

The correct answer is b. The **%TYPE** declaration allows flexibility in that it automatically allows an increase or decrease in the size columns in a table or allows changes in the size or data type of a column. Answer a is incorrect because you don't care about unused columns. Answer c is incorrect because nothing except an **ALTER TABLE** command will force a change in a table column. Answer d is incorrect because constraints are never applied to variables.

Question 59

The correct answer is b. Answer a is incorrect because this statement uses a **BETWEEN**, and thus doesn't check for inequality (greater or less than). Answer c is incorrect because after **order_date** it uses the greater-than operator (>) and not the less-than operator (<), as would be required to find a date before the specified value. Answer d is incorrect because it limits the values to only those that are 0.25 or 10.00, not a range of values.

Question 60

The correct answer is d. The partitioning clause will fail. In Oracle8, you cannot use types in a partitioned table. Answers a, b, and c are incorrect because the clauses or statements they refer to have the correct syntax.

Glossary

ACCEPT—A SQL*Plus command that enables a SQL program to prompt a user for a variable at runtime and accept an input.

ALTER—A DDL (Data Definition Language) command that is used to change database objects.

analysis—In the system development process, the step in which the users' needs are gathered and analyzed to produce documentation used to design a program system. (This step is usually paired with the strategy step.)

archive log—An archive copy of the redo log. The archive log is used to recover to an earlier point in time or to roll forward from a backup to the present time.

attribute—A detail concerning a thing of significance (entity). For example, a PERSON entity may have the attributes of name, address, and date of birth.

audit trail—In Oracle, a defined set of actions that are specified to be audited with system audit tools. For example, you can audit connections to the database.

BFILE—A new data type that is actually a pointer to an external binary file that uses a previously defined **DIRECTORY** entry.

BLOB—A new data type that is an internally stored binary large object. A **BLOB** can be stored inline with other data if it is smaller than 4,000 bytes. If a **BLOB** is larger than 4,000 bytes, it must be stored in a special **LOB**-storage data structure.

buffer—In Oracle, a memory area used to hold data, redo information, or rollback information. Usually, you specify the buffers by using the **DB_BLOCK_BUFFERS, DB_BLOCK_SIZE,** and **LOG_BUFFER** initialization parameters.

cache—A memory area that is self-managing and is used to hold information about objects, locks, and latches. The caches are usually contained in the shared pool area of the SGA (system global area). A cache's size is based on internal algorithms that control how the shared pool memory is allocated.

cardinality—A term used in relational analysis to show how two objects relate; it tells how many. For example, "A person may have zero or one nose" shows a cardinality of zero or one. "A person may have zero, one, or many children" shows a cardinality of zero to many. And "A person has one or many cells" shows a cardinality of one or many. In reference to indexes, cardinality shows how many rows in the indexed table relate back to the index value. A low cardinality index, such as a person's sex (M or F), should be placed in a bitmapped index if it must be indexed. A high cardinality value, such as a person's Social Security number or employee ID, should be placed in a standard B-tree index.

CHUNK—The unit of storage for a **LOB** data type when it is placed in a **LOB** storage area.

CLOB—A character large object data type. The **CLOB** has the same restrictions as does a **BLOB**. (See *BLOB*.) A **LOB** is limited to a maximum of 4 gigabytes or the size limit for your operating system files.

collection—A UDT (User-Defined Type) that is either a nested table or a **VARRAY**.

column—Part of a table's row. A column will have been mapped from an attribute in an entity. Columns have data types, and they may have constraints mapped against them.

COMMIT—A transaction control statement, a **COMMIT** marks a transaction as completed successfully and causes data to be written first to the redo logs and then, after the DBWR process writes, to the disk. A **COMMIT** isn't complete until it receives word from the disk subsystem that the redo-log write is complete. Committed data cannot be rolled back with the **ROLLBACK** command, but must be removed with other DML (Data Manipulation Language) commands.

CONNECT—A Server Manager (SVRMGRL), SQL*Worksheet, or SQL*Plus command that enables a user to connect to the local database or to a remote database.

control file—The Oracle file that contains information on all database files and maintains System Change Number (SCN) records for each file. The control file must be present and current for the database to start up properly. Control files may be mirrored; mirrored copies are automatically updated by Oracle as needed. The control file helps you maintain system concurrency and consistency by providing a means of synchronizing all database files.

conventional path load—The most-used form of the SQL*Loader database load. A conventional path load uses DML (Data Manipulation Language) statements to load data from flat operating system files into Oracle tables.

CREATE—A DDL (Data Definition Language) command used to create database objects.

DANGLING—In a child object table, a record whose parent record has been deleted is said to be **DANGLING**. You must use the **IS DANGLING** clause to handle dangling records.

data dictionary—A collection of C structs, tables, and views that contain all of the database *metadata* (information about the database's data). The data dictionary is used to store information used by all database processes to find out about database data structures.

DCL (Data Control Language)—A classification of SQL commands used to specify grants and privileges in an Oracle database.

DDL (Data Definition Language)—A classification of SQL commands that are used to create or manipulate database structures. Examples are the **CREATE**, **ALTER**, and **DROP** commands.

DELETE—A DML (Data Manipulation Language) command used to remove data from the database tables by rows (generally speaking).

DESCRIBE—A SQL*Plus or Server Manager command that is used to retrieve information on the database structure. Packages, procedures, functions, and tables (including those in clusters) can be described.

DIRECTORY—An internal database object that acts as a pointer to an external operating system directory where **LOB** files are stored.

direct path load—In SQL*Loader, a direct path load disables all triggers, constraints, and indexes, and loads data directly into the table by building and then inserting database blocks. It does not use DML (Data Manipulation Language) commands. There are conventional path loads and direct path loads in SQL*Loader.

discarded record—A record that SQL*Loader rejects for loading; the rejection is based on internal rules for data validation and conversion.

DML (Data Manipulation Language)—A classification of SQL commands that are used to manipulate database structures. Examples are **INSERT, UPDATE, DELETE,** and **SELECT.**

DROP—A DDL (Data Definition Language) command used to remove database objects.

Dynamic SQL—SQL used to build SQL. Essentially, queries are issued against data dictionary tables using embedded literal strings to build a set of commands. Usually, dynamic SQL is used to automate a long series of virtually identical commands acting on similar types of database objects. An example would be creating a script that uses the **DBA_TRIGGERS** table and a single SQL statement to disable or enable all triggers for a set of database tables.

entity—In relational modeling, a thing of significance. Examples of entities are PERSON, CAR, and EXPENSE. Entities are singular in nature and are mapped to tables. Tables contain multiple instances of entities.

equijoin—A statement using equality comparisons to join two or more tables.

ERD (entity relationship diagram)—A pictorial representation—using a standard symbol set and methodology (such as Chen or Yourdon)—of a relational database.

extended ROWID—A new 10-byte format **ROWID** used in Oracle8.

external function—An externally stored function, usually written in C for Oracle8, contained in a shared library, such as a DLL (dynamic link library), and referenced through a PL/SQL call or an internally stored **LIBRARY** object.

external procedure—An externally stored procedure, usually written in C for Oracle8, contained in a shared library, such as a DLL (dynamic link libarary), and referenced through a PL/SQL call or an internally stored **LIBRARY** object.

foreign key—A value or set of values mapped from a primary or parent table into a dependent or child table and used to enforce referential integrity. A foreign key must either be **NULL** or exist as a primary or unique key in a parent table.

function—One of several structures, either an implicit function that is provided as a part of the SQL language or an explicit function is one that is created by the user using PL/SQL. A function must return a value and must be named. As part of the SQL standard, a function cannot change a database's or package's state, but can act only on external variables and values.

GET—A SQL*Plus command that loads SQL or PL/SQL commands from an external operating system file into the SQL*Plus command buffer.

index—A structure that enhances data retrieval by providing rapid access to frequently queried column values. Indexes can be either B-tree structured or bitmapped. The two general types of index are unique and nonunique. A unique index forces all values entered into its source column to be unique. A nonunique index allows for repetitive and null values to be entered into its source column. Generally speaking, a column with high cardinality should be indexed using a B-tree index (the standard, default type of index), whereas a column with low cardinality should be indexed using a bitmapped index. An index can be either for a single column or on multiple columns. A multiple-column index is known as a concatenated index.

index-only table—An index-only table (IOT) stores all data in a B-tree format. The table itself is the index in an IOT. Data in an IOT can be stored either inline or in an offline storage table. Higher efficiency is achieved when all the table data can be stored inline in the IOT itself.

INITIAL—A storage parameter that sets the size of the **INITIAL** extent allocated to a table, index, rollback segment, or cluster. The size is set in bytes (no suffix), kilobytes (K suffix), or megabytes (M suffix).

INITRANS—A storage parameter that reserves space in the block header for the transaction records associated with a table's blocks.

INSERT—A DML (Data Manipulation Language) command that places new records into a table.

INSTEAD OF trigger—In Oracle8, a new form of trigger is allowed, known as the **INSTEAD OF** trigger. An **INSTEAD OF** trigger is placed on a view instead of on a table; this trigger is used to tell Oracle what base tables to modify rather than have Oracle attempt to operate against the view.

LOGGING—A keyword used to tell Oracle that actions taken against a table, cluster, object, or objects in a specified tablespace should be logged to redo logs to allow for recovery of those actions.

MAP method—A special type of UDT method used to map a set of type attributes into a single value to allow comparisons between **TYPE** values. To perform this mapping of **TYPE** values, you can use either a **MAP** or an **ORDER** method, but not both. An **ORDER** method must be called for every two objects being compared, whereas a **MAP** method is called once per object. In general, when you're sorting a set of objects, the number of times an **ORDER** method would be called is more than the number of times a **MAP** method would be called.

MAXEXTENTS—Sets the maximum number of extents an object can grow into. The **MAXEXTENTS** value can be altered up to a virtually unlimited value; however, the maximum number of extents allowed should still be based on block size to prevent chaining of the reference blocks.

MAXTRANS—A companion to the **INITRANS** storage parameter, **MAXTRANS** sets the maximum number of transactions that can access a block concurrently.

NCLOB—A national character **LOB** used for storing multibyte characters. Its size limit is the same as for other **LOB** datatypes—4 gigabytes or the maximum size allowed for your operating system, whichever is smaller.

nested table—A form of UDT (User-Defined Type) that must utilize a storage table to be used. A nested table allows an unrestricted number of rows, based on its base type, to be stored in a single row's column. (Actually, a pointer to the nested table is stored.) Along with **VARRAY**, a nested table forms objects known as collections.

NEXT—Storage parameter that specifies the size of the **NEXT** extent allocated to a table, index, rollback segment, or cluster. The size is set in bytes (no suffix), kilobytes (K suffix), or megabytes (M suffix). The **NEXT** parameter is used with the **PCTINCREASE** parameter to determine the size of all extents after the **INITIAL** and **NEXT** extents.

NOLOGGING—A keyword used to tell Oracle that actions taken against a table, cluster, object, or objects in a specified tablespace should not be logged to redo logs. Using this keyword prevents the recovery of those actions.

object auditing—The specification of auditing options that pertain to database objects rather than to database operations.

object identifier —In Oracle8 and Oracle8i, each object (i.e., table, cluster, and so on) has a 16-byte object identifier. This object identifier (OID) is guaranteed to be globally unique across all databases in your environment. It is a 16-byte, base-64 number that allows for a ridiculously high number of objects to be identified. (In the peta-region of countability—a petillion?—the maximum is: $2^{**}128$.)

object view—A special form of view that is based on a type that exactly mirrors the structure of a base relational form table. An object view is used to provide object identifiers (OIDs) to standard relational tables so they can be used in **REF** type relationships with object tables.

Optimal Flexible Architecture (OFA)—A standard, developed by internal Oracle Corporation experts, that tells how to optimally configure an Oracle database.

ORAPWD—The Oracle Password Manager utility, which is used to create and maintain the external password file. The external password file is used to tell the Oracle Enterprise Manager (OEM) and Server Manager who is authorized to perform DBA functions against a specific database.

ORDER method—A special type of UDT (User-Defined Type) method used to map a set of type attributes into a single value to allow comparisons between **TYPE** values. To perform this mapping of **TYPE** values, you can use either a **MAP** or an **ORDER** method, but not both. An **ORDER** method must be called for every two objects being compared, whereas a **MAP** method is called once per object. In general, when you're sorting a set of objects, the number of times an **ORDER** method would be called is more than the number of times a **MAP** method would be called.

OSDBA—A role that is assigned to users who are authorized to create and maintain Oracle databases. If a user is given the **OSDBA** role, he or she is also given an entry in the external password file.

OSOPER—A role that is assigned to users who are authorized to maintain Oracle databases. If a user is given the **OSOPER** role, he or she is also given an entry in the external password file.

outer join—A type of join in which data not meeting the join criteria (that is, the join value is **NULL**) is also returned by the query. An outer join is signified by using the plus sign inside parentheses (+) to indicate the outer join column for the table deficient in data.

package—A stored PL/SQL construct made of related procedures, functions, exceptions, and other PL/SQL constructs. Packages are called into memory when any package object is referred to. Packages are created or dropped as a unit.

partition—A physical subdivision of a table or index into subsections based on a predefined range or ranges of a list of columns.

partition key—The list of columns used to partition a table.

PCTFREE—Used by Oracle to determine the amount of space reserved for future updates in an Oracle block to rows that already exist in the block. A **PCTFREE** value that's too low can result in row-migration for frequently updated tables; a value that's too high requires more storage space.

PCTINCREASE—After **INITIAL** and **NEXT**, determines the percentage that each subsequent extent grows over the previously allocated extent.

PCTUSED—Determines when a block is placed back on the free block list. When used space in a block drops below **PCTUSED**, the block can be used for subsequent new row insertion.

permanent tablespace—A tablespace that holds permanent data structures such as tables, indexes, and clusters. By default, all tablespaces are permanent unless they are created specifically as temporary tablespaces or are altered to be temporary tablespaces.

PGA (process global area)—Represents the memory area allocated to each process that accesses an Oracle database.

Primary key—In a relational database, the unique identifier for a table. A primary key must be unique and not null. A primary key can be either *natural* (derived from a column or columns in the database) or *artificial* (drawn from a sequence).

privilege auditing—Auditing of what privileges are granted, by whom they're granted, and to whom they're granted.

procedures—Stored PL/SQL objects that may, but aren't required to, return a value. Procedures are allowed to change database or package states. Procedures can be placed into packages.

production—The final stage of the system development cycle. The production stage consists of normal maintenance and of backup and recovery operations in a developed system.

profiles—Sets of resource allocations that can be assigned to a user. These resources are used to limit idle time, connect time, memory, and CPU usage.

PROMPT—A SQL*Plus command used to pass a string out of a SQL script to the executing user. The **PROMPT** command can be used with the **ACCEPT** command to prompt for values needed by the script.

RECOVER—A command used in Server Manager to explicitly perform database recovery operations.

REF—Short for **REFERENCE**. A pointer from a child object to a parent object; this pointer usually consists of the parent object's OID.

referential integrity—The process by which a relational database maintains record relationships between parent and child tables via primary key and foreign key values.

rejected records—In SQL*Loader, records that don't meet load criteria for the table being loaded; rejections occur due to value, data type, or other restrictions.

relationship—A named association between two things of significance. For example, if I say that a wheeled vehicle has one or many wheels, *has* is the relationship. If I say that an employee works for one or more employer, *works for* is the relationship.

resources—The database and system resources that are controlled by the use of profiles.

reverse key index—An index in which incoming key values have their bytes reversed in order. This reversal of bytes forces a random distribution of the key values throughout the index, preventing hot-blocks from being formed. A reverse key index can be used only for single-row lookups or full-index scans. A reverse key index cannot be used in an index range scan.

ROLLBACK—A DML (Data Manipulation Language) command used to undo database changes that have not been committed.

rollback segment—A database object that contains records used to undo database transactions. Whenever a parameter in the database refers to **UNDO**, it is actually referring to rollback segments.

SAVE—A SQL*Plus command used to store command-buffer contents in an external operating system file.

SCOPED REF—A REF whose range of values is limited to the OIDs contained in the defined **SCOPE** object table.

SELECT—A DML (Data Manipulation Language) command used to retrieve values from the database.

SELF—A keyword used to tell Oracle that you are referring to the current value of a UDT (User-Defined Type). Known as selfish nomenclature. All **TYPE**s are self aware.

Server Manager line mode—Server Manager has a GUI mode and a line mode. In line mode, all commands are entered at the command line.

SET—A SQL*Plus command used to change the values of SQL*Plus environment parameters such as line width and page length.

SGA (system global area)—Consists of the database buffers, shared pool, and queue areas that are globally accessible by all database processes. The SGA is used to speed Oracle processing by caching data and structure information in memory.

SHOW—A SQL*Plus command used to show the value of a variable that's set with the **SET** command.

SHUTDOWN—A Server Manager command used to shut down the database. **SHUTDOWN** has three modes: **NORMAL, IMMEDIATE,** and **ABORT. NORMAL** prohibits new connections, waits for all users to log off, and then shuts down. **IMMEDIATE** prohibits new connections, backs out uncommitted transactions, and then logs users off and shuts down. **ABORT** shuts down right now and not gracefully.

SPOOL—A SQL*Plus command used to send SQL*Plus output to either a printer or a file.

SQL buffer—A memory area used to store the last SQL command. The SQL buffer can store only the last command executed, unless the buffer is loaded with the **GET** command. A SQL*Plus command such as **SET, DESCRIBE,** or **SPOOL** is not placed in the SQL buffer.

STARTUP—A Server Manager command used to start up the database. A database can be started in one of several modes: **MOUNT, NOMOUNT, OPEN, EXCLUSIVE,** or **PARALLEL.**

statement auditing—Audits statement actions such as **INSERT, UPDATE,** and **DELETE.**

STORAGE—A clause that Oracle uses to determine current and future settings for an object's extents. If a **STORAGE** clause isn't specified, the object's storage characteristics are taken from the tablespace's default storage clause.

strategy—In the system development cycle, the step in which the overall methodology for the rest of the development effort is mapped out. (This step is usually paired with the analysis step.)

SYSDBA—See *OSDBA.*

SYSOPER—See *OSOPER.*

table—The structure used to store data in an Oracle database. Entities map to tables in relational databases.

tablespace—The unit of logical storage in Oracle. All tables, clusters, and indexes are stored in tablespaces. Tablespaces are composed of physical data files.

temporary tablespace—This type of tablespace is not allowed to contain any permanent structures, such as tables, clusters, or indexes; instead, it holds temporary segments only.

transition—In the system development cycle, the step in which users test the application, and support of the application moves from development to production personnel.

TRUNCATE—A DDL (Data Definition Language) command used to remove all rows from a table. Because it is a DDL command, it cannot be rolled back.

TRUNCATE (functions)—There are both string and date functions called **TRUNCATE;** both are used to shorten the external representations of internal data.

TYPE—May be referred to as a User-Defined Type (UDT). This is a user-defined internal storage structure that may include data types, other UDTs, and methods that act upon the specified attributes and types.

UDT (User-Defined Type)—See *TYPE*.

UGA (user global area)—Used to store user-specific variables and stacks.

UID (unique identifier)—Uniquely identifies a row in a table and usually maps to the natural primary key value. Each entity must have a unique identifier to qualify as an entry in a relational table.

UPDATE—A DML (Data Manipulation Language) command that allows data inside tables to be changed.

variable—A user-defined or process-defined storage area used to hold a value that will probably be different each time a script or procedure is executed.

VARRAY—A form of UDT (User-Defined Type) used to store multiple occurrences of the base type inline with the other data in a row. A **VARRAY** is used when the number of occurrences is small and you know it won't exceed a specified maximum value. Along with nested tables, **VARRAY** makes up the *collections* type of object in Oracle8.

view—A preset **SELECT** statement used against one or more tables. The view is stored in the database and has no physical representation. A view is also known as a *virtual table*.

virtual table—See *view*.

Index

. . . .

Look for All of the Exam Cram Brand Certification Study Systems

ALL NEW! Exam Cram Personal Trainer Systems

The Exam Cram Personal Trainer systems are an exciting new category in certification training products. These CD-ROM based systems offer extensive capabilities at a moderate price and are the first certification-specific testing product to completely link learning with testing.

This Exam Cram Study Guide turned interactive course lets you customize the way you learn.

Each system includes:

- A Personalized Practice Test engine with multiple test methods,
- A database of nearly 300 questions linked directly to the subject matter within the Exam Cram on which that question is based.

Exam Cram Audio Review Systems

Written and read by certification instructors, each set contains four cassettes jam-packed with the certification exam information you must have. Designed to be used on their own or as a complement to our Exam Cram Study Guides, Flash Cards, and Practice Tests.

Each system includes:

- Study preparation tips with an essential last-minute review for the exam
- Hours of lessons highlighting key terms and techniques
- A comprehensive overview of all exam objectives
- 45 minutes of review questions complete with answers and explanations

Exam Cram Flash Cards

These pocket-sized study tools are 100% focused on exams. Key questions appear on side one of each card and in-depth answers on side two. Each card features either a cross-reference to the appropriate Exam Cram Study Guide chapter or to another valuable resource. Comes with a CD-ROM featuring electronic versions of the flash cards and a complete practice exam.

Exam Cram Practice Tests

Our readers told us that extra practice exams were vital to certification success, so we created the perfect companion book for certification study material.

Each book contains:

- Several practice exams
- Electronic versions of practice exams on the accompanying CD-ROM presented in an interactive format enabling practice in an environment similar to that of the actual exam
- Each practice question is followed by the corresponding answer (why the right answers are right and the wrong answers are wrong)
- References to the Exam Cram Study Guide chapter or other resource for that topic

CORIOLIS™

Certification Insider Press